BATTLECRUISER REPULSE

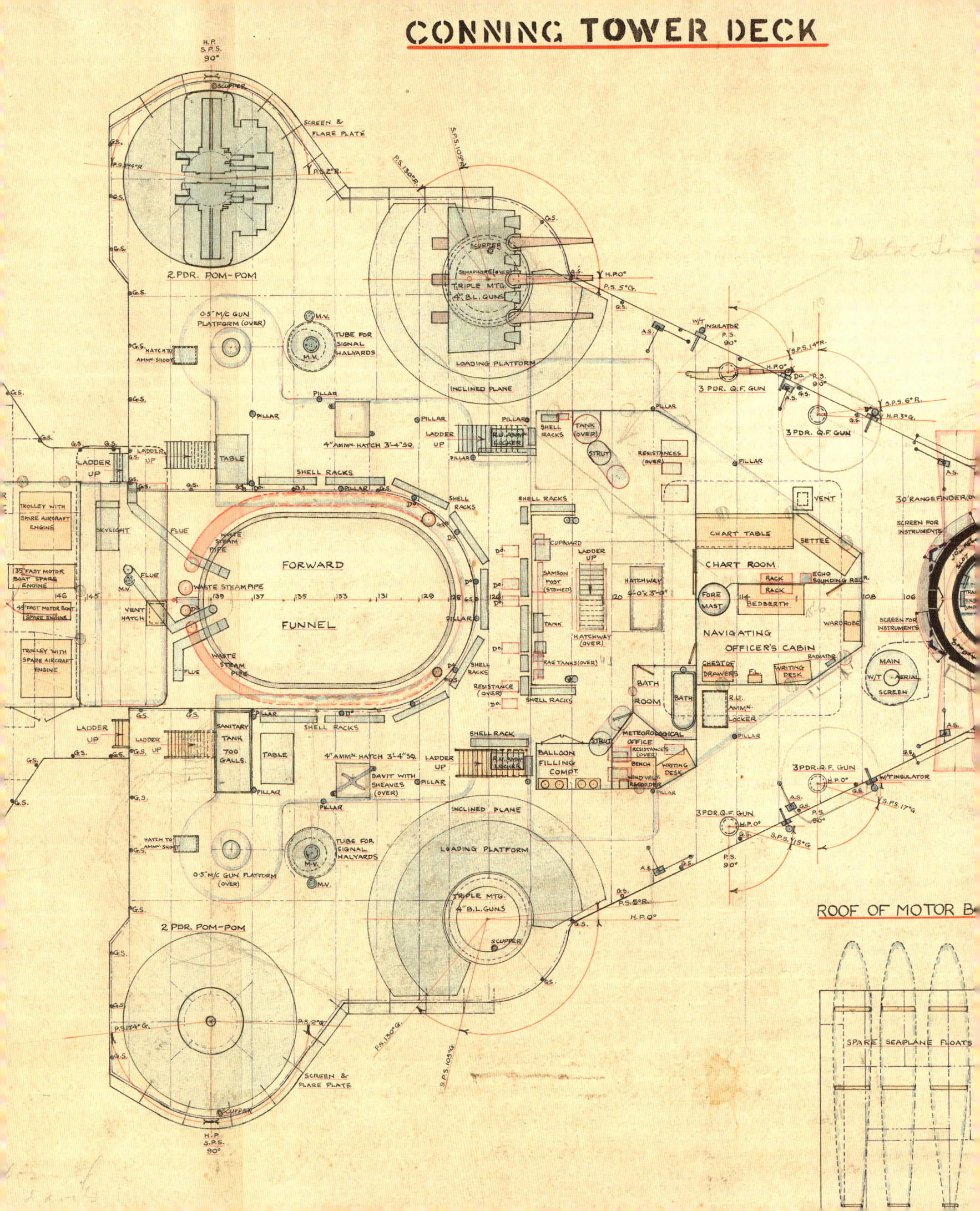

BATTLECRUISER REPULSE

detailed in the original builders' plans

JOHN ROBERTS

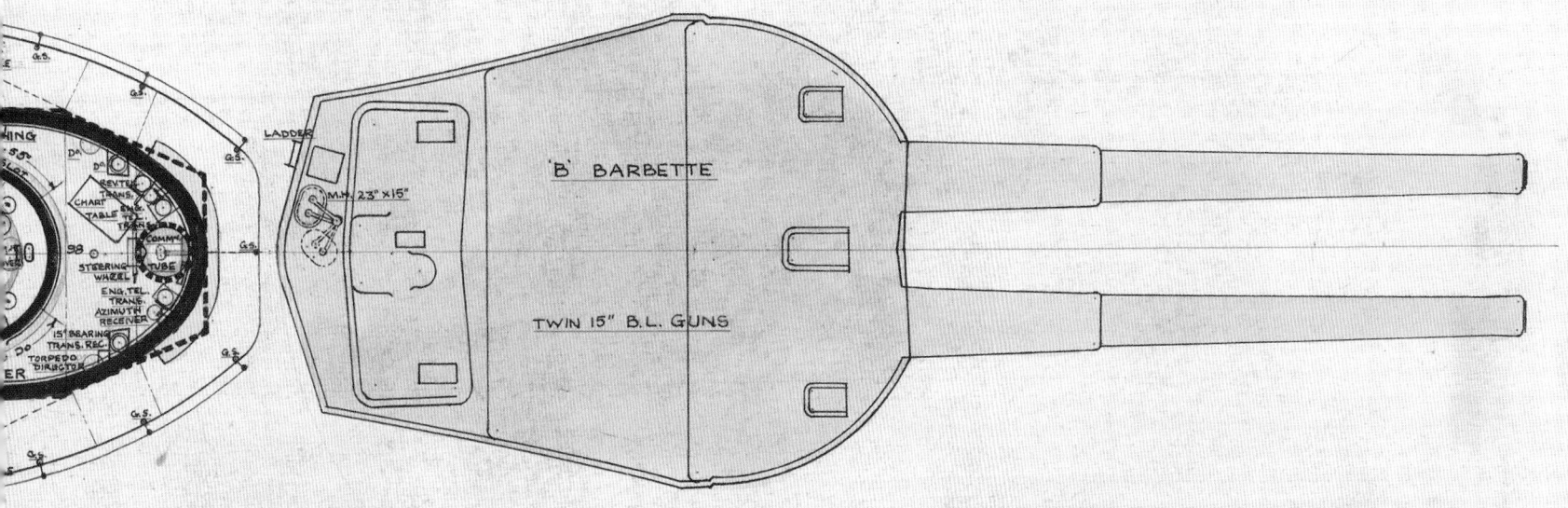

NATIONAL MARITIME MUSEUM GREENWICH

Seaforth PUBLISHING

Half title image: The eagle-and-rock badge was carried by HMS *Repulse* for the vast majority, if not all, of the ship's career, which is attested to by photographs of the tompions and the bridge front. The field is usually blue, although there is one surviving example with the field painted red. There is some uncertainty because the battlecruiser's successor, the Polaris-armed SSBN, had an entirely different badge, described heraldically as: blue field; castle gold, on which flies the Union Flag, proper, on two wavelets, silver. The ship's motto *Qui tangit frangitur* translates as 'Who touches me is broken'. A E Weightman's *Heraldry in the Royal Navy* lists the castle design as 'earlier' than the eagle, but the official sealed design shows the eagle, with pencil annotations dated 8/7/41 saying 'NOT TO BE USED' and 'See new badge'. This may suggest that the battlecruiser was due to be assigned the new castle badge just before she was sunk. (Drawing by Stephen Dent)

Frontispiece: *Repulse* as fitted 1936, conning tower deck (© National Maritime Museum, Greenwich (part of J9434)

ACKNOWLEDGMENTS

This book owes more to co-operation between publisher and author than is normally the case and on that basis my thanks are due to both Robert Gardiner of Seaforth Publishing, who was responsible for creating this series in the first place, and to Steve Dent for his considerable skill in the book's design and the occasional corrective comment. While most of my text is based on research gathered over a lengthy period and not originally linked to this project, I would also like to express my considerable gratitude to Andrew Choong and Jeremy Michell of the Photograph and Ship Plans Department of the National Maritime Museum, Greenwich for the assistance and friendly cooperation they have provided for me over many years. Lastly, I owe thanks to Jean, my wife, who has always been supportive of my apparently insane obsession with the details of warship design and has never regarded the Royal Navy as a rival!

Copyright © Seaforth Publishing 2019
Ship plans © National Maritime Museum, Greenwich

This edition first published in Great Britain in 2019 by
Seaforth Publishing,
An imprint of Pen & Sword Books Ltd,
47 Church Street,
Barnsley
South Yorkshire S70 2AS

www.seaforthpublishing.com
Email: info@seaforthpublishing.com

Published in association with Royal Museums Greenwich,
the group name for the National Maritime Museum,
the Royal Observatory, the Queen's House and *Cutty Sark*.

British Library Cataloguing in Publication Data
A catalogue record for this book is available from the British Library

ISBN 978 1 5267 5728 9 (Hardback)
ISBN 978 1 5267 5730 2 (Kindle)
ISBN 978 1 5267 5729 6 (ePub)

All rights reserved. No part of this publication may be reproduced or transmitted in any form or by any means, electronic or mechanical, including photocopying, recording, or any information storage and retrieval system, without prior permission in writing of both the copyright owner and the above publisher.

Pen & Sword Books Limited incorporates the imprints of Atlas, Archaeology, Aviation, Discovery, Family History, Fiction, History, Maritime, Military, Military Classics, Politics, Select, Transport, True Crime, Air World, Frontline Publishing, Leo Cooper, Remember When, Seaforth Publishing, The Praetorian Press, Wharncliffe Local History, Wharncliffe Transport, Wharncliffe True Crime and White Owl.

Typeset and designed by Stephen Dent
Printed and bound in China

CONTENTS

ORIGINS   6
- Design   8
- Structure   9
- Armament   10
- Fire Control   13
- Protection   13
- Machinery   14
- General   14
- The Plans   16

DECKS, AS FITTED 1916   18
- Shelter Deck, Flying Deck and Bridges   18
- Forecastle Deck and Upper Deck   20
- Main Deck and Lower Deck   22
- Platform Deck and Hold   24

ENLARGED PROFILE AND SECTIONS, AS FITTED 1916   26
- Stern to Station 303   26
- Stations 303 to 289   28
- Stations 289 to 280   30
- Stations 280 to 270   32
- Stations 270 to 258   34
- Stations 258 to 249   36
- Stations 249 to 227   38
- Stations 227 to 199   40
- Stations 199 to 165   42
- Stations 165 to 115   44
- Stations 115 to 95   46
- Stations 95 to 80   48
- Stations 80 to 66   50
- Stations 66 to 54   52
- Stations 54 to 43   54
- Stations 43 to 27   56
- Station 27 to stem   58

MODIFICATIONS 1916–1930   60
- Flying Deck and After Night Control Position   62
- Mainmast and Funnel Platforms   64
- Conning Tower Platform   66
- Admiral's, Forward Night Control, and Compass Platforms   68
- Foremast Upper Platforms   70

GATEFOLD PLANS   72
- Profile, as fitted 1916 (modified in January 1921)   72
- Profile, as fitted 1936   75
- Rig, as fitted 1936   79

MODERNISATION 1933–1936   82
- Career Summary   83
- Aircraft Arrangements   85

ENLARGED PROFILE AND SECTIONS, AS FITTED 1936   90
- Stern to Station 303   90
- Stations 303 to 294   92
- Stations 294 to 289   94
- Stations 289 to 280   96
- Stations 280 to 270   98
- Stations 270 to 258   100
- Stations 258 to 249   102
- Stations 249 to 227   104
- Stations 227 to 198   106
- Stations 198 to 165   108
- Stations 165 to 115   110
- Stations 115 to 95   112
- Stations 95 to 80   114
- Stations 80 to 66   116
- Stations 66 to 54   118
- Stations 54 to 43   120
- Stations 43 to 32   122
- Stations 32 to 27   124
- Station 27 to stem   126

ENLARGED DECKS, AS FITTED 1936   128
- After Superstructure Decks   128
- Midships Superstructure Decks   130
- Forward Superstructure Decks   132
- Bridge Platforms   134
- Forecastle Deck   136
- Upper Deck   140
- Main Deck   144
- Lower Deck   148
- Platform Deck   152
- Hold   156

BIBLIOGRAPHY   160
ACKNOWLEDGEMENTS   160
LIST OF PLANS   160

ORIGINS

During the decade before 1914 the most influential personality in the development of British warship design was Admiral Sir John Fisher (1st Sea Lord 1904–1910). His forceful and positive approach served to accelerate the rate of technical advance generating what was to become known as the 'dreadnought' revolution. While the *Dreadnought* may have initiated this revolution, it actually encompassed a much broader range of technological, strategic and tactical ideas than those simply concerned with battleship construction. Fisher's undoubted genius and foresight brought substantial advantages to British naval administration and development but his faith in the correctness of his views on ship construction contained the danger of assuming that their success was a foregone conclusion. Foremost among his pet schemes was the introduction, in parallel with *Dreadnought*, of the all-big-gun armoured cruiser of which three (*Invincible*, *Inflexible* and *Indomitable*) were included in the same 1905–06 Construction Programme. These ships followed Fisher's obsessive belief that high speed in warships was of paramount importance. His demands for priority in speed were employed with religious fervour whenever an opportunity to express his vision presented itself. In effect he saw the *Indomitable* class, which were 4 knots faster than *Dreadnought*, as the basis for the capital ships of the future. He did not view their considerably lighter protection as a problem or see that many of the advantages of high speed would be lost if matched by new ships of a potential enemy. His essential requirements were for speed and gun-power. Armour followed up a poor third, utilising whatever weight was available on the displacement allowed by the financial limitations of the time.

Fisher was a master of employing persuasion, intrigue and threats (usually to resign) to get his own way but he was not all-powerful and was dependent on the support of both his political masters and the senior officers of the Admiralty. In consequence there was no change in construction priority and the battleship remained the primary unit of fleet power. Consequently the construction programmes for 1906–07 and 1907–08 included no armoured cruisers, in part due to political demands for economy. For much the same reason the 1908–09 Programme included only one battleship and one conventional armoured cruiser with 9.2in guns. However, at this point in time Germany embarked on a substantially increased warship construction programme that included her first all-big-gun armoured cruiser (the German designation was *großen kreuzer* = large cruiser), *Von Der Tann*, laid down in March 1908. This initiated the pre-war naval race between Britain and Germany which began in earnest in 1909 and gave Fisher his chance to press again for ships that would outclass their rivals in both speed and gun-power. With the need for economy overridden by the threat to Britain's naval supremacy the next three programme years provided for the construction of 14 battleships and 6 armoured cruisers – size steadily increased, gun calibre was stepped up from 12in to 13.5in and, in the case of the 13.5in-gunned armoured cruisers, speed raised to 28 knots. In 1911 the all-big-gun armoured cruisers were officially re-designated 'battle cruisers'.

When Fisher stepped down as 1st Sea Lord in January 1910 he had not achieved his prime objective in regard to speed. All the battleships constructed during his tenure of office retained the standard 21-knot speed of *Dreadnought* while the speed of the armoured cruisers more-or-less equalled rather than exceeded contemporary German designs. However, being out of office did not put him out of the picture and he continued to campaign for those items of naval administration, strategy and technology that he viewed as critical to the continuation of British naval supremacy. His efforts were substantially enhanced when Winston Churchill, having been appointed 1st Lord of the

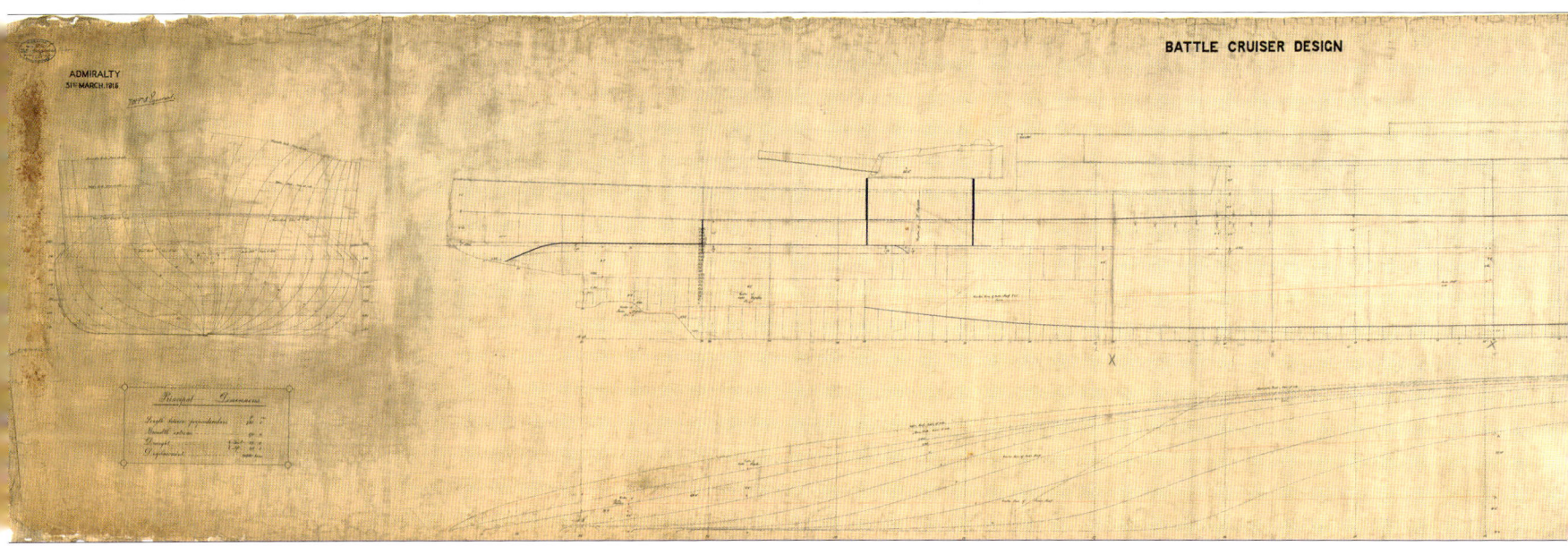

ORIGINS

Admiralty in October 1910, solicited his advice. This developed into a close relationship in which Fisher provided guidance on a variety of naval subjects including his strong views on the advancement of ship design. Even here, however, Fisher failed to win round either Churchill, or possibly the Board of Admiralty via Churchill, to his view that the heavily armed battlecruiser, with a speed substantially in excess of foreign contemporaries, was an essential fleet requirement. The last of the pre-war battlecruisers, *Tiger* of the 1911–12 Programme, demonstrates the relatively limited extent of Churchill's application of Fisher's views in the adoption of a modification of the machinery design to allow sufficient overload power to provide a design speed of 30 knots (in practice she could not achieve more than 29 knots). The fact that none of the remaining pre-war construction programmes included a battlecruiser also serves to indicate the Admiralty's loss of confidence in the value of the type which resulted in the introduction of the fast battleships of the *Queen Elizabeth* class in the 1912 Programme. These ships were intended to serve as the fleet's fast wing but not for the cruiser functions (scouting and trade protection) assigned to the battlecruisers. The only points in which they fulfilled Fisher's desires were a further increase in gun-power by adopting the 15in calibre and the provision of oil fired boilers. It is worth noting that late in 1911 Fisher was advocating the adoption of the same eight-gun 15in armament for a 30-knot battlecruiser design – it is not clear if this proposal served to initiate the development of the 15in gun or that his choice of calibre was simply prompted by some inside knowledge of developments at the Admiralty. Any doubt in regard to the immediate pre-war capital ship construction policy of the Admiralty is provided by the programmes of 1913–14 and 1914–15. The former consisted of the five 15in gun, 21-knot *Royal Sovereign* class battleships and the latter of three more slightly modified vessels of the same class and a single repeat of the *Queen Elizabeth* design. Thus by 1914 Fisher's battlecruiser concept was as good as dead – but fate, in the shape of the outbreak of war in August 1914, was to intervene and allow him to initiate the construction of exactly what he wished for.

At the end of October 1914, following a loss of confidence in the naval leadership of the Admiralty during the first few months of war, the 1st Sea Lord, Admiral Prince Louis of Battenberg, was obliged to resign. Churchill offered the post to Fisher who, despite his age of 73, was still seen as capable of providing the same energetic leadership he had so ably demonstrated in the past. The choice was, at least initially, justified. On the material side he immediately set in train a large building programme that included destroyers, submarines, sloops, patrol craft and amphibious warfare vessels which proved invaluable in the subsequent prosecution of the naval war. In particular, Fisher accelerated the production process by bypassing the Admiralty's standard bureaucratic system and consulting with suppliers directly – leaving whatever red-tape was required to follow. He also began a campaign for a return to the construction of battlecruisers, but Churchill rejected his proposals on the grounds that large ships would absorb too much of the available construction resources and could not, in any case, be completed in time to take part in the war which, at this time, was not expected to extend beyond the latter part of 1915. Not to be thwarted, Fisher continued to lobby for support using a variety of arguments. He expressed the view that several naval actions of the war thus far had clearly demonstrated the great advantages of the battlecruiser concept, especially the Battle of the Falkland Islands on 8 December 1914 and the need of the Grand Fleet for newer and faster ships of the type to face the battlecruisers nearing completion in Germany. In a letter to Admiral Jellicoe, CinC Grand Fleet, on the 23 December soliciting for support he wrote 'The new German *Lützow* battlecruiser, with possible 14in guns, or even 16in, will certainly have over *28-knots speed!* We must have 32-knots speed to

SHEER DRAWING, MARCH 1915

One of a number of general arrangement design drawings prepared by the DNC's department as general guidance for the shipbuilders. This illustrates the hull form by means of the sheer profile and plan and a body plan. It also indicates the positions of the decks, frames and bulkheads together with the ship's primary dimensions, including the heights between the underside of the decks (*ie*, to the tops of the deck beams at the side) and the positions of various items (such as the gun axis) in relation to the LWL. (J9432)

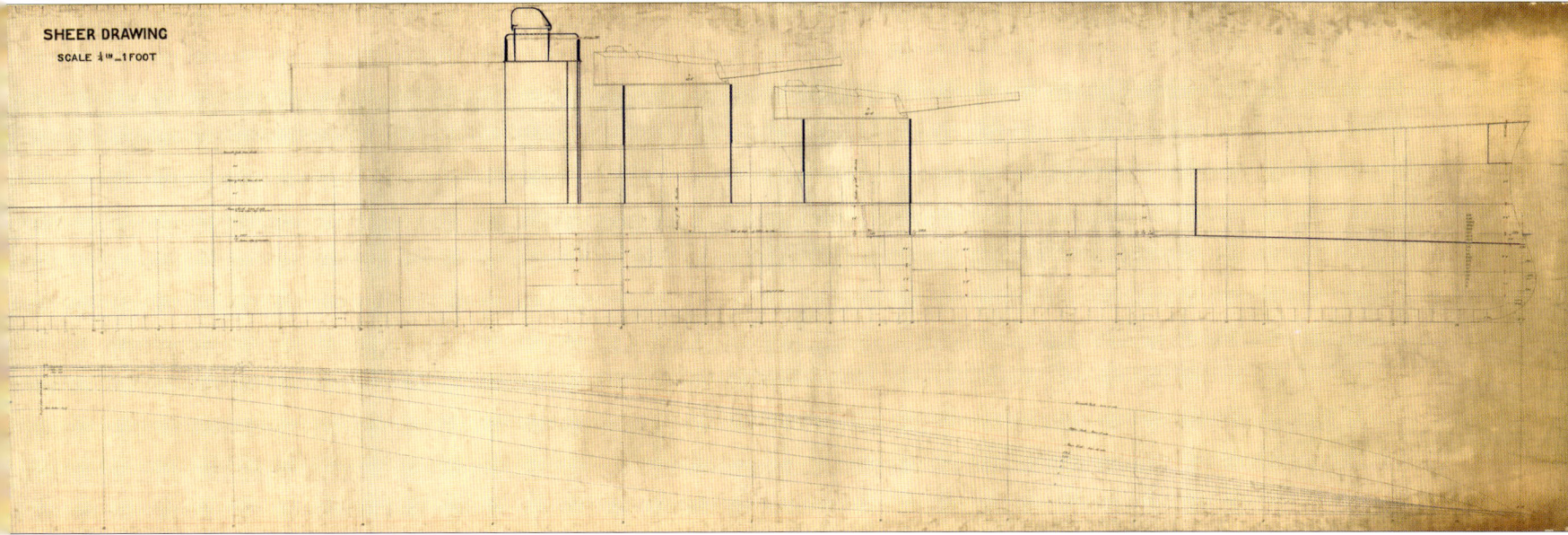

give us a margin for being long out of dock, and to give the necessary speed to CATCH a 28-knot ship! ... SPEED IS EVERYTHING ...' His remarks on the speed and armament of *Lützow* were somewhat exaggerated but he was always more concerned with impact than with accuracy when it came to making a point.

DESIGN

It would seem that the Admiralty's wartime regime did not provide the same restraint on Fisher's more far-reaching proposals for warship development as it had done pre-war. There appears to be no record of dissenting voices regarding his re-introduction of the battlecruiser concept or the fact that he effectively restored the type to the form he originally envisaged for it in 1905, including the limited protection and light anti-torpedo-boat (ATB) armament. He certainly seems to have had little time for consulting the naval members of the board on his proposals. His thoughts and requirements for ship design were generally discussed directly with the Director of Naval Construction, Sir Eustace D'Eyncourt, who recorded that he made a practice of making Admiral Tudor, who as 3rd Sea Lord was responsible for material, '... fully aware of any discussions I had had with Lord Fisher' – implying that without this information Tudor would not have been fully aware of the development of these new designs until they came up for discussion by the Board of Admiralty. In preliminary discussions with D'Eyncourt, Fisher proposed a design for a light battlecruiser – three ships each armed with two of the twin 15in mountings originally ordered for the 1914–15 Programme battleships. Work on this design was temporarily halted (it later re-emerged, in modified form, as the large light cruisers of the *Courageous* class) when Fisher decided instead on two ships, each with three 15in mountings. This may have been prompted by a change of emphasis caused by Fisher's reactions to current events in the war at sea. D'Eyncourt described the original purpose of the four-gun design as hunting down cruisers raiding the sea lanes, this being a particular problem at the time, whereas the request for a six-gun design dates from 19 December, shortly after the Falkland Islands Battle, which, in Fisher's view, vindicated the battlecruiser concept in its original 1905 configuration. The requirement was also influenced by Admiral Beatty's concerns about the strength of the Battle Cruiser Fleet vis-à-vis the German 1st Scouting Group and the latter's bombardment raids against Yarmouth on 3 November and the Yorkshire coast on 16 December.

Apart from the increase in the number of 15in guns, the addition of two torpedo tubes and an increase in size, the outline requirements Fisher requested from the DNC were almost identical to those of his earlier four-gun proposal – namely a speed of 32 knots, a long, high, flared bow, an anti-torpedo-boat armament of twenty 4in guns protected with light shields, mounted high up on the superstructure, oil fired boilers and armour on the same scale as that provided in the 12in gun battlecruiser *Indefatigable*. Work on a sketch design and a model of the proposed ship were completed within a few days and served to convince the Board to accept Fisher's arguments for the need of such ships. Churchill obtained cabinet approval for their construction on 28 December, a decision possibly influenced by Fisher's contention that the war would last much longer than originally assumed and that he could, in any case, get these ships built quickly as he had done with *Dreadnought* in 1905–6.

The increased rate of construction was to be assisted by utilising the existing contracts for the 1914–15 battleships *Repulse* and *Renown* which had been placed with the shipbuilders Palmers and Fairfield respectively. Neither ship had been laid down, their construction having been suspended on 26 August, but material had been delivered to the yards, much of which could be used in the new ships. (The two other battleships of the programme, *Resistance* and the fast battleship *Agincourt*, had been assigned to Devonport and Portsmouth Dockyards respectively but had been cancelled rather than suspended.) The new vessels retained the names of the ships they replaced but, in the case of *Repulse*, not the builder. Palmers did not have a slip long enough to accommodate the new ship so the contract, and any suitable sub-contracts (including 6000 tons of steel plate, hull castings and auxiliary machinery), were transferred to John Brown's Clydebank yard in early January 1915.

From 28 December, when D'Eyncourt was ordered to proceed with the design, progress was rapid. Fisher interviewed the contractors on 29 December and obtained agreement to complete the ships in a remarkable 15 months. On the following day the legend of particulars received Board approval. Construction information was supplied to the builders in priority order from early January so they had sufficient information to lay down both ships on 25 January 1915, from which point on the construction gradually accelerated. All the drawings, calculations and specifications normally supplied by the Admiralty prior to construction were completed on 12 April 1915, at which time *Repulse* already had 1200 tons of steel on the blocks. Ten days later the design received its formal Board approval. Fisher did not continue to oversee his cherished project as he resigned his post on 15 May 1915 following serious disagreements with Churchill over the Dardanelles Campaign. The pressure for early completion did, however, remain. In September, a large number of the shipyard workers employed on the battleship *Ramillies* at Beardmore's yard in Dalmuir were transferred to the construction of *Repulse* and *Renown*. *Repulse* was launched on 8 January 1916 and completed eight months later, commissioning on 8 August 1916. Although her construction time was actually slightly short of 19 months, 4 months longer than that negotiated by Fisher, it was still a remarkable achievement, especially under wartime conditions. It is worth noting that the construction of the battlecruiser *Queen Mary*, also built by John Brown, took 30 months. Despite all the effort, the Grand Fleet did not greet their new acquisitions with much enthusiasm. At the Battle of Jutland on 31 May 1916 three battlecruisers had been destroyed by magazine explosions. Given that these losses were, at that time, primarily blamed on weak protection, the obviously limited provision of armour in the *Repulse* and *Renown* was subject to severe criticism.

Whatever the initially perceived value of these ships as naval assets, they were a remarkable demonstration of both the skill of British naval architects and the efficiency of her shipyards, together with the many industries that supported them. Their major faults – limited

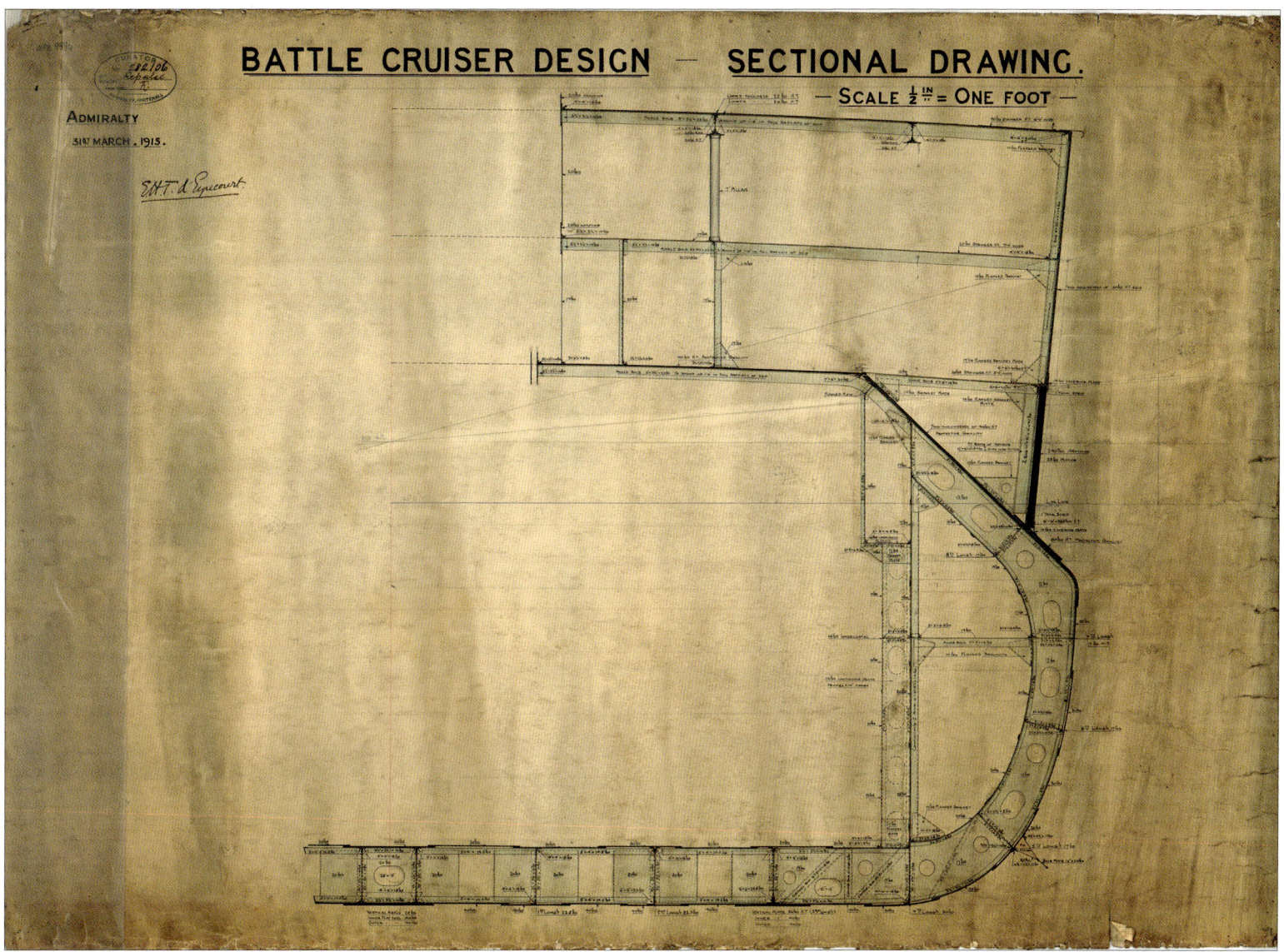

STRUCTURAL SECTION, AMIDSHIPS MARCH 1915
Presumably due to the need to complete the design drawings quickly, this single section appears to be the only design drawing produced for the structural arrangements. It illustrates well the unusual form of the hull with its semi bulge, integrated with the protective deck, and outward sloping upper side – the primary purpose of which was to improve sea-keeping. Of note is the adoption of heavy framing spaced at 4ft behind the side armour in preference to using lighter main frames with local intermediate frames. This arrangement saved weight without compromising the support provided. Despite this the ship retained the standard frame numbering system of a ship with intermediate frames (ie, main frames every other number over length of main belt). (M1003)

protection and the acceptance of a six-gun main armament, which was not ideal for fire control – were faults of concept rather than design. D'Eyncourt was justly proud of his department's achievement in both their design and the speed at which it was developed. Both ships subsequently had their protection improved in major refits and from 1922 provided, together with *Hood* (and *Tiger* until 1930) the only ships of the fleet's operational battlecruiser force. Whatever the technical view might be, these large, fast and powerful, headline-grabbing ships held a special place in the nation's perception of its navy.

STRUCTURE

Although Fisher, and others, often referred to *Repulse* and her sister as 'lightly built' their comparative hull weight (allowing for the altered dimensions) and scantlings did not in fact vary greatly from earlier battlecruisers. If anything, they were slightly heavier in build, reflecting the fact that they were the longest ships thus far designed for the Royal Navy. The general structure employed the standard 'longitudinal' framing system in which the main fore-and-aft members were continuous while the transverse frames were worked between them. Being derived from the cruiser class, battlecruisers did not have a Middle Deck like battleships. From the *Indefatigable* onward the upper strength deck amidships was therefore made the Forecastle Deck rather than the Upper Deck as in battleships, which provided a similar depth to the hull girder. The lower section of the hull girder gained its primary strength from the keel and double bottom structure. The keel in this case adopted a box section with two vertical keels rather than one, an innovation first proposed for the un-built battleships of the 1914–15 Programme.

ARMAMENT

The 15in guns were standard production firing, initially, a 1920 lbs projectile to a maximum range of 24,350yds at 20° elevation. However, the elevation was dictated more by the need to provide for continuous aim with the ship rolling than any need for what, at this time, would have been well beyond existing expectations of action requirements. The revolving weight of each 15in turret was 741.5 tons, including the guns (200 tons) and half the weight of the roller ring and rollers (20 tons). Power was supplied to the mountings by three hydraulic pumps, two forward and one aft, supplying distilled water mixed with a small amount of lubricant.

The original intention to fit twenty single 4in mountings for the ATB armament was changed early in the design process to triple mountings, which was intended to ease the problems of providing a workable distribution of the mountings free of blast and with good arcs of fire. The ship was fitted with seventeen guns on five triple mountings and two on singles, all with light spray shields. The triple mountings were not an unqualified success, primarily due to the difficulty of organising their large gun-crews for the loading and firing of three closely spaced guns, which substantially reduced the potential volume of fire.

The remaining gun armament consisted of two 3in Mk I QF guns on single HA Mk II mountings and two Hotchkiss 3pdr QF saluting guns, all fitted in the Shelter Deck – the former abreast the second funnel and the latter abreast the fore funnel. The ship was actually allocated four 3pdr guns but only two were carried during the war. She was also allocated a 12pdr field gun and carriage but this was only intended to be supplied to the ship when on foreign service. The ship was also equipped with two submerged torpedo tubes, located on the Platform Deck forward and an outfit of ten 21in torpedoes.

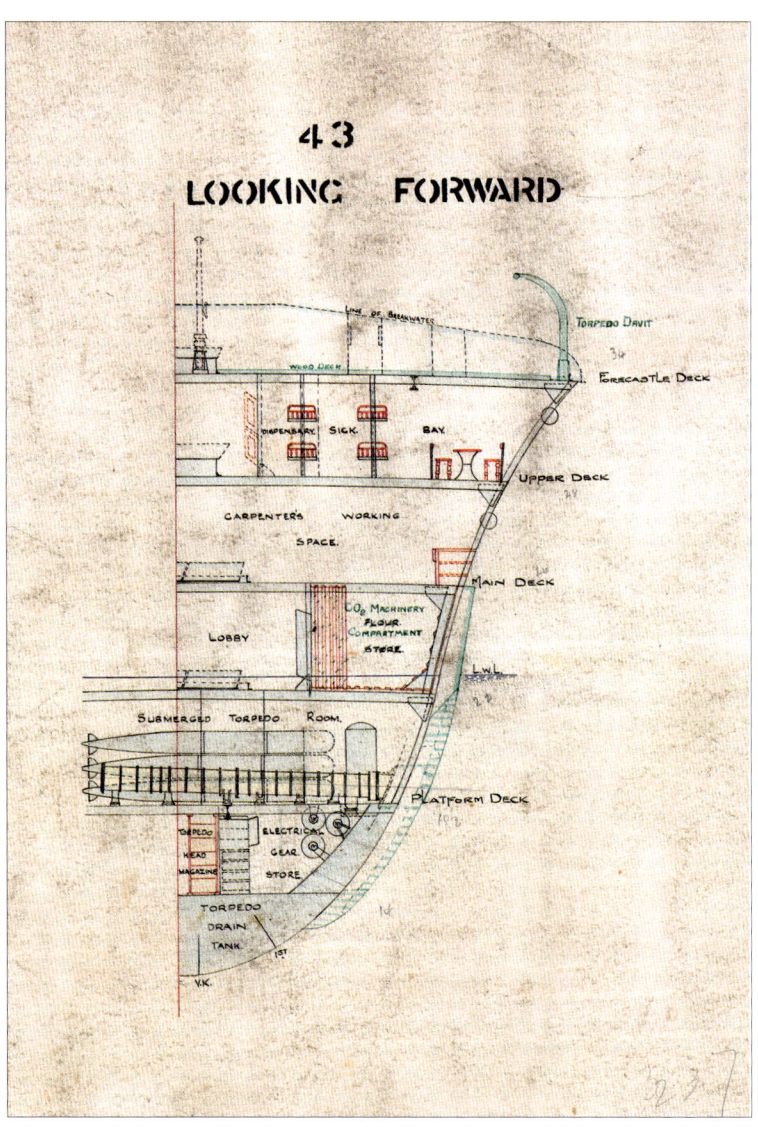

SUBMERGED TORPEDO TUBE COMPARTMENT

The initial torpedo outfit of ten 21-inch Mk II HB torpedoes was replaced in 1917 with new production Mk IV and IV* HB torpedoes. The items in the plan view with red outlines indicate that they are overhead which includes four of the torpedo bodies. Note that although the drawing shows the torpedoes with their warheads, the latter were in fact normally stowed separately in the warhead magazine immediately below. Items added during 1918–21, identified in green, including an additional, possibly spare, torpedo body stowed on the floor, four warheads (due to insufficient space in warhead room since the addition of AW tubes), extension of tube outlets (as a result of the fitting of bulges) and a re-routing of the firing reservoir pipe to the after tube. (details from M1102 & J9374)

ARMAMENT

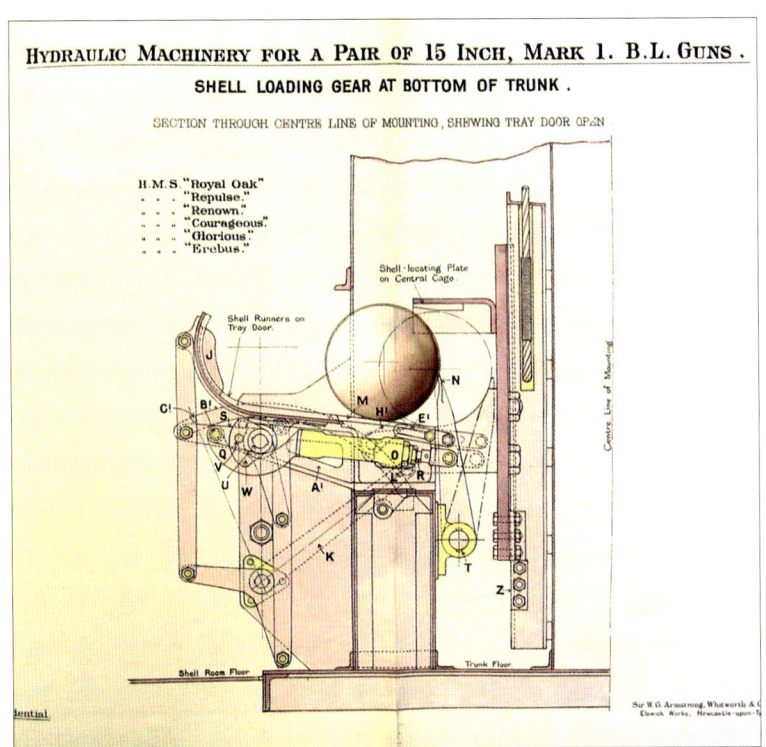

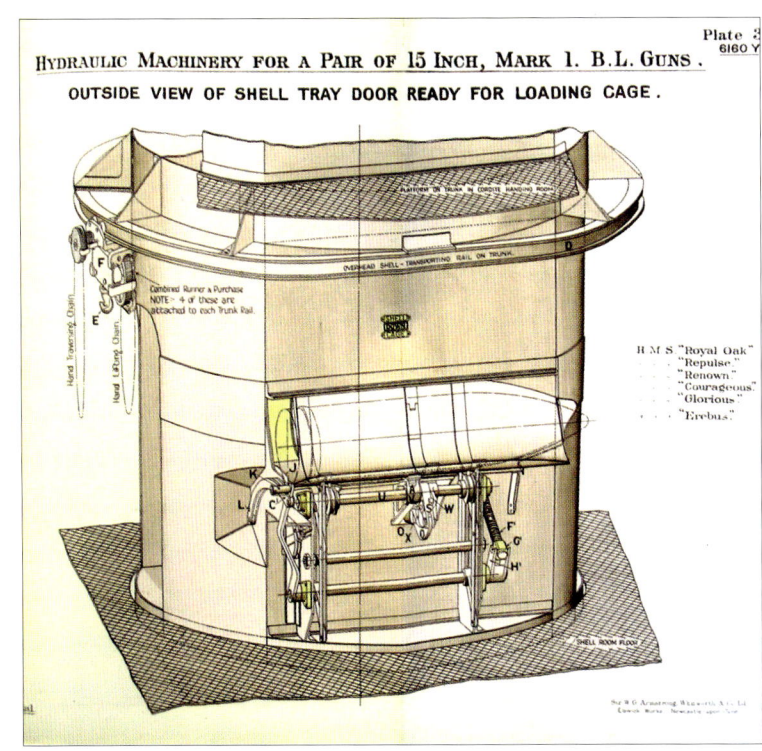

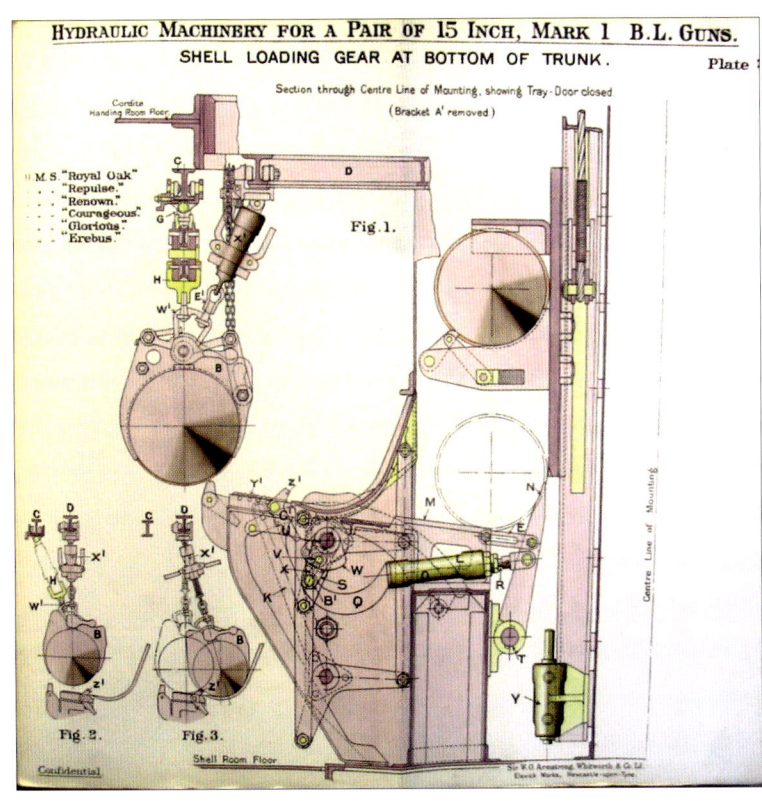

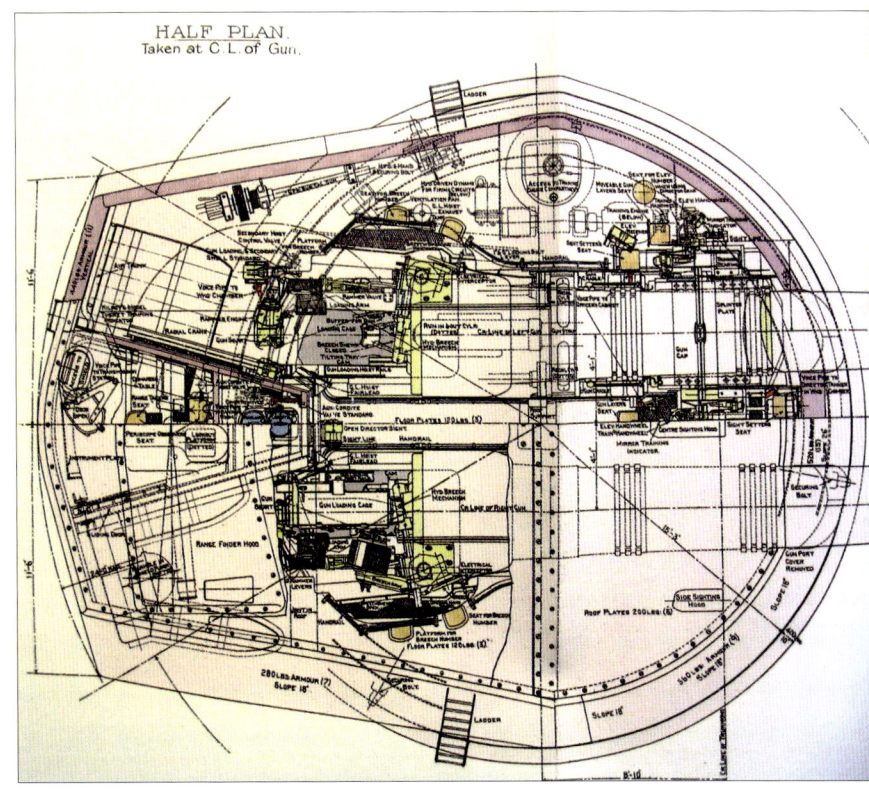

15-INCH MK I AND I* TWIN MOUNTINGS

The 15in mountings originally allotted to *Repulse* were Mk I* ordered in May 1914. The star indicated the adoption of 'Kenyon' doors for loading shells into the central hoist. The need to expedite the completion of *Repulse* resulted in the substitution of Mk I mountings, intended for *Royal Oak*, for two of her turrets. *Repulse* was officially listed as having one Mk I* and two Mk I turrets throughout her career but all three had 'Kenyon' doors. Oddly, the shell loading arrangement was still given officially as the 'only' difference between Mk I and Mk I* in 1943.

The 'Kenyon' door was a combined loading tray and door seal. It can be seen in the closed position in the drawings at top right and bottom left and in the hoist loading position at top left. *Repulse*'s turrets also differed from earlier Mk I turrets in having a thinner shield armour and circular, as opposed to faceted, front plates. In other respects they were of the same design as those in *Warspite* which can be seen in detail in the volume in this series for that ship.
(Plates from 15in Gunnery Manual)

TRIPLE MOUNTING MARK I. FOR 4 INCH B.L. GUNS.
GENERAL ARRANGEMENT
SCALE 1/8
SIR W. G. ARMSTRONG, WHITWORTH & Co LTD
SECTIONAL ELEVATION
REAR END VIEW
ORDER AND W. No 2103/1 TO 22 D
DRG No 16760

TRIPLE MOUNTING MARK I. FOR 4 INCH B.L. GUNS.
SIR W. G. ARMSTRONG, WHITWORTH & Co LTD
GENERAL ARRANGEMENT.
SCALE 1/4
SIDE ELEVATION
PLAN
ORDER AND W. No 2103/1 TO 22 D
DRG No 16759

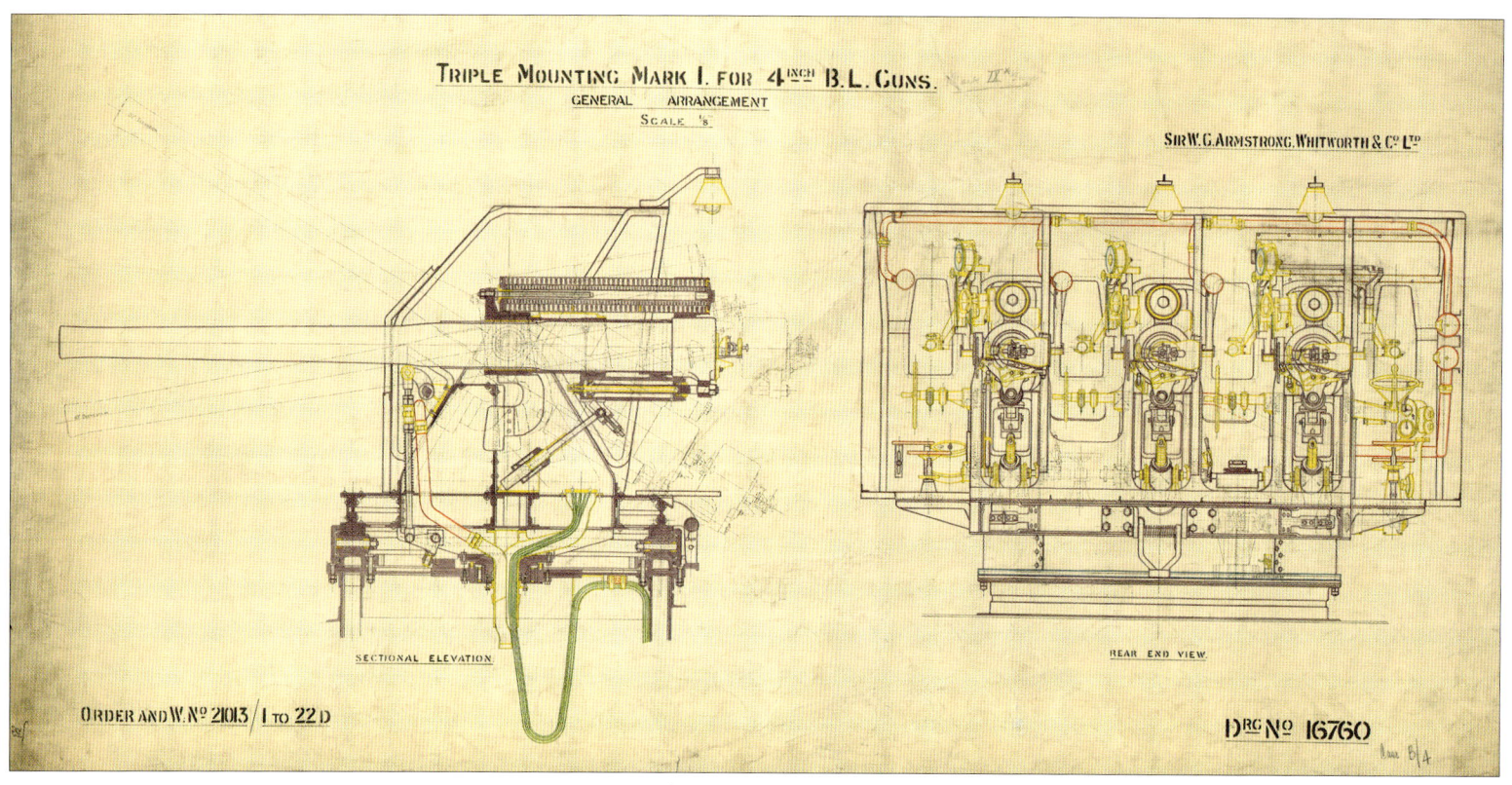

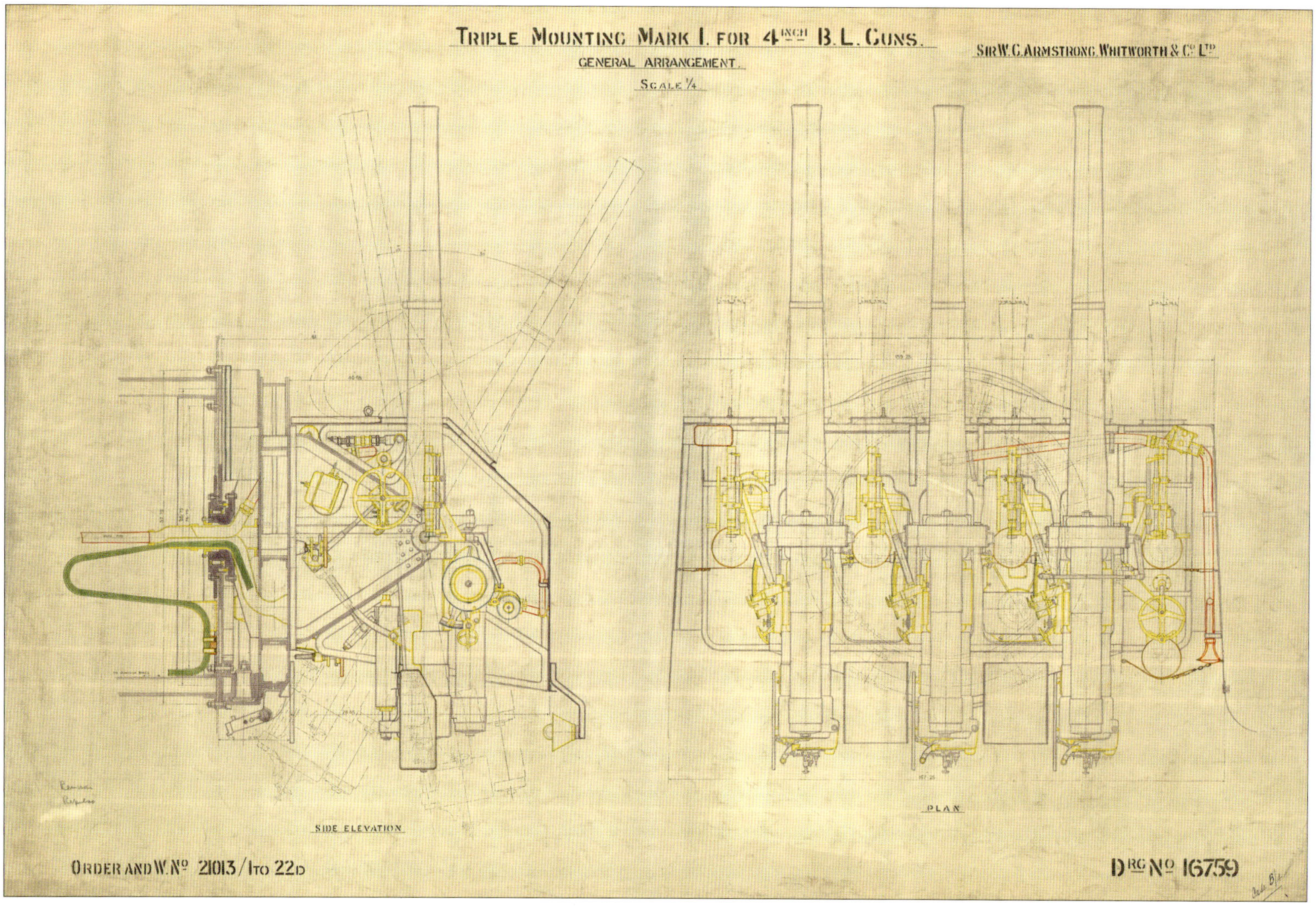

FIRE CONTROL

Primary main armament direction was provided from two positions – a director tower fitted on a platform below the fore-top and an armoured director tower fitted above the GCT in the conning tower. Both contained Scott/Vickers tripod type directors, either of which could control all the 15in guns via follow-the-pointer instruments. In divided control, 'A' and 'B' turrets could be directed from the aloft director and 'Y' turret from the armoured director. In addition, both forward turrets could be controlled from 'B' turret, with 'Y' under local control, or all three turrets could be controlled locally. Primary control for the directors and turrets was supplied from a Dreyer Mk IV★ fire control table located in the Transmitting Station (TS) abaft 'B' magazine on the Platform Deck. Ranges were provided from five rangefinders – four 15ft FT24, one in each turret on MG8 mountings, and one in the armoured director tower on a MW1 mounting, and one 12ft FQ2 in the spotting top. These, together with observed information on the target's course, speed and inclination, plus various ballistic and spotting corrections, and own-course control from the gyro compass, were processed by the Dreyer table into range and deflection information for transmission to the director sights and gun sights. Each turret also had a Dreyer turret control table for use, in combination with the turret's rangefinder and sighting gear, for local control.

The 4in armament was also provided with two director positions for day control, one on a platform below the 15in director tower on the foremast and one on the mainmast, both employing Vickers pedestal type directors, a light version of the tripod type. The two single 4in gun mountings were not compatible for control purpose with the director transmission system of the triple mountings and were supplied with range and deflection information via telephones or voice-pipes rather than follow-the-pointer instruments. For night control, the ship was provided with three night defence positions (NDP), two (port and starboard) on the bridge, below the Compass Platform and one in the night control tower on the mainmast. Each of the 4in triple mountings was treated as a group for control purposes: the two forward were group 1 port and group 1 starboard, with the three centre line mountings, from forward to aft, providing groups 2, 3 and 4. Either the 4in TS or spotting top could control all the guns in day control but the forward NDP controlled only groups 1 and 2 and after NDP only groups 3 and 4. Night communication was via voice-pipe and telephone, it did not use the director system.

Primary torpedo control was initially provided from the armoured torpedo control tower abaft the mainmast, which included a revolving hood for a 9ft rangefinder, a torpedo director on each side and a torpedo plotter, together with the necessary instruments to communicate with the submerged torpedo room. Torpedo directors were also provided forward, one on each side in the conning tower.

PROTECTION

The negotiations between the Admiralty and the armour firms for the supply of armour for the new battlecruisers were completed in January 1915 – the usual bureaucratic process of drawing up contracts took somewhat longer. The majority of that for *Repulse* was manufactured by her builder, John Brown, at their Atlas Works in Sheffield. The only exceptions were the roof for the conning tower and the communication tube (supplied by Thomas Firth) and the roof of the torpedo control tower (supplied by Cammell Laird).

Although Fisher specified armour on the same scale as that of *Indefatigable*, the arrangement adopted was much the same as that in first ships of the battlecruiser type – the *Indomitable* class. The earlier arrangement had the advantage over that in *Indefatigable* of not thinning the 6in side armour abreast the forward and after magazines. Compared to *Indomitable* the height of the belt in *Repulse* was 4ft 3in less, although this reduction was partially compensated by an extension of the protective plating of the Main Deck to a point 5ft below the lower edge of the side armour. There were also differences in the distribution of protection beyond the central citadel due to changes in the relative importance and extent given to vertical and horizontal protection. The upper barbette armour was the same as that of *Indomitable* except for being generally thinner below the Main Deck. One major omission in *Repulse* was the lack of any form of longitudinal protective bulkheads as defence against torpedoes. In March 1915 Fisher decided that this omission should be corrected and plans were put in hand to increase the thickness of the longitudinal bulkheads from ⅜in to 2in (lower half) and 1½in (upper half). Surprisingly, when the DNC pointed out that this would add 700 tons to the displacement and 7in to the draught and cause some loss in speed, Fisher insisted that the sacrifice was necessary. When, however, Tudor suggested that the change should be dropped since it would result in a two-month delay in the ship's completion, Fisher agreed.

Shortly after Jutland it was decided to increase the thickness of the flat of the Main Deck above the 15in magazines to 2in and this work was carried out during the final stages of fitting-out. Further improvements as listed below, were made by John Brown while the ship was docked at Rosyth during November–December 1916.

- Main deck over engine and condenser rooms on flat and for a distance of 5ft down the slopes increased to 3in.
- Lower Deck over 15in magazines and for 8ft outboard of their longitudinal bulkheads, increased to 2in.
- Lower Deck over steering gear increased to 3½in.
- Lower Deck abaft 'Y' barbette to Station 292 increased to 2½in on flat and slope.
- Lower Deck immediately forward of 'A' barbette to Station 43 increased to 2½in.
- Enclosing bulkheads of lower conning tower fitted with 2in plating.

4-INCH BL MK I TRIPLE MOUNTING

Despite the title above, the mounting was normally listed in official documents as simply 'TI'. Looking at the spacing of the guns it is not too difficult to see why the loading crews tended to get in each other's way – especially since, being a BL gun, it employed separate ammunition. The mounting was only fitted in *Repulse*, *Renown*, *Courageous* and *Glorious* (and briefly in the monitor *M27* during 1919) so became firstly unique to the *Renown* class when the latter pair were converted to aircraft carriers and finally to *Repulse* alone when *Renown* was modernised during 1936–39. (J9423 & J9424)

These changes added 475 tons to the displacement and 4⅓in to the draught, compensation for which was obtained by reducing the maximum amount of oil fuel carried by 600 tons (to 86 per cent of full capacity).

MACHINERY

It was originally intended to provide an entirely new 110,000shp machinery design with a HP and LP turbine on each of four shafts, higher pressure boilers and a reduced condenser plant. Since this proposal conflicted with the need to complete the ships quickly it was decided instead to install the same Brown-Curtis turbine machinery as that in the battlecruiser *Tiger* for which the design and patterns were immediately available. This involved accepting an increase in weight to accommodate an increase in the length and width of the engine rooms and an additional boiler room at the fore end of the machinery spaces to accommodate three extra boilers to provide an ample reserve of power. In January 1915, the Deputy Engineer-in-Chief indicated that this power would be 120,000 compared with the 112,000shp given in the legends of both December 1914 and March 1915. However, the DNC's description of the design accompanying the latter document stated that the machinery would develop 110,000 to 120,000shp (the former figure being added in pencil) and that it was estimated that slightly under 32 knots would be obtained in deep water (60 fathoms or more) at legend draught and about 31.25 knots at deep draught with 120,000shp.

It having been established that high power trials over shallow water resulted in a loss of speed, *Repulse* ran her steam trials over a new deep water course off the east coast of the Isle of Arran, in the Firth of Clyde. During the contractor's four-hour run on 15 August 1916 she developed a mean power of 117,000shp during the first two hours and 120,700shp in the second two hours, the maximum power attained being a little over 125,350shp during the final 30 minutes. Displacement at the time was 28,200 tons, 1700 tons above the design load. Apart from a mean figure of 31.63 knots at 118,850shp for the entire four-hour run, no record of the speeds obtained seems to have survived. The series trials – progressive double runs over the measured mile in opposite directions, starting at 12,000shp and working up through ten stages to full power – were run on 15 September 1916. The mean result for the two full power runs gave a speed of 31.73 knots at 119,025shp with 275rpm. The fact that 32 knots was not reached is unsurprising given that the ship was 3300 tons above her designed load, that the high-power trial was run in a Force 8 gale and that the power she developed was less than that achieved on 15 August. It was concluded that at designed load the ship could make 32.5 knots with 120,000shp, although this should be tempered by the fact that such a performance required ideal conditions.

GENERAL

Whatever the fighting value of *Repulse* and *Renown*, the DNC's department was justly proud of their achievement, having given Fisher precisely what he asked for in record time. The department's comment on the design origin was pure Fisher

... conceived as direct result of the Falkland Islands Battle and also of the experience gained during the [Helgoland Bight] actions fought on 28th August 1914, which showed the immense value of very high speed with long range powerful gunfire and large radius of action which qualities, in association, enable a ship to run down those of the enemy under any circumstances, with the power of enforcing or declining action, as may be considered desirable. Features of such magnitude could only be obtained if the armour protection were comparatively light, unless very great size of ship were accepted ... (DNC Records of War Construction, May 1918).

Fisher put forward multiple purposes for the construction of his new battlecruisers including trade protection, fleet scouting and inshore support of amphibious operations in the Baltic. Much has been made of the last named as the primary purpose but it is a more likely to have been all of the above with varying order of priority depending on with whom and for what he was arguing at the time. Ultimately they joined the Grand Fleet's heavy scouting force as the 2nd Division of the 1st BCS in the latter part of 1916.

On the plus side, the ships were certainly fast, heavily armed and proved very good sea-boats due to the substantial flaring of the hull side and high freeboard. Some strengthening of the forward structure was required following early experience in heavy weather and they did have a tendency to ship water over the quarterdeck, but they could maintain high speed in most conditions without difficulty. Their speed and 15in guns were certainly seen as an asset to the Battle Cruiser Force, but serious criticism was directed at their weak protection against both shellfire and torpedoes and at the limited number of both their 15in guns and torpedo tubes. In September 1918 Rear-Admiral H F Oliver, commanding the 1st BCS with his flag in *Repulse*, submitted a paper on the dispositions to be adopted if his squadron found itself in action with German battlecruisers. The accepted disposition of the time was with the 2nd Division (*Repulse* and *Renown*) astern of the 1st Division (*Lion*, *Princess Royal* and *Tiger*). Oliver argued the 2nd Division should be in the van in order to be in a position to utilise their greater speed to pursue enemy ships, should they decline action. He also pointed out that, should the enemy turn back, the 2nd Division had enough speed to fall back on the 1st – closely following Fisher's idea of being able to enforce or decline action. He also suggested that in good visibility, if the German battle-cruisers were willing to stand and fight, the 2nd Division should, due to their 'very inferior armour', engage at a range beyond the effective range of the German 12in and 11in guns. This involved stationing the 2nd Division well ahead and off the bow of the lead ship of the 1st Division (*Lion*), the latter at an initial range of 16,000yds. The 2nd Division was to engage the leading ships of the enemy at a range of about 18,000yds until the fire of the latter was sufficiently diminished to reduce the danger of closing. It also offered a good position for the firing of torpedoes providing the *Lion* was sufficiently clear of the line of fire. The commander of the Battle Cruiser Force, Vice-Admiral W Pakenham, while generally agreeing with Oliver's paper, considered

PARTICULARS, JANUARY 1917

Builder:	John Brown, Clydebank
Laid down:	25 January 1915
Launched:	8 January 1916
Completed:	August 1916
Cost:	£2,949,087
Displacement (tons):	26,058 light, 27,333 load, 31,659 deep, 32,071 extreme deep
Length:	750ft 1in pp, 794ft 2½in oa, 790ft 2½in wl
Beam;	89ft 11½in max
Mean Draught:	25ft 1in light, 26ft 2in load, 29ft 8½in deep, 30ft 0½in extreme deep
Gun Armament:	6 x 15in/42cal BL Mk I, two twin Mk I and one twin Mk I* mounting (120rpg)
	17 x 4in/44.35cal BL Mk IX, five triple TI and two single PXII mountings (120 rpg)
	2 x 3in/45cal QF Mk I AA, single HA Mk II mountings (200 rpg)
	2 x 3pdr saluting, single mountings (100 rpg)
Torpedo Tubes:	2 x 21in submerged broadside (10 torpedoes)
Small Arms:	Five 0.303in Maxim machine guns (field and boat) and 168 rifles (40 for seamen and 128 for marines)
Armour:	Side: 6in amidships, 4in forward, 3in aft
	Bulkheads: 4in and 3in
	Barbettes: 7in, 6in, 5in and 4in
	15-inch gun shields: 9in front, 7in sides, 11in rear, 4¼in roof
	Conning tower: 10in walls, 3in roof
	Conning tower support: 3in sides 2in ends
	Gun control tower: 6in
	Revolving director hood: 6in front and sides, 3in rear and roof
	Communication tube: 3in
	Torpedo control tower: 3in sides, 2in roof
Protective Plating:	Side above belt: 1½in
	Funnel uptakes: 1½in sides and 1in ends
	Forecastle Deck: from 'A' barbette aft 1⅛in, with 1½in stringer plates
	Main Deck: 1in flat, 2in slope over boiler rooms; 2in flat and slope over magazines; 3in flat, 3in and 2in slopes over engine and condenser rooms.
	Lower Deck: 2½in and ¾in fore and aft; 2in over magazines; 2½in above 15in magazine abaft 'Y' barbette and forward of 'A' barbette; 3½in over steering gear.
	Conning tower floor: 3in.
	Torpedo control tower floor: 1in
	Lower CT: 2in bulkheads
Machinery:	42 Babcock and Wilcox large-tube boilers (max working pressure 285psi). Two sets of Brown-Curtis direct drive turbines, each consisting of an IP ahead and a HP astern on the wing shafts and HP ahead, LP ahead and LP astern on the inner shafts
	120,000shp = 32 knots at design load draught and 31¼ knots at deep draught for 4 hours; 112,000shp = 31.5 knots at load draught and 31 knots at deep draught for 8 hours; normal sea going maximum 100,000shp = 29.5 knots (figures with clean bottom and in deep water)
Oil Fuel Capacity:	3830 tons normal, 4243 tons max
Endurance (approx) with max oil fuel stowage:	1700nm at 30 knots; 2700nm at 25 knots; 3800nm at 20 knots; 4000nm at 18 knots; 4200nm at 15 knots; 4700nm at 12 knots
Complement:	953 (980 as flagship)

that the 'distant detachment' of the 2nd Division was 'not to be contemplated' unless the enemy ships were substantially inferior in number. He did accept that *Repulse* and *Renown* should be in the van, where they could concentrate their fire on the leading enemy ships. He added that for this purpose they would be more effective employing full 6-gun broadsides rather than 3-gun salvoes.

THE PLANS

The official plans for *Repulse* consist of a design set, an as-fitted set for the ship as completed in 1916 and a second as-fitted set showing her in 1936 after modernisation. There are also a number of detail drawings but, unlike most other ships in the Admiralty collection, these are very limited in extent. The primary plans, and those made greatest use of in this book, are the as-fitted sets; those for 1916 were produced by John Brown following her completion and those for 1936 by Portsmouth Dockyard following her major modernisation. It is worth noting that the as-fitted plans were simply a record of the completed ship – a useful reference for the Admiralty and the dockyards. They were not always 100 per cent accurate, although errors were usually of a minor nature and unsurprising given the amount of work involved, although in the case of *Repulse*'s 1916 set there are more errors than one would normally expect – no doubt due to the pressure of both wartime production and the need to complete the ship at an early date.

Occasionally the as-fitted drawings were modified to bring them up to date. Originally more than one set of as-fitted plans was produced but since only one set is, with rare exception, included among the surviving plans it is a matter of luck if it is a modified version. Fortunately, this is the case with the surviving original set for *Repulse* where alterations were made in green ink following her major refit of 1918–21 (removed items having their outlines crossed through with short dashes, also in green ink). It should be noted that such alterations include all changes up to the specified date so would include all surviving alterations from 1916–18 as well as those made during the refit. However, this only applies at the date of modification so any alterations made after the completion of the original plans but no longer in the ship at the time of modification would not be shown. In the captions references to the items in green indicate that they were made during the 1918–21 refit unless specifically referred to as being made either earlier or at an unknown date. The originals are drawn to a scale of ⅛in = 1ft: a 50 per cent reduction on what was standard for the as-fitted drawings of large ships pre-war. This no doubt resulted from the increasing size of ships and served to ease the problems of drawing and handling very large plans. Nevertheless, the original profile and deck plans for *Repulse* are still 9ft long. The same remarks can be applied to the 1936 as-fitted plans except that these are unmodified and therefore indicate clearly the condition of the ship in 1936 complete with the surviving modifications made during 1922–32. The following passages describe some of the standard conventions employed in the as-fitted plans.

Profile: Both the 1916 and 1936 profiles are drawn assuming the ship is at its original 'as designed' (1915) LWL draught of 25ft forward and 26 ft aft. The designed trim by the stern was common to all British battlecruiser designs with the exception of *Tiger* which, like battleships, was designed assuming a level keel. Height dimensions above the LWL, such as the gun axis heights, are also design figures although the length pp, while still taken from the intersection of the stem and the

ABBREVIATIONS IN TEXT

ac	Alternating Current [electric power]	HA/LA	High Angle/Low Angle	NDP	Night Defence Position
A/F	As-Fitted [plan]	HACP	High Angle Calculating Position	NWTD	Non Water Tight Door
AP	Admiralty Pattern [anchor]	HACS	High Angle Control System	oa	Overall
APC	Armour Piecing Capped [projectile]	HB	Hook Bracket [torpedo]	PO	Petty Officer
atb	Anti Torpedo Boat	HC	Hose Connection	pp	Between Perpendiculars
ATD	Air Tight Door	HEDA	High Explosive [projectile] Direct Action [fuse]	p & s	Port and Starboard
BCS	Battle Cruiser Squadron			QF	Quick Firing [gun]
BL	Breech Loading [gun]	HETF	High Explosive Time Fused [projectile]	RAF	Royal Air Force
CinC	Commander in Chief	HF/DF	High Frequency Direction Finder	rpm	Revolutions Per Minute; and Rounds Per Minute
CPC	Common Pointed Capped [projectile]	H/F D/F	High/Frequency Direction/Finder		
CPO	Chief Petty Officer	HP	High Power [turbine]	RYPA	Roll, Yaw and Pitch Apparatus
crh	Calibre Radius Head	HT	High Tensile [steel]	SAP	Semi Armour Piercing [projectile]
dc	Direct Current [electric power]	IP	Intermediate Pressure [turbine]	shp	Shaft Horse Power
D/F	Direction Finder	kW	Kilowatts	SL or S/L	Searchlight
DNC	Director of Naval Construction	LCS	Light Cruiser Squadron	SL	Side Lug [torpedo]
DNO	Director of Naval Ordnance	LP	Low Power [turbine]	TCT	Torpedo Control Tower
EM	Escape Manhole	LWL	Load Water Line	TD	[Weather] Tight Door
FAA	Fleet Air Arm	MF/DF	Medium Frequency Direction Finder	TS	Transmitting Station
F/C	Fire Control	MS	Mild Steel	TSR	Torpedo, Spotter, Reconnaissance [aircraft]
FMB	Fast Motor Boat	MV	Muzzle Velocity	WC	Water Closet
GCT	Gun Control Tower	MVO	Mineral Vaporising Oil	wl	Water Line
HA	High Angle	NC	Non-Cemented [armour]	WTT	Water Tight Trunk

designed LWL, is that established from the measurements of the hull at the time of launch while the freeboard aft is 1in greater than the design figure. The decks and platforms were arranged parallel to the LWL except for the sheer of the forecastle and upper decks forward and the upper and middle decks aft. In addition, the above description of 'horizontal' applies to the lengths of the main, upper and forecastle decks at the deck edge, the camber of the decks creating a curved rise along the middle line which reduced toward the bow and stern as the beam narrowed. The use of a horizontal line at the deck edge had value where this defined the upper or lower edges of side armour since this allowed uniformity in the height of the majority of armour plates (although still variable forward and aft due to variation in the flare of a ship side). This did not apply to the forecastle deck of *Repulse,* since there was no side armour, but it is likely that it still served to simplify construction – an important consideration for a ship that needed to be completed quickly. It was not unusual in other ships for the middle line to be horizontal (causing a downward curve to the deck edge due to camber) where no side armour was involved.

Decks: Items fitted 'over', that is in the deck above (such as hatches, skylights, manholes, vent openings, etc), immediately under the deckhead or simply raised well above deck level are outlined in red. Such items are often, but not always, provided with the helpful annotation '(over)'. Red lines are used to indicate the outline of decks and platforms 'over' where they extend beyond the outline of the subject deck or platform. The location of bulkheads and transverse and longitudinal beams fitted under the deck are shown in blue dashed or dash-dot lines. On the mess decks the dashed red lines with an arrow at each end indicate the rigged positions of hammocks.

General: Naval terminology suffers from inconsistency and generally the terms used in the original drawings have been employed in the accompanying captions. For example, the 'spotting top' (a true reflection of its function) might also be called 'foretop' or 'control top' (the as-fitted drawings of *Renown* refer to it as the 'spotting tower'). Such things are further complicated by variations in terms used by those who designed and built ships and those who served in them. Boats are only shown in outline and the positions of the light guns are often only indicated by the base of their mountings (particularly noticeable in the 1916 deck plans where only one mounting of each type is shown in full). The conventions for colour do not apply to the modifications made in 1921 where all the additions and deletions are indicated in green ink except for a few minor anomalies where green corrections have been altered or deleted in black ink. A number of the abbreviations listed below are in some cases given on the plans in full or only partially abbreviated.

ABBREVIATIONS USED ON THE AS-FITTED PLANS

AADO	Assistant Air Defence Officer	**GM**	General Mess [locker]	**PO**	Petty Officer
ADO	Air Defence Officer	**GS**	Guard Rail Stanchion	**POS**	Position
AP	After Perpendicular	**HA**	High Angle	**RR**	Rifle Rack
AS	Awning Stanchion	**HSWTD**	Horizontal Sliding Water Tight Door	**RS**	Rail Stanchion (Variation on GS)
AW	Above Water [torpedo tube]	**HW**	Hot Water [tank] (also used for Hand Wheel)	**RU**	Ready Use
BD	Between Decks [gun mounting]			**SL**	Searchlight
BL	Breech Loading (also used for Bread Locker)	**HYD**	Hydraulic	**SR**	Shell Rack
		KL	Kit Locker	**SUP**	Supply [fan]
CO₂	Carbon Dioxide	**KT**	Kneehole Table	**SW**	Salt Water [tank]
COMPT	Compartment	**LKR**	Locker	**V**	Vent
CPO	Chief Petty Officer	**LWL**	Load Water Line	**WC**	Water Closet
CUPB	Cupboard	**M/A**	Motor Alternator	**WO**	Warrant Officer
D/F	Direction Finder	**MAA**	Master at Arms	**WR**	Wardrobe
DRS	Drawers	**M/C**	Machine	**WT**	Water Tight
E	Electrical [resistance box]	**M/G**	Motor Generator	**W/T**	Wireless Transmitter
ER	Engine Room	**MH**	Manhole	**WTB**	Water Tight Bulkhead
ERA	Engine Room Artificer	**MR**	Mess Rack	**WTC**	Water Tight Compartment
ERT	Engine Room Telegraph	**MV**	Mushroom Vent	**WTD**	Water Tight Door
EXHT	Exhaust [fan]	**OA**	Ordnance Artificer	**WTEM**	Water Tight Escape Manhole
F&B	Fire and Bilge [pump]	**OF**	Oil Fuel [pump]	**WTF**	Water Tight Frame
FL	Folding Lavatory	**OFF**	Oil Fuel Filling [connection]	**WTH**	Water Tight Hatch
FP	Forward Perpendicular	**OTB**	Oil Tight Bulkhead	**WTM**	Water Tight Manhole
F/T	Flash Tight	**OTM**	Oil Tight Manhole	**WTSS**	Water Tight Sliding Shutter
FW	Fresh Water [tank]	**P**	Pillar	**WTSV**	Water Tight Slide Valve

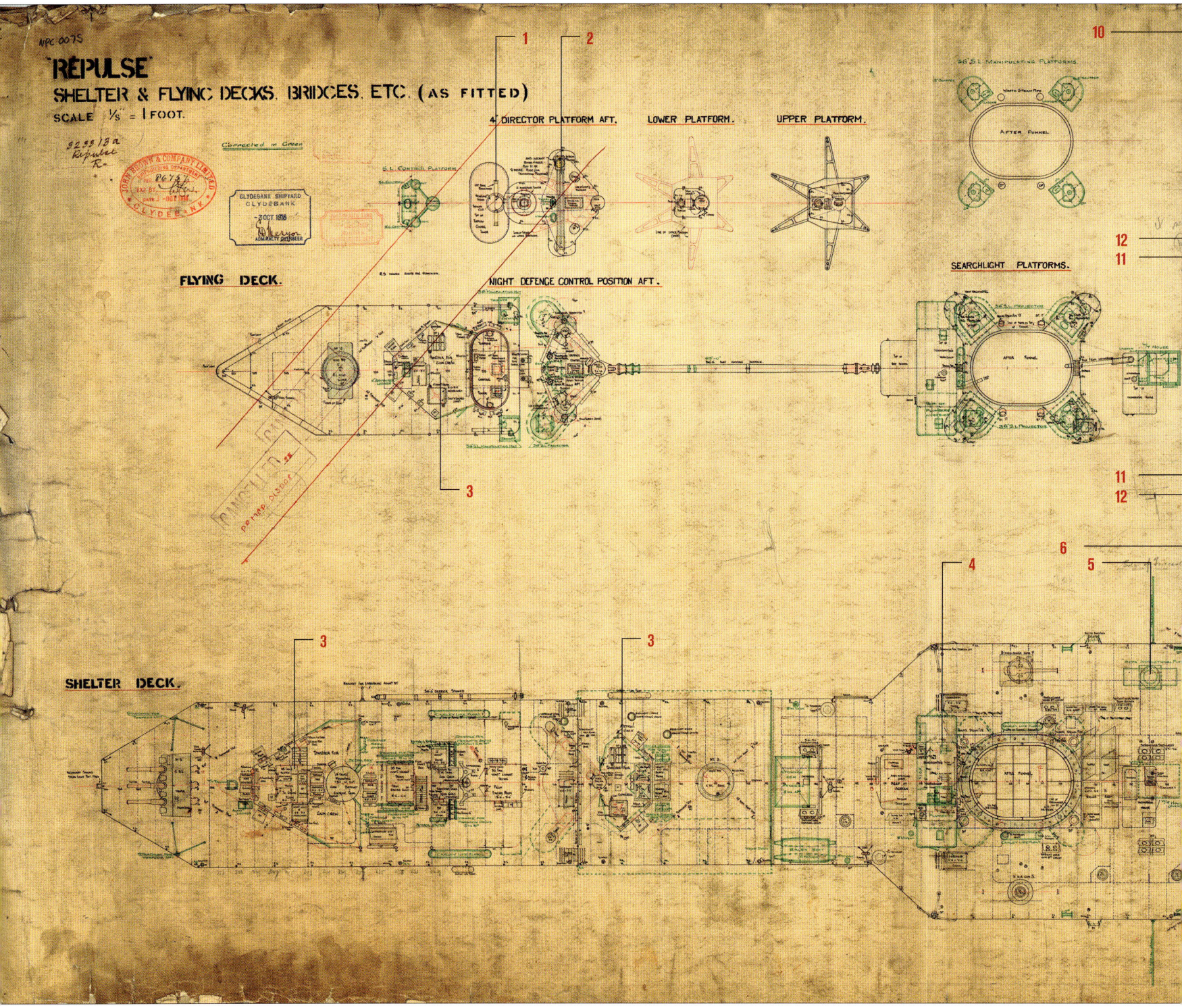

SHELTER DECK, FLYING DECK AND BRIDGES
(J9373)

1. **9ft FQ2 rangefinder** in the TCT has not been corrected – it was replaced by a 15ft FT24 rangefinder on MG10 mounting in 1918.
2. **After 4in director platform** also accommodates the ship's FT29, 2m HA rangefinder. Its MT6 mounting was carried on traversing rails so that it could be operated from either side of the platform.
3. **4in gun-crew shelters** on the shelter, flying decks and CT platform were originally partly enclosed with canvas screens. These were replaced with steel screens in 1917.
4. **The blacksmith's workshop** has been extended to port and starboard and divided to provide for a plumber's workshop on the starboard side. This necessitated moving the blacksmith's forge further to port. Despite the fact that the blacksmith now had more space, an additional 'blacksmith's shop' has been added further forward on the starboard side (the green rectangle just abaft the fore funnel).
5. **RYPA** (Roll, Yaw and Pitch Apparatus) was a training platform for mounting either a 9ft rangefinder or secondary armament director intended to reproduce the effects of ship movement for instructional purposes (it also provided for course changes). There was a larger version of this equipment for main armament directors but this seems to have been limited to shore training establishments.

SHELTER DECK, FLYING DECK AND BRIDGES

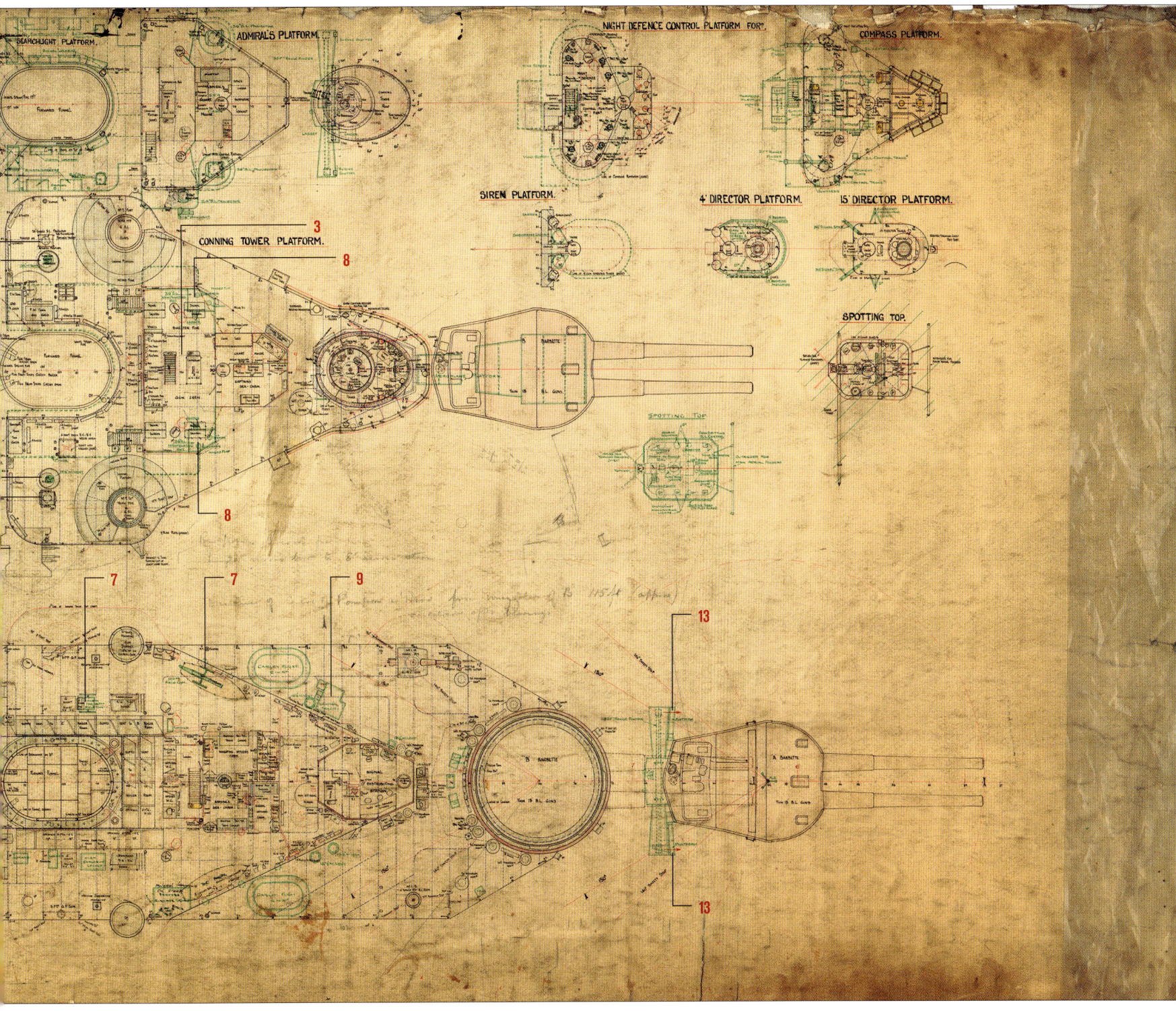

6. **Proposed pom-pom position** indicated in faint pencil outline for the starboard mounting fitted during the ship's 1933–36 Modernisation.
7. **12pdr field gun and limber** shown in their intended stowage positions. Under normal circumstances this equipment was only carried while on foreign service.
8. **The S/L manipulating huts** (p & s) were fitted in early 1918 and served to control the elevation and training (via rod gearing) of the new 36in S/Ls fitted on the admiral's platform above.
9. **Loading teacher** for training 4in gun-crews.
10. **Flag deck** added in 1918 as an extension of admiral's platform provided a new flag and signal deck which replaced the wartime signal stations on each side of the main deck.
11. **Flag signal tube** (p & s) via which flag signals were passed up from the signal stations on the main deck. When the signalling arrangements were moved to the bridge, the tops of these tubes were blanked and fitted with MT vents to serve as vent trunks.
12. **24in signalling projectors** (p & s), shown in their stowed positions, were mounted on portable trolleys. Although not shown as deleted, it is probable that they were removed either in 1918, when 24in signalling projectors were fitted on the admiral's platform, or during her major refit when two further 24in projectors were provided on the new flag deck.
13. **Access platforms** (p & s) ran along the fore sides and below the 30ft rangefinder fitted to the rear of 'A' turret. The platforms were fitted to the rangefinder housing supports and had steps down from the turret roof (see profile, page 53). A similar arrangement was provided for the 30ft rangefinder on 'Y' turret but, since this was positioned higher, the platform was level with the edge of the turret roof and did not require the steps.

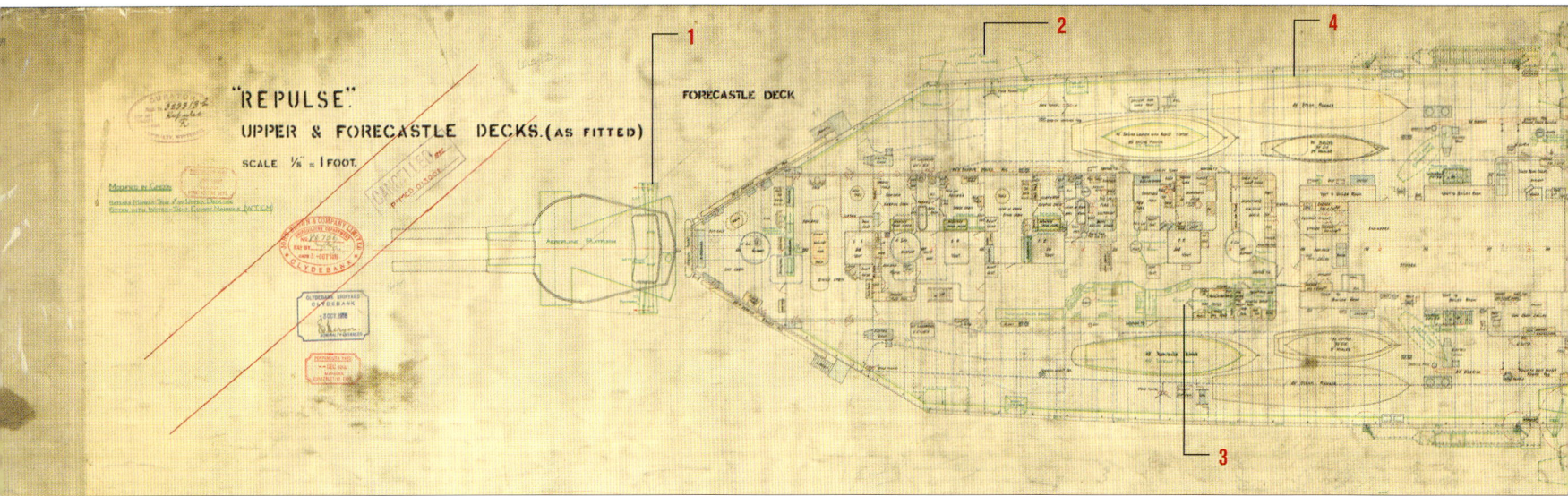

FORECASTLE DECK

Paravanes were supplied to the ship in Aug–Sep 1916 but only the chocks on which they were stowed are shown on the plan as originally drawn. The chocks are located on each side of the forecastle just forward of the torpedo davits abreast 'A' turret and just abaft the flag signal tube abreast the fore funnel. There is also a fifth position on the after starboard side of the forward breakwater, although the standard outfit of paravanes was four. All these chocks, apart from the starboard after one, were crossed through when the drawing was corrected and it seems probable that this correction should have been applied to all five. The two paravanes added as a correction (housed on the underside of the shelter deck at Station 158 port and 133 starboard) represent only two of the four Type CIV** allocated to the ship; the location of the other two is not known. (J9372)

1. **The 30ft FX2 rangefinder** in 'Y' turret, unlike that in 'A' turret, replaced the original 15ft FT24 on MG8 mounting. The mountings for the 30ft turret rangefinders differed (MG14 in 'Y' turret and MG18 on 'A' turret) due to the fact that the forward mount was external to the turret.

2. **Harbour position for one of the 30ft gigs.** Earlier capital ships generally had several of these, usually with davits on both sides for gigs, whalers and dinghies. *Repulse* was built without any, probably because the rapid construction requirements included the omission of any fittings or equipment that that were not essential to the efficient running of the ship. This single pair of davits was added during her 1918–21 refit.

3. **Additional officer accommodation** provided for the fleet surgeon, displaced from the upper deck as a result of the fitting of the after, port side pair of torpedo tubes, the navigating officer (additional to his cabin on the bridge) and the 1st lieutenant who does not appear to have had a previously dedicated cabin. Note the table for a model of the ship just aft of the navigating officer's cabin – judging by its length, the model was probably to a scale of ¼in = 1ft (ie 16ft 6in long).

4. **The edge of the wood planking** added to the forecastle and quarter decks during the 1918–21 refit are marked by a shaded green line set 2ft inboard of the ship's sides. Note that the forecastle planking ends at the aft side of the cable holders.

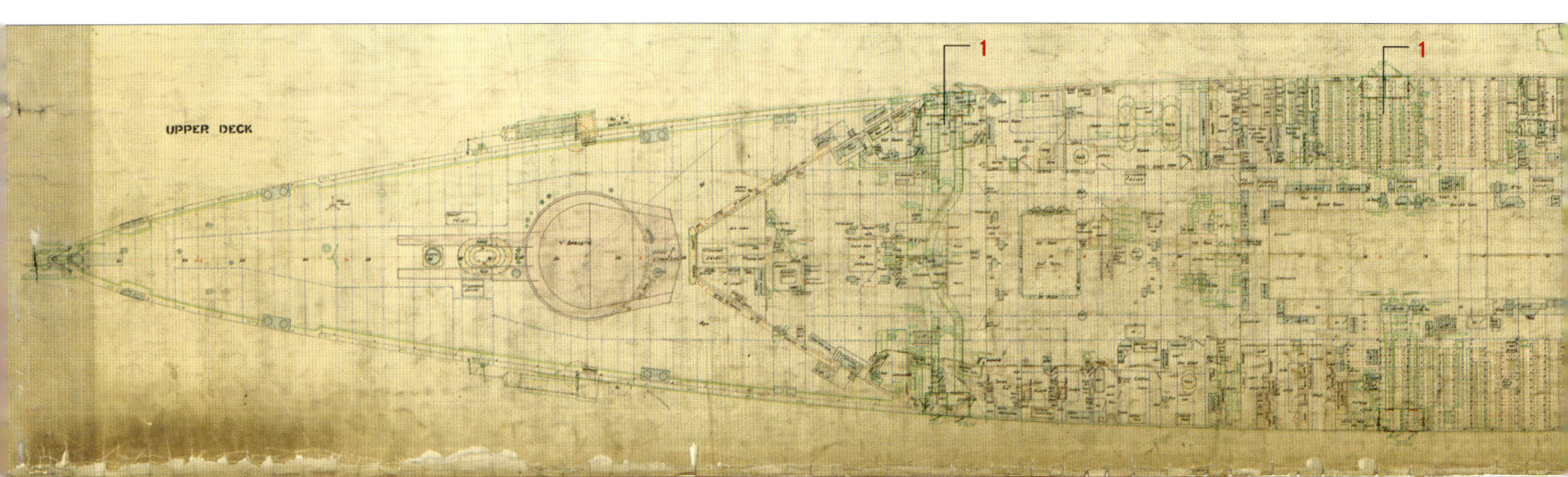

UPPER DECK

This deck and the main deck below were the primary accommodation areas. Officer accommodation was arranged hierarchically from the top down. The admiral and his staff occupied most of the after block of the superstructure on the forecastle deck above, the senior officers, the ward room and its sub compartments, occupying the sides of this deck; and the junior officers, midshipmen and warrant officers the main deck from the stern and then forward along each side. Forward of this, the upper and main decks provided the mess spaces for the ship's crew, their petty officers and the marines together with the usual washing and dressing facilities, etc. I have often wondered what use was made of the very large area provided for an admiral when such ships were not serving as flagships. (J9372)

FORECASTLE DECK AND UPPER DECK

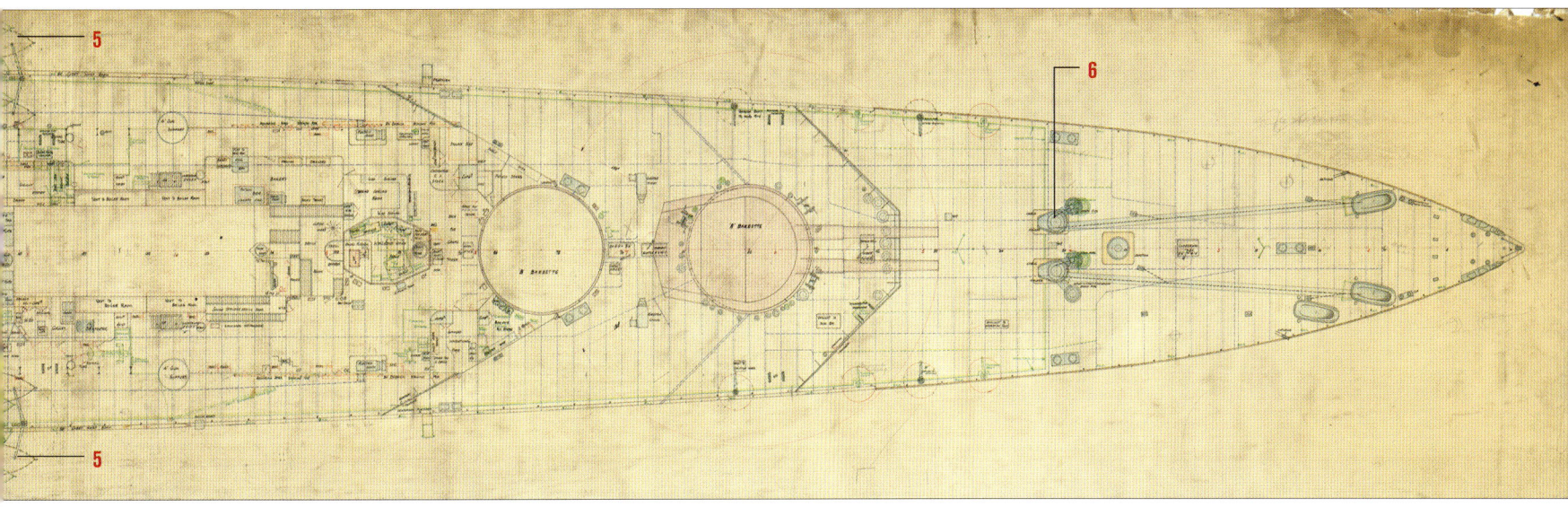

5. **The 32ft life cutters** (p & s) have had their davits relocated outboard of the ship's side in order to give sufficient clearance over the newly fitted bulges. Similar changes were required for the ship's main boat boom (increased in length from 60ft to 63ft), the accommodation ladder platforms (extended outboard c1ft), the torpedo and paravane davits (abreast 'A' turret and the forecastle breakwater respectively) moved further forward and the relocation of the heel of the sounding boom from the side of the fore superstructure to brackets extending outboard from the forward triple 4in gun mounting supports (note that these brackets are just below the level of the shelter deck).

6. **The cable holders.** These are only provided for the bower anchors, none being fitted for the sheet anchor. If the latter was used, weighing it would have required the transfer of its chain to the starboard 'bower' cable holder. It seems probable that this omission was another case of saving on construction time. Note that the chain pipes for the bower anchors are shown relocated further forward, an alteration probably made during the 1918–21 refit. It is not clear why this was done, especially as no such alteration was made in *Renown*.

SHIP'S BOATS, OCT 1916

2 x 50ft steam pinnaces
1 x 45ft admiral's barge
1 x 42ft sailing launch with auxiliary motor
1 x 36ft sailing pinnace
3 x 32ft cutters
1 x 32ft galley
2 x 30ft gigs
2 x 27ft whalers
2 x 16ft dinghies
1 x 13ft 6in balsa raft
5 x Carley life floats
 (2 pattern 20, 1 pattern 19 and 2 pattern 18)

Of the above, the 45ft barge, 32ft galley and one of the 16ft dinghies were allocated for her service as a flagship (1916–18). In 1921, when she was no longer serving as such, the barge was replaced with a 40ft steam pinnace and the galley omitted but, according to the amended plans, she retained the second dinghy. The dinghies had been moved from the shelter deck to the forecastle deck by 1921 (note that they were hung from the underside of the shelter deck).

By Jan 1921 the number of Carley floats had increased to nine pattern 18. There were a number of variations in type and location for the Carley floats during 1916–18

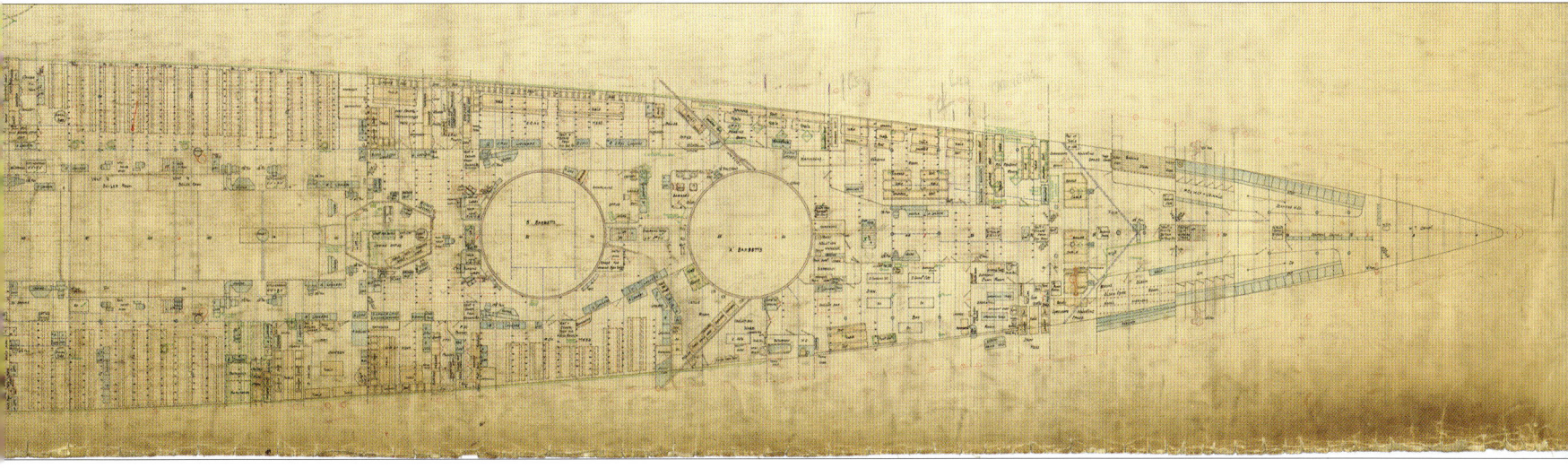

1. Four 21in AW torpedo tubes were fitted (p & s) on the upper deck during the 1918–21 refit. For these the ship was allocated sixteen 21in Mk IVA – IV*A SL torpedoes. These were the same as those provided for the submerged tubes except that they were fitted with side lugs (hence the 'SL' designation) rather than hook brackets ('HB'), the former required for AW tubes and the latter for submerged tubes. Eight of the torpedo bodies were stowed in the tubes while the spares were hung from the transport rails above them. The warheads were kept in the torpedo head magazine in the hold (see page 25) and were normally only fitted to the bodies in wartime when action was expected. The boxes, shown in thick green line, fitted around the ends of the tubes indicate splinter protection for the warheads (including the spare). They were 2in thick on the ship's side (giving a total of 3½in including the side plating) and 1½in thick elsewhere.

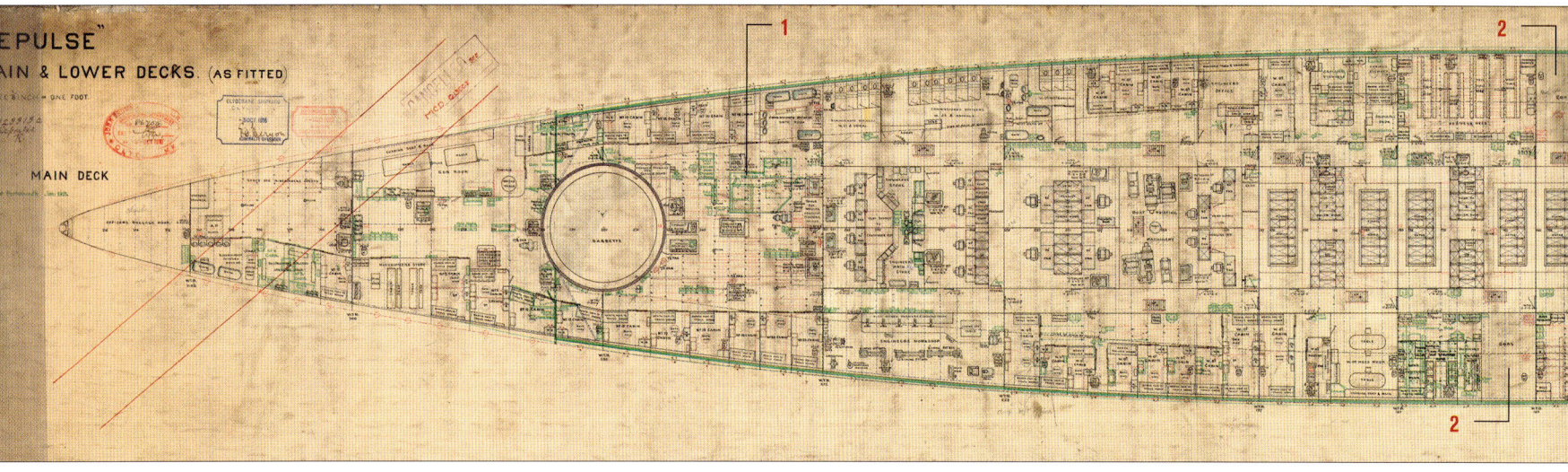

MAIN DECK

The main deck has been subject to a considerable amount of detail correction covering additions to the minor subdivision, the distribution of furniture and the designations of various compartments. In most cases it is impossible to say how much of this was carried out during her major refit and how much beforehand. As this is the main protective deck, all the ventilation trunks and the funnel uptakes are fitted with armour gratings, indicated individually by the blue lines crossing each grating from corner to corner. Note that the access ladders in the boiler uptakes and ventilation trunks are provided with hinged armour gratings but these are only indicated by dashed outlines. (M1001)

1. **Second W/T office** for the Type 2* set. There is also an auxiliary W/T office on the upper deck just abaft the mainmast which probably housed the Type 9 short-range set. It is difficult to be absolutely precise about the locations of the ship's W/T sets given the total absence of any form of rig drawing for the ships prior to 1936.
2. **The coal bunkers** (p & s) may seem surprising in an oil-fired ship, but were required for the ship's steam-powered boats, the galleys and the stoves in the officer accommodation.
3. **The flag signal station** (p & s) was intended to provide a protected position below decks for war service. In this case the protection was minimal since the ship's side was only 1½in thick. Nevertheless, the personnel and their

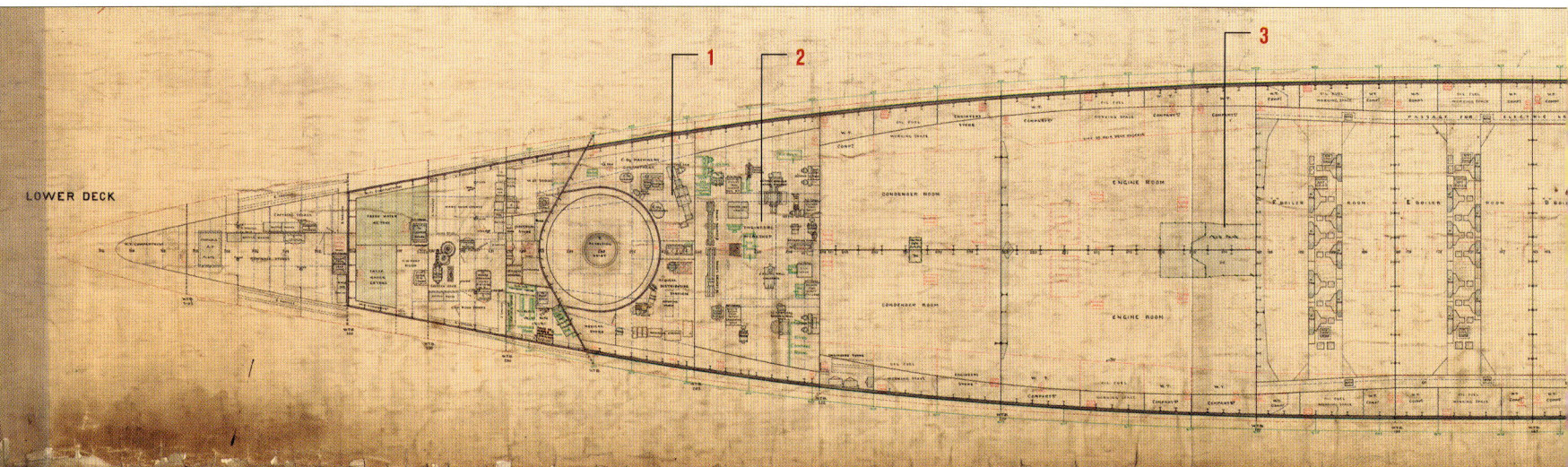

LOWER DECK

This plan shows along the sides of the ship the outlines of the upper compartments of the bulge, and their watertight frames. Inboard of this, the green line added along the outer edges of the main side armour is intended to indicate its increased thickness. The framing shown behind the side armour serves to illustrate its 4ft spacing which only reduced to 2ft where it was necessary to fit an intermediate frame to support armour butts that did not coincide with the main frames. The majority of these frames consisted of 10in 'I' bars (8in behind the 4in and 3in side armour) but where the butts occurred these were increased to 12in. The 'I' bars were not fitted at bulkheads but where a bulkhead coincided with a butt the bulkhead was reinforced with a 12in wide, ¾in plate with double 4in x 4in boundary angles. (M1001)

1. **This CO_2 machinery compartment** contained the cooling plant for 'Y' 15in magazine. A similar plant was provided for the forward magazines between Stations 58 and 68. These served to maintain the temperature of the ship's cordite charges within limits that would help to maintain their long-term consistency, both for stability and ballistic performance. As further insurance against deterioration it was standard practice for samples from cordite lots (especially older ones) to be landed for quality checks.
2. **The engineers' workshop** is equipped with sufficient machinery to set up a small engineering factory – especially if you add the second engineers' workshop on the deck above (port side above the condenser room) and the armourers' and electricians' workshops forward between Stations 68 and 76.
3. **The feed tank** shown here as deleted is in fact still there. This appears to be the result of the draughtsman who modified the drawings deciding that this was an error since the top of the tank is actually 3ft below the level of the lower deck.

MAIN DECK AND LOWER DECK

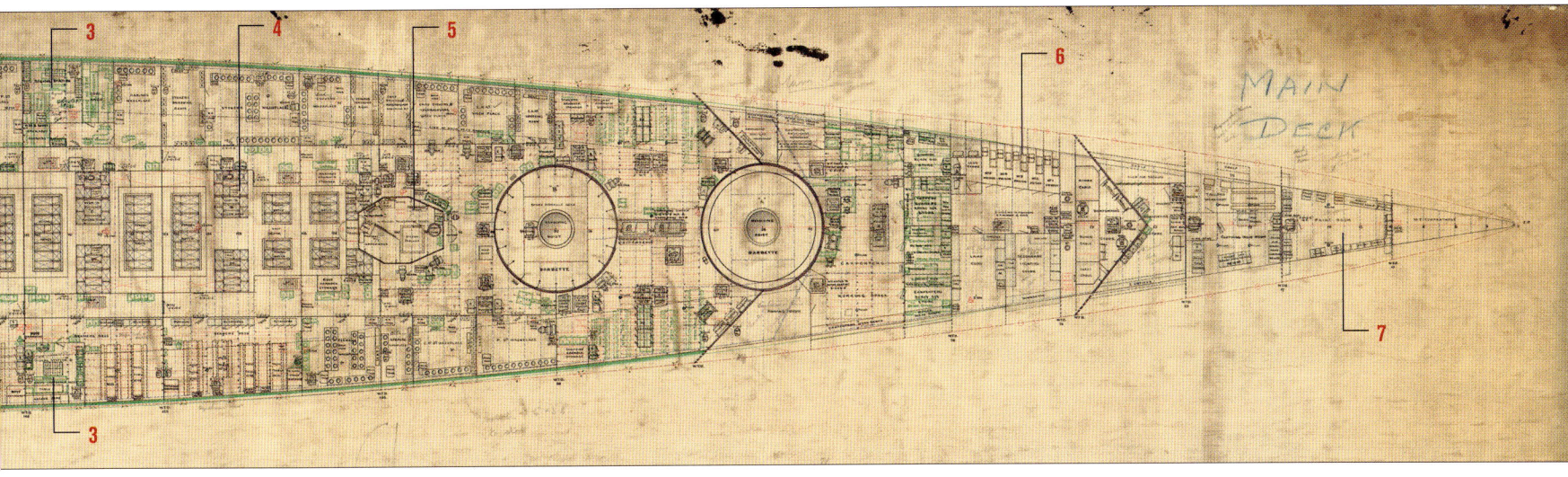

equipment would still have been less exposed to weather, blast and to splinter damage than they would have been on an open flag deck. One suspects that tradition and a desire for a position with a better view prompted their replacement with a bridge flag deck. The original positions, now, ironically, behind 6in armour, were converted to mess spaces.

4. **Boiler room access** was provided either via ladders into the boiler room fan chambers or lifts in the port side passageway. Both routes were provided with airlocks, since the boiler rooms were pressurised, those for the lifts being in the passageway while those via the vent trunks were fitted between the fan chambers and the boiler room.

5. **The main W/T office** at the base of the CT support contained the Type 1-16 combined set with its aerial trunk on the aft side of the compartment. She was also fitted with a Type 34 main set, either in 1918 or during the 1918–21 refit, which may have been located in the new W/T cabinet added in the intelligence office, two decks above.

6. **The ship's prisons** were certainly not intended for comfort. Each cell was only 4ft wide, had minimal natural light from a small side scuttle and the only furniture was a combined bed/seat and a small table.

7. **The paint stores** were located well forward, the remote location a reflection of the flammable nature of their contents (note that there is a second paint store immediately below on the lower deck).

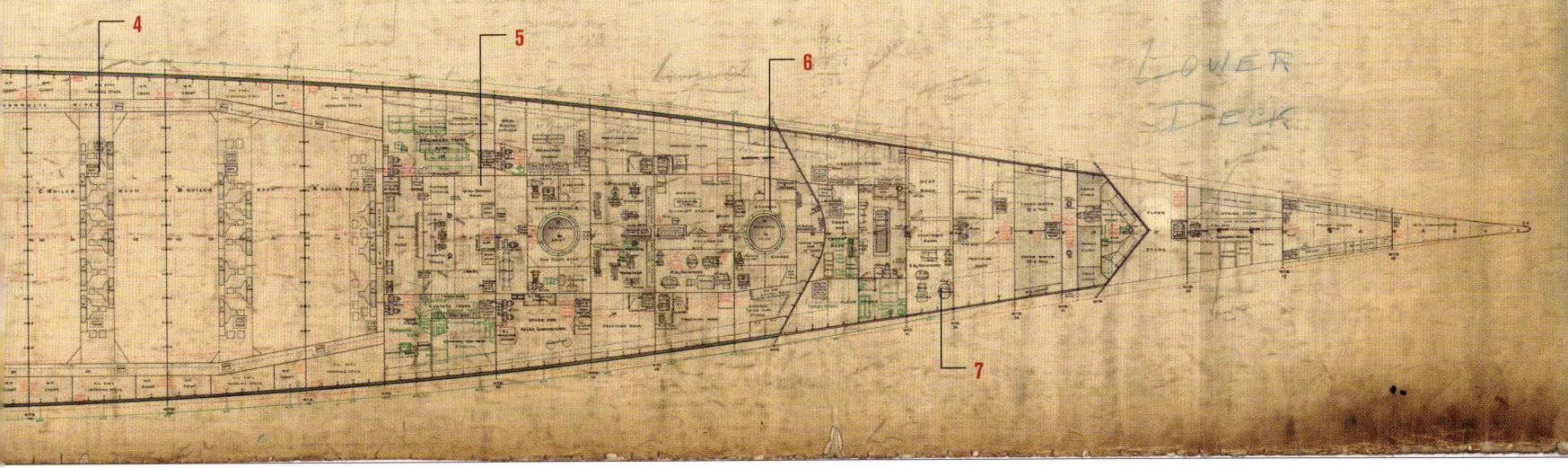

4. **The fan chambers** in boiler rooms 'C' to 'F' each contained eight 81in diameter fans, while the smaller 'B' and 'A' boiler rooms contained seven and three respectively, for a total of 42 fans, each driven by a vertical single cylinder steam reciprocating engine. These drew air down through the vent trunks into the boiler rooms to maintain sufficient pressure to provide a forced draught to the boilers.

5. **The gyro compass room** originally contained two Sperry master compasses but the addition of a second gyro compass room in the fore, starboard corner of the engineers' workshop (probably during her 1918–21 refit) would imply that one of the two was relocated (the alternative of a third master compass seems unlikely). This may have been to reduce the chance of both instruments being disabled by action damage but it is worth noting that this alteration was not applied to *Renown*.

6. **The green rings** around the hoist trunks of 'A' and 'B' mountings are 2in protective plating tubes, extending 5ft above the deck, intended to shield the circular opening for the hoist trunk. These were added in combination with the 2in protective plating fitted on the lower deck above the magazines, in 1916–17. This alteration was not required for 'Y' mounting as its barbette armour extended down to the lower deck.

7. **The CO_2 machinery compartment** between Stations 38 and 41 provided the refrigeration and cooling of the adjacent meat (or cold) room and vegetable (or cool) room. The second, additional, CO_2 machinery compartment abaft it served another cool room in the space marked in green as the 'flour store' (Stations 44–50) – the error has been corrected in pencil.

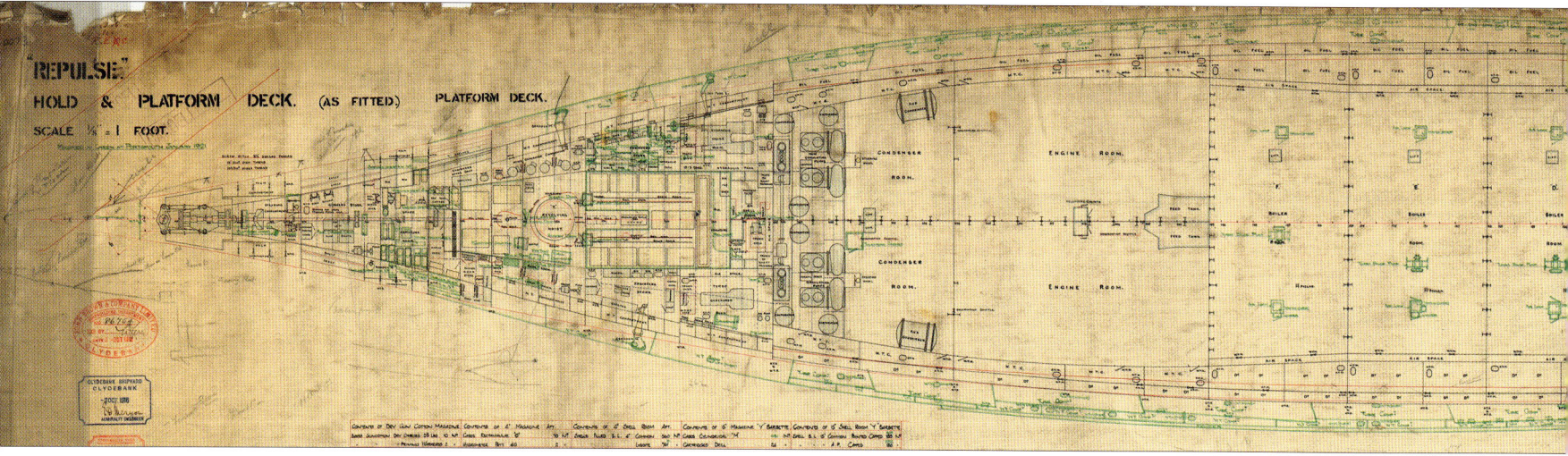

PLATFORM DECK

The platform deck's name derives from the fact that it was not in fact a continuous deck but a series of platforms fitted between the main bulkheads and often fitted at differing levels (the latter most noticeable in this case between 'A' boiler room and the watertight bulkhead at Station 31 – see profile drawings).

The deck level coincides with the widest part of the added bulges, which extend for 550ft along each side of the ship covering the full length of the magazine and machinery spaces. The main centre section from Stations 141 to 250 had inner and outer compartments, the former being packed with sealed 9in diameter steel tubes with wood plugs in each end while the outer compartments were void. The tubes and the inner compartments which contained them were intended to collapse under pressure (note the use of angled bulkheads and the deliberate lack of structural continuity) to absorb the impact of an underwater explosion, and serve to slow splinters that might otherwise penetrate the hull proper. The main bulges forward of Station 141 were formed as single compartments, the foremost being void while the remainder were filled with tubes. The main compartments aft of Station 250 were also single but all were void.

The deck accommodates all the primary auxiliary machinery that is not associated with the main propulsion plant. The electric generators include two Browett Lindley steam reciprocating engines driving Rees Rototurbo 200kW dynamos, one on the centre line (Stations 31–38) and one on the port side (Stations 88–104, starboard); a Mirrlees Diesel driving a 175kW Laurence Scott dynamo (Stations 88–104 port); a Brotherhood steam turbine driving a 202.5kW Westinghouse dynamo (Stations 252–262 starboard); and, added on

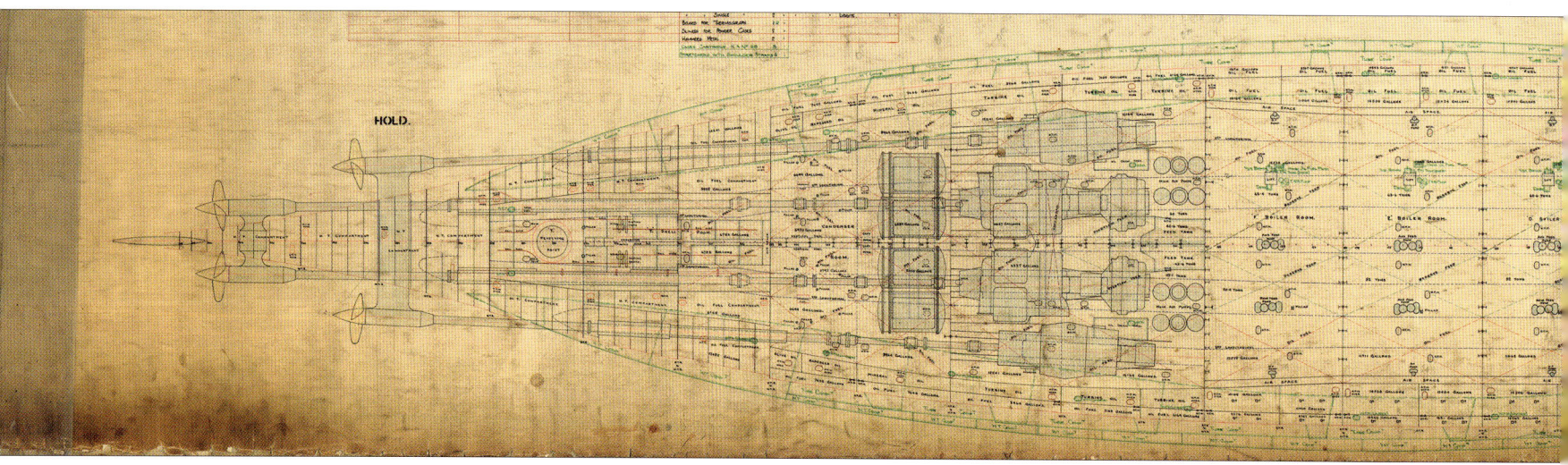

HOLD

The framework shown in 'A', 'B' and 'C' boiler rooms is the support structure for the boilers. It is not shown in the remaining boiler rooms because they are all identical to 'C' boiler room. The compartments in the double bottom which contain oil fuel or feed water are indicated by dashed lines running from corner to corner of their enclosing oil-tight or watertight transverse and longitudinal frames. Note that there is a single frame space 'cofferdam' at each end of the run of feed water tanks down the middle of the ship. The wing and double bottom compartments along the side of the ship containing oil fuel do not have diagonal lines since, at the level of the hold, they are not 'hidden' by structure above them. Note that the capacity of the oil fuel tanks is given in gallons and that for the feed water tanks in tons. (M1002)

1. **The tables** list the contents of the shell rooms and the magazines on the platform deck and in the hold. They have been subjected to few changes. The primary alteration is the adjustment of the proportions of 15in APC and CPC shell in favour of the former (from 50 to 75 per cent) as a result of the lessons of the Battle of Jutland. Only the battlecruisers retained CPC projectiles since they were likely to engage with cruisers – in the battleships the entire outfit was changed to APC (excluding a small number of shrapnel and practice projectiles).

PLATFORM DECK AND HOLD

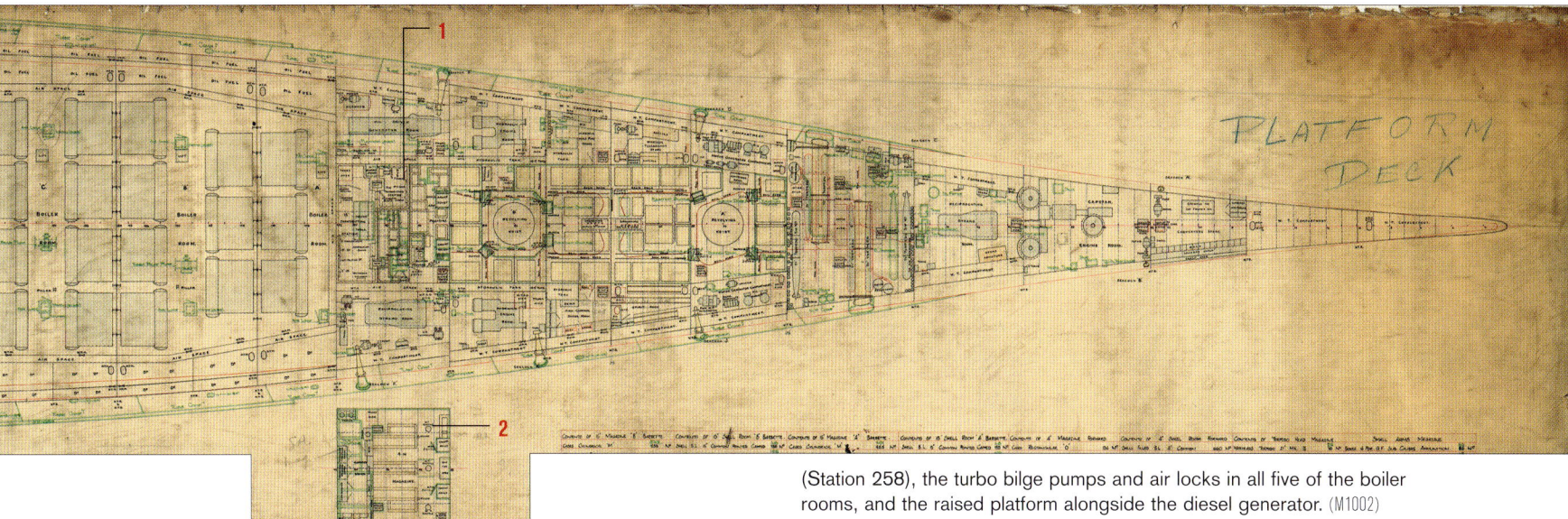

the port side during the 1918–21 refit, a Parsons steam turbine driving a second Westinghouse dynamo (Stations 264–276). The main electrical supply was rated at 225volts dc. Three hydraulic pumps served to power the 15in gun mountings, two forward abreast 'B' mounting and one aft between Stations 252–262 port. Also the steam piston engine driving the fore capstan and cable holders (Station 23–31) and finally the steering gear aft.

Several of the modifications in green on this deck are actually restorations of items omitted from the original drawings – these include the bulkhead abaft the steering gear (Station 310½), the condenser in the turbo generator room (Station 258), the turbo bilge pumps and air locks in all five of the boiler rooms, and the raised platform alongside the diesel generator. (M1002)

1. **This area accommodated** the main 15in TS, the 4in TS and the magazine for the 3in HA guns. At some point during 1917–18 the HA magazine was moved down to the platform below, the space freed being used to enlarge the main TS and add a Type 31 fire control W/T cabinet in its starboard, forward corner. At the same time the Dreyer Mk IV* F/C Table was moved forward about 1ft 6in presumably to provide more space for the operators.
2. **This rectangle represents** an additional platform level fitted centrally between bulkheads 88 and 102. It accommodated the 4in magazine and gunners' store until the store was modified for service as the 3in magazine displaced from the platform above when the TS was re-arranged.

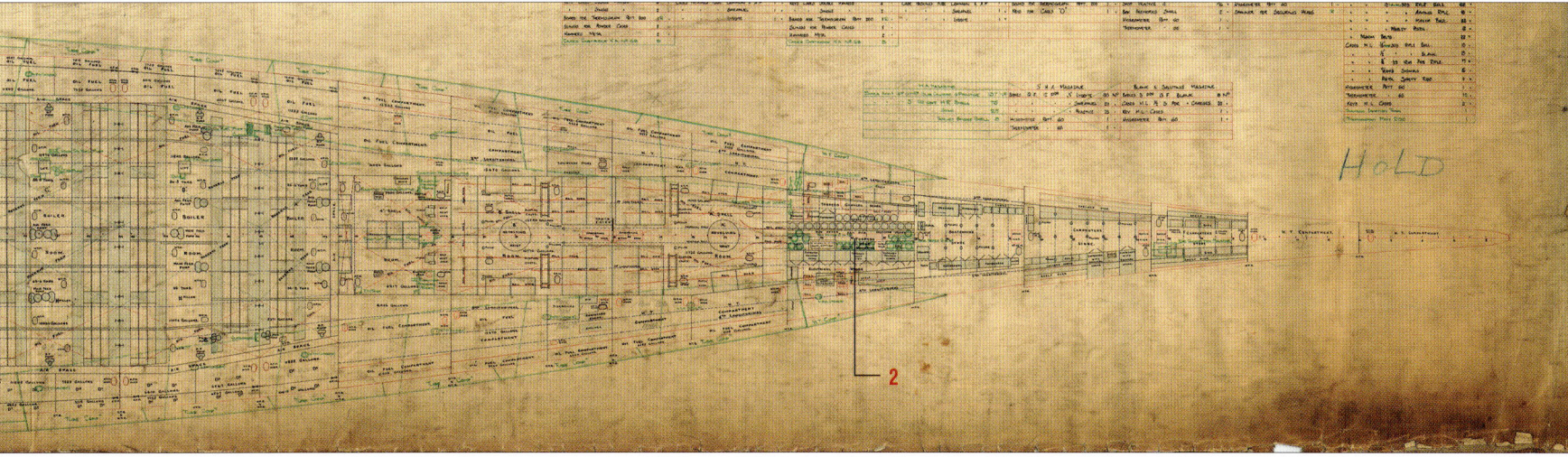

2. **The torpedo head magazine** originally contained ten warheads (the row of circles to the left) and five collision heads for exercise (on the right) – the row of similarly sized circles to port are not warheads but mine sinkers in the adjacent torpedo gunners' store. The green circles are the 16 warheads required to complete the outfit after the addition of the eight AW torpedo tubes. Note that the table for the torpedo head magazine indicates Mk II warheads, as supplied for the original Mk II torpedoes, but this should have been corrected to Mk IV following the ships resupply with Mk IV torpedoes.

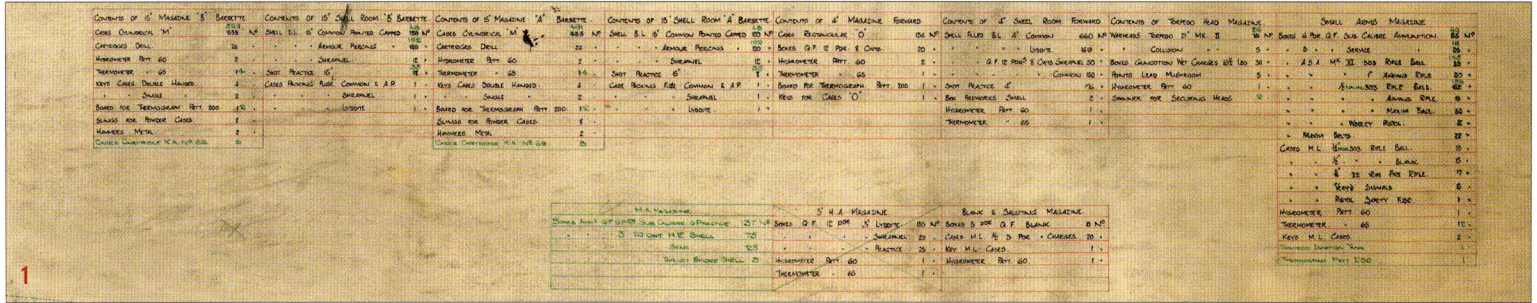

STERN TO 303 STATION

The sections reproduced in this and the following pages are all derived from a single plan (J9374). Each section is provided with the appropriate part of the main 1916 profile (J9371) which is reproduced in full in the gatefolds. The sections are transverse half sections with their position identified by Station (frame) number, those forward being for the starboard side looking forward and those aft for the port side looking aft. Since ships were not necessarily symmetrical in their internal arrangements, the detail on the other, blind, side of the ship can only be accurately ascertained by reference to the plan views.

The dominant features of the stern area are the rudder and propellers. The steering arrangements consisted of a single rudder operated by the then standard screw steering gear. The main steering engines were in the condenser room, about 135ft further forward. The rudder area was 320ft^2 which provided a tactical diameter of just over 1000yds with the rudder at full helm (35°). Speed had little effect on the tactical diameter but naturally the helm angle did. At 30 knots the full 32-point circle, with 35° helm, took 5 minutes to complete. The *Repulse* and *Renown* were the first modern capital ships to reintroduce the single rudder, all the earlier British dreadnought battleships and battlecruisers having been fitted with twin rudders. Although the latter provided more total rudder area and reduced the tactical diameter, the difference was not as great as one might expect (for example the tactical diameter of *Lion* at 24kts was 840yds but she had a total rudder area of 570 ft^2 and was 90ft shorter than *Repulse*). The single rudder would have been much easier to fit into the limited space at the after end of such a fine-lined ship than a double rudder and, given the need to complete the ship quickly, would also have helped towards the reduction of work involved.

The Wasteneys Smith's 60cwt (3-ton) stream anchor in the stern hawse pipe was provided with an alternative stowed position at the after end of the upper deck early in 1917. At the same time a gantry, overhanging the stern, was fitted for lifting the anchor out of and into its new position. The short post at the end of the gantry carries the stern light. The gantry was removed in the late 1920s.

The ensign staff shown in its 'peace position' has actually been deleted at the time the drawing was modified in green while its 'war position' on the after superstructure, which should have been the one deleted, remains untouched.

The protective deck from the 3in armour bulkhead at Station 300 to Station 315 was constructed of two thicknesses of 1¼in HT steel. The area above the steering gear as far as the bulkhead at Station 310½ was increased during the ship's Nov 1916 – Jan 1917 refit to 3½in by the addition of 1in HT plate.

A Williams-Janney auxiliary engine, fitted at the fore end of the steering compartment, provided an alternative electrical drive for the steering gear for emergency use (an alternative to the old system of employing multiple hand steering wheels).

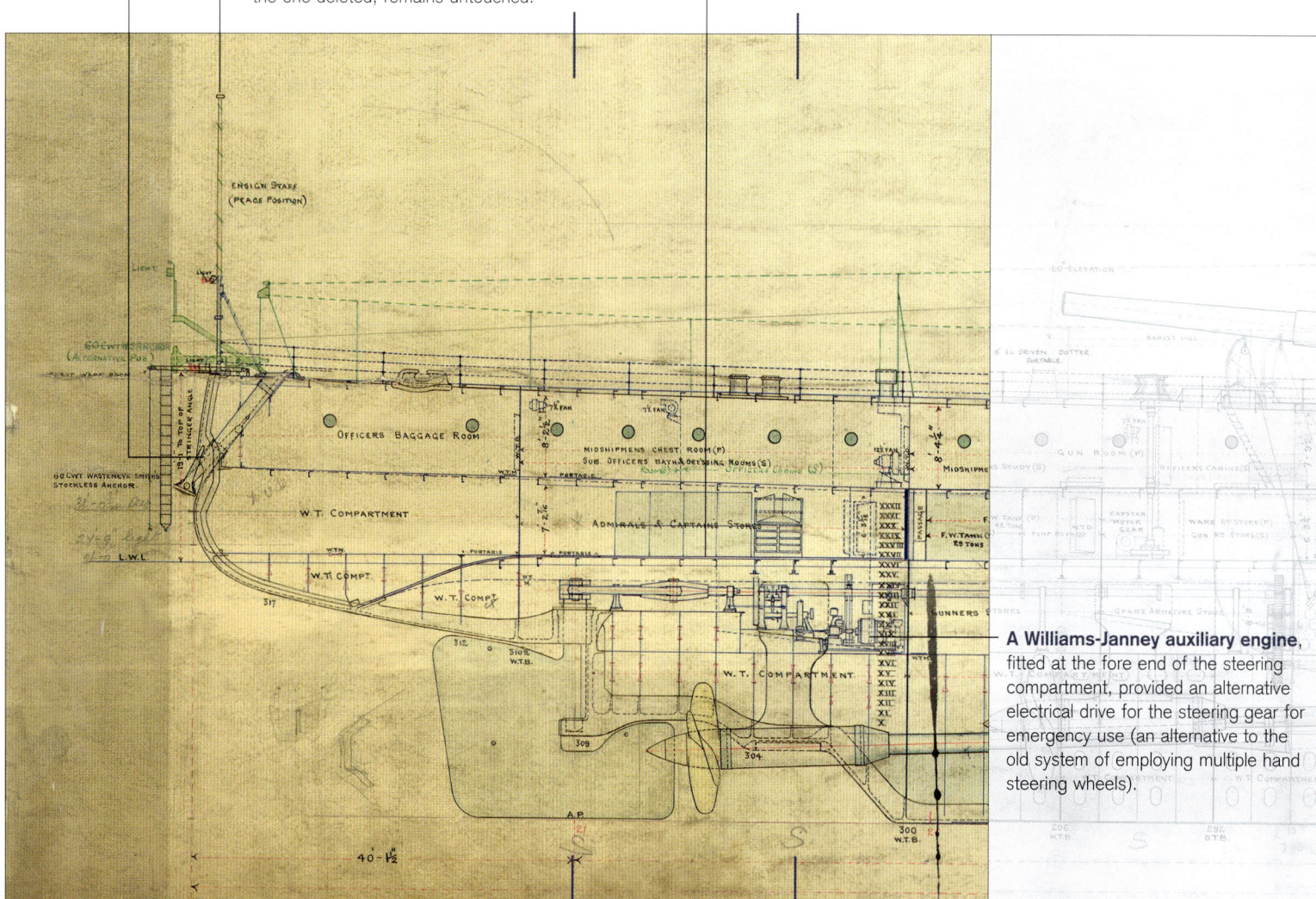

309 STATION   **303 STATION**

SECTIONS AT STATIONS 309 AND 303, PORT SIDE, LOOKING AFT

The section at 309 coincides with the axis of the rudder post or after perpendicular, while that at 303 is close to the centre of the support struts for the inner propeller shafts.

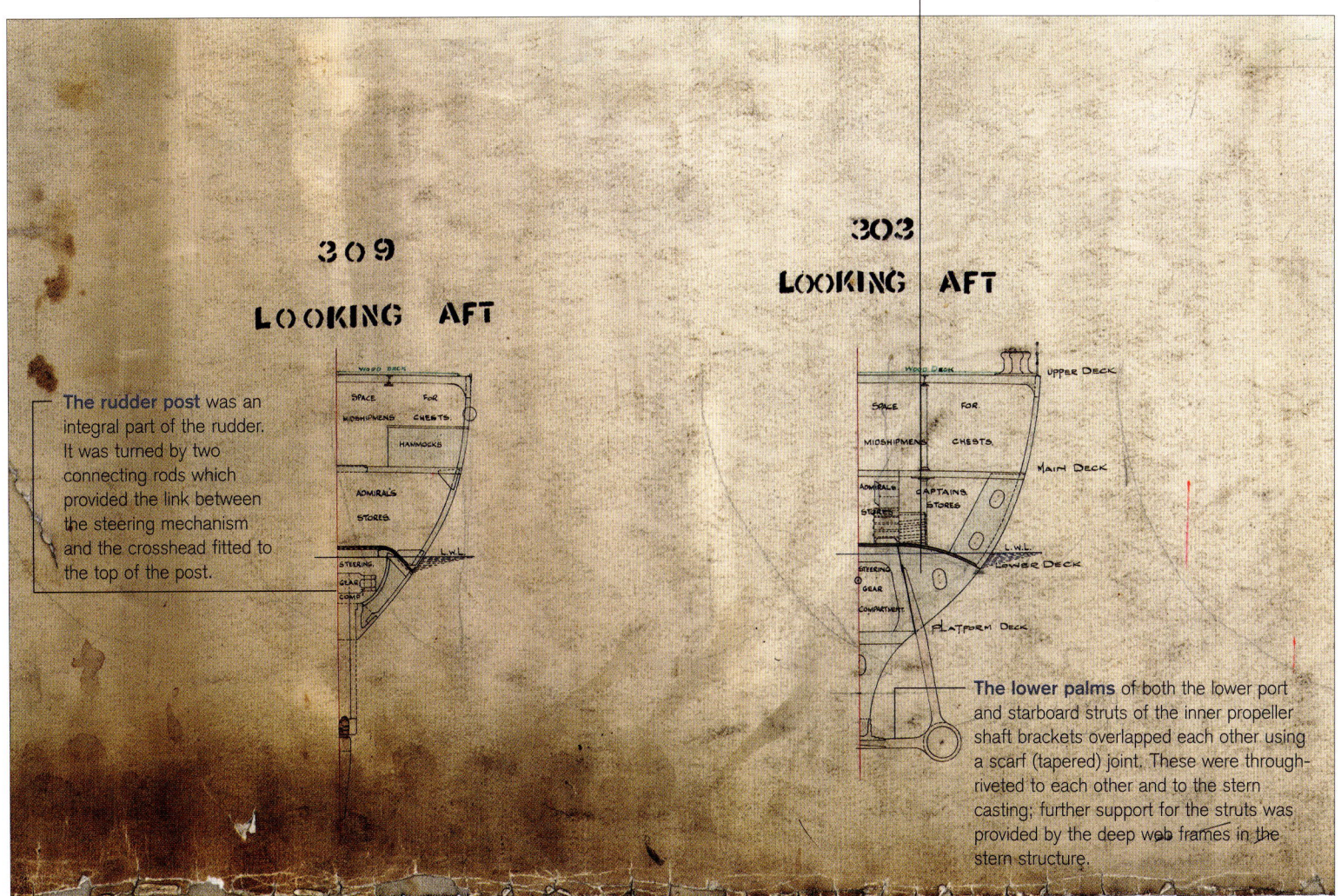

The palm compartment provided the securing point for the upper strut of the inner propeller shaft 'A' bracket. The palm was a wide section of the arm which was riveted to the thick and heavily supported inner bulkhead of the compartment.

The rudder post was an integral part of the rudder. It was turned by two connecting rods which provided the link between the steering mechanism and the crosshead fitted to the top of the post.

The lower palms of both the lower port and starboard struts of the inner propeller shaft brackets overlapped each other using a scarf (tapered) joint. These were through-riveted to each other and to the stern casting; further support for the struts was provided by the deep web frames in the stern structure.

STATIONS 303 TO 289

As originally built the main and lower decks from 'Y' barbette to the 3in NC bulkhead at Station 300 were both constructed of ¾in HT plating. Since the after end of the 15in magazine below the lower deck projected beyond the protection of the after barbette, 'Y' magazine was seriously vulnerable to shellfire at even shallow angles of descent. This was partially corrected in two stages. Prior to completion the main deck was increased to 1¾in HT by adding 1in plating from 'Y' barbette to Station 293 across a width of about 25ft and, during Nov 1916 to Jan 1917, the lower deck was increased to 2½in HT on the flat and slope between 'Y' barbette to Station 292. The thickness of the flat of the lower deck was further increased to 3½in during the ship's refit of 1918–21.

The after fresh water tanks. The port tank has a capacity of 42 tons and that to starboard 29 tons, the latter being reduced to provide space for the compartment containing the 10-ton fresh water pump (see page 22). Two more tanks, each of 37.8 tons were provided forward between Stations 31 and 34 with a 10-ton fresh water pump located in the adjacent provision compartment (see page 23). The system had a gravity tank on the shelter deck at Station 227 (see page 18) and two more at the after end of the CT platform to port of the fore funnel (see page 19). The fresh water service supplied water for drinking, cooking and washing (except for showers), etc.

Location for a 15in portable dotter. A harbour training device used to train gun layers to keep their sights on target by employed a vertically reciprocating aiming point to represent ship movement. The name is derived from a pencil dot created on the target when the gun layer pressed his trigger. Earlier versions of this apparatus were driven by hand or clockwork, but this one was driven electrically.

The steering drive gears. Between Stations 290 and 291 is a set of four gears which transferred the drive from the shaft running aft from the steering engines to a second drive shaft fitted on the deck above connecting the gears to the steering gear. These gears also transferred the axis of the drive from about 7ft 6in to starboard to the middle line since the drive from the steering engines had to be offset to clear the revolving hoist of 'Y' 15in gun mounting.

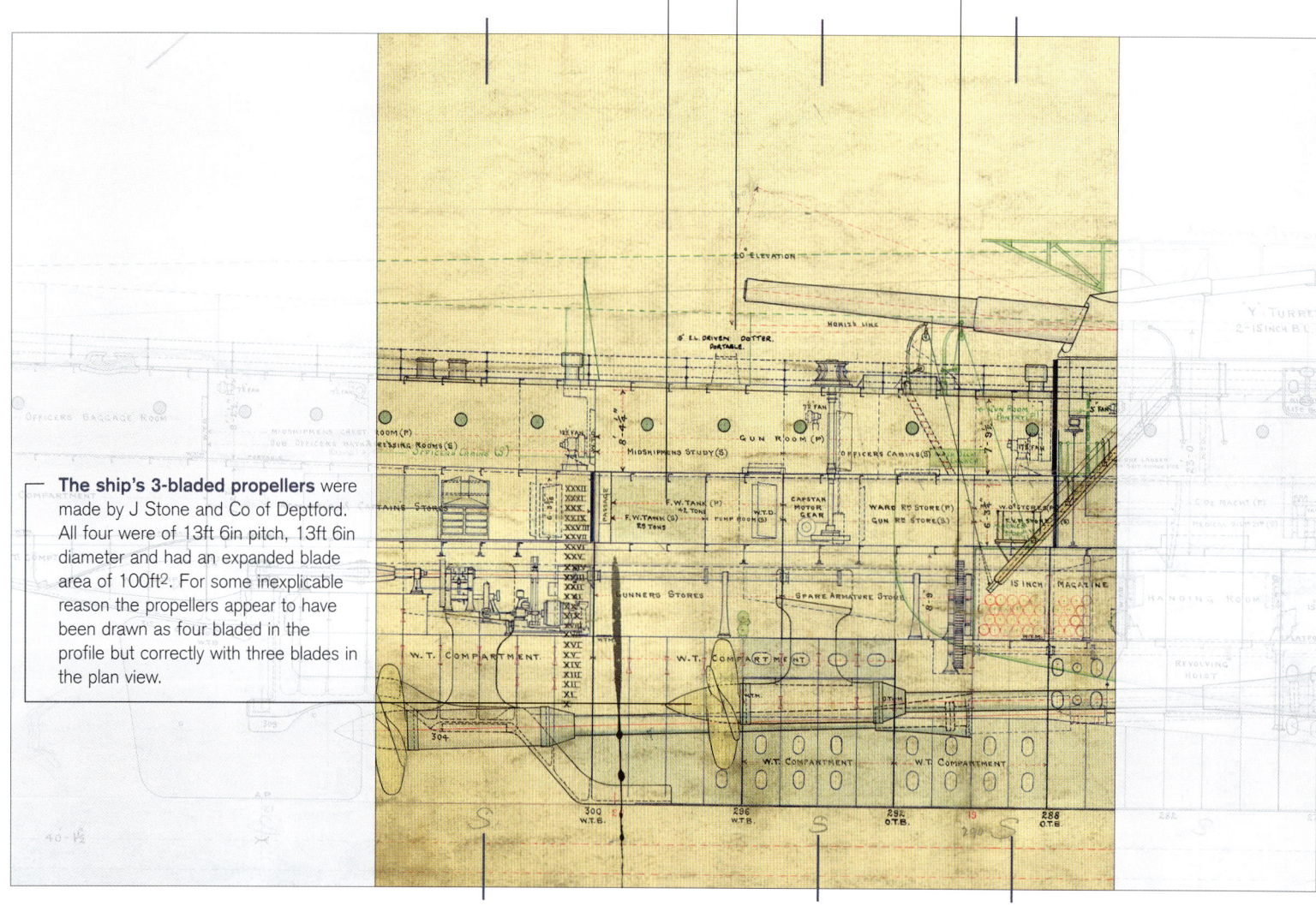

The ship's 3-bladed propellers were made by J Stone and Co of Deptford. All four were of 13ft 6in pitch, 13ft 6in diameter and had an expanded blade area of 100ft². For some inexplicable reason the propellers appear to have been drawn as four bladed in the profile but correctly with three blades in the plan view.

303 STATION   **294 STATION**   **289 STATION**

STATIONS 303 TO 289

SECTION AT STATION 294, PORT SIDE, LOOKING AFT

The section at Station 294 passes through the middle of the support struts of the outer propeller shafts. The construction is much the same as that for the struts of the inner shafts (see page 27) except that the lower palms are fixed to a thick plate inside the hull in the same fashion as the upper palms.

SECTION AT STATION 289, PORT SIDE, LOOKING AFT

This section makes very clear the vulnerability of the after end of 'Y' magazine at the time the ship completed. The only structure between it and the outside world is, vertically, the narrow strip of 3in side armour between the main and lower decks and the 1½in HT side behind and above it and, horizontally, the ½in MS (HT for the stringer) upper deck, and ¾in main and lower decks. It is likely that a heavy shell could easily have reached the magazine without losing much more than its cap and even if it did explode before reaching the magazine this could still have been penetrated by splinters. The risk was somewhat reduced by later additions to the main and lower decks but even in 1936, following the addition of NC armour to the main deck, the after magazine remained at higher risk than those forward.

Section 289 lies exactly on the line of the fore bulkhead of the gun room. Consequently, the sliding door to the gun room in that bulkhead is shown together with the gun room pantry, which was forward of the bulkhead. The watch table is inside the gun room, hence shown in broken line, while the wavy, red, vertical line to port of the table indicates the position of a surrounding curtain. When the 4in armour bulkhead at Station 286 was added during the 1918–21 refit it cut off the fore end of the pantry, which was then converted to a cabin. To restore the after section of the pantry to a reasonable size it was extended inboard, the new bulkhead and its door being shown in green.

The after capstan served to handle the stream anchor and mooring and towing cables etc. It was driven by electrically powered machinery on the lower deck. In the event of power failure, the drive spindle could be disconnected and the capstan pushed around manually by capstan bars (shown in red dashed line) fitted in sockets around its upper rim. When in use the bars were linked to each other by a 'swifter' – a rope joining the outer ends of the bars.

The gun room provided the mess space for the ship's most junior officers (midshipmen and sub-lieutenants). The name derives from the accommodation space for junior officers in the wooden ships of the sailing navy – a space associated with, but not occupied, by guns.

The net shelf shown here, and on the section at 294, are in error since no such shelves were fitted to the ship. It was intended that that Repulse and Renown should be fitted with torpedo net defence but this was cancelled while the ships were under construction, saving 115 tons in weight and a little construction time. This may be a simple case of the draughtsmen picking up details from the design drawings since they probably served as templates for the production of the as-fitted drawings.

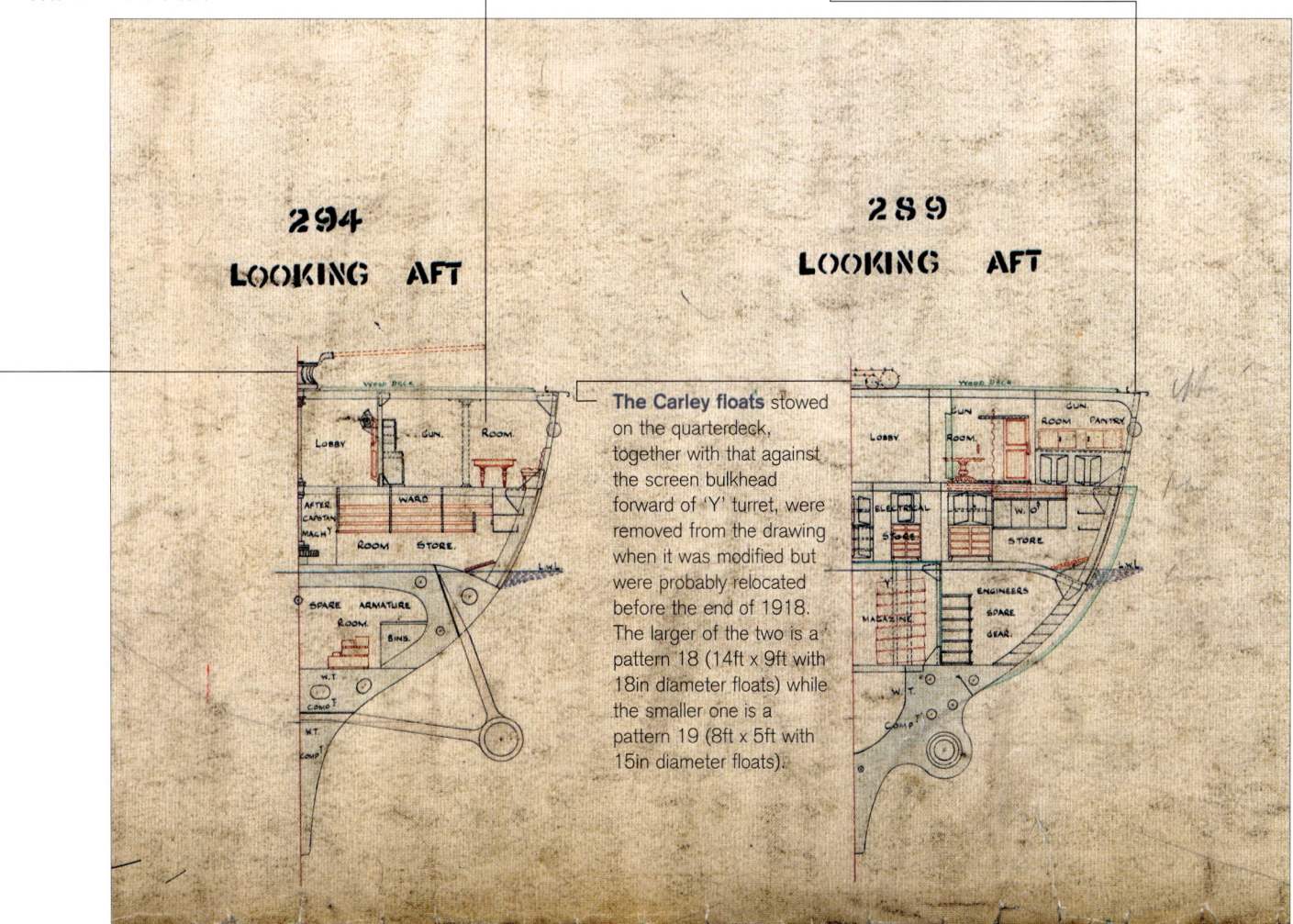

The Carley floats stowed on the quarterdeck, together with that against the screen bulkhead forward of 'Y' turret, were removed from the drawing when it was modified but were probably relocated before the end of 1918. The larger of the two is a pattern 18 (14ft x 9ft with 18in diameter floats) while the smaller one is a pattern 19 (8ft x 5ft with 15in diameter floats).

STATIONS 289 TO 280

The aircraft flying-off platform on the roof of 'Y' turret was installed early in October 1917. A successful flight was made from this platform on 8 October in a Sopwith Pup flown by Squadron Commander F J Rutland – the second such flight from the ship since the first was made from 'B' turret, also by Rutland, a few days before. The ramp differed from that fitted forward in that it was arranged to launch the aircraft over the rear of the turret. This according to the DNC's history of war construction was adopted in order '... to limit the training of the turrets' when launching on forward bearings (the most likely direction). It did, however, have another advantage since the rear end of the ramp could overhang the 15in guns without restricting their elevation and thus provide for a longer take-off run than was then possible from 'B' turret. This platform remained in place until the start of the ship's major refit of 1932–36.

The accommodation ladder. Two were provided for the quarterdeck, one on each side, unlike that amidships which was a single fitting that could be rigged on either side. The addition of the bulge required it to be relocated further outboard. It was also necessary for it to be shortened to allow for the increase in the ship's draught and, judging from the drawing, to raise the landing platform somewhat higher above the waterline than originally arranged. The combined effect of the bulge and length reduction resulted in the relocation of the ladder's after davit both outward (which moved the heel fitting to the ship's side) and further forward.

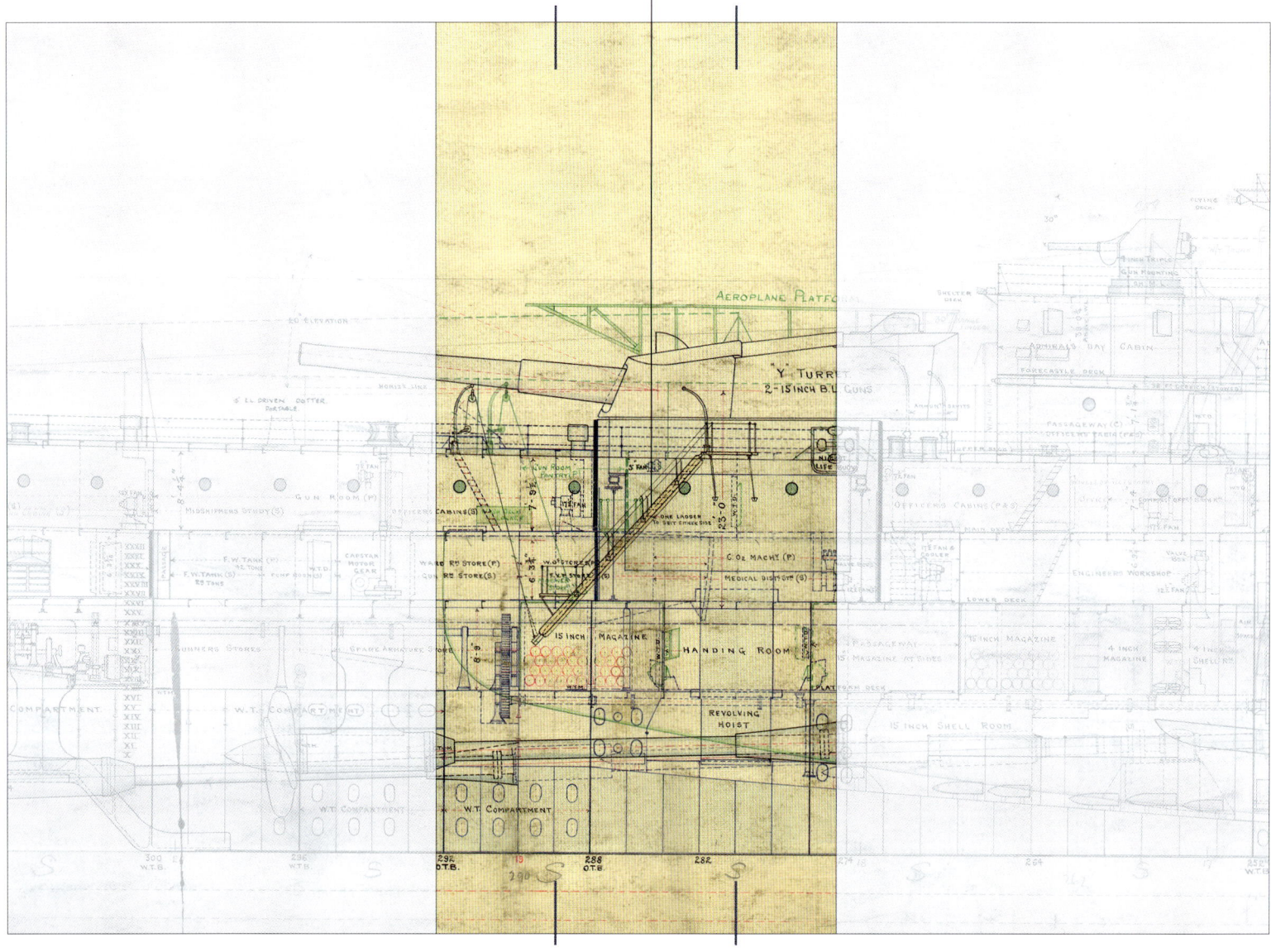

289 STATION **280 STATION**

STATIONS 289 TO 280

SECTION AT STATION 280, PORT SIDE, LOOKING AFT

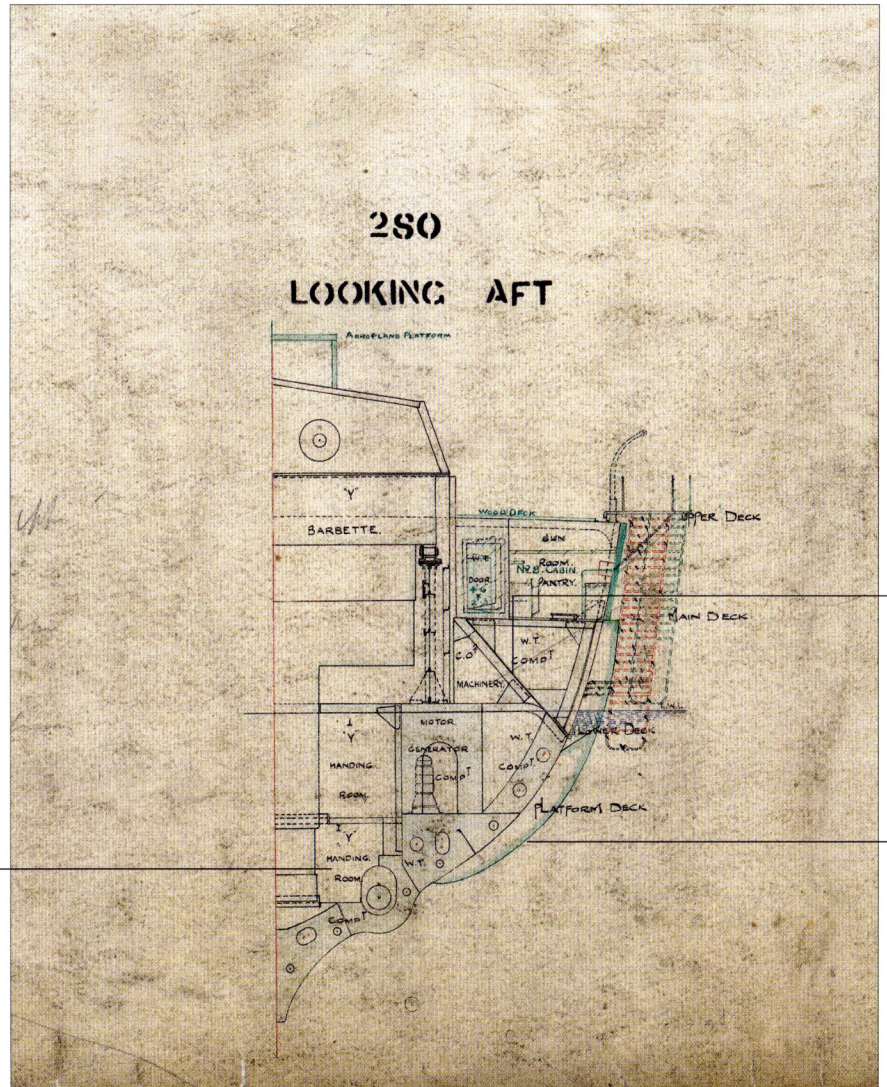

The shell room. Oddly, the draughtsman has seen fit to identify this area of the shell room at the base of the revolving hoist of 'Y' turret as the 'handing room', a term which, at this period of time, applied exclusively to a space through which propellant charges were transferred from the magazine to the hoist. This is not a separate enclosure, which would have justified the use of the term, but simply the fore end of the shell room which extended forward to within 2ft of the after bulkhead of the condenser room. The fact that all the shells in 'Y' shell room are forward of the hoist is merely a reflection of the limited space available in the after part of the ship.

The slope of the protective deck at this point is set at a slightly steeper angle than that along the remainder of the deck in order to accommodate the extension of 'Y' barbette beyond the knuckle line between the flat and slope of the deck.

The after section of the bulge was entirely void. The green diagonal line indicates the division plate between its upper and lower WT compartments.

STATIONS 280 TO 270

On the middle line of the upper deck just abaft 'Y' barbette there is a 6ft 6in x 2ft 6in hatch, the topmost of a series of similar hatches that extended down to the hold. These served for ammunition embarkation and as access and escape hatches for the magazine and shell room crews. There was also a circular scuttle on the upper deck, to starboard of the embarkation hatch, used to embark cordite charges down, through the medical distributing station hatch, and then to 'Y' magazine via a second circular scuttle on the lower deck. The route for the magazine crews was somewhat torturous – down from the main deck through a trunk to a passageway on the platform deck, then aft through an arched opening into the handing room where access to the forward and after sections of 'Y' magazine was made via their small 3ft x 2ft 6in doors (the after section of the magazine also had a single 5ft x 2ft 6in access door but this had been changed to a standard 3ft x 2ft 6in door during the 1918–21 refit). After the installation of flash-tight scuttles these doors would have been permanently closed while the ship was in action or exercising the main armament. The only possible alternative means of escape were the cordite embarkation scuttle in the deck-head of the fore section of the magazine and a hatch in the handing room floor which gave access to the shell room, below, and its embarkation hatch. The ship is recorded as being fitted with F/T scuttles (referred to on drawing as 'hoppers') for passing charges from magazine to handing room during her Nov 1916–Jan 1917 refit. However, the 'hoppers' are shown in the as-fitted drawings (dated October 1916) and they are referred to in an August 1916 report, by HMS *Excellent*, on the ship's gunnery equipment. The 1921 modification of the drawings includes a different form of F/T scuttle which, given the above discrepancy, may have replaced the originals anytime between late 1916 and late 1920.

The night life buoys, consisting of a wood cross with a copper float on each arm, were carried on angled metal frames located on each side of the quarterdeck. In the event of a man overboard or similar emergency in the dark hours they could be released from the frame to slide into the sea. In the process the frames pulled off the seals of calcium canisters, fitted to each side of the buoy. The calcium ignited on contact with the sea and would burn for about 30 minutes producing smoke and flame to aid location. Both buoys had been moved to the after end of the forecastle by the end of 1917 – possibly viewed as a safer position given that at night they were supposed to be provided with a sentry while the ship was at sea.

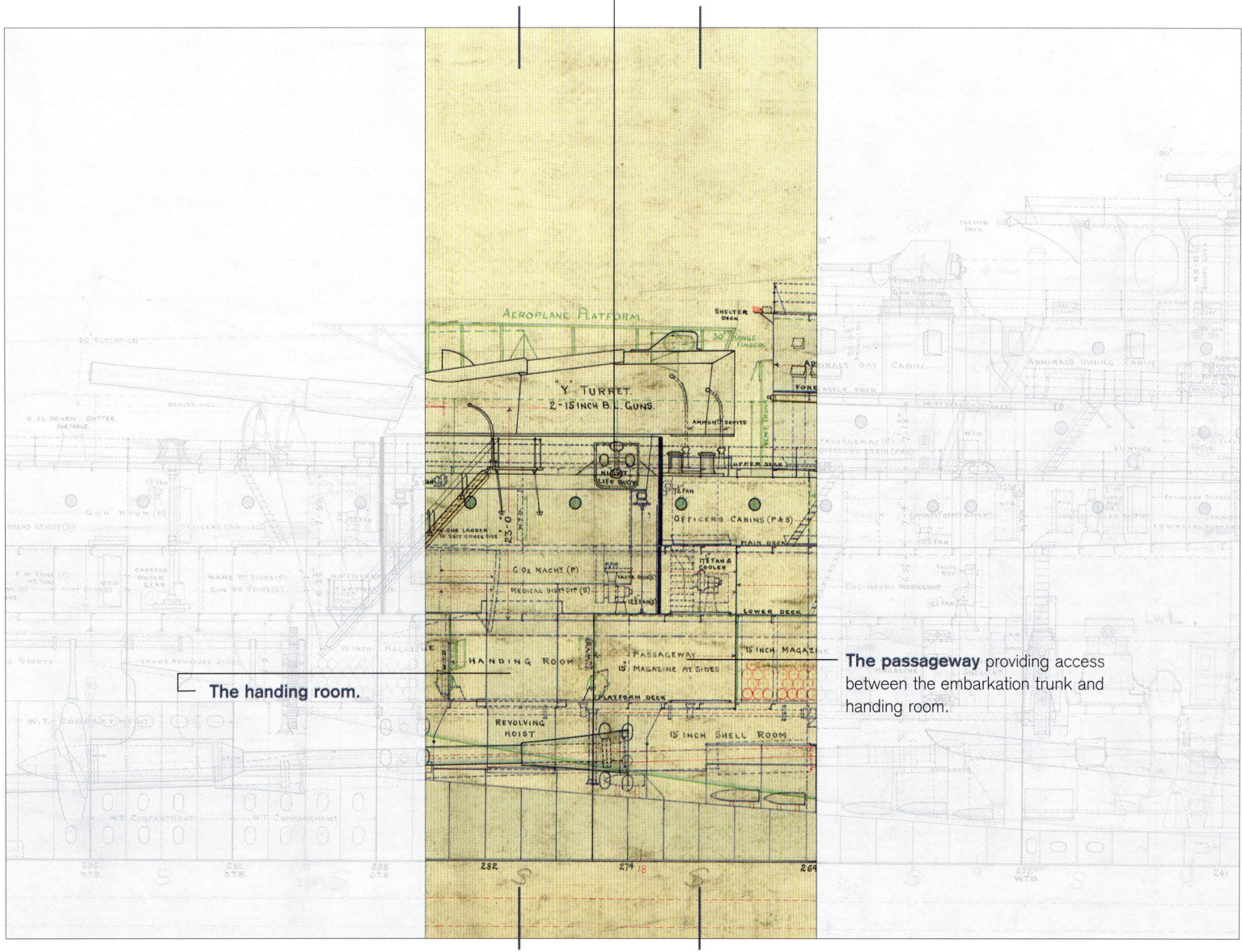

The handing room.

The passageway providing access between the embarkation trunk and handing room.

280 STATION   **270 STATION**

STATIONS 280 TO 270

SECTION AT STATION 270, PORT SIDE, LOOKING AFT

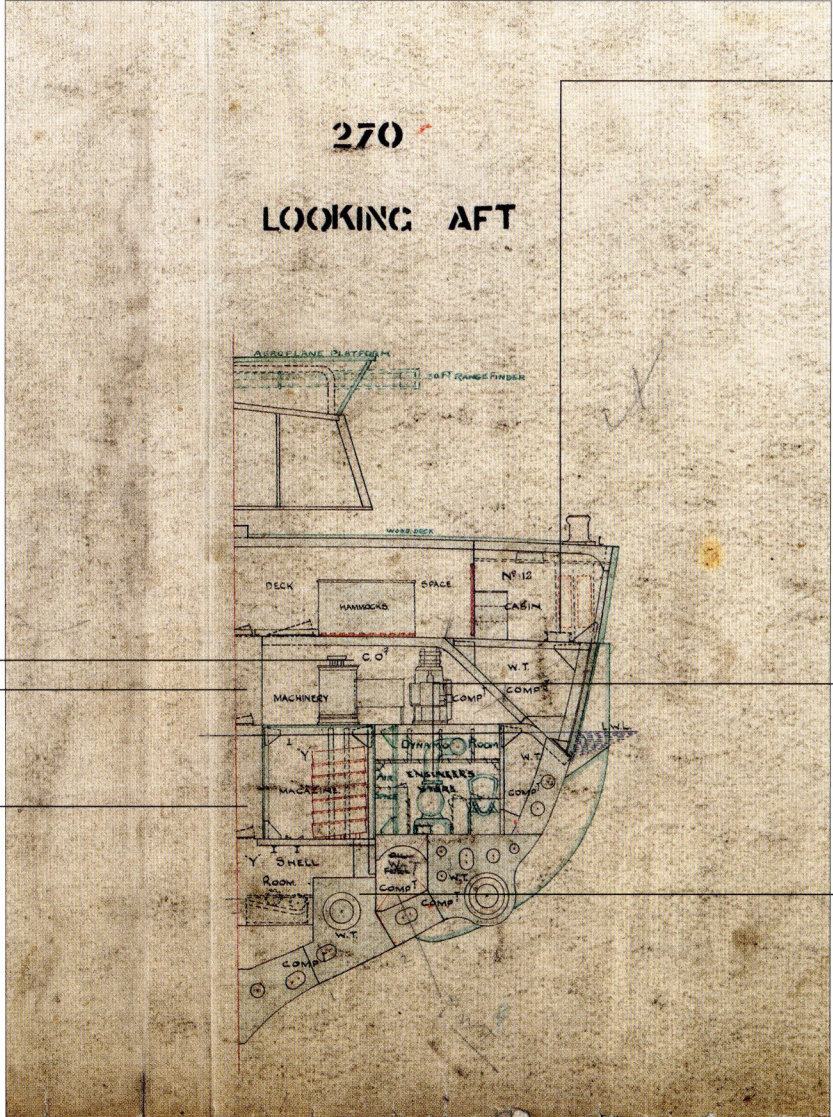

The cooling plant for 'Y' magazine, showing the CO_2 evaporator to the left and CO_2 compressor to the right.

The Ammunition embarkation trunk between the main and lower decks.

The fore and aft passage within, but sealed from, 'Y' magazine gave direct access to the handing room aft and, via the hatch, to the shell room below.

This manhole with raised coaming in No 12 cabin, is typical of several located along the sides of the main deck to provide access to the WT compartments above the slope of the main deck. Manholes without coamings, fitted flush to decks, bulkheads and platforms, were also common. Both types were normally bolted down since they were only required for the inspection, cleaning or repair of normally closed compartments (including those for oil fuel, water, etc) and were rarely opened. The primary exception is the escape manholes fitted in hatch covers which were necessarily hinged and clipped. The standard size for the manhole opening was 23in x 15in – variations in size were rare but not unknown.

The ship's second turbo generator, fitted during 1918–21 in what was originally one of the engineers' stores. Note the addition of an air space on the inboard side to provide heat insulation between this compartment and 'Y' magazine.

The enclosures for the inner propeller shafts (also seen in different forms in the sections at Stations 280 and 258) encroached on the limited space available for 'Y' shell room. As a result, the shell room was both longer and more restricted than those for 'A' and 'B' magazines.

STATIONS 270 TO 258

The deck protection above the magazines from the after bulkhead of the condenser rooms (Station 252) to 'Y' barbette and the armour bulkheads abreast 'Y' barbette was increased in thickness in several stages. Shortly before completion 1in HT plating was added on the main deck providing a total of 2in HT on the flat and slopes of the deck. During Nov 1916 to Jan 1917 2in HT (1in + 1in) was fitted on the lower deck above the magazines and for 8ft outboard of their longitudinal bulkheads. Finally during her 1918–21 refit the main deck was further increased by the addition of another 1in HT layer on the flat and 2in (1in + 1in) HT on the slope bringing the total to 3in on the flat and 4in on the slope.

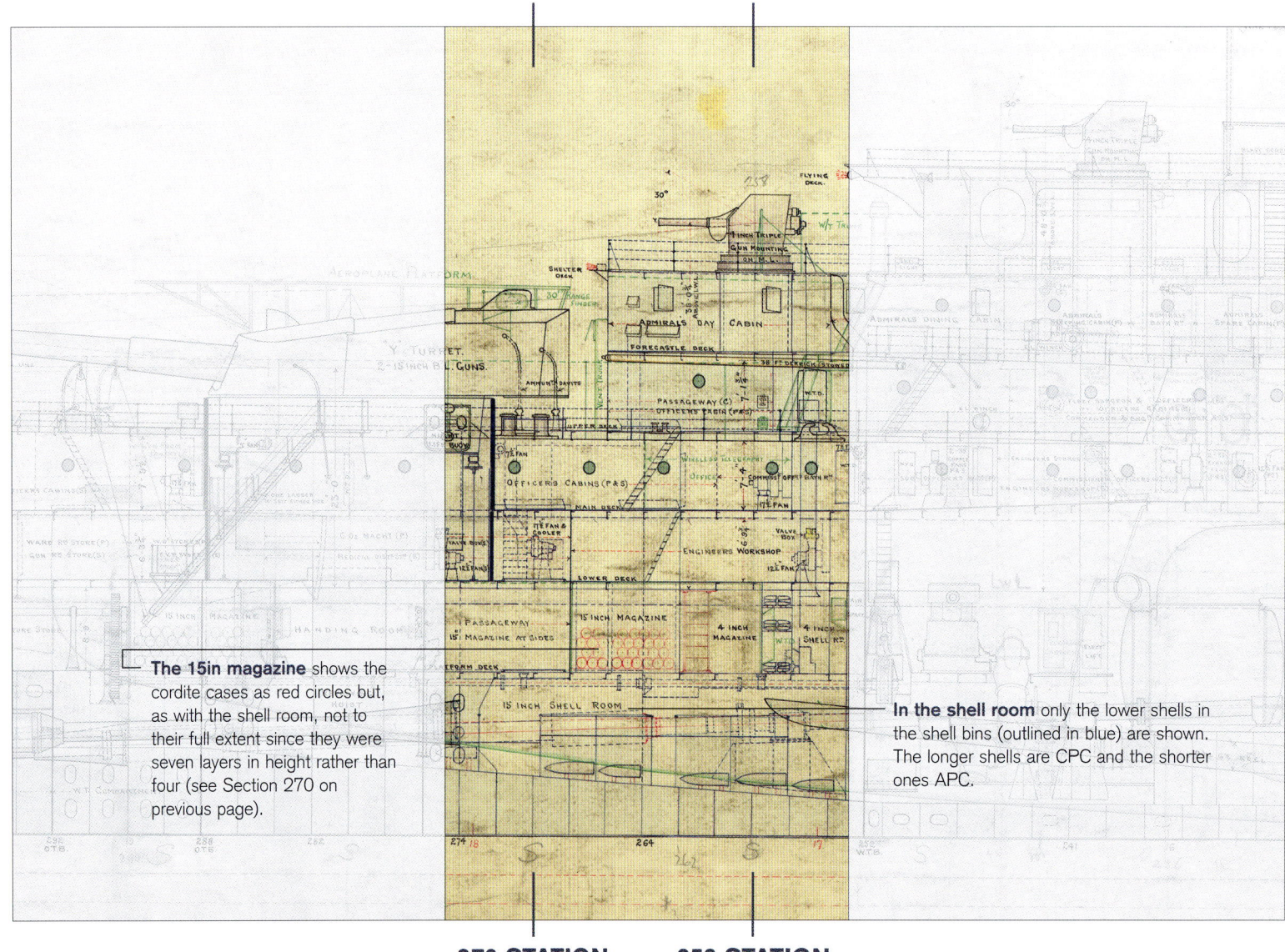

The 15in magazine shows the cordite cases as red circles but, as with the shell room, not to their full extent since they were seven layers in height rather than four (see Section 270 on previous page).

In the shell room only the lower shells in the shell bins (outlined in blue) are shown. The longer shells are CPC and the shorter ones APC.

270 STATION   **258 STATION**

SECTION AT STATION 258, PORT SIDE, LOOKING AFT

The triple 4in mounting only appears twice in the sections, here, showing the aftermost mounting, and at Station 299, showing the midship mounting. Both are drawn in profile rather than facing along the centre of the ship and only this one is shown with a shield. The original intention to fit twenty single 4in mountings for the anti-torpedo-boat (atb) armament was changed early in the design process, the adoption of triple mountings serving to ease the problems of providing a workable distribution of the mountings free of blast and with good arcs of fire. A new 4in semi-automatic gun, the Mk V QF, faster firing, more accurate and more reliable than the earlier 4in Mk VII BL gun (employed as atb weapons in capital ships prior to the adoption of the 6in gun) helped in some small degree to compensate for Fisher's decision to revert to the smaller calibre. However, Fisher wanted director control for the 4in which presented a problem since the Mk V gun had percussion-firing only and director control required electric-firing. This was at first resisted by both the 3rd Sea Lord (Admiral Tudor) and the DNO (Rear-Admiral Singer) but in April 1915 Fisher suggested reverting to the Mk VII BL, which could be fired electrically. When Tudor pointed out that the advantages of the semi-automatic gun would be lost Fisher commented that it was his understanding that improvements in the accuracy of the BL gun was under consideration. Tudor then asked the DNO to make proposals for a solution which resulted in the cheap and quick expedient of developing a new gun consisting of the body of the Mk V with its breech end modified to take the breech mechanism of the Mk VII. This was approved by Fisher on 24 April, the final design adopting seventeen such guns, which became the 4in BL Mk IX; fifteen were mounted on five triple TI mountings and two on single PXII mountings, all with light spray shields.

The after hydraulic pumping engine, like the two fitted forward, was driven by a steam piston engine. This pump supplied the ring main for 'Y' magazine while the two forward supplied a common ring main for 'A' and 'B' mountings. The two mains were linked by pipes run along the starboard side for supply and port side for return so that if required any of the pumps could be arranged to supply either ring main. The hydraulically powered machinery included that for the 15in mountings, 15in shell rooms and the training motor for the director hood mounted on the GCT. The hydraulic medium was distilled water with a small amount of lubricant. Each pump had its own hydraulic tank located alongside the inboard side of its compartment, that for the after pump having a capacity of 18.3 tons and each of those forward 19.8 tons. After passing through the hydraulic machinery the exhausted fluid was returned to the tanks for re-use. Loss of fluid was made up from the ship's distilling plant. In an emergency salt water could be admitted to the system but its use involved acceptance of deterioration in the operation and components of the machinery.

A horizontal boring and milling machine in the engineers' workshop on the lower deck. The two rectangles on each side of this machine are not identified nor is there anything in the plan view that coincides with either their shape or position. That to the left may be a work bench since there is an unlikely lack of these in the original plan except where several have been added when the drawing was modified.

This L shape is a steel angle bar – these would have provided the inner boundary of the torpedo net shelves but for the fact that it was decided not to fit the nets. They remained in place because they also served as spurn-waters. They extended along the forecastle from Station 42 to its after end and along the quarterdeck from the break of the forecastle to Station 301. Beyond these points, both fore and aft, the deck edges were fitted with smaller stringer angles. Forward of the forecastle breakwater the stringer angles had wood spurn-waters fitted along their inner edge – probably because this gave a vertical barrier to water on the deck, rather than the sloped one that resulted from the uprights of the stringer angles being bent outward to follow the flare of the hull sides.

The after 4in magazine, together with the 4in shell room forward of it, supplied the three after triple 4in mountings. Charges were passed from the magazine into the shell room where they were lifted by whip hoist (driven by a winch in the shell room) via an ammunition trunk to an ammunition lobby on the upper deck. The shells were transferred separately to the upper deck by dredger hoist. From here the ammunition was transferred aft to six pairs of hoist trunks fitted with Miller's hatches and overhead davits. Each pair of hatches, arranged one to port and one to starboard of the middle line, supplied one of the 4in mountings.

STATIONS 258 TO 249

Repulse was originally provided with seven derricks for handling boats and for taking in ammunition and stores. Those furthest aft, two 38ft (actually 38ft 2in) were primarily intended for ammunition embarkation. That on the starboard side can be seen here stowed against the after screen bulkhead at the break of the forecastle. The remaining derricks were 34ft (actually 34ft 2in), the altered length due to their heels being closer to the ship's side. Two (again primarily for ammunition) were fitted abreast the forward superstructure on the forecastle and three more – two worked from derrick posts on the forecastle deck amidships and one on the port side of the forecastle deck aft – were intended primarily for boat handling. Each was powered by a nearby electric winch. The latter in the case of the aftermost derricks was fitted behind the screen bulkhead with its drum outboard of the screen. The odd derrick on the port side of the forecastle was stowed against the after superstructure but was operated from a heel socket on the forecastle deck just aft of Station 221. It was obviously intended that there should also be a matching derrick on the starboard side since this position also had a winch and a heel socket. The port derrick had been removed by the end of 1918 at the latest but both winches remained to provide additional service with the 38ft derricks.

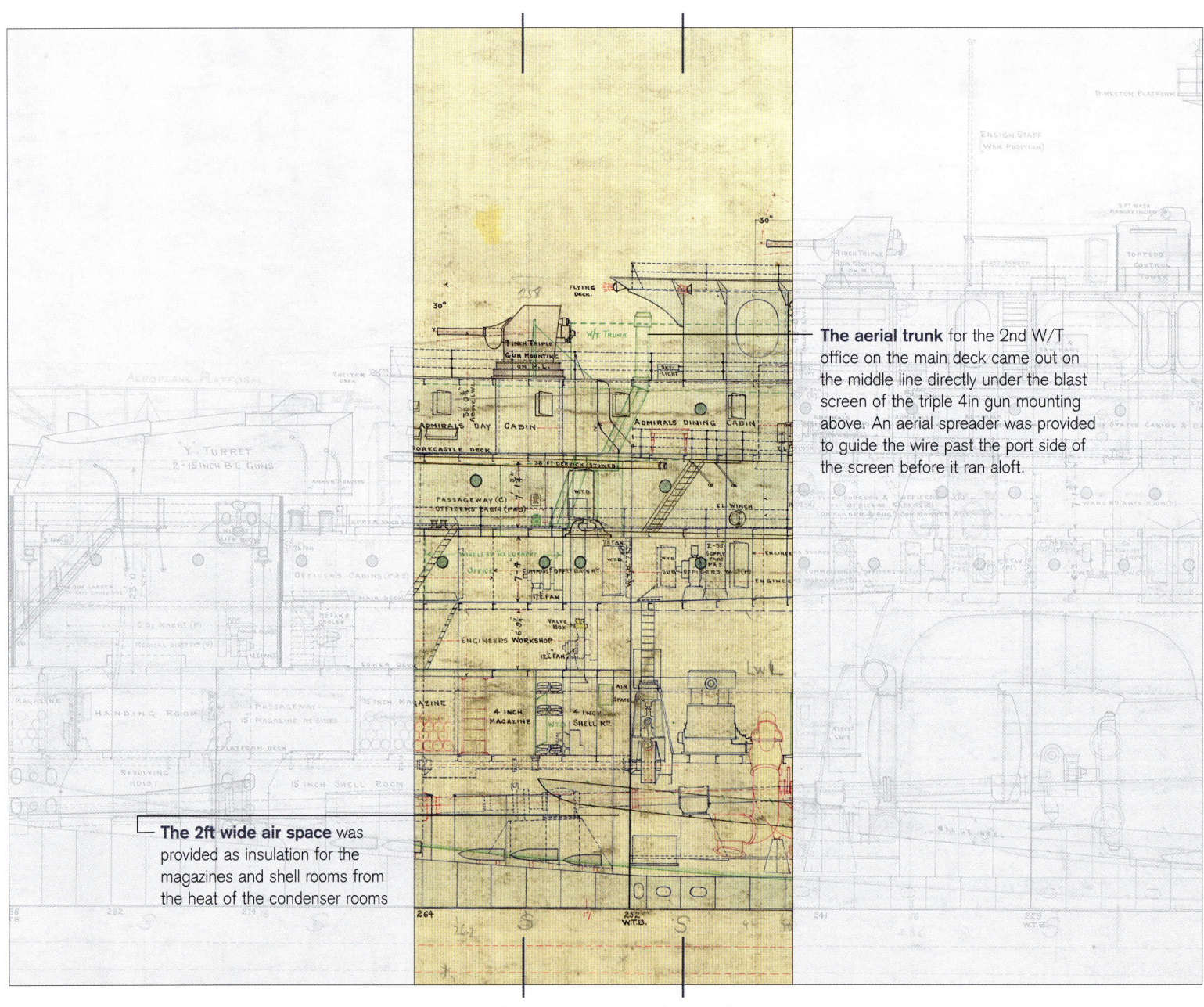

The aerial trunk for the 2nd W/T office on the main deck came out on the middle line directly under the blast screen of the triple 4in gun mounting above. An aerial spreader was provided to guide the wire past the port side of the screen before it ran aloft.

The 2ft wide air space was provided as insulation for the magazines and shell rooms from the heat of the condenser rooms

258 STATION   249 STATION

STATIONS 258 TO 249

SECTION AT STATION 249, PORT SIDE, LOOKING AFT

This section includes the condenser room, the aftermost compartment of the main machinery compartments. Since all these remained virtually unmodified throughout the ship's career comment on their detail has been limited to the as-fitted plans produced in 1936 since they are both clearer and contain a little more information. There were, however, changes to the oil stowage arrangements abreast the engine rooms. As built the lubricating oil tanks (olive, rapeseed, mineral and turbine oil) were arranged along the outboard lower sides of the condenser and engine rooms. These tanks were later changed to oil fuel tanks and the lubricating oil moved to the upper-most double bottom oil fuel tanks from Station 215 to Station 252. It is uncertain when this was carried out but the refit of 1925–26 seems likely since there is no correction of this on *Repulse*'s 1916 plans (apart from some faint pencil alterations probably made prior to the start of her 1933–36 refit) and the fact that the *Renown* had also been modified in this way by 1926.

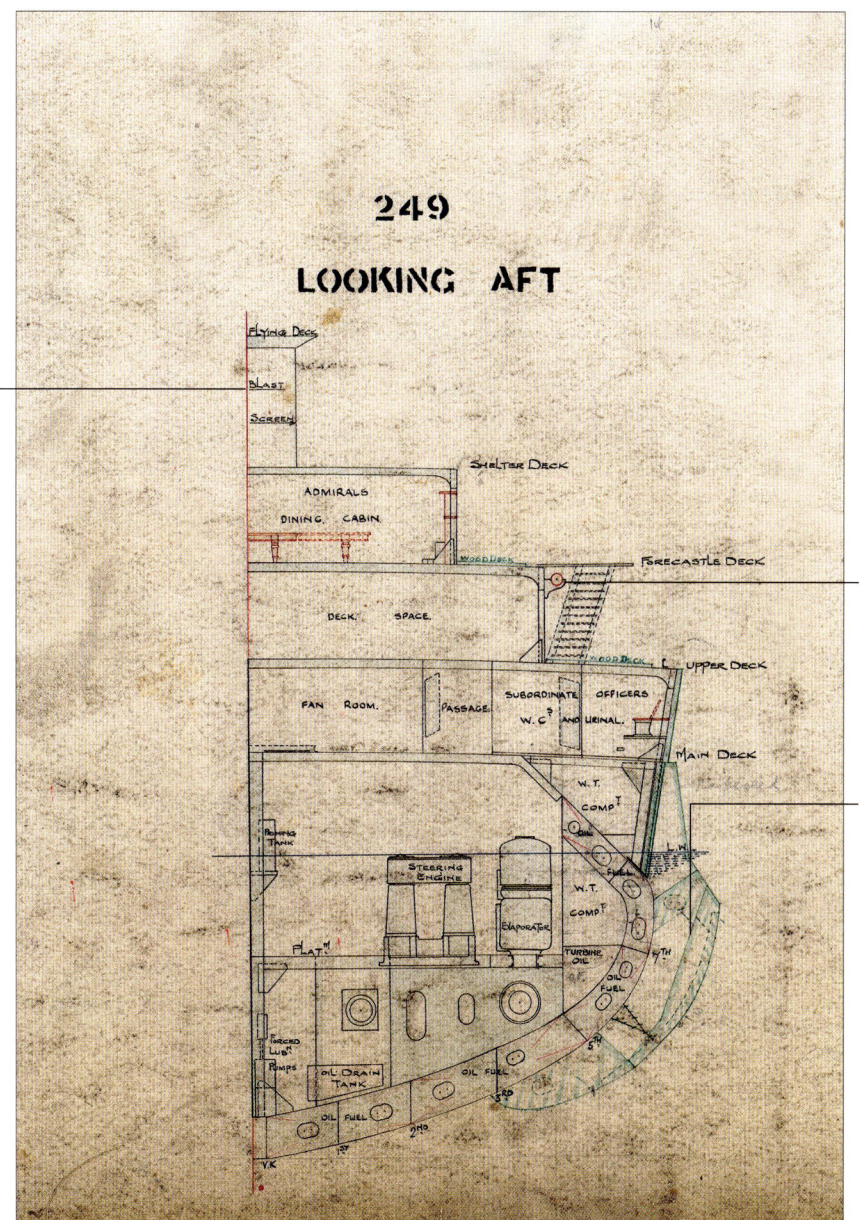

This blast screen formed the forward part of the gun-crew shelter for No 5 4in triple mounting. The after end of the shelter contained the tops of the ammunition hoists for No 5 mounting.

The red circle represents the port 38ft derrick in its stowed position.

The lower bulge was divided into inner and outer compartments from Stations 141 to 250, the inner compartment being filled with 9in diameter crushing tubes and the outer compartment void. *Repulse* was the last ship to adopt crushing tubes since water was substituted for the tubes in all subsequent bulging refits and in new construction. The water was considered equally effective and considerably more convenient since the water could be pumped in or out as convenient and there was a considerable saving in construction, maintenance and running costs.

STATIONS 249 TO 227

This section of the profile encompasses the condenser room, the workshops and fan rooms above it and part of the senior officer accommodation on the upper and forecastle decks. Note the extension to the after end of the flying deck and its raised sides which served as a blast screen to protect the crew of No 5 triple 4in gun mounting from the blast from No 4 mounting when the latter was firing on after bearings.

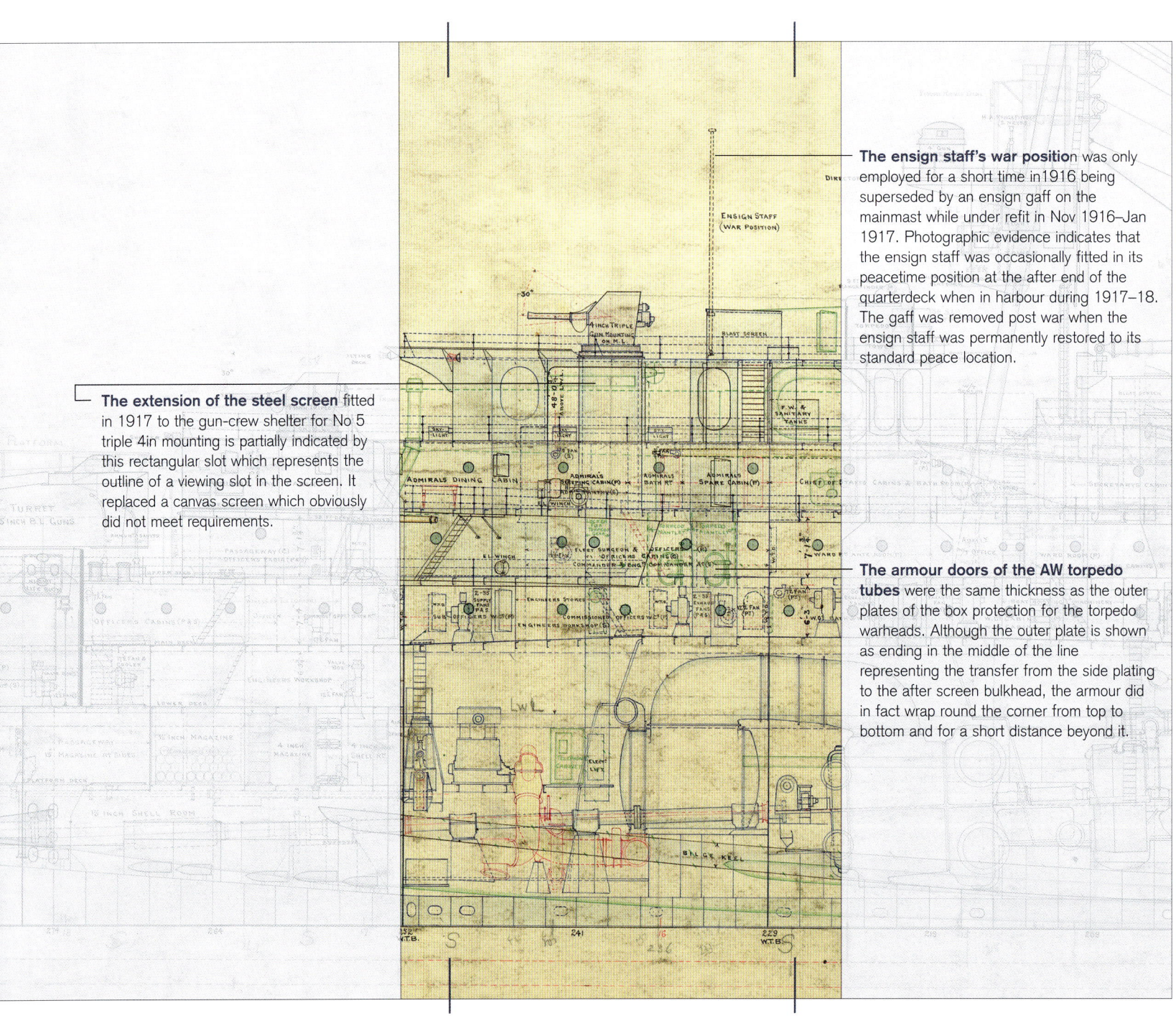

The ensign staff's war position was only employed for a short time in 1916 being superseded by an ensign gaff on the mainmast while under refit in Nov 1916–Jan 1917. Photographic evidence indicates that the ensign staff was occasionally fitted in its peacetime position at the after end of the quarterdeck when in harbour during 1917–18. The gaff was removed post war when the ensign staff was permanently restored to its standard peace location.

The extension of the steel screen fitted in 1917 to the gun-crew shelter for No 5 triple 4in mounting is partially indicated by this rectangular slot which represents the outline of a viewing slot in the screen. It replaced a canvas screen which obviously did not meet requirements.

The armour doors of the AW torpedo tubes were the same thickness as the outer plates of the box protection for the torpedo warheads. Although the outer plate is shown as ending in the middle of the line representing the transfer from the side plating to the after screen bulkhead, the armour did in fact wrap round the corner from top to bottom and for a short distance beyond it.

249 STATION **227 STATION**

STATIONS 249 TO 227

SECTION AT STATION 227, PORT SIDE, LOOKING AFT

This section is partially in error since the part above the main deck is correct but that below it, showing the forward section of the condenser room should, at least, be at Station 229 (the transverse bulkhead between the engine and condenser rooms). The problem had been noticed since there is a faint pencil circle around 227 with a leader to the number 229. No correction was, however, made since the 1936 as-fitted sections have the same error.

The blast screen shown here formed the after extremity of the gun-crew shelter of No 4 triple 4in mounting. Despite being shown in green it was present in the ship at the time of her construction and this is simply a correction of its omission. It is shown as an original installation in the profile on the previous page.

The ammunition trunk for No 4 4in triple mounting provided the local supply from the upper deck to the flying deck. The Miller's (self-closing) hatch was fitted at the top of the trunk with hoist motors for the whips on the upper deck. Both the hoist motors for this trunk can been seen just below, and on each side, of the bottom of the trunk.

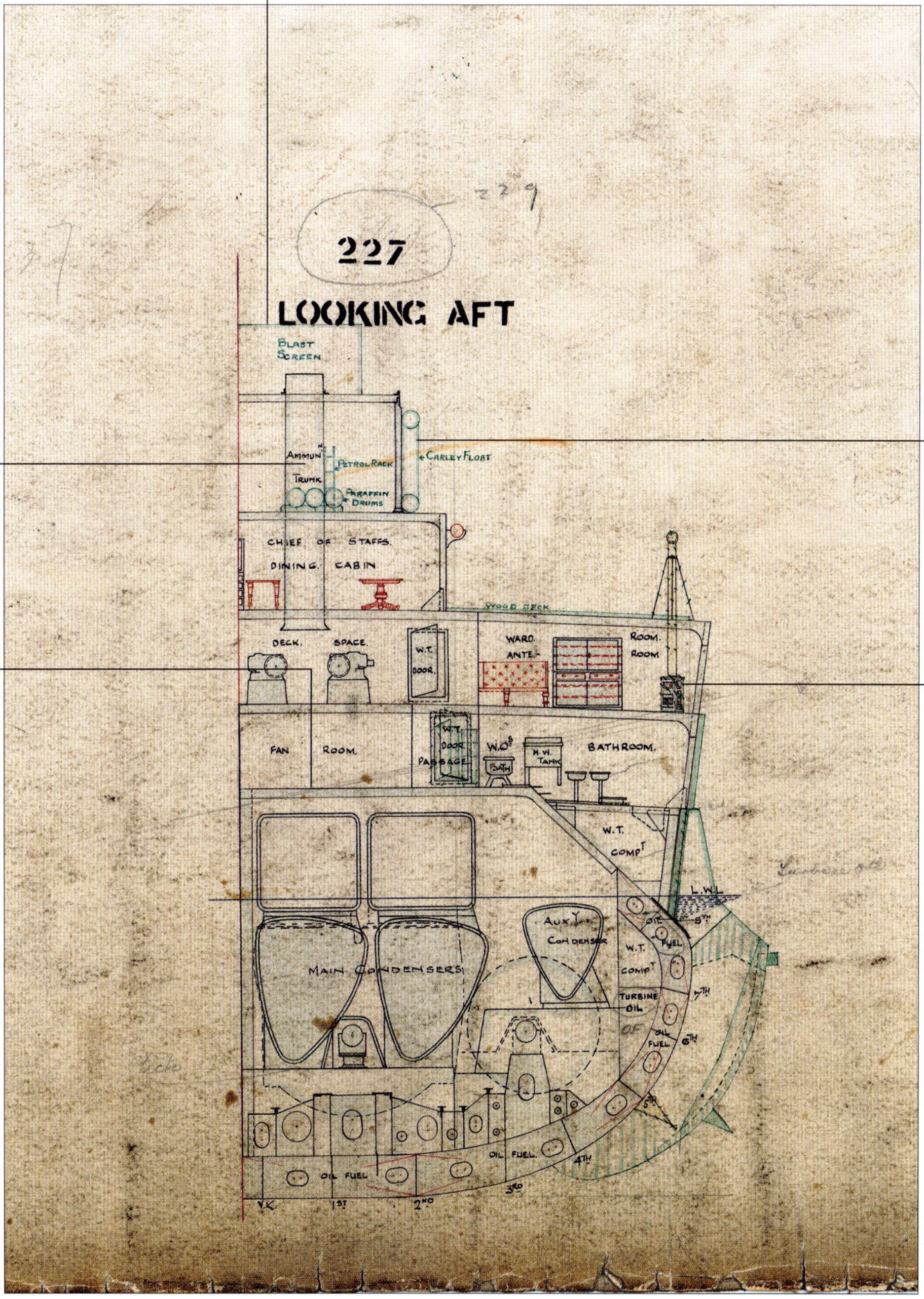

The main deck is raised in this area to give clearance above the bends (the large rectangular trunks) which carry exhaust steam from the LP turbines to the condensers. Note that the deck has no camber in this area while the flats at the side of the ship remained at the level of the decks fore and aft, necessitating the steps in the WOs' bathroom between the raised part of the deck and the flat (steps were also fitted in some of the adjacent compartments in this area – see main deck plan on pages 144–145).

This pattern 18 Carley float, together with one to starboard, replaced a pair of pattern 20 (10ft x 5ft) floats located one deck lower (and stowed vertically) during 1916–18. It can be seen in profile on page 40.

The coal-fired heating stove in the ward room ante-room was a common feature of officer accommodation at the time of the ship's construction. That part of its funnel above the upper deck was portable, the deck opening having a cover plate. It has been deleted from this position because it was moved a few feet further forward.

STATIONS 227 TO 199

This part of the ship is dominated by the mainmast, a substantial structure supporting several important functions, including fire control, communication, night defence and boat handling. The steel lower mast was 90ft 7in in length and 3ft in diameter, the upper (or starfish) platform at its top being 100ft above the ship's designed LWL. Wood provided the material for the 55ft 6in main topmast, 49ft 5in topgallant mast and the 30ft main W/T yard. The total height to the top of the topgallant mast, including the 2ft 6in height of the lightning conductor, was recorded in 1921 as 181ft 6in above an estimated LWL of 27ft 3in. It is worth noting that such figures could vary over time depending on whether they measured to the design or actual LWL, if the upper masts had been subjected to alteration or replacement, if a change had been made to the position of the topmast (the heel had a rack which engaged with a pawl on the lower platform allowing about 2ft in the adjustment of height), or simple miscalculation. As completed she had no topgallant mast and the wireless yard, as can be seen here, was positioned at the top of the main topmast. The topmast was removed during her Nov 1916–Jan 1917 refit and not restored until her major refit of 1918–21, at which time the topgallant mast was added. The reason for the reduction in the rig during 1917–18 was that the height was only necessary for long-range W/T communication which was not a requirement while the fleet was restricted to operating within the confines of the North Sea.

The TCT is, like that in the plan view, unmodified despite the fact that its original 9ft rangefinder was replaced by a 15ft rangefinder in 1918.

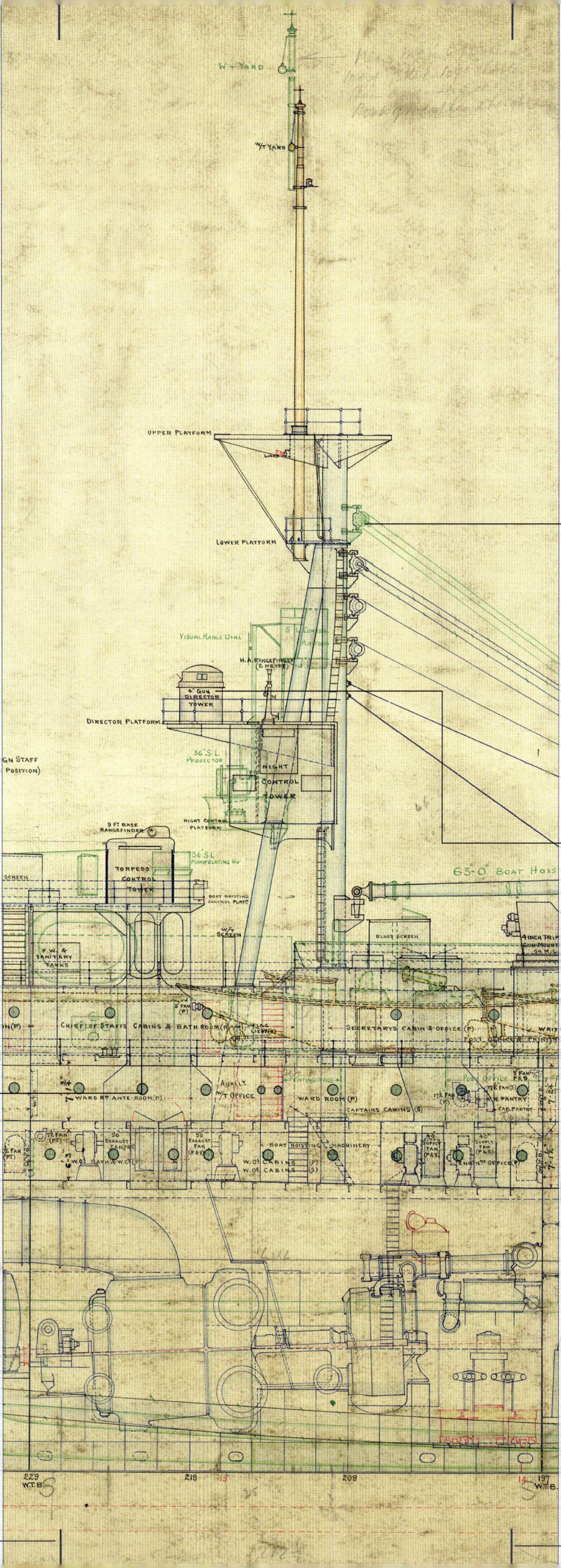

The upper (double) topping-lift block of the steel boat derrick was raised by about 5ft 6in at the same time as the derrick was lengthened to clear the bulges. The lower (single) topping lift block, and the purchase lift block below that, remained in their original positions. In simple terms the topping lift blocks raised and lowered the boom while the purchase lift operated the boat purchase blocks – shown on page 42 under the end of the boom with their hook linked to a deck plate.

The after 4in gun director tower contained a standard, pedestal type, secondary armament director.

227 STATION — 199 STATION

STATIONS 227 TO 199   41

SECTION AT STATION 199, PORT SIDE, LOOKING AFT

The side armour in most as-fitted drawings is drawn in solid black but the original here only provided an outline which allowed the use of a green tint (plus an additional outer line) to indicate the replacement of the 6in belt with a 9in one. The 6in belt above this was mainly, but not entirely, provided from the original lower belt. Although this is shown neatly arranged between the top of the 9in armour and the upper deck, it did in fact extend about 1ft above the edge of the upper deck (an error corrected in the 1936 as-fitted set). There were also sloped fairing plates at the tops of both the 9in and 6in side armour (partially included in some of the forward sections).

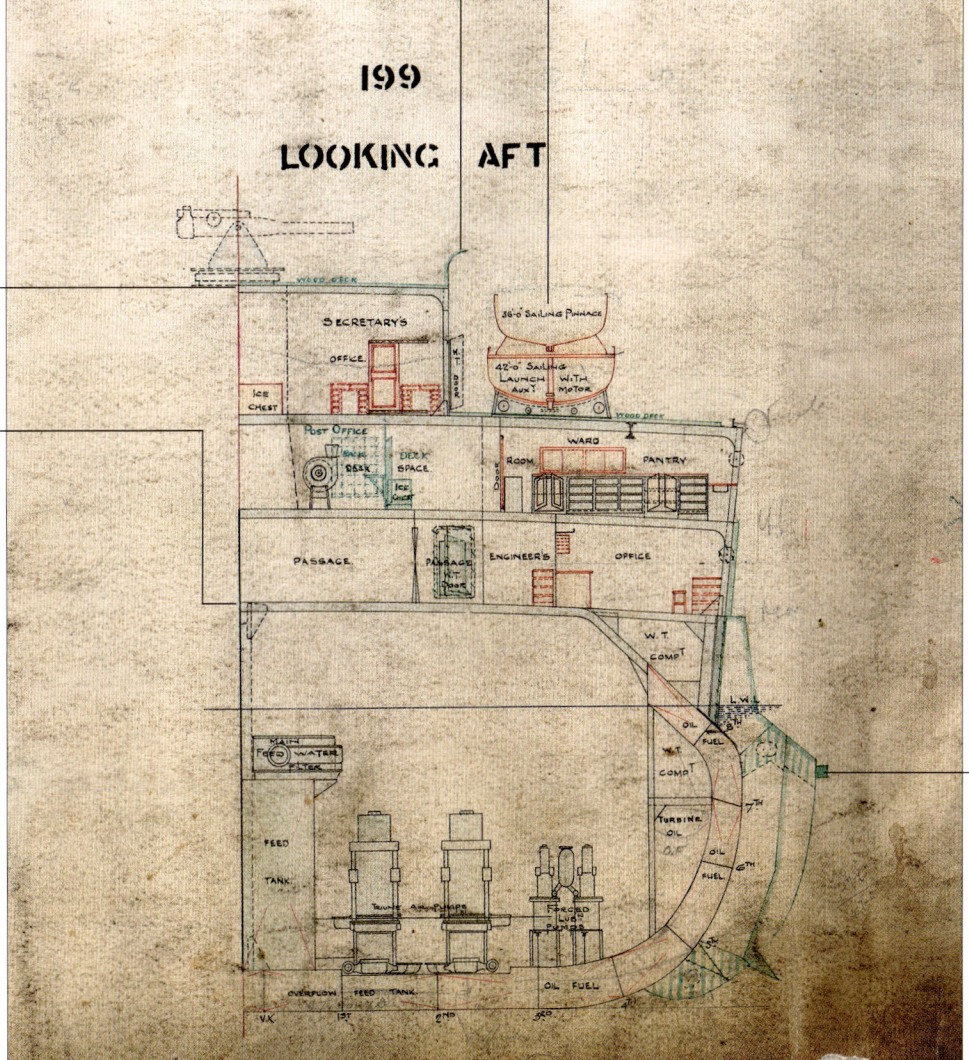

This curved bulwark replaced the guardrails that were originally fitted to the ship abreast No 3 triple 4in mounting, an alteration made in 1917.

The 42ft launch and the 36ft sailing pinnace stowed above it were standard boats for all Royal Navy capital ships of the period. A relatively recent innovation was the fitting of an auxiliary motor to the 42ft launch but, apart from this, they represented the largest pulling and sailing boats normally to be found in the Navy's larger ships.

The shelter deck in the vicinity of No 3 triple 4in mounting was provided with wood planking from about 12ft forward of the centre of the mounting to the point at which the shelter deck stepped down 2ft 6in just abaft the mainmast. Otherwise the addition of deck planking during the 1918–21 refit was limited to the forecastle and quarterdeck.

The deck camber gave a rise of 18in at the maximum designed beam of the ship (90ft). The curve thus produced was followed consistently on all the decks from the main deck upward (except for the raised section of the main deck above the condenser and engine rooms) and in all the primary superstructure platforms. No camber was provided for the platform deck, the smaller superstructure platforms (including the compass and NDP platforms) or the thick floor plates of the CT.

The wood fenders fixed outboard of the bulges extended from Station 107 to Station 231. They added 18in to the maximum width of the ship.

STATIONS 199 TO 165

This area encompasses the length of the two after boiler rooms ('E' and 'F'). The protective quality of deck above all the boiler rooms was never improved, remaining at 1in HT on the flat and 2in HT on the slopes throughout the ship's life. The engine and condenser rooms on the other hand were increased, with additional layers of 1in HT, to a total of 3in on the flat and for 5ft down the slopes during her Nov 1916–Jan 1917 refit (mostly replaced with NC armour in 1933–36). Apart from a reluctance to accept the additional weight involved, it was probably considered that the low level of horizontal protection for the boiler rooms was an acceptable risk given that six boiler rooms greatly reduced the possibility of the total loss of steam power.

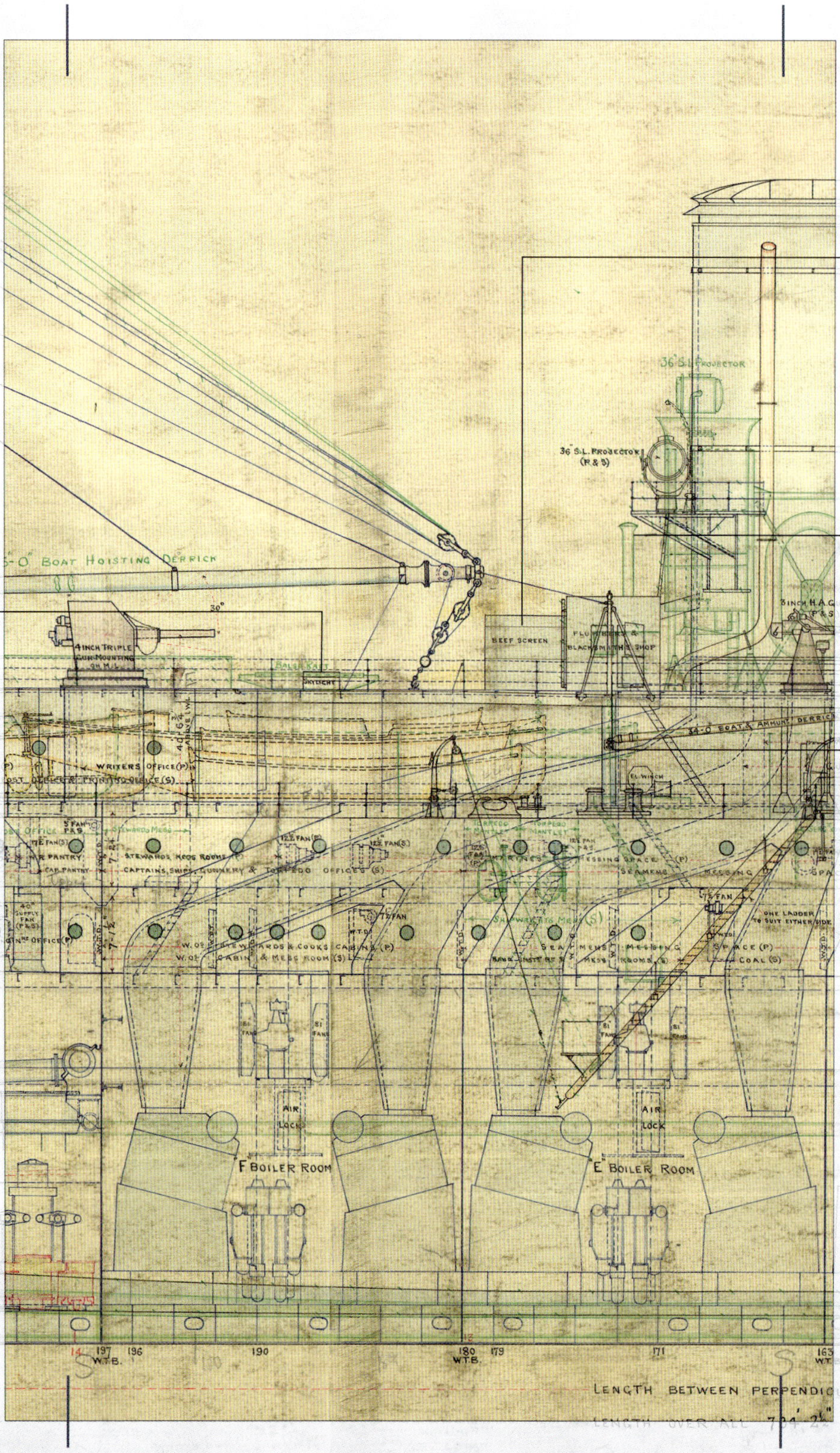

The balsa raft is shown in the position it occupied in January 1921. At the time of completion it was stowed vertically against the starboard side of the coppersmith's workshop, just abaft the fore funnel. Such portable items were easily moved and where the ship's personnel decided to stow them could vary from time to time.

The beef screen was in effect the ship's butcher shop. Meat was brought here from the cold room to defrost before being prepared for issue to the galleys. The upper half of the walls of the enclosure were fitted with close-mesh wire screens to allow the free flow of air but limit the entry of insects.

The flue of the blacksmith's forge projects through the roof of his shop. Previously the flue passed into the after funnel and then upward but was relocated when the forge was moved to port, as described on page 18.

A heavy-duty stanchion, and a matching one on the port side, supported the rigging of the 34ft boat derricks mounted on the posts below. These stanchions also served to hold the securing guys attached to the end of the main boat derrick to prevent it moving sideways when stowed. A second pair of securing guys was attached between the main derrick's forward support ring and the sides of the shelter deck. Note that the main boom had two support rings for the support lifts attached to the mainmast just below the purchase block. These served to fix the lowest possible elevation of the main boom for safety purposes.

199 STATION   **165 STATION**

SECTION AT STATION 165, PORT SIDE, LOOKING AFT

This section through the fore end of 'E' boiler room and the centre of the after funnel provides a clearer view of the form and construction of the four S/L towers (also known as trunks), fitted around the funnel in Oct–Nov 1917, than that of the profile where they are confused by being superimposed over the original S/L platforms. The one shown here is the after port tower; the other three were exactly the same except that those forward were fitted higher to provide the searchlights with a clear arc on after bearings. The 36in S/Ls were Type B, controlled in both elevation and training from the manipulating platform at the bottom of the tower. The S/L was directly attached to the stalk running down the centre of the tower and rotated with it. Elevation was controlled by a geared input in the manipulating position to drive a control rod that passed up the centre of the stalk to the S/L where it was geared to its elevating arc. The base of the stalk was provided with seats and binocular sights and the tower with an observation slot fitted with roller blinds. If required or if the remote control failed, the S/L could be disconnected and operated locally. At the time of introduction these S/L were often referred to as '15ft searchlights' because this was the length of the stalk. The earlier Type A S/L and stalk arrangement was essentially the same except that its weight was supported on the S/L platform with the stalk hanging below it while in the Type B it was supported on the manipulating platform at the base of the stalk. Direction of these S/Ls was provided in the NDPs and from the compass platform utilising Evershed bearing transmitters. The original outfit of 36in S/Ls was operated remotely from S/L control pedestals in the NDPs.

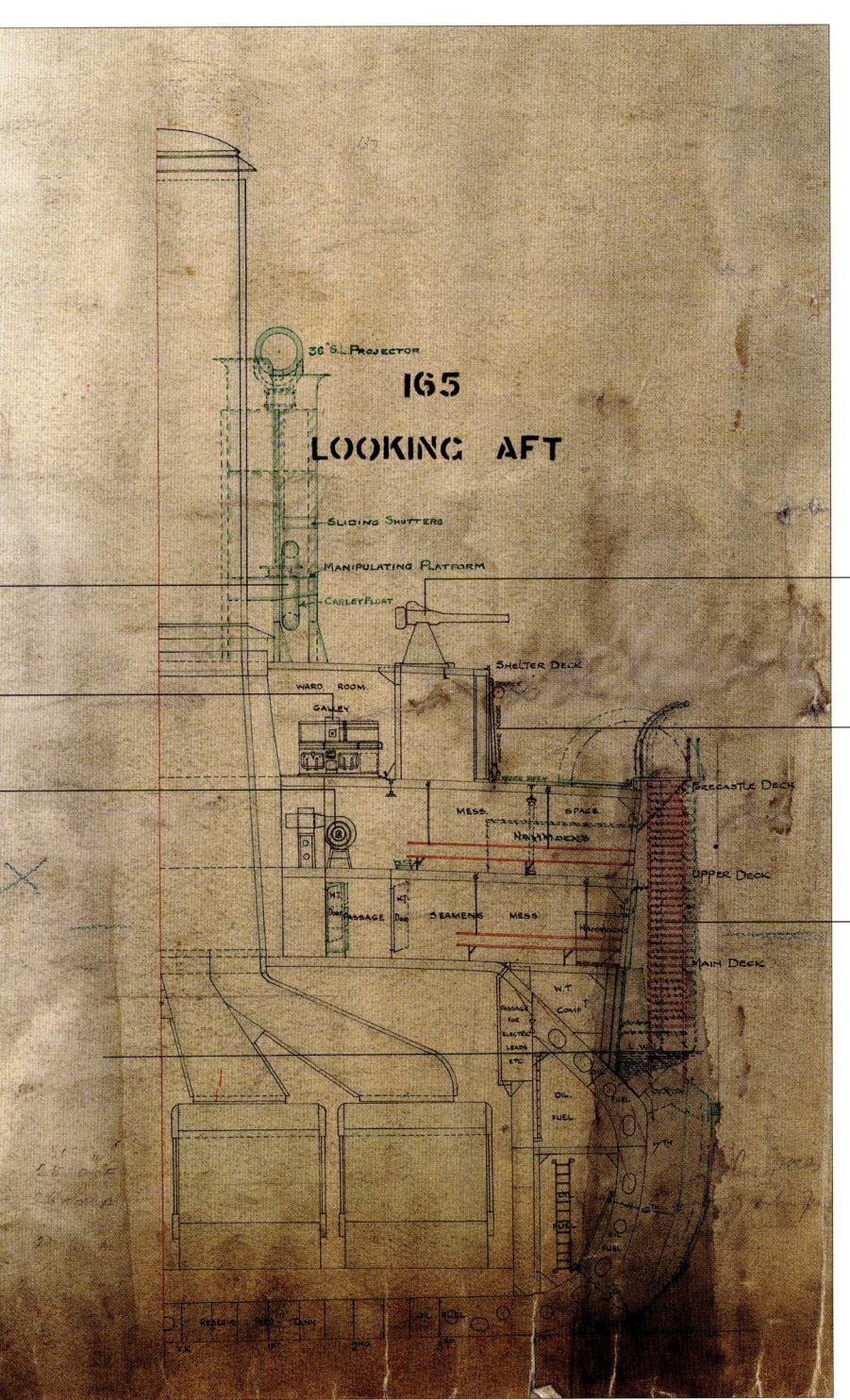

The Carley float illustrated here is too small since those fitted against the after funnel were 14ft x 9ft pattern 18 stowed vertically (it is shown correctly in the profile on page 44). There was a third pattern 18 stowed against the after side of the funnel.

The cooking range at the after end of the ward room galley.

This Sirocco 17½in ventilation supply fan is one of many located around the ship, primarily in accommodation spaces with their output via an electric heater for cold weather use; in this case the heater is on the fan's inboard side. There were also 12½in fans (20in in the case of the capstan engine room forward) for auxiliary machinery compartments which provided exhaust since these compartments normally had a natural air supply. The 12½in fans, and some of 7½in, were also fitted to provide air to store rooms, and working areas (shell rooms, workshops, torpedo room, TS, etc).

The port 3in/20cwt Mk I QF gun on Mk II HA mounting, one of the ship's only pair of AA mountings until she was upgraded to four 4in in 1924.

Admiralty pattern 12cwt kedge anchor stowed against supports to the overhang of the shelter deck. A second such anchor of 16cwt was stowed in the same position on the starboard side.

The midships accommodation ladder, like that aft, has been moved to clear the top of the bulge and reduced in length, the upper platform being extended outboard and the lower platform raised by c7ft. The arc lines (one original and one for the extended platform) curving inboard from the end of the upper platform indicate the path it sweeps when swung over onto the deck.

44

STATIONS 165 TO 115
This area of the profile covers the length of all the boiler rooms except the aftermost one. It provides a clear impression of the complexity and extent of the uptakes between the boilers and the ship's two funnels. The plan shows the fore funnel after it had been increased in height at Portsmouth Dockyard in Aug–Sep 1916 although the section on the next page only notes 'funnel raised 6'- 0" higher [than shown]', presumably because the drawing was complete before the decision to increase the funnel height had been made. The steam pipes on the sides of the after funnel are unusual in that these were normally placed on the forward and/or after sides of funnels as with those shown here on the forward funnel. The arrangement served as a means of identifying *Repulse* from *Renown* since the latter's after funnel steam pipes were *c*2ft 6in shorter.

Square side ports providing light and ventilation to the gun room, ship's and WOs' galleys are represented by the rectangles along the sides of the superstructure. Two similar ports on the port side served the ward room galley.

The incinerator was employed to burn rubbish which could not otherwise be disposed of and was of particular importance in disposing of secret or sensitive documents such as operational and fleet orders, memoranda, etc which were commonly headed with the words 'to be destroyed when complied with'. Its flue is run into the after funnel to exhaust out through its top.

This flue from the ship's galley is actually one of several that fed into the fore funnel. There were two from the galley's ovens and a third from its boiler, together with two smaller ones from the forge and furnace in the coppersmith's shop. All can be traced on the plan views on page 66.

The sanitary tank is one of two (the other being located on the after shelter deck) which served as gravity tanks for the ship's salt water system for the heads, WCs and showers.

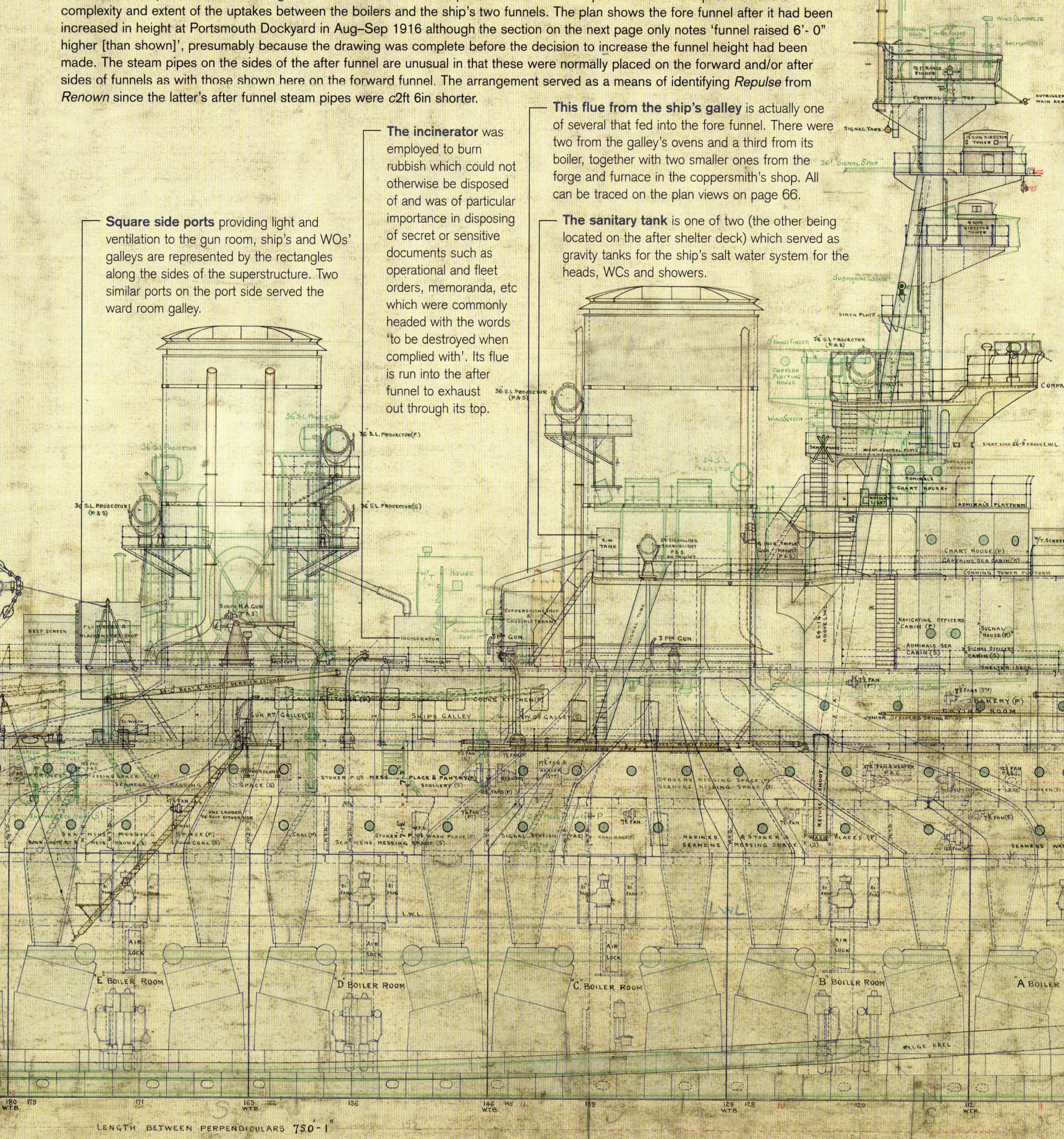

STATIONS 165 TO 137

SECTION AT STATION 137, PORT SIDE, LOOKING AFT

This section passes through the fore end of 'C' boiler room and the centre of the fore funnel. The annotations around the outer bottom indicate the port vertical keel (VK) and the 1st to 8th longitudinal frames, although the 4th is actually a continuation of a longitudinal bulkhead that ran the full length of the boiler rooms. Note that the red lines to the corners of the oil fuel and reserve feed water tanks in the double bottom serve to indicate which longitudinals are oil-/watertight and which are not.

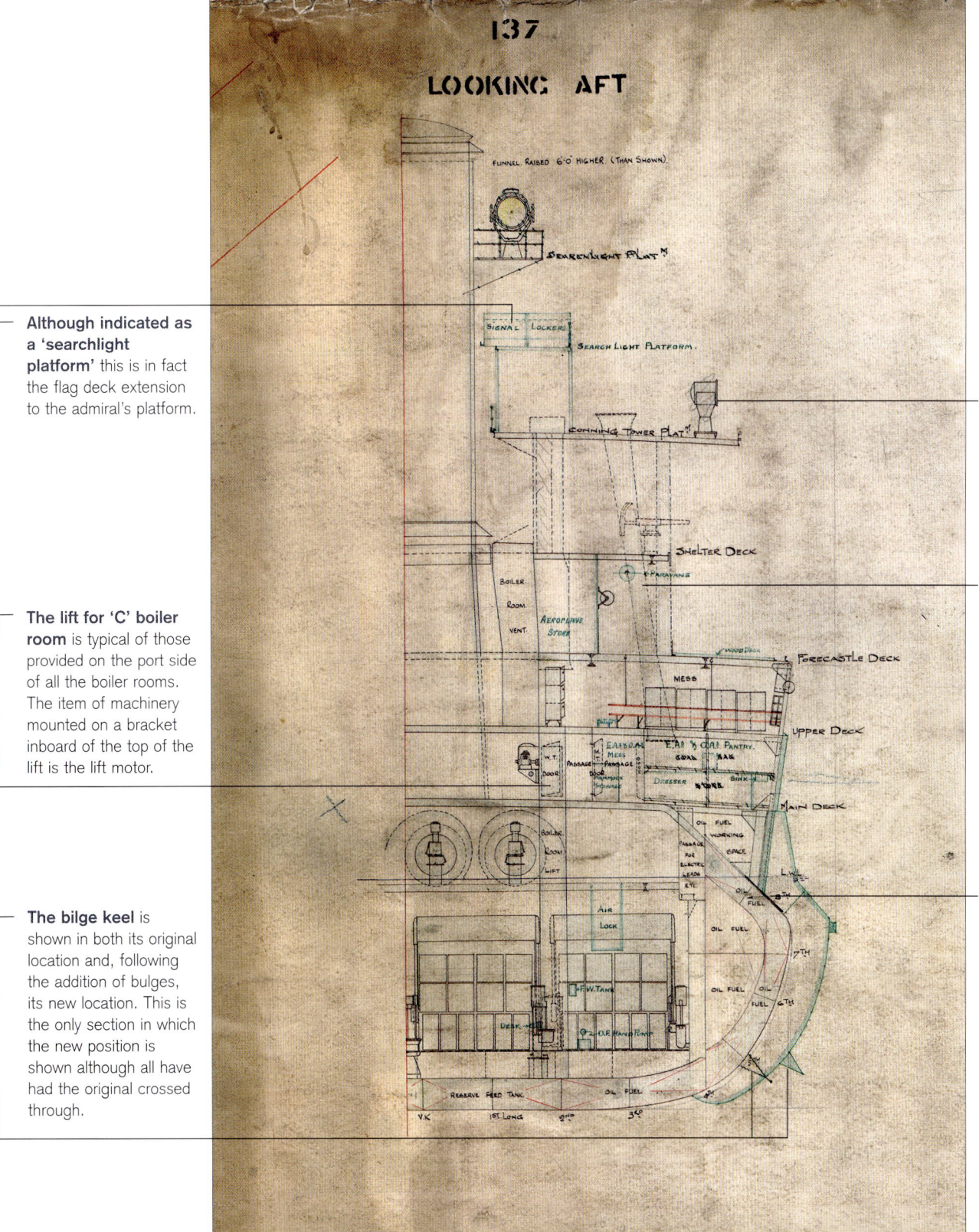

Although indicated as a 'searchlight platform' this is in fact the flag deck extension to the admiral's platform.

The lift for 'C' boiler room is typical of those provided on the port side of all the boiler rooms. The item of machinery mounted on a bracket inboard of the top of the lift is the lift motor.

The bilge keel is shown in both its original location and, following the addition of bulges, its new location. This is the only section in which the new position is shown although all have had the original crossed through.

The 24in signalling projector on its portable trolley is shown moved further outboard than in the plan view (page 19) probably representing an operating, rather than stowed, position.

The signal flag tube, via which flag signals were passed from the signal stations on the main deck to the signal yard below the fore top. The yard was replaced by signal spars on each side of the 15in director platform during the ship's Nov 1916–Jan 1917 refit.

The thick black line represents a 2in HT plate on which the side armour rested. This was in addition to the 2in (1in + 1in) HT plating of the slope of the main deck effectively increasing the vertical depth of the side armour by 2ft at 4in thickness and a further 3ft for the 2in thickness.

SECTION AT STATION 115, STARBOARD SIDE, LOOKING FORWARD

This section is taken down the centre of the foremast and incorporates the primary bridge platforms but not the structure above the compass platform. The NDP below the compass platform originally contained the remote controls for the six foremost 36in searchlights. These were removed when the new 36in S/Ls were fitted in 1917–18, the remote control being relocated to the manipulating positions at the base of the S/L towers on the funnel and, for the two bridge S/Ls, to the CT platform. These arrangements, and modifications, were repeated in the after NDP except that the original remote controls only served the after 36in S/L on the after funnel. During the 1918–21 refit the compass platform was fitted with two S/L control transmitters on each side to serve as the forward position of the S/L directing arrangements, the after position being that fitted to the mainmast (see page 40).

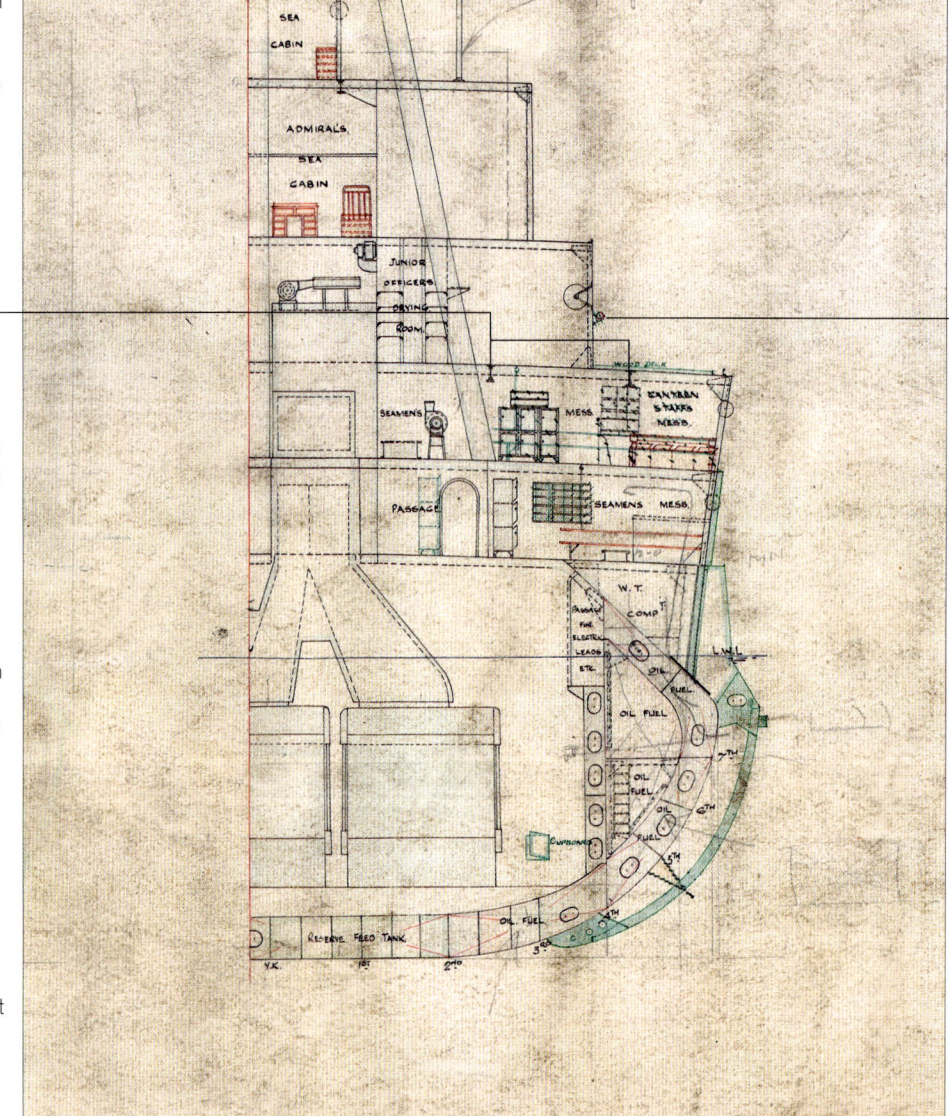

The 36in S/L mounted above the admiral's platform in 1918 was intended to provide coverage on forward bearings. The adjacent 24in signalling projector and the platform on which it stands should not be included here since it is about 9ft abaft the centre of the foremast.

Heavy longitudinal girders, two on each side extended along the underside of the forecastle deck to Station 102. These stiffened and supported the primary upper strength member of the hull girder. The deck itself was generally 1¼in HT (½in + ¾in) with a 6ft wide, 1½in (½in + 1in) stringer plate as far as 'B' barbette and then gradually reduced to ½in at its forward end. The girders were built up with a ½in vertical plate and 4in x 4in angles to join it to the deck above and to a ¾in HT horizontal rider plate at the bottom. They were supported at regular intervals by 7in diameter pillars and, occasionally, by short lengths of fore and aft compartment bulkheads.

The outer screen of the NDP had been fitted with large wind screens by mid-1917. They have not been added in this drawing but are in the profile on the next page and in the plan view on page 19.

The 38ft sounding boom is indicated here in its original stowed position. The boom was relocated when bulges were fitted; the original and new positions can be seen in the profile on the next page and in the plan view on page 21.

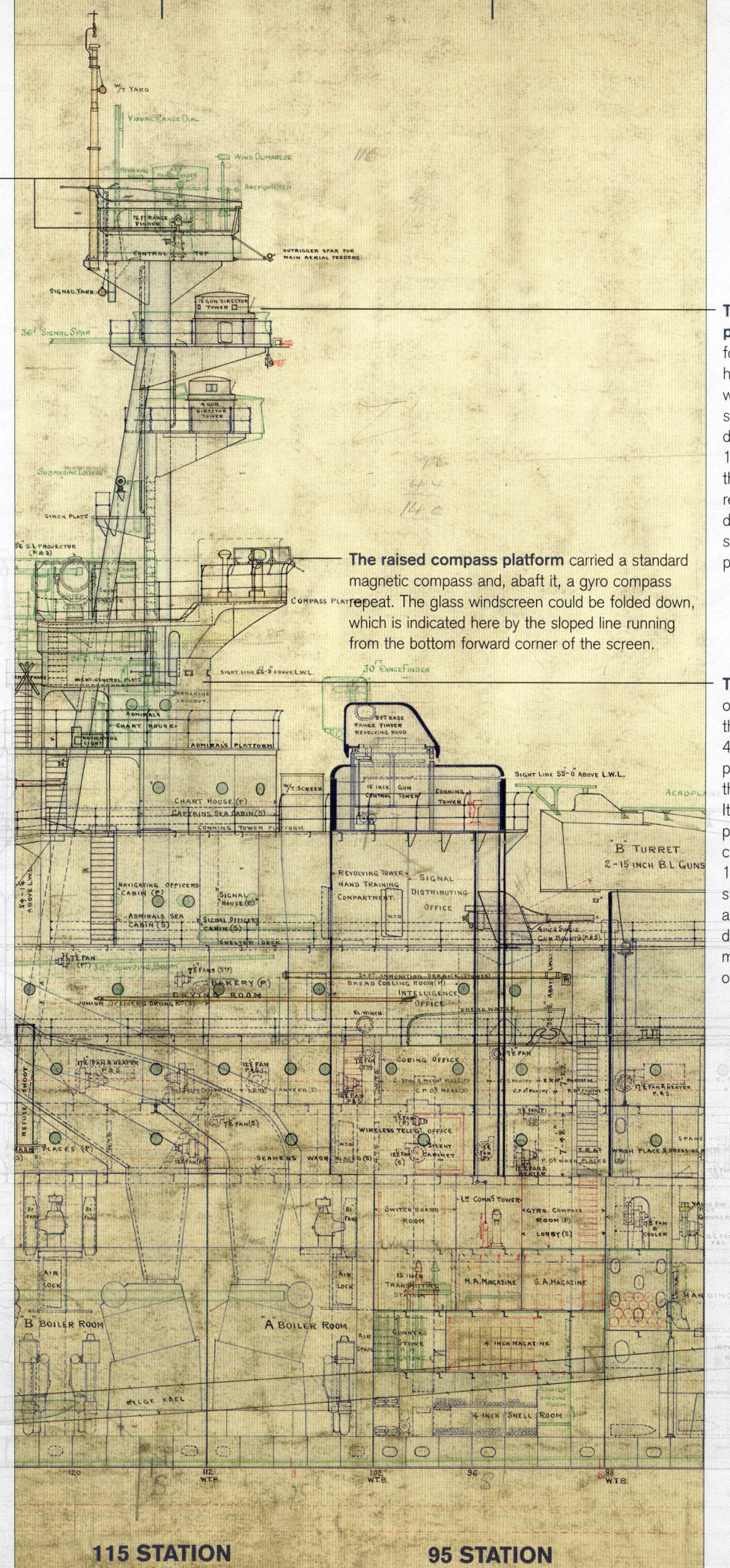

The 12ft rangefinder in the spotting top is shown in both its original location and, in green, in the new position fitted in 1917 to raise it above the roof of the top. This gave the instrument an all-round view without the need of the transfer rails that allowed the pedestal to be moved from side to side in the top. The revolving hood provided the rangefinder and its operators with protection against the weather.

STATIONS 115 TO 95

The bridge structure accommodated the primary control positions of the ship for fire control, conning, navigation and signalling, together with sea accommodation for the ship's senior officers. Its only rival in this respect was the armoured CT which provided control and spotting for the 15in guns and for torpedo fire together with communication and navigation equipment. However, there was a tendency for senior officers to prefer the unprotected (other than by splinter mattresses) compass platform which provided a higher and wider point of observation.

The steel foremast had a length of 98ft 1in, a diameter of 37in and, to the floor of the spotting top, a height of 113ft 6in above an estimated LWL of 27ft 3in. The wood fore topmast was 26ft 3in in length, its height above the 27ft 3in LWL being 142ft 6in (including the 4ft 6in lighting conductor). A wireless yard (length unknown) was fitted to the fore topmast and a 50ft signal yard to a post under the after end of the spotting top. The signal yard was replaced by a 36ft signal spar on each side of the 15in director platform during the ship's Nov 1916–Jan 1917 refit.

The raised compass platform carried a standard magnetic compass and, abaft it, a gyro compass repeat. The glass windscreen could be folded down, which is indicated here by the sloped line running from the bottom forward corner of the screen.

The main 15in director platform and that of the forward 4in director below it had their guardrails replaced with steel screens, shaped to serve as wind deflectors, during the ship's Nov 1916–Jan 1917 refit. Note that the tipped green rectangle just abaft the 4in director is a glass wind screen which can be seen in plan view on page 19.

The submarine lookout is on a raised area forward of the admiral's chart house and 4ft above the admiral's platform but accessed from the NDP platform above it. It contained six lookout positions giving overlapping coverage from right ahead to 19° abaft the beam on each side. The 'sight line' indicated at '66ft 9in above [the designed] LWL' is actually measured to the lower edge of the sighting ports.

115 STATION   **95 STATION**

SECTION AT STATION 95, STARBOARD SIDE, LOOKING FORWARD

This section is, nominally, down the centre of the communication tube. The arrangement of the deck protection is the same as that described on page 34 for the after magazine group except here it also covers the 15in TS, 4in TS, lower steering position, gyro room and switchboard. The termination of the thicker protection at the fore bulkhead of 'A' boiler room made the arrangement vulnerable to plunging shell coming from abaft the beam since it could pass through the thin deck protection over the boilers, through the forward bulkhead of 'A' boiler room and reach the 4in magazine.

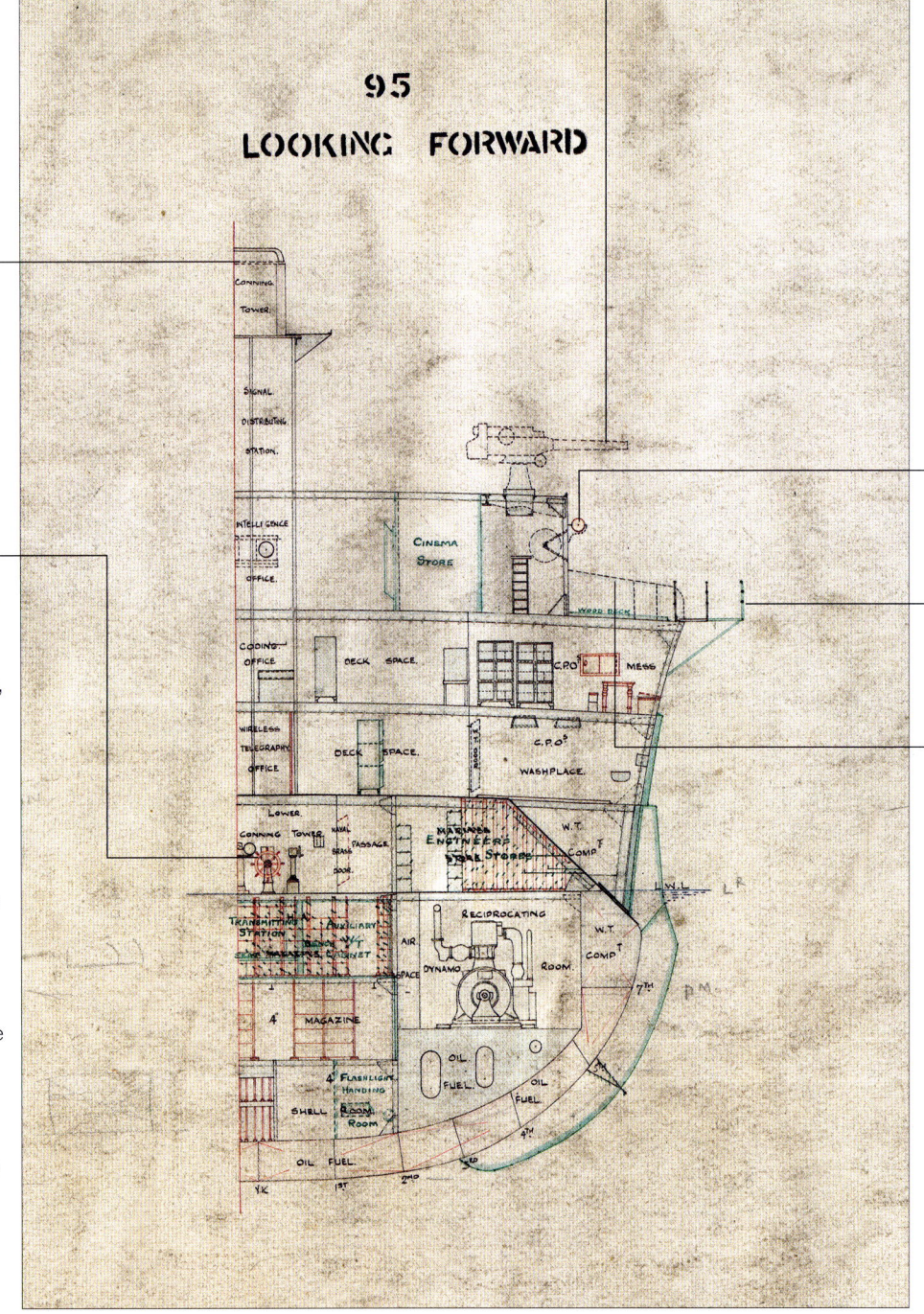

The sighting slot in the CT was 55ft above the designed LWL, a measurement made to the bottom edge of the slot.

The lower conning tower showing its primary items of equipment – the magnetic compass binnacle on the middle line, and starboard steering wheel and engine room telegraph which were matched on the port side. The two steering wheels were alternatives to each other, only one being in use at any given time. The steering wheel in the CT could be connected to either via a control rod passing down the communication tube. There were also two alternative sets of telemotor pipes (port and starboard) connecting the wheels to the steering engines in the condenser rooms; both could be connected to either wheel by means of change-over valves in the lower conning tower

The starboard 4in BL Mk IX gun on its single Mk XII LA mounting is shown here without its shield. The shield is, however, shown in the profile view on the next page.

The forward 34ft ammunition derrick is indicated in its stowed position by this red circle.

The leadsman's platform has been extended outboard 3ft to give clearance over the bulge.

The breakwater is shown in dashed line, presumably to show that it passes diagonally through Station 95. The vertical lines indicate the position of the portable section of the breakwater which when required could be removed to allow personnel fore and aft access.

STATIONS 95 TO 80

If anything deserves the title nerve centre of the ship it is the armoured structure that extends downwards from the CT to the main deck. Oddly there is no sign on these plans, or on those of *Renown* or in the ship's armour contracts, of the CT being fitted with an armour door. The GCT did have a 2in HT sliding door but the opening in the 10in wall of the CT itself only had a thin double door on the inside of its entrance. Presumably the fact that the GCT effectively blocked the opening on the inside was considered sufficient defence against a shell detonating abaft the CT.

The CT surrounds the 6in armour tube of the GCT which supported the revolving armoured hood containing a 15ft rangefinder and one of the ship's two Vickers tripod directors. Note that the 30ft rangefinder added at the rear of the hood, together with its enclosure, are completely exterior to the hood and unprotected except against the weather. The platform around the CT was originally intended to be the primary conning position and was equipped with gyro compass and engine room telegraph repeats together with screens on the after sides of the CT for instruments and voice pipes. In addition, abaft the CT, on each side of the CT platform, was an Evershed bearing indicator and a portable chart table. The arrangement was not popular, officers preferring to con the ship from the compass platform and there is little indication that the chart tables were ever fitted in place after 1916. The compass platform quickly became the official primary conning position while the platform around the CT was only expected to be used when the ship was in action.

The armoured support structure of the CT, extending down to the main deck, was 3in thick at the sides and 2in thick at the ends. It enclosed the primary communication compartments of the ship – from top to bottom, the signal distributing office, intelligence office, coding office and the main W/T office. Under the protection of the main deck, were the main switchboard room, the main telephone exchange (to port of the lower conning position) and the gyro compass room (also to port) on the lower deck. Below this, on the upper platform deck, were the TS for the 15in armament and, to port of the HA magazine, that of the 4in armament.

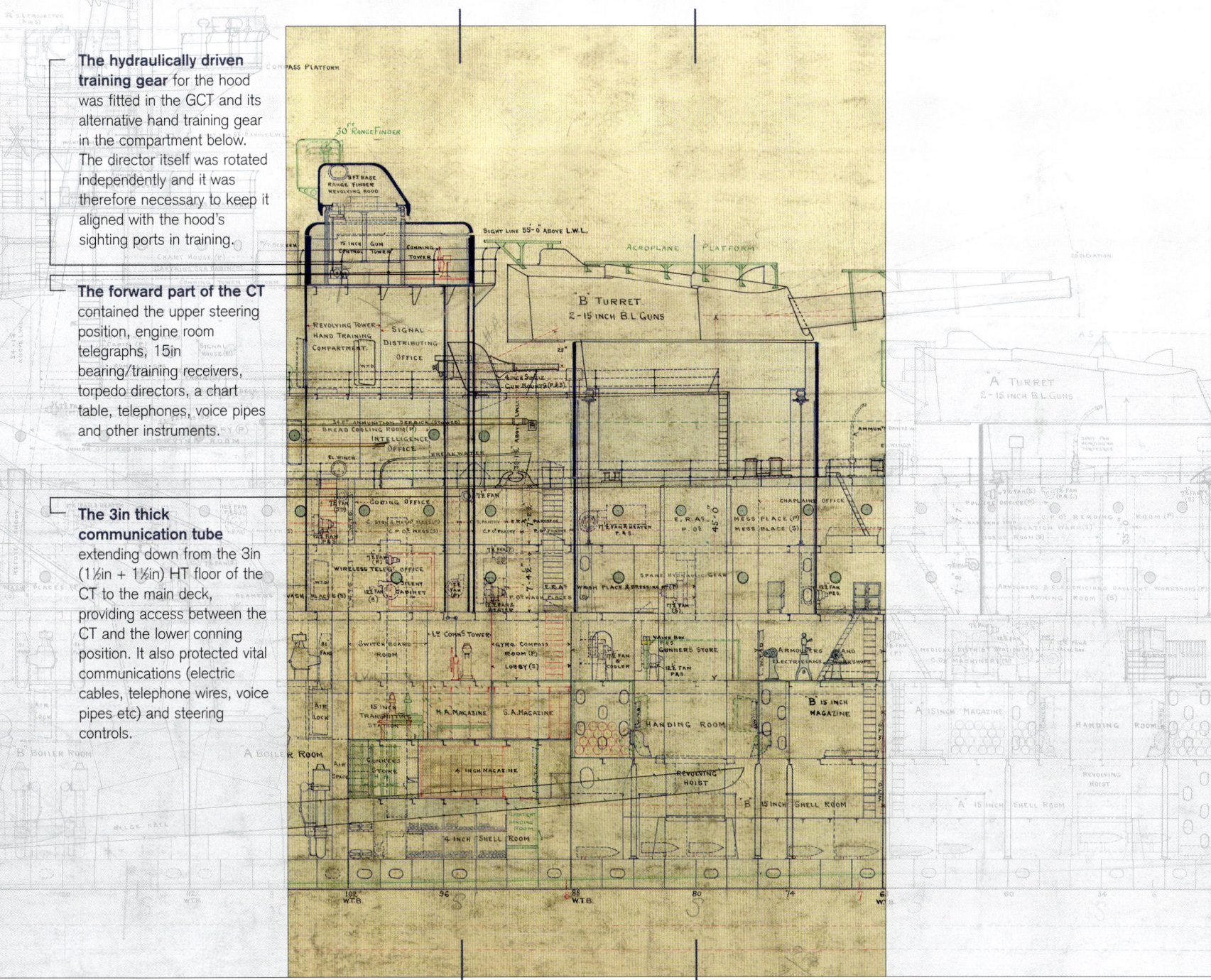

The hydraulically driven training gear for the hood was fitted in the GCT and its alternative hand training gear in the compartment below. The director itself was rotated independently and it was therefore necessary to keep it aligned with the hood's sighting ports in training.

The forward part of the CT contained the upper steering position, engine room telegraphs, 15in bearing/training receivers, torpedo directors, a chart table, telephones, voice pipes and other instruments.

The 3in thick communication tube extending down from the 3in (1½in + 1½in) HT floor of the CT to the main deck, providing access between the CT and the lower conning position. It also protected vital communications (electric cables, telephone wires, voice pipes etc) and steering controls.

95 STATION   **80 STATION**

SECTION AT STATION 80, STARBOARD SIDE, LOOKING FORWARD

The barbette armour of British battleships and battlecruisers of the First World War period tended to be a somewhat complex arrangement of varying thicknesses according to the likely direction of attack and whether or not it was also shielded by side or bulkhead armour and adjacent barbettes. In *Repulse* it was a little simpler particularly because no tapered armour was employed – possibly one of the concessions made to reduce construction time. This section is cut through the centre of 'B' barbette, the deepest of the three in the ship. From the top to the upper deck it was uniformly 7in thick and between, the forecastle and main decks, 6in with the exception of a 4in 36° wide portion on the fore and after sides. 'A' barbette was 7in from the top to the upper deck, while between the upper and main deck the forward 180° was 7in while the after 180° stepped down from 6in forward to 5in and then 4in across the after portion, each of the five sections involved occupying 36°. 'Y' barbette was uniform 7in down to the main deck and 4in between the main and lower deck.

A total of 48 flanged and tapered forged steel rollers on a pitch diameter of 27ft supported the entire revolving, 741.5-ton, nominal weight of the 15in twin mountings. They were carried in a roller ring and travelled round a lower roller path fixed to the top of a heavily supported ring bulkhead that extended, in the case of 'B' mounting, down to the upper deck. The upper roller path was fixed to the underside of the turntable floor. During construction the lower roller paths were machined in situ to get them as flat as possible (noting that they sloped to match the taper of the rollers) but such was the desired accuracy for fire control purposes it was still necessary to install tilt correctors in the elevation controls to correct for any slight variations around the turrets' training arcs which might affect the accuracy of the guns' elevation. The inside diameter of the barbette was 30ft.

From the fore bulkhead of 'A' boiler room to the angled armour bulkhead abreast the fore end of 'A' barbette the double bottom no longer followed the underside of the slope of the main deck but turned vertically at the lower deck/7th longitudinal and terminated part way up the slope of the main deck.

The bulge protection forward was similar to that fitted aft, consisting of single upper and lower compartments, but differed in being filled with crushing tubes – except for the extreme forward end, which was void.

STATIONS 80 TO 66

On 1 Oct 1917 a take-off by Squadron Commander F J Rutland in a Sopwith Pup from a ramp fitted to 'B' turret of *Repulse* marked the initial trial that resulted in the adoption of such ramps in all the battlecruisers of the Grand Fleet, and the majority of its battleships, during 1917–18. However, the Pup was a fighter, primarily intended for air defence and not entirely suited for reconnaissance and fire-control that ideally required a two-seat aircraft. Such aircraft, being heavier, required a longer take-off run and in Mar 1918 an attempt was made to launch a Sopwith 1½ Strutter from 'B' turret with the ramp extended over the 15in guns by a covered, flexible wire mattress. This was a total failure but a subsequent experiment from the battlecruiser *Australia* resulted in the adoption of a portable wood platform supported by steel frames clamped to the turret's guns. The 'B' turret ramp in this profile is that finally adopted and not the original fitted in 1917. It has a tail support above the turret rear, the main ramp on the roof and the support structure for the portable wood platform above the gun barrels. The aircraft allocated to *Repulse* during 1917–18 were: two Sopwith Pups (Oct 1917–Jan 1918); two Sopwith 2F1 Camels (Feb–Mar 1918); one 2F1 Camel and one Sopwith 1½ Strutter (Mar – Oct 1918). In Oct–Nov 1918 a Parnall Panther (for trial) replaced the 1½ Strutter. These were not carried continuously it being regular practice to transfer aircraft ashore when in harbour. In Nov 1921 she embarked another Panther which was wrecked during the take-off procedure on 9 November. During 1922–32 she does not seem to have been provided with aircraft except for a short period in 1928 when she embarked an Armstrong Whitworth Siskin IIIA fighter for evaluation purposes (she was also equipped with a Fairey Flycatcher at this time).

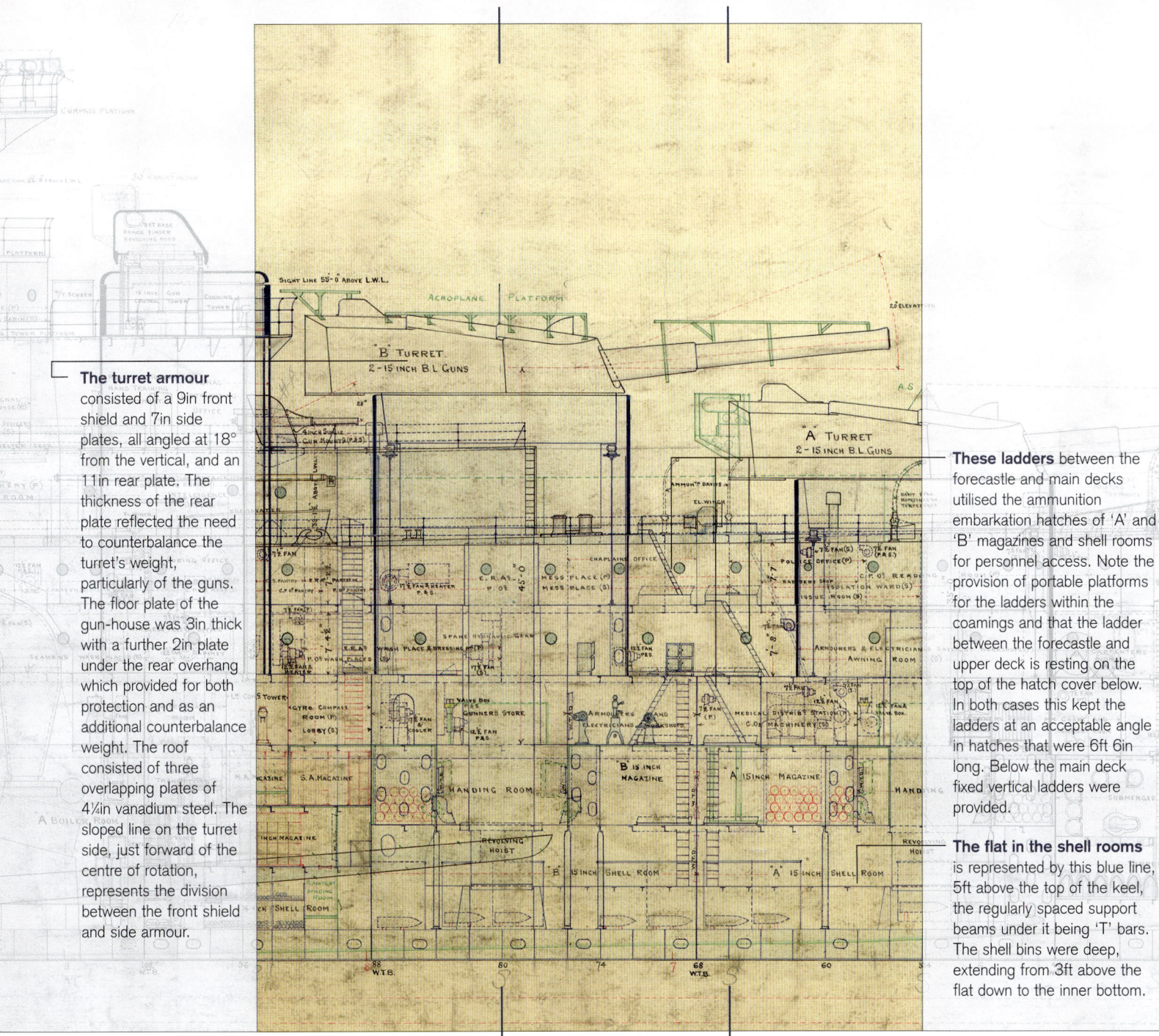

The turret armour consisted of a 9in front shield and 7in side plates, all angled at 18° from the vertical, and an 11in rear plate. The thickness of the rear plate reflected the need to counterbalance the turret's weight, particularly of the guns. The floor plate of the gun-house was 3in thick with a further 2in plate under the rear overhang which provided for both protection and as an additional counterbalance weight. The roof consisted of three overlapping plates of 4¼in vanadium steel. The sloped line on the turret side, just forward of the centre of rotation, represents the division between the front shield and side armour.

These ladders between the forecastle and main decks utilised the ammunition embarkation hatches of 'A' and 'B' magazines and shell rooms for personnel access. Note the provision of portable platforms for the ladders within the coamings and that the ladder between the forecastle and upper deck is resting on the top of the hatch cover below. In both cases this kept the ladders at an acceptable angle in hatches that were 6ft 6in long. Below the main deck fixed vertical ladders were provided.

The flat in the shell rooms is represented by this blue line, 5ft above the top of the keel, the regularly spaced support beams under it being 'T' bars. The shell bins were deep, extending from 3ft above the flat down to the inner bottom.

80 STATION **66 STATION**

52 ENLARGED PROFILE AND SECTIONS, AS FITTED 1916

SECTION AT STATION 66, STARBOARD SIDE, LOOKING FORWARD

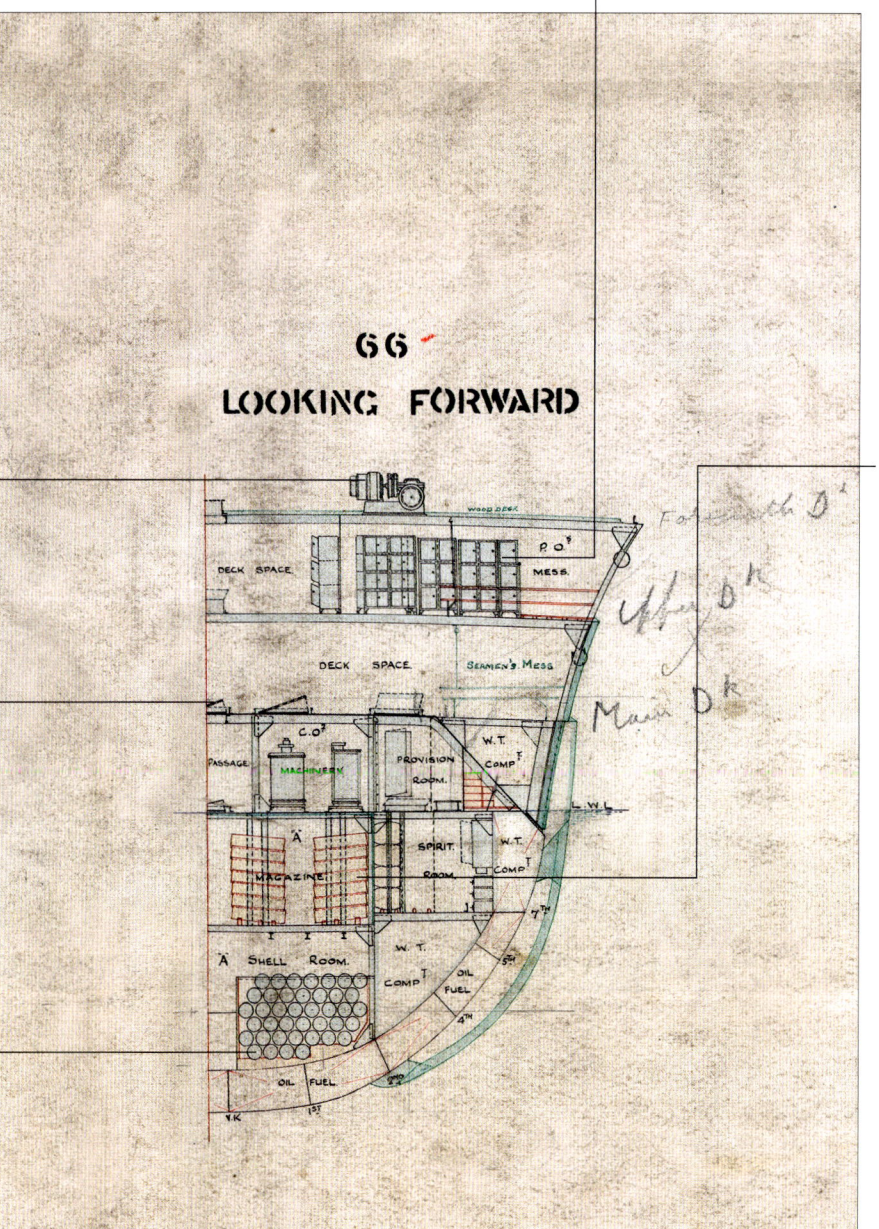

Kit lockers of the type shown here can be found in considerable numbers on the mess decks. These were steel cabinets of similar design but with varying arrangements of lockers (one or two wide and two or three high being the more common variants). In the plan views the number of lockers in each cabinet (or group of cabinets) is indicated by a number.

The No 1 (p & s) electric winches were mainly employed (together with the No 2 winches abreast the CT on the forecastle deck) in conjunction with the forward 34ft ammunition derricks.

Armour hatches in the protective main deck were of the same thickness and material as the deck and fitted flush with the deck, a raised coaming being fitted around them. These two are the ammunition embarkation hatch on the middle line and, to starboard of it, the access hatch to the CO_2 machinery room.

This shell bin accommodates 39 APC projectiles and is located slightly forward of the intended position since Station 66 actually passes through a bin for 42 CPC projectiles.

The cordite cases were stowed in racks and sloped at 5° to ease the removal of the charge. These are cylindrical 'M' cases each accommodating two quarter charges of 107lbs MD cordite. There is a common misconception that these storage cases were Clarkson's cases, which they were not. The 'M' cases stayed in the magazine racks and were only removed or installed when ammunition was landed or embarked. In normal operation the cordite was removed from the cases in the magazine and the bare charges passed into the handing room via a flash-tight scuttle. Clarkson's cases were transport cases re-introduced post Jutland for use between the magazines and mountings of medium calibre BL guns, including the 4in in *Repulse* (noting that even in this case they were not employed for magazine stowage).

STATIONS 66 TO 54

The heavy weight of the 15in gun mountings required a substantial level of structural support, particularly as the accuracy of the guns depended upon, among other things, a stable platform from which to fire. This included heavy pillars fitted in the shell rooms, visible here at Stations 50 and 60 (both being fitted port and starboard), and the large fore-and-aft plates fitted in both shell rooms and magazines on the centre-line between floor and deck-head and recognizable by their oval lightening holes. One is visible in this view at the fore end of 'A' shell room and two more in 'A' magazine, one at its forward end (between the fore bulkhead of 'A' magazine and the fore bulkhead of 'A' handing room) and one further aft (between the after bulkhead of the handing room and an 8ft wide transverse plate at Station 60).

The short awning stanchion is located on the centre of rotation of 'A' turret and supports the after end of the forecastle awning ridge rope. This and all the other awning stanchions were added to the plans when they were modified. As completed *Repulse* had no awning stanchions and there does not appear to be any photographic evidence, including any sign of the heel fittings, that these were provided at any time during 1916–18 apart from a 1918 photograph that shows an awning rigged between the after end of the forecastle and the after funnel. This could be the result of the fitting of a standard arrangement or of something extemporised by the crew. The ship was, however, built with a large 'awning room' on the main deck to starboard of 'A' barbette.

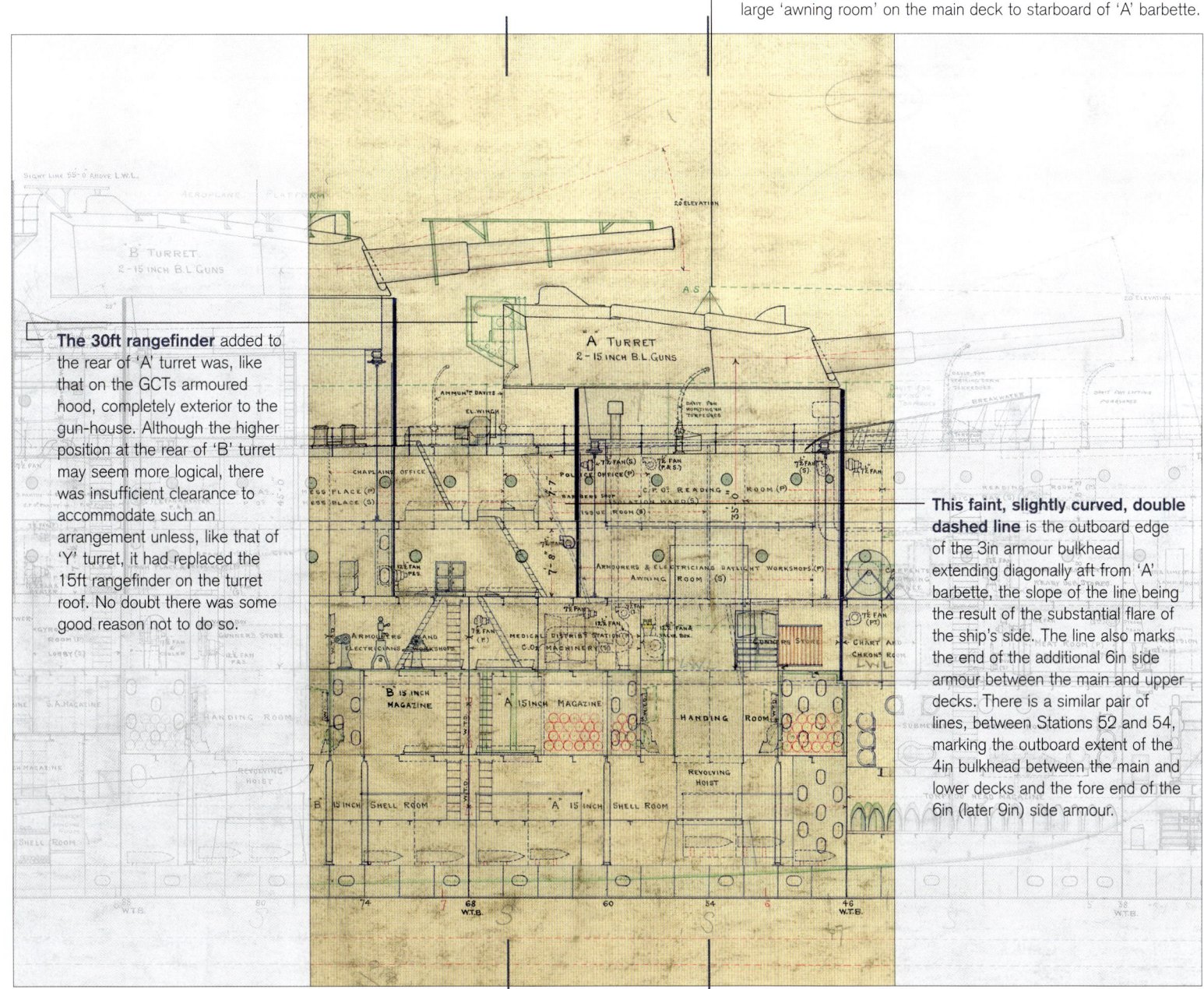

The 30ft rangefinder added to the rear of 'A' turret was, like that on the GCTs armoured hood, completely exterior to the gun-house. Although the higher position at the rear of 'B' turret may seem more logical, there was insufficient clearance to accommodate such an arrangement unless, like that of 'Y' turret, it had replaced the 15ft rangefinder on the turret roof. No doubt there was some good reason not to do so.

This faint, slightly curved, double dashed line is the outboard edge of the 3in armour bulkhead extending diagonally aft from 'A' barbette, the slope of the line being the result of the substantial flare of the ship's side. The line also marks the end of the additional 6in side armour between the main and upper decks. There is a similar pair of lines, between Stations 52 and 54, marking the outboard extent of the 4in bulkhead between the main and lower decks and the fore end of the 6in (later 9in) side armour.

66 STATION   54 STATION

SECTION AT STATION 54, STARBOARD SIDE, LOOKING FORWARD

This section taken across the centre of 'A' 15in gun mounting contains one of the ship's three motor generator compartments. Another was located on the port side opposite this one while the third was located aft on the lower deck, to port side of 'Y' mounting. Each of those forward contained two motor generators for the forward 36in searchlights, a smaller motor generator for the 24in signalling projectors, a motor alternator for the main W/T set and an isolator (in this context a form of motor generator – probably for the Evershed system). The port room also contained two motor alternators for the turret danger signals while that to starboard had had a second isolator added by 1921. The after motor generator compartment contained four motor generators for the after 36in searchlights and a motor alternator (possibly for the auxiliary W/T set). All were driven by mains electric motors to drive lower voltage generators for dc current or alternators for ac current. The ship also had six motor generators in the main switchboard room supplying the 15-volt low power switchboard located against its after bulkhead. Apart from the items already mentioned, the low power system supplied the telephones, fire control instruments, gyro compass and the bell and buzzer circuits.

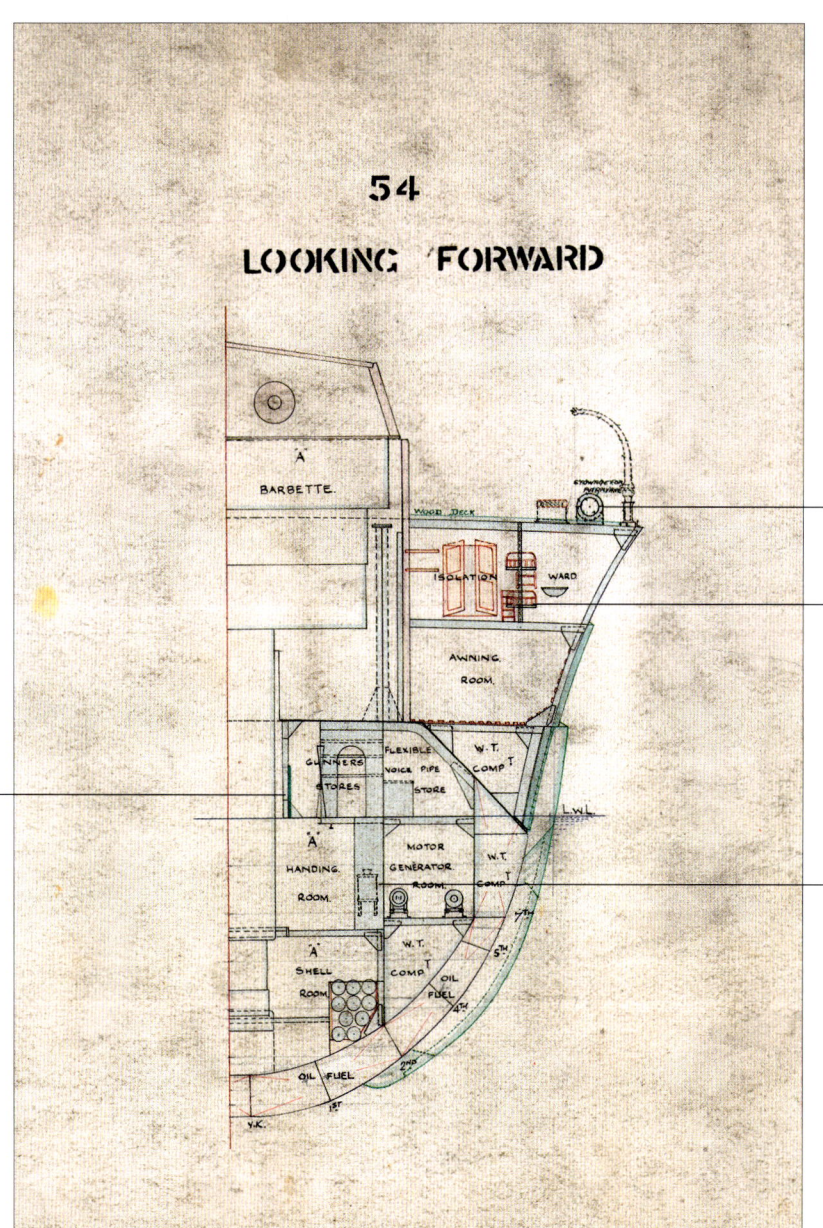

The thick green line indicates the addition of a fixed ring of 2in HT protective plating fitted at the same time as the extra protective plating added to the lower deck in 1916–17. It served to screen the hoist trunk opening in the deck; the same addition for 'B' mounting can be seen on page 50.

One of the ship's four paravanes is shown here, in end view, stowed adjacent to one of its davits.

The isolation ward showing an end view of its two cots and the double doors that led to the sick bay (which had ten cots) at its fore end. The vertical lines through the ends of the cots represent the posts to which the cots were fixed.

The fresh water tank in 'A' handing room is fixed to the aft side of a vertical, structural, support frame (shaded). This frame is not shown in the plan of the platform deck for 1916 but is shown in that for 1936.

STATIONS 54 TO 43

The fore end of 'A' magazine, like that for the after end of 'Y' magazine, was vulnerable to plunging shellfire, although not to the same degree since it did not project so far beyond 'A' barbette and, where it did, the crown of the magazine was 1½in rather than ¾in and the side armour was 4in rather than 3in. The increase in the thickness of the main deck over the magazines to 2in, carried out shortly before completion, was continued for a short distance forward of 'A' barbette to Station 44, which reduced the vulnerability to a very limited extent. Further improvement was made during the ship's Nov 1916–Jan 1917 refit when the lower deck from the 4in bulkheads angling aft from the base of 'A' barbette were increased to 2½in HT, but only as far as Station 43. No further improvement was made in this area (which contained the torpedo head magazine) until the ship's 1933–36 refit. The remainder of the main and lower decks as far as the forward 4in armour bulkhead was ¾in HT.

The submerged torpedo room provides end views of the ship's two 21in tubes, starboard tube aft and port tube forward. Given the limited value of being able to fire only one torpedo at a time on each beam the subsequent addition of eight above-water tubes is easier to understand than the logic of the original installation. The keyhole shape of the tube results from the combination of a circular opening to the left, for the torpedo, and an elongated slot to the right for the torpedo bar. The bar (contained within the tube structure) was extended outboard to guide the torpedo until it was clear of the ship, preventing it being forced sideways by the ship's passage through the water and getting damaged and/or jammed in the tube. Also visible are all of the torpedo bodies of the ship's outfit: four stowed just below the deck-head, and three in vertical racks at each end of the room. The eleventh (spare?) body stowed at the fore end of the platform, is something of a mystery since there does not appear to be any official document that lists more than ten torpedoes for the ship's submerged tube outfit.

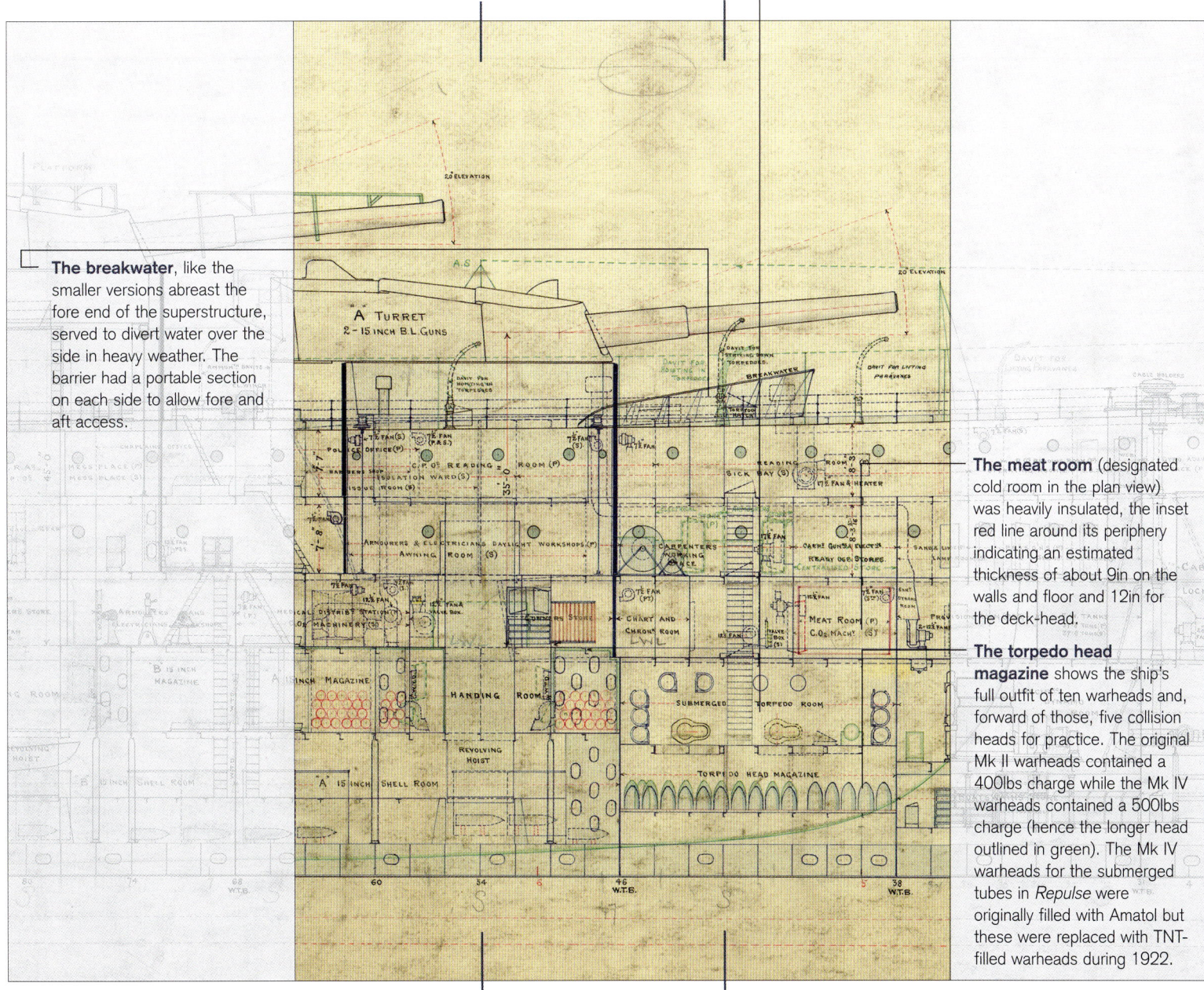

The breakwater, like the smaller versions abreast the fore end of the superstructure, served to divert water over the side in heavy weather. The barrier had a portable section on each side to allow fore and aft access.

The meat room (designated cold room in the plan view) was heavily insulated, the inset red line around its periphery indicating an estimated thickness of about 9in on the walls and floor and 12in for the deck-head.

The torpedo head magazine shows the ship's full outfit of ten warheads and, forward of those, five collision heads for practice. The original Mk II warheads contained a 400lbs charge while the Mk IV warheads contained a 500lbs charge (hence the longer head outlined in green). The Mk IV warheads for the submerged tubes in *Repulse* were originally filled with Amatol but these were replaced with TNT-filled warheads during 1922.

54 STATION **43 STATION**

SECTIONS AT STATIONS 43 AND 32, STARBOARD SIDE, LOOKING FORWARD

The original torpedo outfit of *Repulse* consisted of ten 21in, RNTF, Mk II****/Mk II***** HB torpedoes, which had standard range settings of 14,000yds at 24kts (23kts for the Mk II****) and 4500yds at 44.5kts; the former was the standard long-range setting and the latter for night and low visibility conditions. Two torpedoes of the outfit were newly introduced extended-range (ER) versions with an additional setting of 17,000yds at 19kts (18kts for the Mk II****). Later almost all Mk II torpedoes were converted to ER, prompting the reclassification of the standard long-range setting to 'medium' range. These ranges were the nominal maximums with the air vessel charged to a working pressure of 2500psi. This could be raised to an action pressure of 2650psi which provided sufficient over-run to ensure the torpedo would exceed the working pressure range and that the speed would not reduce excessively until beyond that point. The maximum expected over-run at the high speed setting was 300yds and at the other speeds 1000yds.

During 1917 the Mk II outfit was replaced by new production Mk IV-IV* torpedoes. These had three speed settings providing ranges of 4200yds at 44.5kts, 14,000yds at 25kts and 17,000yds at 21kts at 2500psi (the over-runs at 2650psi were the same as those for the Mk II). Depth keeping problems with the high-speed setting resulted in its 'temporary' reduction to 35kts, for a range of 6000yds at action pressure, pending the introduction of improved depth gear. The latter was available by early 1918 but, following opinion from officers of the Grand Fleet, it was decided to retain the lower speed since this was viewed as providing positive gains against the moderate advantages of the higher speed (the 35kt setting was also adopted in the Mk II torpedo). The Mk IV* torpedo had some minor changes to its mechanism and introduced a fourth range setting – 10,750yds (11,000yds with action pressure) at 29kts. In 1920 The Mk IV and IV* torpedoes were re-rated to 14,500yds at 25kts, 11,000yds at 29kts and 8500yds at 35kts, all at a working pressure 2500psi.

The section at Station 32 provides an alternative view of the dynamo and the access, escape and ventilation trunk to the dynamo room. The hull at this point has minimal protection – 4in side armour between the ¾in thick main and lower decks. The section also provides a view of one of the ship's cable holders.

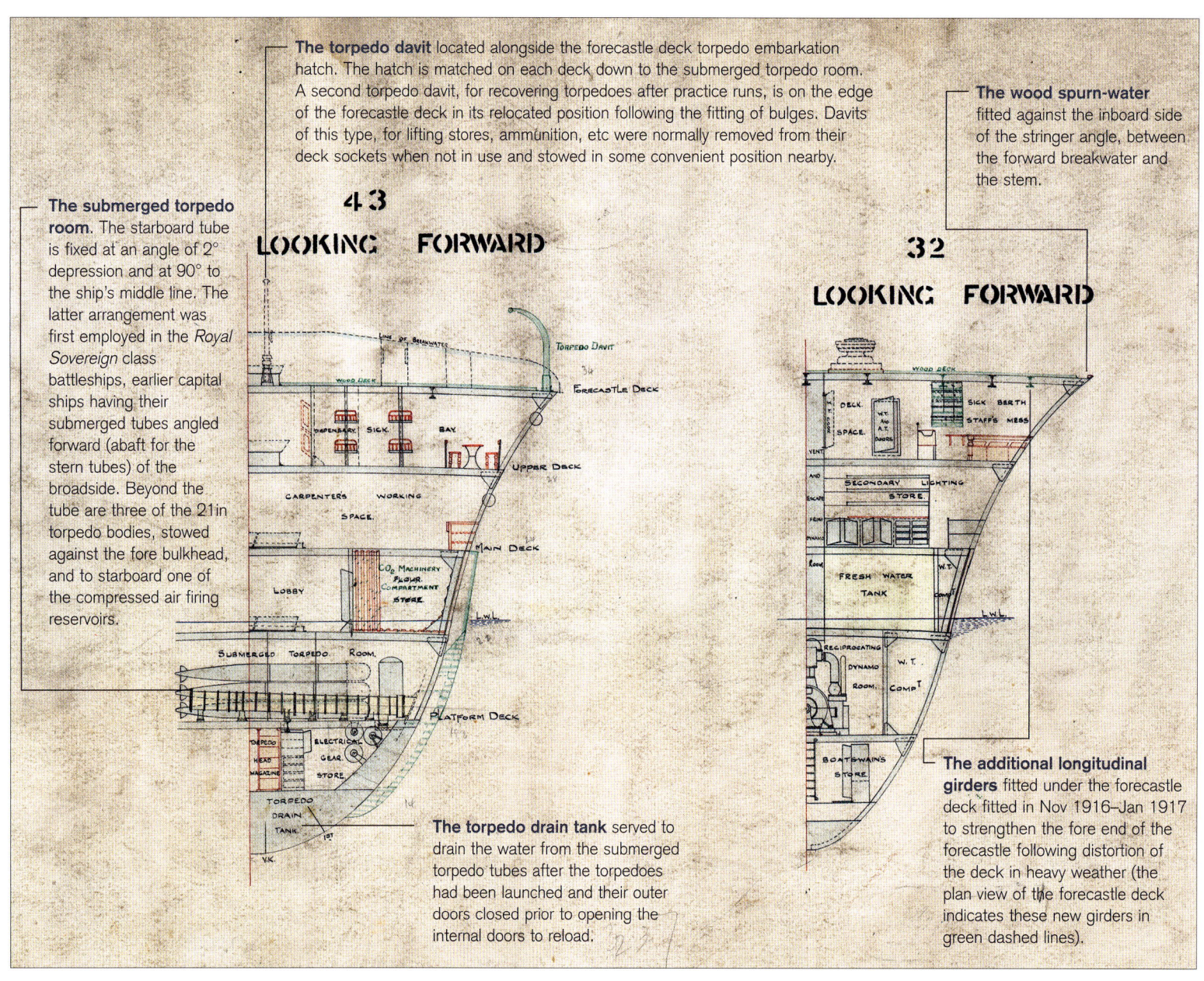

STATIONS 43 TO 27

Compared with the section on page 58, this part of the profile provides a more detailed view of the capstan engine room with its two-cylinder steam engine driving three worm wheels – one forward for the capstan and two aft for the cable holders. The room had a similar access and escape trunk to that described below for the dynamo room except that the ladder in the trunk is vertical and there is an armour hatch at the bottom.

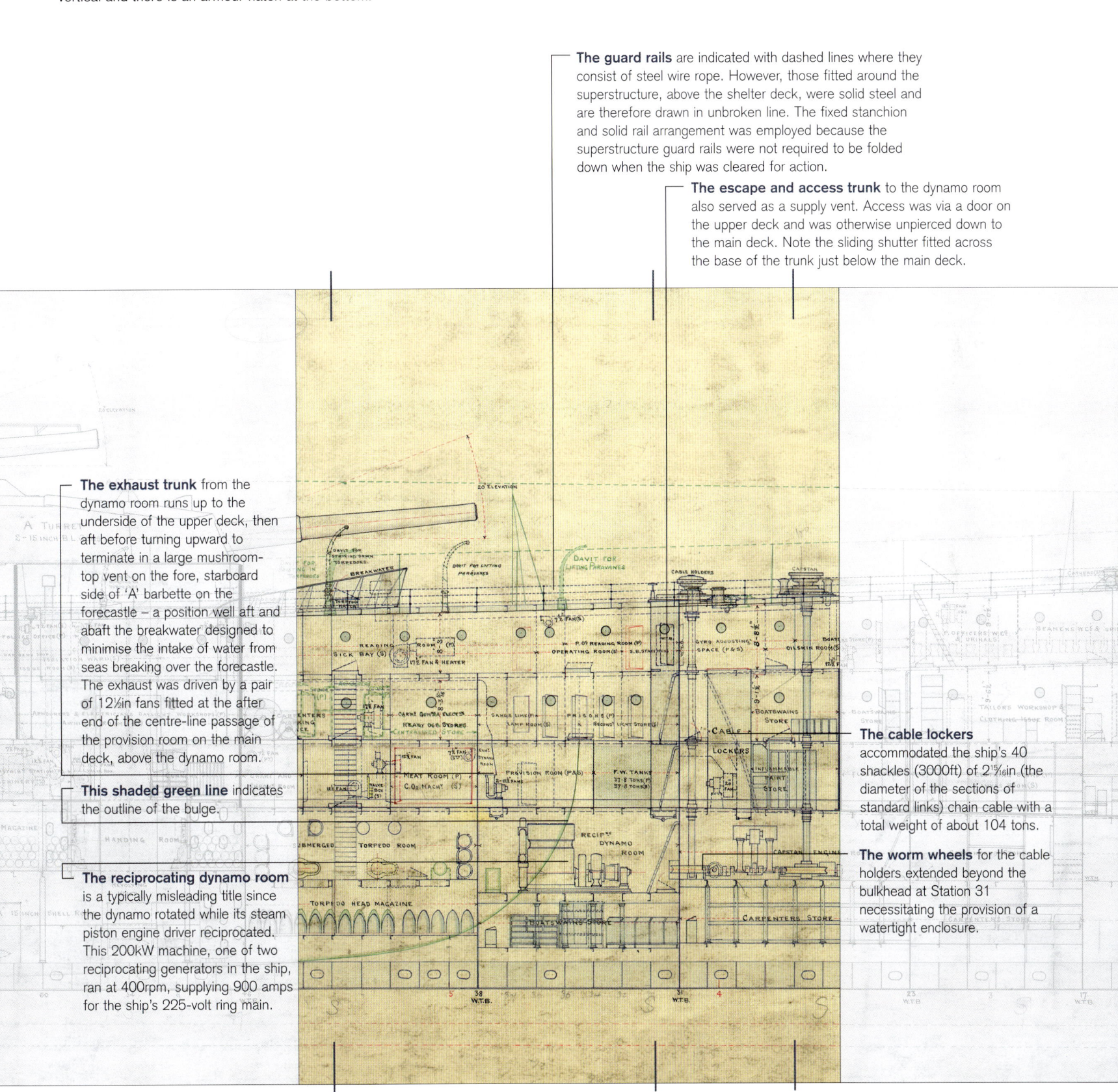

The guard rails are indicated with dashed lines where they consist of steel wire rope. However, those fitted around the superstructure, above the shelter deck, were solid steel and are therefore drawn in unbroken line. The fixed stanchion and solid rail arrangement was employed because the superstructure guard rails were not required to be folded down when the ship was cleared for action.

The escape and access trunk to the dynamo room also served as a supply vent. Access was via a door on the upper deck and was otherwise unpierced down to the main deck. Note the sliding shutter fitted across the base of the trunk just below the main deck.

The exhaust trunk from the dynamo room runs up to the underside of the upper deck, then aft before turning upward to terminate in a large mushroom-top vent on the fore, starboard side of 'A' barbette on the forecastle – a position well aft and abaft the breakwater designed to minimise the intake of water from seas breaking over the forecastle. The exhaust was driven by a pair of 12½in fans fitted at the after end of the centre-line passage of the provision room on the main deck, above the dynamo room.

This shaded green line indicates the outline of the bulge.

The reciprocating dynamo room is a typically misleading title since the dynamo rotated while its steam piston engine driver reciprocated. This 200kW machine, one of two reciprocating generators in the ship, ran at 400rpm, supplying 900 amps for the ship's 225-volt ring main.

The cable lockers accommodated the ship's 40 shackles (3000ft) of 2 15/16in (the diameter of the sections of standard links) chain cable with a total weight of about 104 tons.

The worm wheels for the cable holders extended beyond the bulkhead at Station 31 necessitating the provision of a watertight enclosure.

43 STATION   **32 STATION**   **27 STATION**

SECTION AT STATIONS 27 AND 19, STARBOARD SIDE, LOOKING FORWARD

All compartments shown at Station 27 are for stores with the exception of the capstan engine room. The capstan drive shaft and its worm wheel are shown but not the capstan engine itself.

The section at Station 19 is also mainly occupied with store rooms with the exception of the heads on the upper deck.

The portable vertical roller was one of two provided to serve as cable guides. They could be fitted in any of four positions provided around the capstan.

The seamen's WC is somewhat lacking in privacy: although there are screens between each cubicle, these were open at the front apart from a longitudinal screen (open at top and bottom) set some distance inboard (the second screen outboard of the latter only extends across the entrance to the WC space). PO and CPO WCs had the privilege of doors. The WCs are on a raised platform because the soil pipes were run along under them.

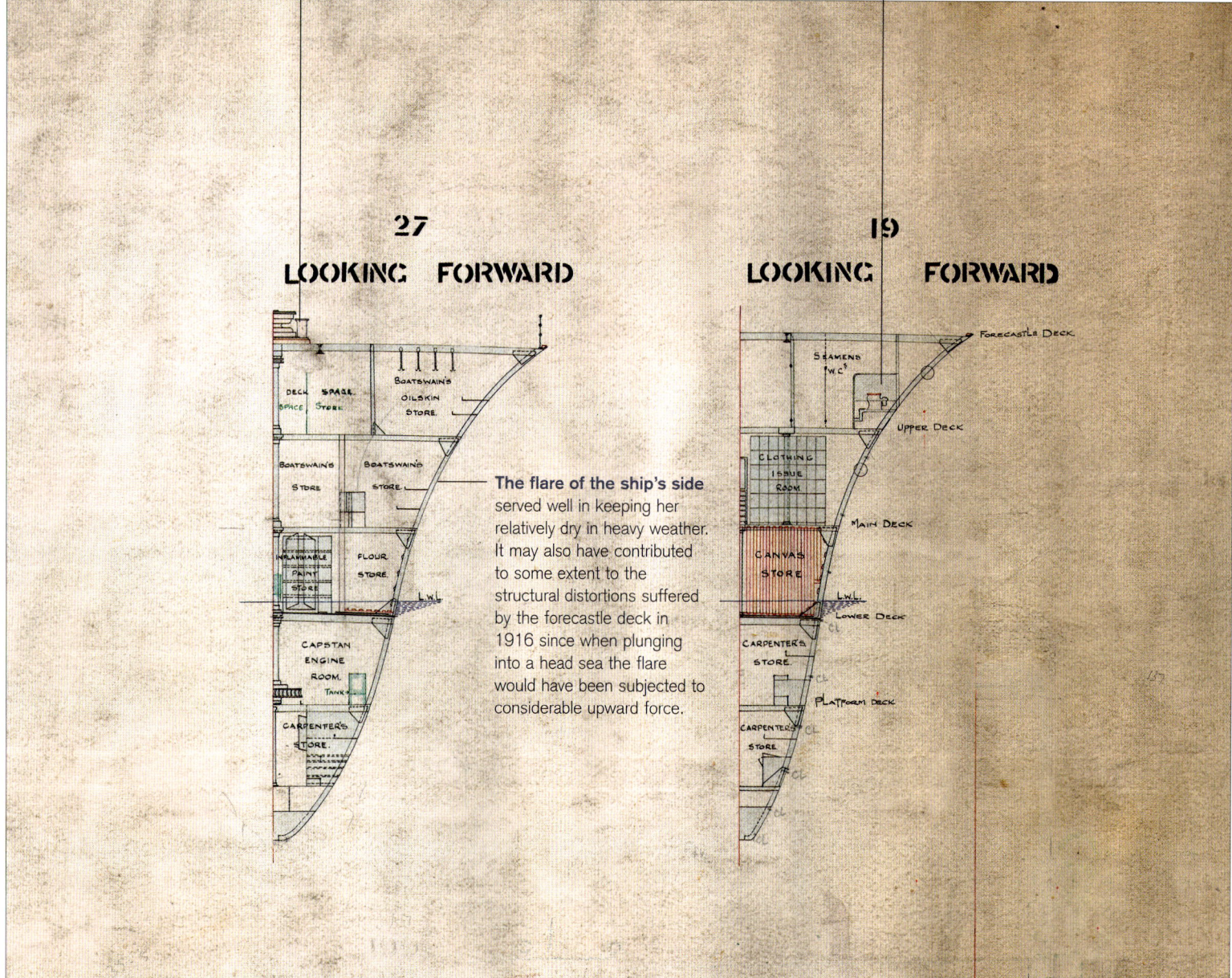

The flare of the ship's side served well in keeping her relatively dry in heavy weather. It may also have contributed to some extent to the structural distortions suffered by the forecastle deck in 1916 since when plunging into a head sea the flare would have been subjected to considerable upward force.

STATION 27 TO STEM

The lack of any side armour beyond the foremost 4in armour bulkhead was compensated to some extent by splinter protection provided by the 2½in HT lower deck extending from the bulkhead to the stem. The bulkhead, as can be seen in the plan views, sloped aft in 'V' form like those abreast 'A' turret, the faint curved lines, where it met the side plating, being visible across the cable locker in the profile on page 57.

The stem casting extended from just forward of Station 6 to the main deck, above which the stem was covered by a contour plate. The casting can be identified by the flanges for attaching and supporting the fore ends of the decks and the dashed line indicating the inner thickness of the casting wall. Unfortunately, the drawing, using the two latter identifiers, implies that the casting extended to the upper deck. This is at variance with standard practice, the design specification, the arrangement in *Renown*, the as-fitted profile of *Repulse* in 1936 and photographic evidence and therefore unlikely.

The Wasteneys Smith's stockless bower and sheet anchors weighed a nominal 145cwt (7¼ tons) each. The plan includes the bower anchor's actual weight (standard practice on as-fitted drawings), the port anchor being 112lbs more and the starboard anchor 70lbs less than the nominal weight. Unusually, no weight is given for the sheet anchor, presumably because this information was not available to the draughtsman at the time he completed the drawing.

The paravane chain pipes (two on each side). Each paravane chain ran through one pipe, down and through the clump, then up to the pipe on the opposite side and back onto the forecastle providing an arrangement via which the paravane towing wire could be lowered or raised. The majority of earlier and later capital ships were fitted with fairleads for the paravane chains and this pipe arrangement only appears to have been employed in *Repulse*, *Renown* and the *Courageous* class. It would seem this arrangement was not entirely successful since the ship had been fitted with paravane fairleads by the end of 1918. The use of chain pipes did reappear in the 1930s, in a somewhat different form, and was employed in the battleships *Anson* (but not her sisters) and *Vanguard*.

The paravane clump fitted on the forefoot shortly before completion provided the lower guide for the paravane chains. (During the initial period of installation the clumps were referred to as 'bow extensions'.)

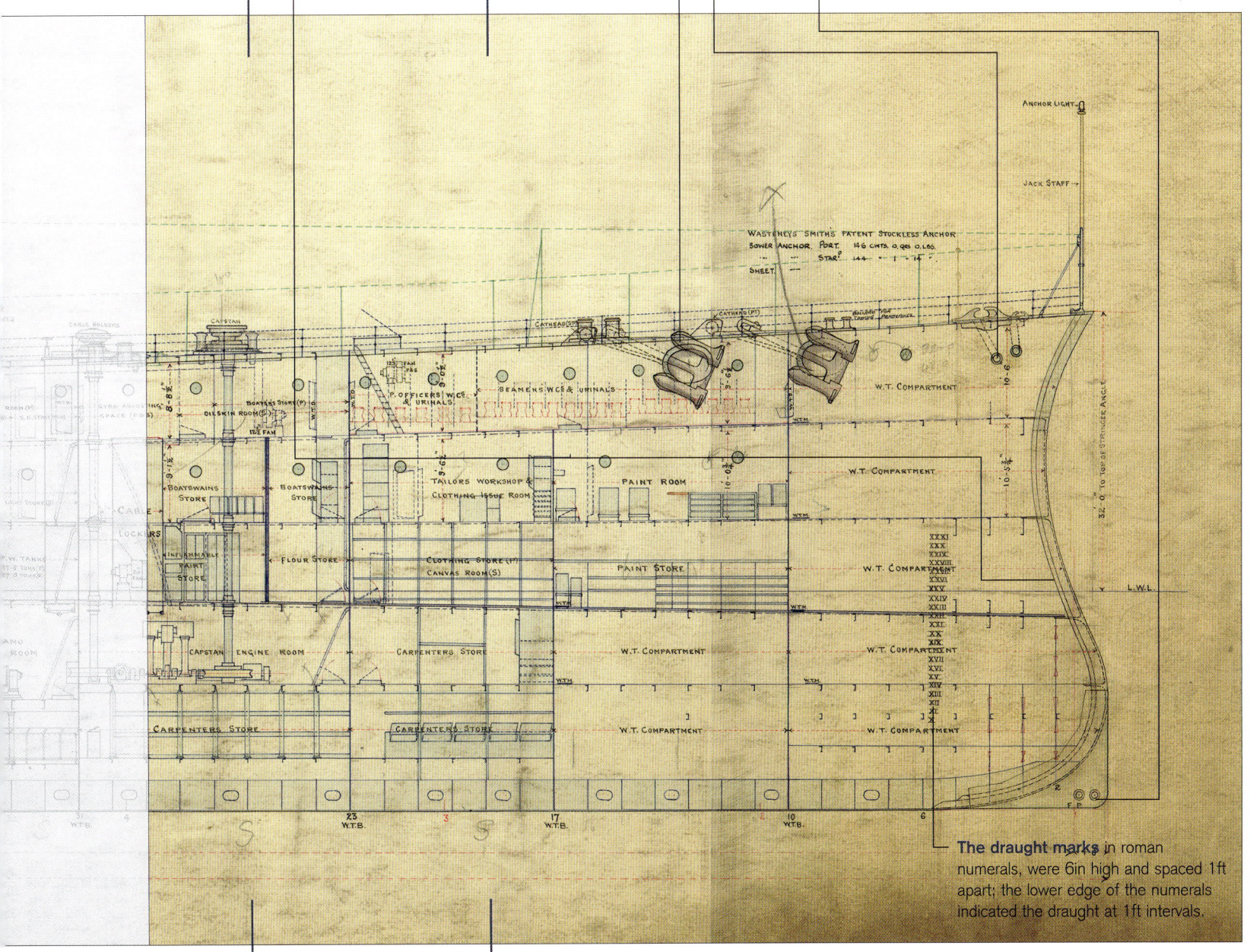

The draught marks in roman numerals, were 6in high and spaced 1ft apart; the lower edge of the numerals indicated the draught at 1ft intervals.

27 STATION   **19 STATION**

MODIFICATIONS 1916–1930

SUMMARY OF MODIFICATIONS 1916–1918

Clydebank June–Aug 1916

Following Battle of Jutland 1in protective plating was added to the flat of the main deck over the 15in magazines while ship was in the final stages of fitting out.

Portsmouth Aug–Sep 1916

Fore funnel raised in height by 6ft it having been found that funnel smoke would under some conditions of wind and speed make the compass platform untenable.

Fitted with paravanes.

Refit at Rosyth Nov 1916–Jan 1917

Additional protective deck plating fitted as a result of further consideration of lessons of Jutland.

Additional stiffening fitted to fore end as a result of weaknesses revealed during heavy weather at time of steam trials.

Main topmast and ensign staff on after superstructure removed. Ensign gaff fitted to lower platform on mainmast.

Fore signal yard removed and replaced with signal spars on aft side of 15in director platform.

Flash-tight scuttles fitted between 15in magazines and handing rooms.

May–Aug 1917

The following three items are in the order that they were implemented. The precise dates are unknown – those above only indicate the period during which the changes were made.

Painted with light/dark grey disruptive camouflage scheme which including diagonal stripes on the funnels and dark areas in various locations on the superstructure all of which remained in place to the end of 1918. Initially it also included two dark panels on the sides (one amidships and one forward) and an area of white at the fore ends. The white and amidships panels were painted out about mid-1918 but the forward dark panel survived until at least March 1918.

Foretop modified and enlarged, 12ft rangefinder raised to project through roof and fitted with a revolving hood.

Bearing scales painted on 'A' and 'Y' turrets and two concentration dials fitted on aft side of night control tower on mainmast.

Rosyth Aug–Sep 1917

Fitted with kite-balloon winch and supplied with balloon (Aug).

Aircraft flying-off platform fitted on 'B' turret.

Rosyth Oct 1917

Aircraft flying-off platform fitted on 'Y' turret.

Rosyth Oct–Nov 1917

Original funnel searchlight arrangements removed and replaced with four searchlights on towers around after funnel. Two new searchlight positions fitted aft on platforms extending from the after corners of the night control tower. Manipulating huts for the latter positioned on the forward corners of the after flying deck.

Compass platform modified to serve as primary torpedo control position. Extended 4ft aft, provided with a torpedo plotting house at the aft end and fitted with a 9ft FQ2 rangefinder on each side. The latter displaced the forward 36in searchlights which were re-located on the admiral's platform below.

Sides of admiral's platform extended outward and fitted with 24in signalling projectors.

Concentration dials on night control tower repositioned on the screens around after searchlight platforms.

Rosyth around Feb–Mar 1918

Aircraft platform on 'B' turret modified.

Portable aircraft hangars located on forecastle and after superstructure.

The background colour of the bearing scales on 'A' and 'Y' turrets changed from medium grey to black.

Around Mar–Nov 1918

Concentration dial fitted on fore side of forward 15in director platform.

15ft rangefinders replaced the 9ft rangefinders in the revolving hoods of the GCT and the TCT.

Admiral's platform modified, being extended aft on each side of the fore funnel to serve as a signal deck.

New 36in searchlights fitted on admiral's platform and manipulating huts provided below them on the CT platform.

De-capping plates fitted to front shields of 15in gun-houses (complete by end of Nov 1918). Work on fitting de-capping plates to barbettes was suspended in December 1918.

MAJOR REFIT DECEMBER 1918 TO JANUARY 1921

The initial steps towards correcting what were seen as the shortcomings of the design began very early with the fitting of the additional deck armour in Nov–Dec 1916. This revealed a reluctance to deviate from Fisher's requirements for the design on the part of the DNC, who commented that the increased displacement and draught involved was '… a very serious addition of weight beyond that considered necessary in this Office after the Jutland Battle' – a view endorsed by the 3rd Sea Lord (Admiral Tudor). This reflected the opinions of both parties that weak deck protection was not a primary cause of the losses to magazine explosions during the battle.

In November 1917 the 1st Sea Lord (Admiral Jellicoe) requested proposals for increases in the protection of *Renown* and *Repulse*, initiating a lengthy debate which did not conclude until the autumn of 1918. The initial proposal by the DNC was for a new form of relatively light weight armour consisting of steel gratings, covered with ½in steel plates (Brown's de-capping plates) to be fitted between the bottom of the main belt and the forecastle over a length covering the magazines and machinery spaces. Following a request from the Director of Plans (Rear Admiral Keyes) for consideration to be given to the underwater protection of the engine and condenser rooms, the DNC proposed the fitting of bulges which, to avoid a trim by the

PARTICULARS, 1921

Generally as in 1917 except for following:

Displacement (tons):	31,150 light, 32,500 load, 36,780 deep, 37,190 extreme deep
Beam:	101ft (102ft 6in max over wood fenders)
Mean Draught:	26ft 10½in light, 27ft 11in load, 31ft 1in deep, 31ft 6in extreme deep
Torpedo Tubes:	2 x 21in submerged, broadside (10 torpedoes), 8 x 21in above-water, broadside (16 torpedoes)
Small Arms:	Five Maxim machine guns (field and boat), 10 Lewis MG and 467 rifles (330 for seamen and 137 for marines)
Armour:	9in lower and 6in upper belt amidships and additional 4in bulkhead closing off aft end of 6in belt.
Protective plating:	Main deck: 3in flat, 4in slopes over magazines. Lower deck: 3½in flat, 2½in slope above 15in magazine abaft 'Y' barbette.
Machinery:	120,000shp = 29½ knots at load draught and 28¾ knots at deep draught.
Complement:	1222

SUMMARY OF MODIFICATIONS 1918–1930

Portsmouth 1918–21 Major Refit

Side armour improved.

Protective plating on main deck above magazines increased to 3in on flat and 4in on slopes.

Protective plating fitted above 15in magazine abaft 'Y' barbette increased to 3½in.

Fitted with bulges.

Fitted with eight above-water 21in torpedo tubes on upper deck.

30ft rangefinders fitted at rears of 'A' turret and the revolving armoured director hood.

15ft rangefinder in 'Y' turret replaced with 30ft rangefinder.

Wood planking fitted on forecastle and quarter decks.

Fitted with additional dynamo.

D/F office fitted on shelter deck between funnels.

Main topgallant mast re-fitted.

New searchlight control platform fitted to mainmast.

New concentration dial control positions fitted in spotting top and after night defence tower.

1921–22

Rails over 15in guns for extension of aircraft ramp on 'B' turret removed (restored briefly c1923).

Two after searchlights on second funnel removed.

De-capping plates removed from front shields of 15in turrets.

Portsmouth Nov–Dec 1924

Two single 4in and two 3in HA mountings replaced with four 4in Mk V guns on single HA Mk III mountings.

Fitted with a large cabin between the funnels, on the starboard side of the shelter deck.

Flagstaff fitted to fore topmast.

(last two items for Royal Tour by Prince of Wales to South Africa and South America, Jan to October 1925).

Portsmouth Nov 1925–Jul 1926

Fitted with new foretop with HACP on roof.

Fore topmast and W/T yard removed – latter supplanted by W/T spurs at rear of foretop platform.

12ft rangefinders fitted in place of the 9ft rangefinders on each side of the compass platform.

Forward night defence control platform modified, windscreen removed and fitted with a wing platform on each side for the 9ft rangefinders removed from compass platform.

Fitted with collective protection (defence against poison gas).

Around 1926–27

Cabin fitted between funnels for royal tour removed.

1928

Aircraft platform extension rails on 15in barrels of 'B' turret re-fitted for trials of Siskin IIIA fighter aircraft.

1929

Flagstaff added to rear of foretop for rear admiral's flag while serving as flagship of BCS, Atlantic Fleet, during April–Sep 1929 (removed c1930).

---

bow, should either be extended well forward of the engine rooms or packed with steel tubes. The details of this discussion were forwarded to the CinC Grand Fleet (Admiral Beatty) in November 1917 who further suggested that the 15in upper barbettes and gun-house front shields required improved protection and that underwater defence would be better if tube-filled bulges were provided for both engine and boiler rooms. Shortly after this the DNC proposed increasing the 6in side armour to 9in by utilising the armour of the former battleship *Almirante Cochrane* (which was in the process of being converted into the aircraft carrier *Eagle*) for one ship and ordering new plates for the other. He also suggested increasing the side protection above the belt to a total of 4in HT plating and using grating armour for the 15in barbettes and shields. These proposals together with the long, tube-filled bulge were estimated to give a 6in increase in mean draught and a loss in speed of about 1¼ knots.

Early in 1918 it was decided that plans for these modifications should be prepared by Portsmouth Dockyard and all necessary material prepared for commencing one ship in August 1918. However, the DNO (Captain Dreyer), who had not previously been aware of these discussions, suggested that further increases in deck protection were required. The proposals were again sent to Beatty in March 1918 and he suggesting that the upper extent of 4in HT side plating should be limited to the upper deck, the weight saved being utilised to increase the thickness of the main deck over the magazines to 3in flat and 4in slope and the crowns of the magazines to 2in. At this point one gets the impression that the DNC was becoming less than happy with the discussion, especially given that the magazines had already been fitted with 2in crowns in 1916, although he limited his remarks to pointing out that both ships '… were already fitted with considerable additional deck protection over engine rooms and magazines'. The following debate produced several variations on additions to the side armour and deck protection with the DNC strongly favouring the adoption of a 9in belt and the 3rd Sea Lord (Rear Admiral Halsey) regarding it as essential that the side plating be increased to 7in. The DNC covered the latter point by proposing to fit the ship's existing 6in side armour above the 9in belt giving a total of 7½in including the side plating. Beatty was informed in May 1918 and agreed to the latest proposals which included his increased deck, barbette and gun shield armour together with a full length bulge. These decisions received Board approval about June 1918 and plans were made to take the first ship in hand during the winter of 1918–19. The DNCs views on increased weight were no doubt mollified by the fact that the increase buoyancy provided by the bulges served to partially compensate the effects of increased protection weights.

Protection was not the only item subject to improvement since the provision of one torpedo tube on each side was viewed as totally inadequate. Apart from this, it was not possible at that time to fire from a submerged tube when running at full speed and slowing down in order to do so was not regarded as a practical option when in action. Proposals to fit AW tubes were first made in September 1916 – initially two on each side. Later this was increased to two sets of three fixed broadside tubes on each side with mantle protection for the warheads, but nothing was done about this until the major refit when, apart from a reduction to double rather than triple tubes, the latter proposal was adopted. Work on the de-capping plates began prior to the refit and was completed for the front shields of *Repulse*, and in part for the barbettes. In December 1918 this work was suspended, pending the results of trials, and in February 1919 all further work on de-capping plates was cancelled as a result of tests showing that the plates were ineffective against the latest designs of APC shell. The de-capping plates thus far fitted to the barbettes of *Repulse* were removed during the refit but she retained the front shield plates until 1922 (these were not added to the modified as-fitted plans).

The decision that *Repulse* would be the first to refit was not made until late in 1918, up to which point it was anticipated that *Renown* would be first. At this time the calculated additional weights were 2310

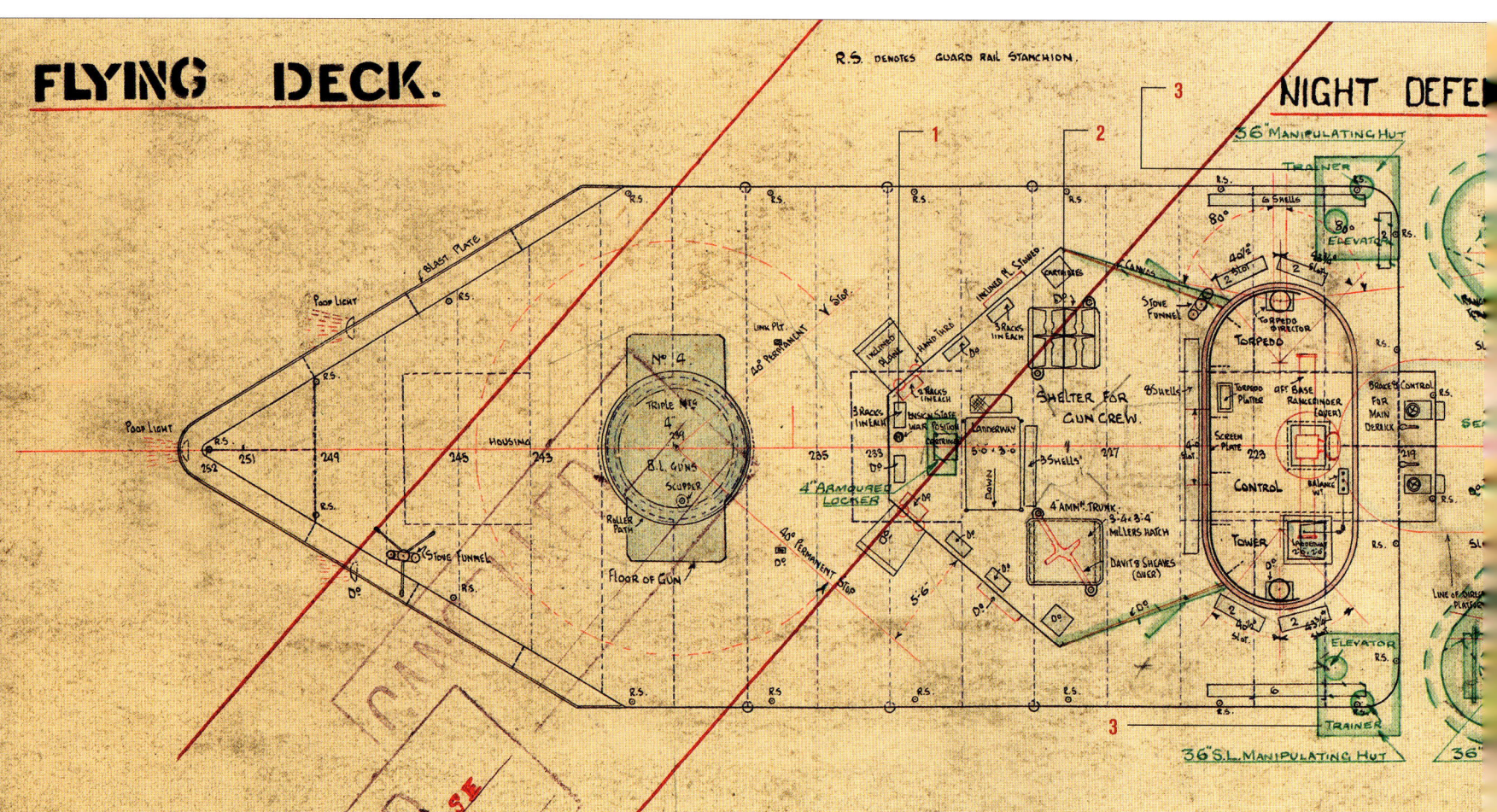

tons for the bulges (of which 1025 tons was for the crushing tubes and packing, etc) and 1624 tons for armour and protective plating. The refit was carried out at Portsmouth between 3 December 1918 and 12 January 1921. On completion the estimated displacement from an inclining carried out in December 1920 was 32,500 tons at a load draught of 27ft 11in and 37,190 tons extreme deep at a mean draught of 31ft 6in. It was estimated that the loss of speed resulting from the addition of bulges and the increased displacement would be about 1¼ knots. A 2½-hour full power trial off Cromarty on 12 October 1921 gave only 26 knots with 111,292shp and 240rpm but the weather was poor, she was 12 months out of dock and running at about 36,700 tons. Four runs on the Arran course on 12 January 1922 in good conditions with a clean bottom and a displacement of about 35,500 tons gave mean figures of 29.63 knots with 117,632shp and 262rpm. However, due to poor light no speed was timed on the fourth run (with the tide) and the accuracy of the other three were subject to a small degree of doubt. The following pages highlight the alterations applied to the superstructure platforms of the as-fitted plans in 1921.

FLYING DECK AND AFTER NIGHT DEFENCE CONTROL POSITION

This drawing and those which follow on pages 64–71 provide enlarged views of the upper superstructure platforms taken from plan J9373 (shown in full on pages 18–19). The term 'flying deck' derives from past use referring to superstructure decks or platforms that bridge decks below them – it was employed extensively in the Victorian era but its use in British warships had more or less died out by the end of the First World War.

1 **The 4in armoured locker** served to store ready-use cordite charges for the 4in guns. As originally built the ship was only provided with ready-use shell for the 4in guns – stowed in racks around the inner walls of the gun-crew shelters. Presumably the supply of cordite from below was initially viewed as sufficient to keep pace with the ready-use shell. It is not clear when the cordite lockers were added – they were also provided for mountings 3 and 5 but there is no indication of them being provided for the triple mountings fitted on the conning tower platform.
2 **The gun-crew shelter** for No 4 triple 4in mounting shows both the original after end steel blast screen and, in green outline, the steel extension (with door) that replaced the canvas screen in this position in 1917. Unlike that for No 5 mounting, this space originally had a canvas roof – also replaced by steel. The shelter for No 3 mounting was similarly altered.
3 **The manipulating huts** on each side of the flying deck controlled the 36in S/Ls fitted at the after corners of the NDP above them. The searchlights were Type B/C, the 'C' indicating their remote control by rod gearing. If the latter failed, the S/Ls could be disconnected and controlled locally.
4 **The range dial control platform**. This square platform, raised about 5ft above the floor of the NDP, served as the control position for a range dial mounted at the top of a post above the NDP. This arrangement, fitted during the 1918–21 refit, replaced the dials originally fitted on the after screen of NDP in 1917. The post, which extended down to the platform, carried the dial's mechanical controls. The range dials – also known as range clocks or concentration dials – served to transmit the range at which the ship's main armament was firing to the ship astern when employing concentrated fire (two or more ships co-ordinating their fire on a single target). For the same purpose 'Y' turret was painted with a bearing scale to indicate the direction and inclination in use.
5 **The main boat derrick** was extended by providing it with a new, steel, heel casting 3ft longer than the original.

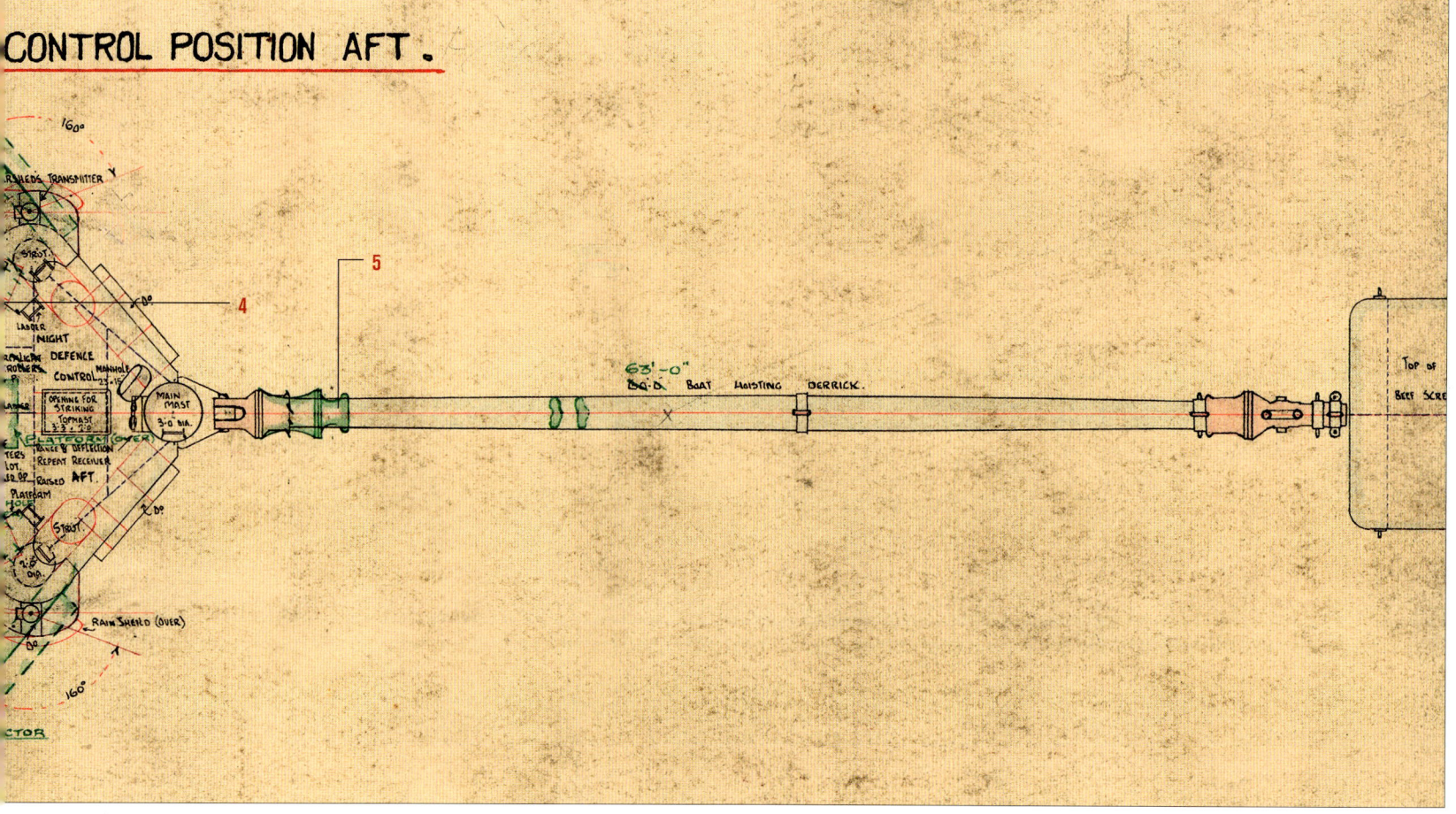

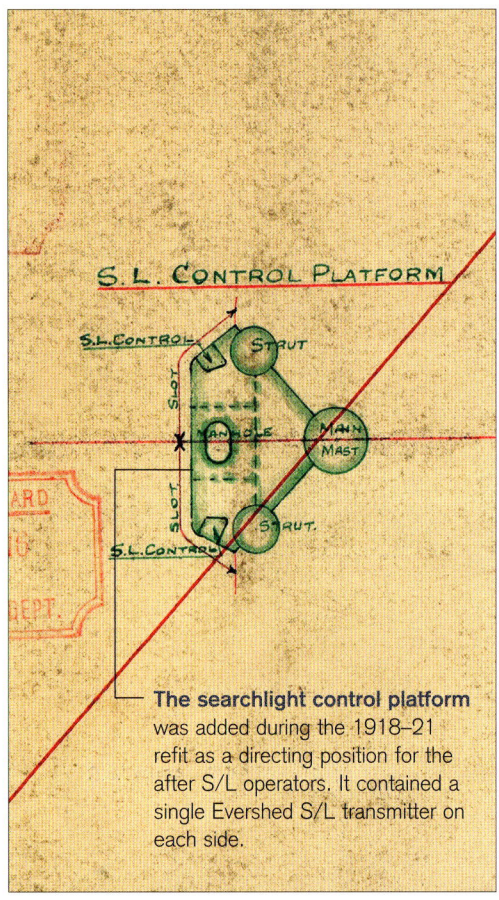

The searchlight control platform was added during the 1918–21 refit as a directing position for the after S/L operators. It contained a single Evershed S/L transmitter on each side.

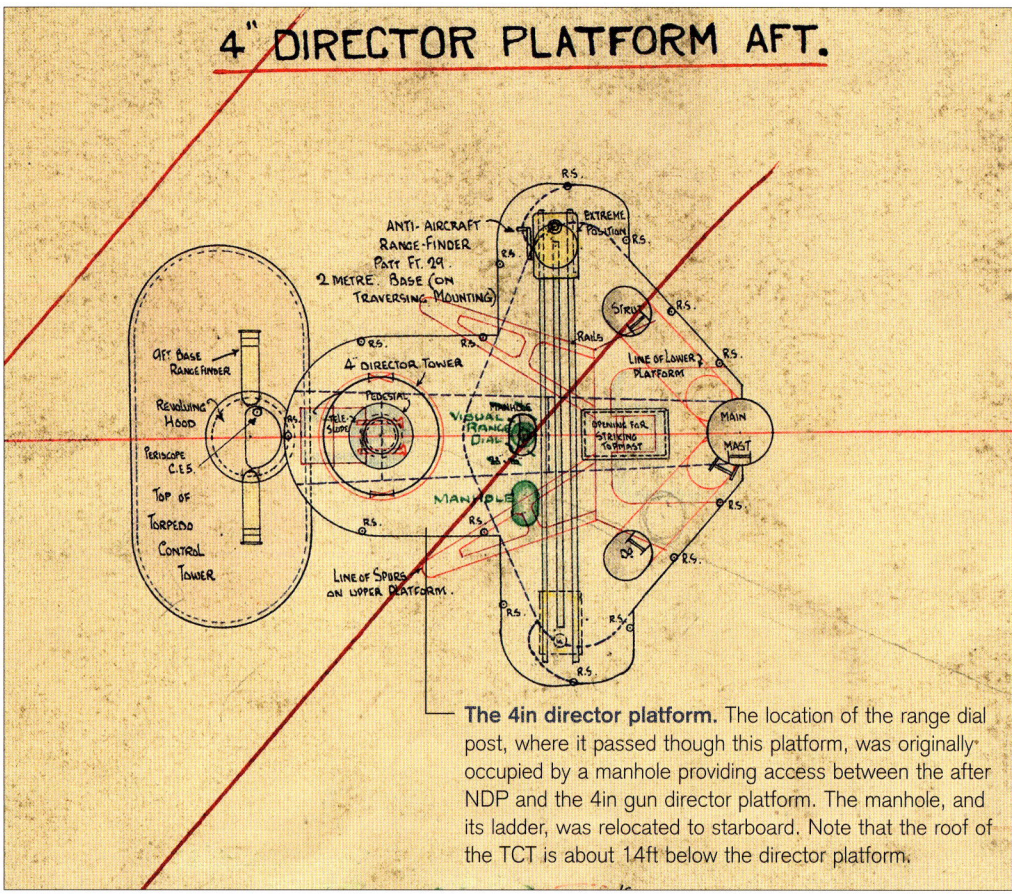

The 4in director platform. The location of the range dial post, where it passed though this platform, was originally occupied by a manhole providing access between the after NDP and the 4in gun director platform. The manhole, and its ladder, was relocated to starboard. Note that the roof of the TCT is about 14ft below the director platform.

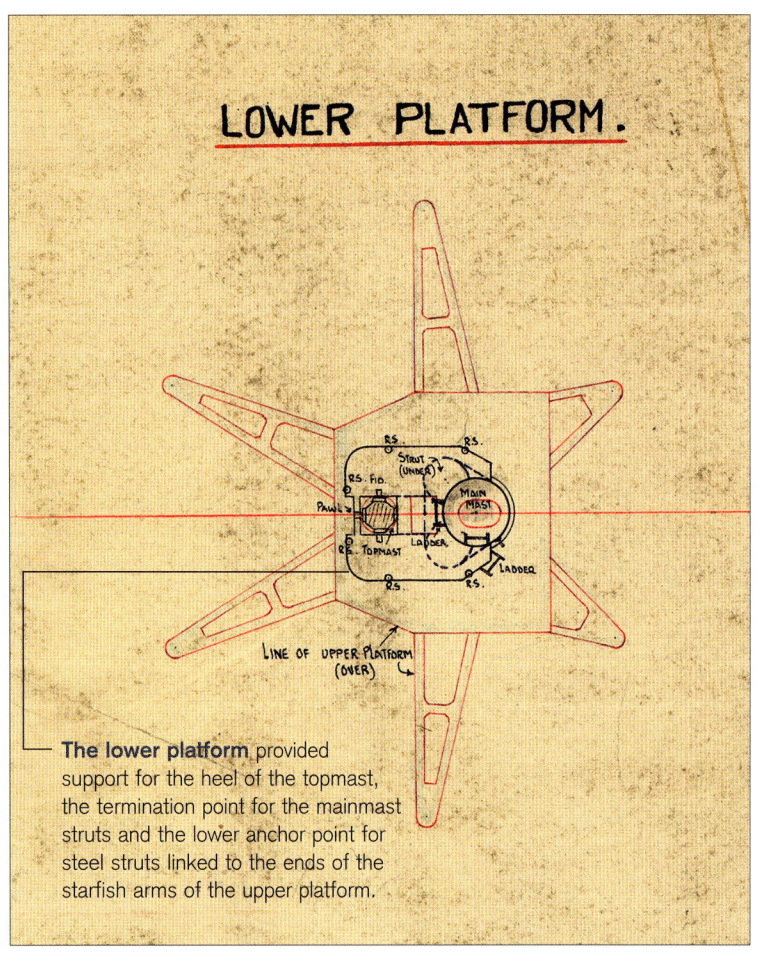

The lower platform provided support for the heel of the topmast, the termination point for the mainmast struts and the lower anchor point for steel struts linked to the ends of the starfish arms of the upper platform.

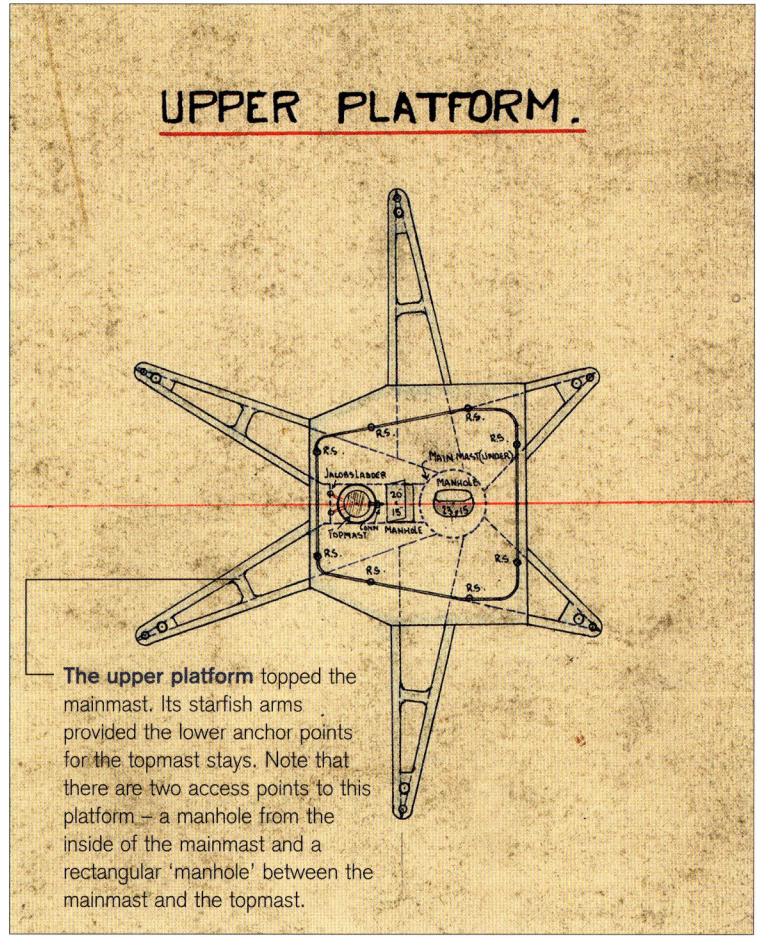

The upper platform topped the mainmast. Its starfish arms provided the lower anchor points for the topmast stays. Note that there are two access points to this platform – a manhole from the inside of the mainmast and a rectangular 'manhole' between the mainmast and the topmast.

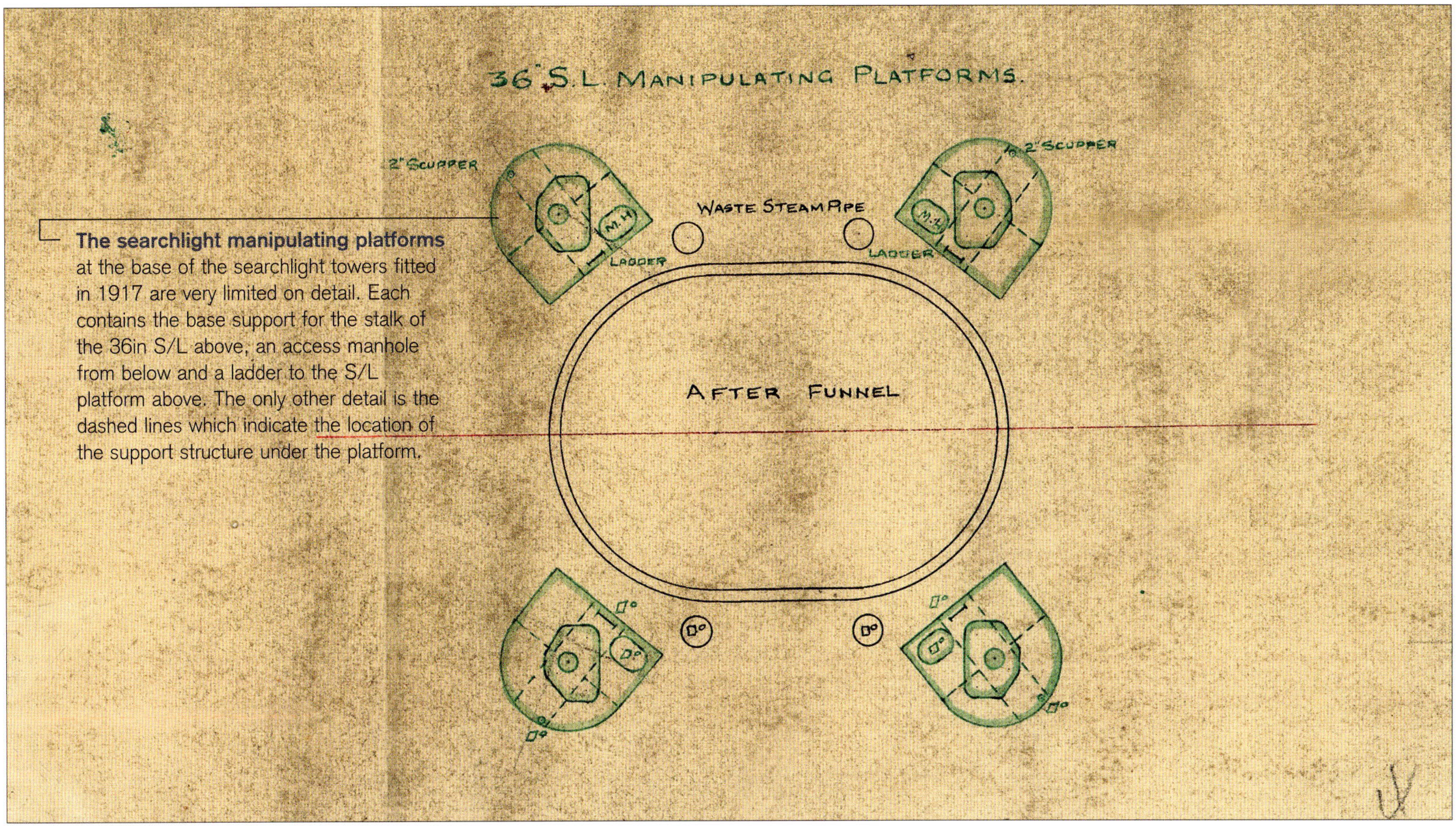

MAINMAST AND FUNNEL PLATFORMS

36" S.L. Manipulating Platforms

The searchlight manipulating platforms at the base of the searchlight towers fitted in 1917 are very limited on detail. Each contains the base support for the stalk of the 36in S/L above, an access manhole from below and a ladder to the S/L platform above. The only other detail is the dashed lines which indicate the location of the support structure under the platform.

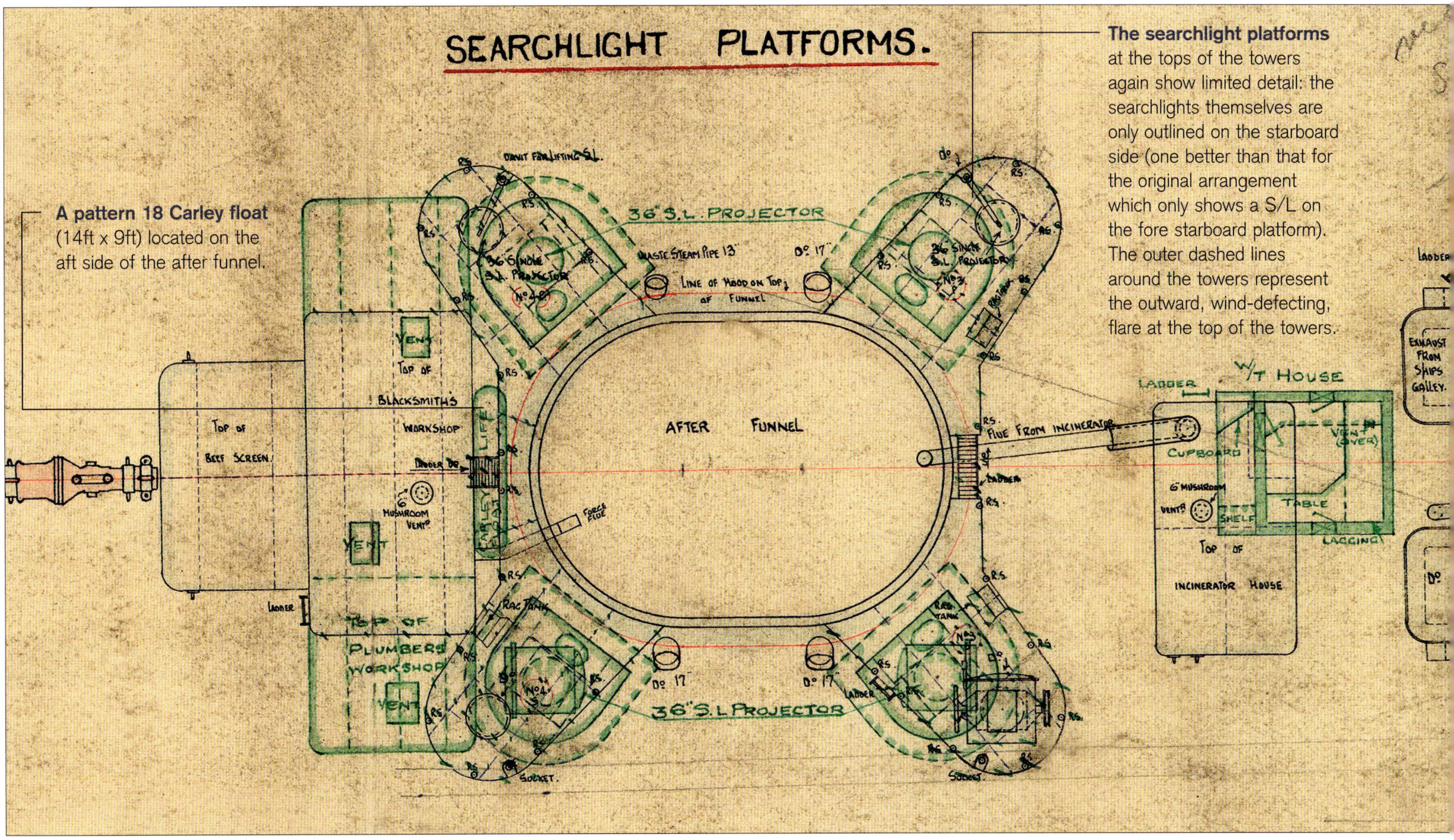

Searchlight Platforms

A pattern 18 Carley float (14ft x 9ft) located on the aft side of the after funnel.

The searchlight platforms at the tops of the towers again show limited detail: the searchlights themselves are only outlined on the starboard side (one better than that for the original arrangement which only shows a S/L on the fore starboard platform). The outer dashed lines around the towers represent the outward, wind-defecting, flare at the top of the towers.

MODIFICATIONS 1916–1930

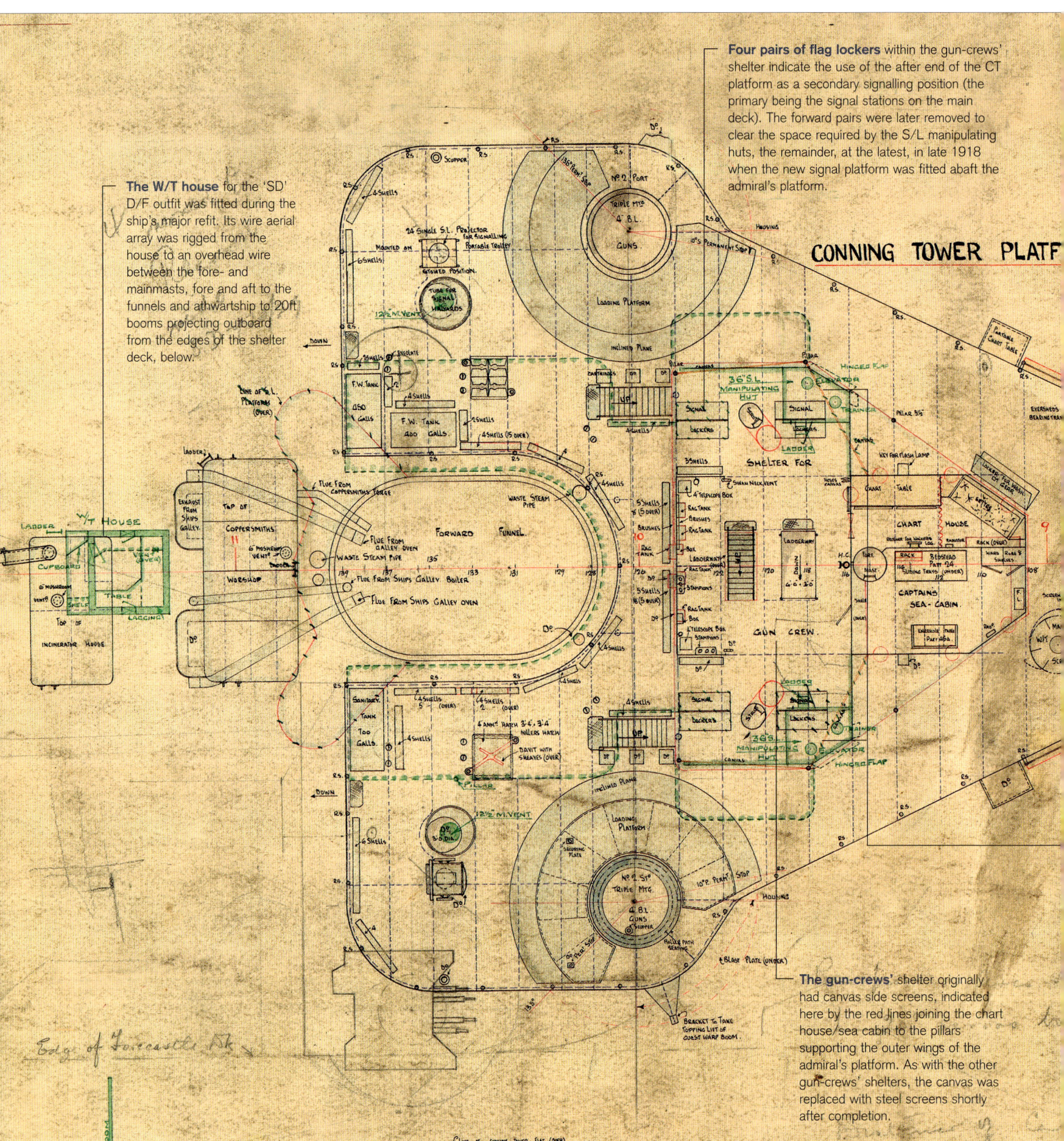

Four pairs of flag lockers within the gun-crews' shelter indicate the use of the after end of the CT platform as a secondary signalling position (the primary being the signal stations on the main deck). The forward pairs were later removed to clear the space required by the S/L manipulating huts, the remainder, at the latest, in late 1918 when the new signal platform was fitted abaft the admiral's platform.

The W/T house for the 'SD' D/F outfit was fitted during the ship's major refit. Its wire aerial array was rigged from the house to an overhead wire between the fore- and mainmasts, fore and aft to the funnels and athwartship to 20ft booms projecting outboard from the edges of the shelter deck, below.

The gun-crews' shelter originally had canvas side screens, indicated here by the red lines joining the chart house/sea cabin to the pillars supporting the outer wings of the admiral's platform. As with the other gun-crews' shelters, the canvas was replaced with steel screens shortly after completion.

CONNING TOWER PLATFORM

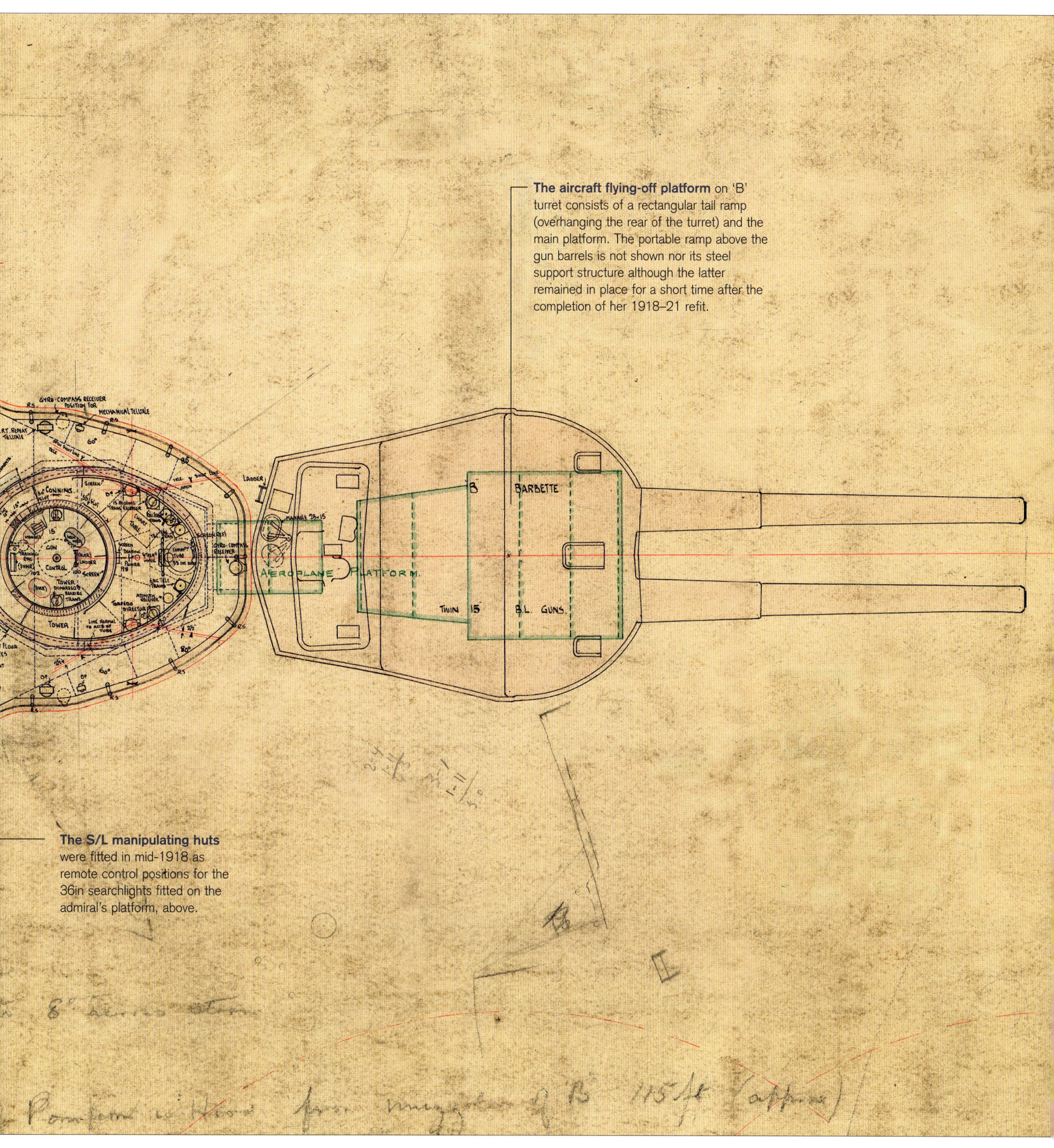

The aircraft flying-off platform on 'B' turret consists of a rectangular tail ramp (overhanging the rear of the turret) and the main platform. The portable ramp above the gun barrels is not shown nor its steel support structure although the latter remained in place for a short time after the completion of her 1918–21 refit.

The S/L manipulating huts were fitted in mid-1918 as remote control positions for the 36in searchlights fitted on the admiral's platform, above.

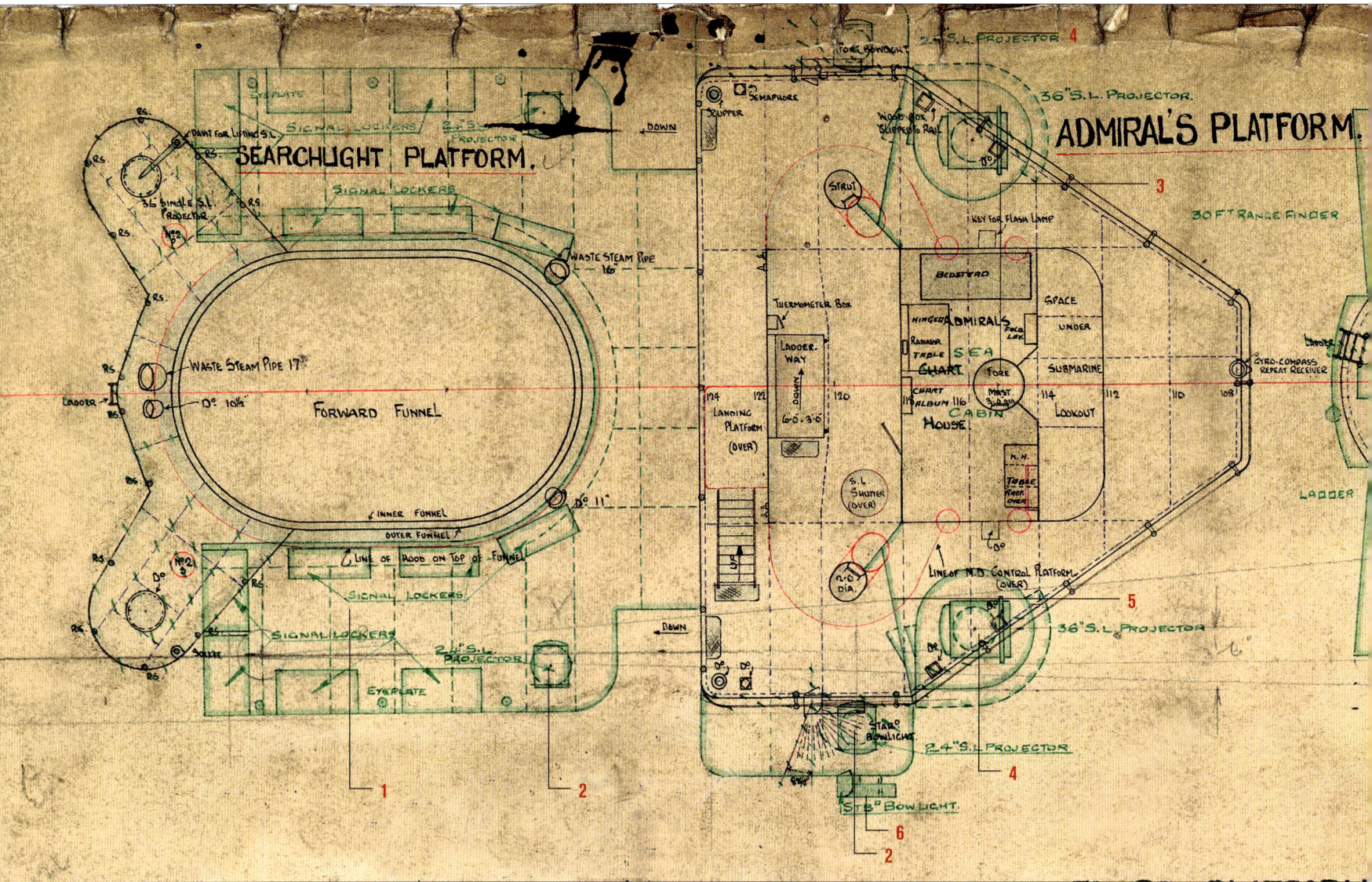

ADMIRAL'S PLATFORM (above)

This platform was extended aft in mid-1918 to provide a new signal deck. The new arrangement superseded the primacy of the signal stations on the main deck and replaced the alternative signal position on the CT platform. Although the main deck signal stations had been converted to other purposes by 1921 it is unclear if this was done prior to or during her major refit but it is probable that they were retained during 1918 for employment when in action.

1. The new flag deck accommodates 14 flag lockers all of which are the same size, the apparent difference in plan view being due to some being tipped back rather than vertical (see pages 44 and 45).
2. The 24in signalling projectors, one on each side of the flag deck and one in each of the side extensions, replaced the portable versions fitted on the CT platform. The new arrangement owed much to the conclusion that the 36in S/Ls should be employed for their primary purpose and not for signalling (note that as built the ship had a signalling shutter for the original 36in S/Ls stowed overhead, just abaft the admiral's chart house, on the starboard side).
3. The admiral's chart house has been renamed as the admiral's sea cabin. Given the unmodified contents included a bedstead, it seems likely that this was no more than a re-designation possibly reflecting its more common use.
4. The forward 36in S/Ls were fitted in mid-1918, on a small platform raised 3ft above the admiral's platform, replacing the original 36in S/Ls which had been moved down from the compass to the admiral's platform in late 1917. The delay in fitting the new forward searchlights was due to an extended debate on the best arrangement to adopt. These were Type B/C which could be controlled either remotely by rod gearing, operated from the manipulating huts below, or locally. By this time the ship had three groups of 36in searchlights – those on the bridge covering forward bearings, those grouped around the after funnel covering a wide angle on the broadside, and those on the mainmast covering after bearings. It was not the intention that these groups should be operated together in night defence since widely spaced lights used in combination were likely to provide an attacking vessel with information as to the ship's course and inclination. The raised platforms were removed and the S/Ls remounted directly on the admiral's platform during a refit at Rosyth in Nov–Dec 1922.
5. These green lines indicate new screens fitted each side between the corners of the admiral's chart house and the foremast struts and from the middle of that screen to the edge of the platform.
6. The bow navigation lights were moved to new positions as a result of the addition of the side signalling platforms.
7. The fan-shaped enclosures to the 30ft rangefinder fitted during the major refit provided the required clearance for the rangefinder to train independently from the revolving tower. This, as with turret-mounted rangefinders, allowed for them to train directly at a target while the structure on which they were mounted was off-set from the target bearing by the deflection set on the gun sights.

FORWARD NIGHT DEFENCE PLATFORM (opposite, top)

1. The Evershed S/L transmitters on each side were retained when the primary S/L control was moved to the compass platform, probably as target indicators for the forward 36in S/Ls.

ADMIRAL'S, FORWARD NIGHT CONTROL, AND COMPASS PLATFORMS

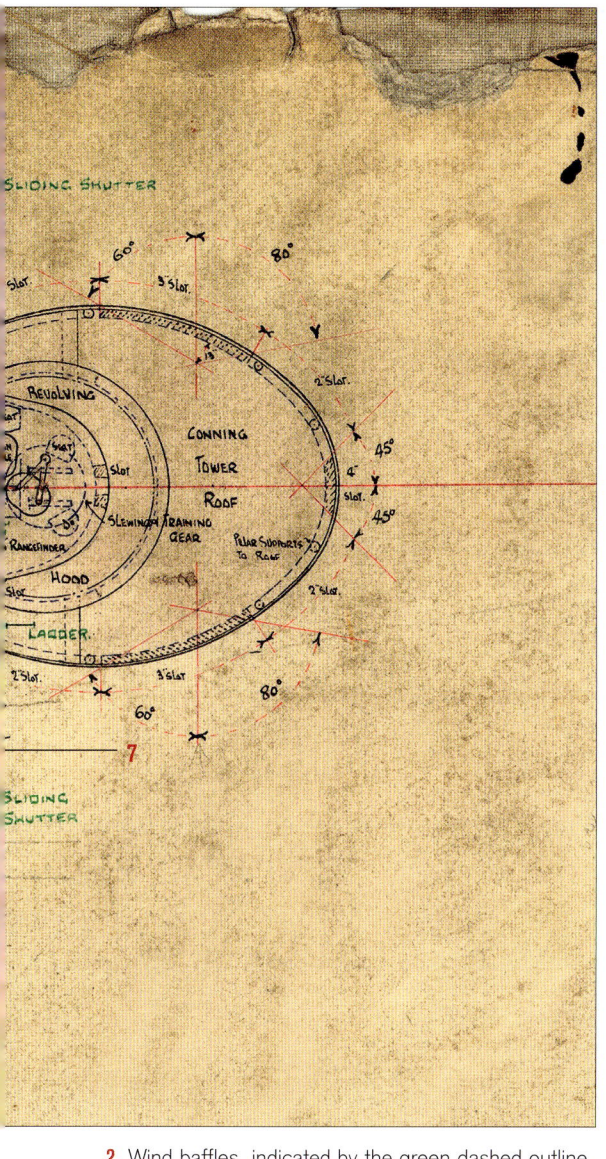

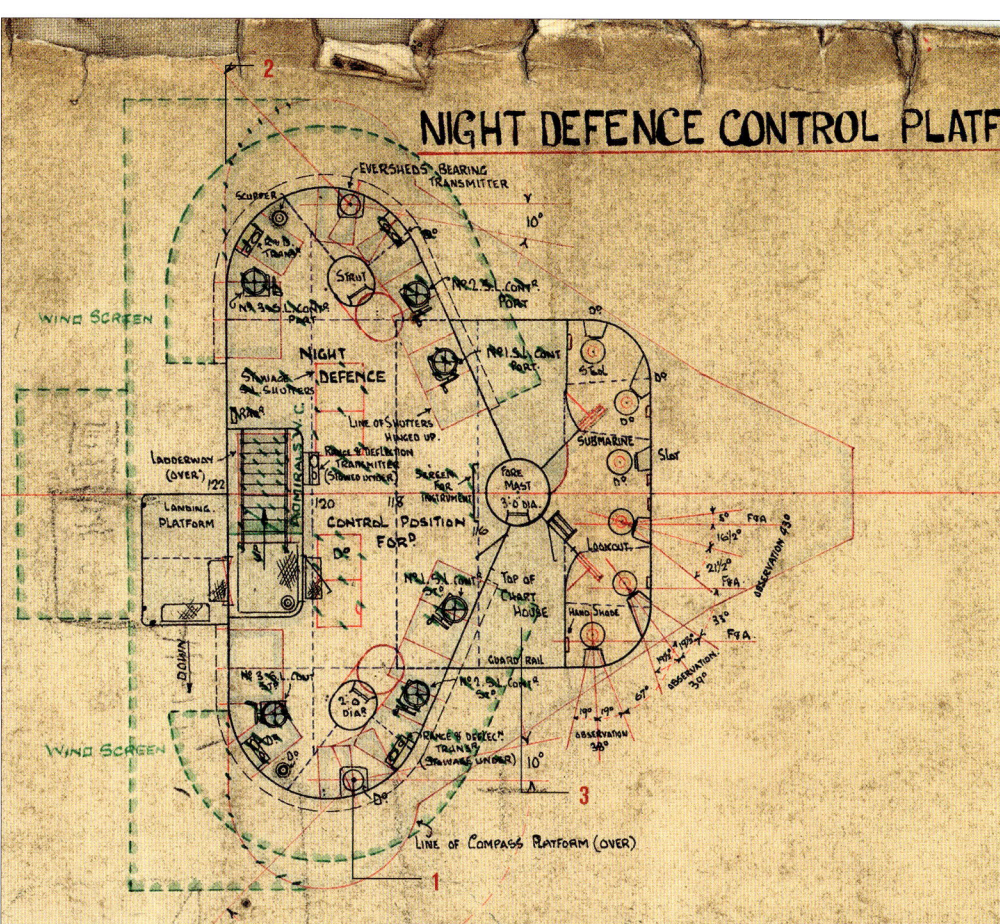

2. **Wind baffles**, indicated by the green dashed outline, were fitted on each side of the forward NDP in 1917. They were removed in 1925–26.
3. The open area on each side of the foremast only had guardrails on the starboard side, since this side provided access from the NDP to the submarine lookout.

COMPASS PLATFORM (right)

The compass platform was extended and modified in Oct–Nov 1917 to serve as the primary torpedo and S/L control position.

1. Torpedo plotting house.
2. 9ft FT24 rangefinders, on MG3 mounting, for torpedo and secondary armament control.
3. Dumaresq instruments.
4. Evershed transmitters for target indication to rangefinders on compass platform and in the TCT.
5. Glass windscreens of raised compass platform shown folded down.
6. The enlarged chart house and added watch cabin are indicative of the restoration of the compass platform as the primary conning position. These additions had been fitted, at least in part, by early 1917.

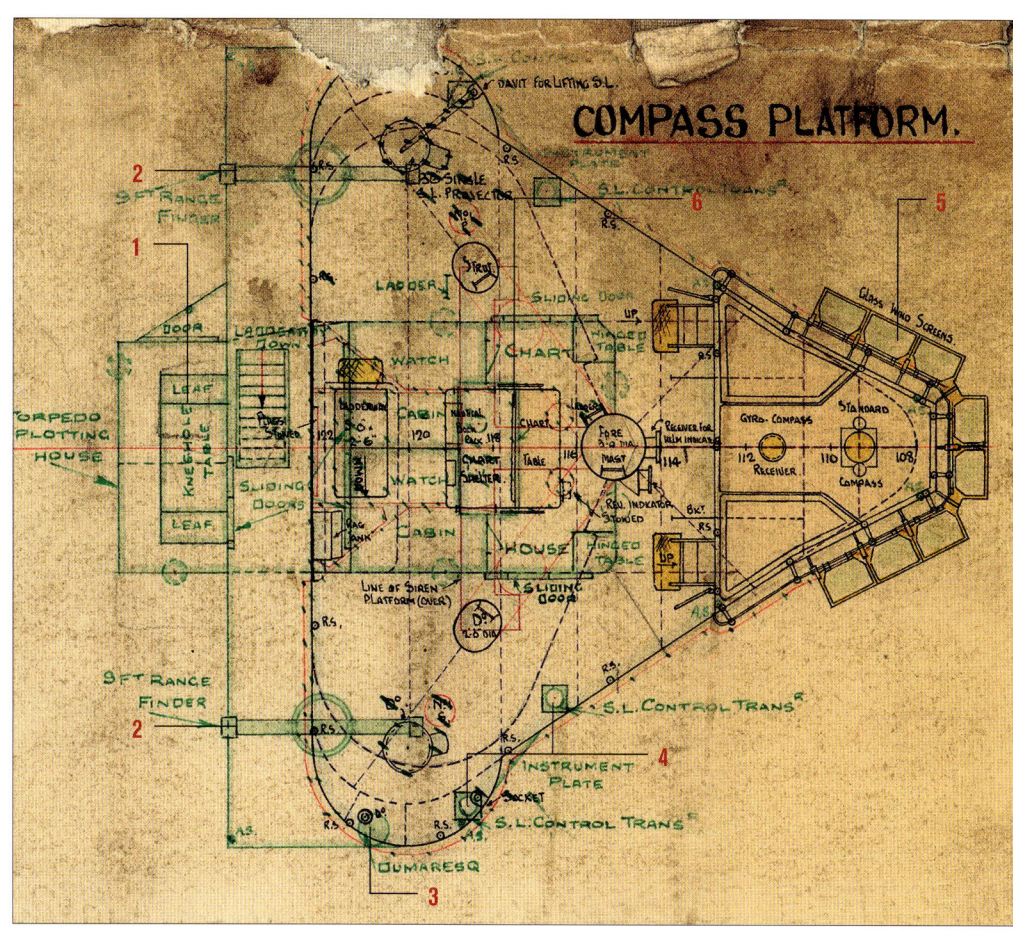

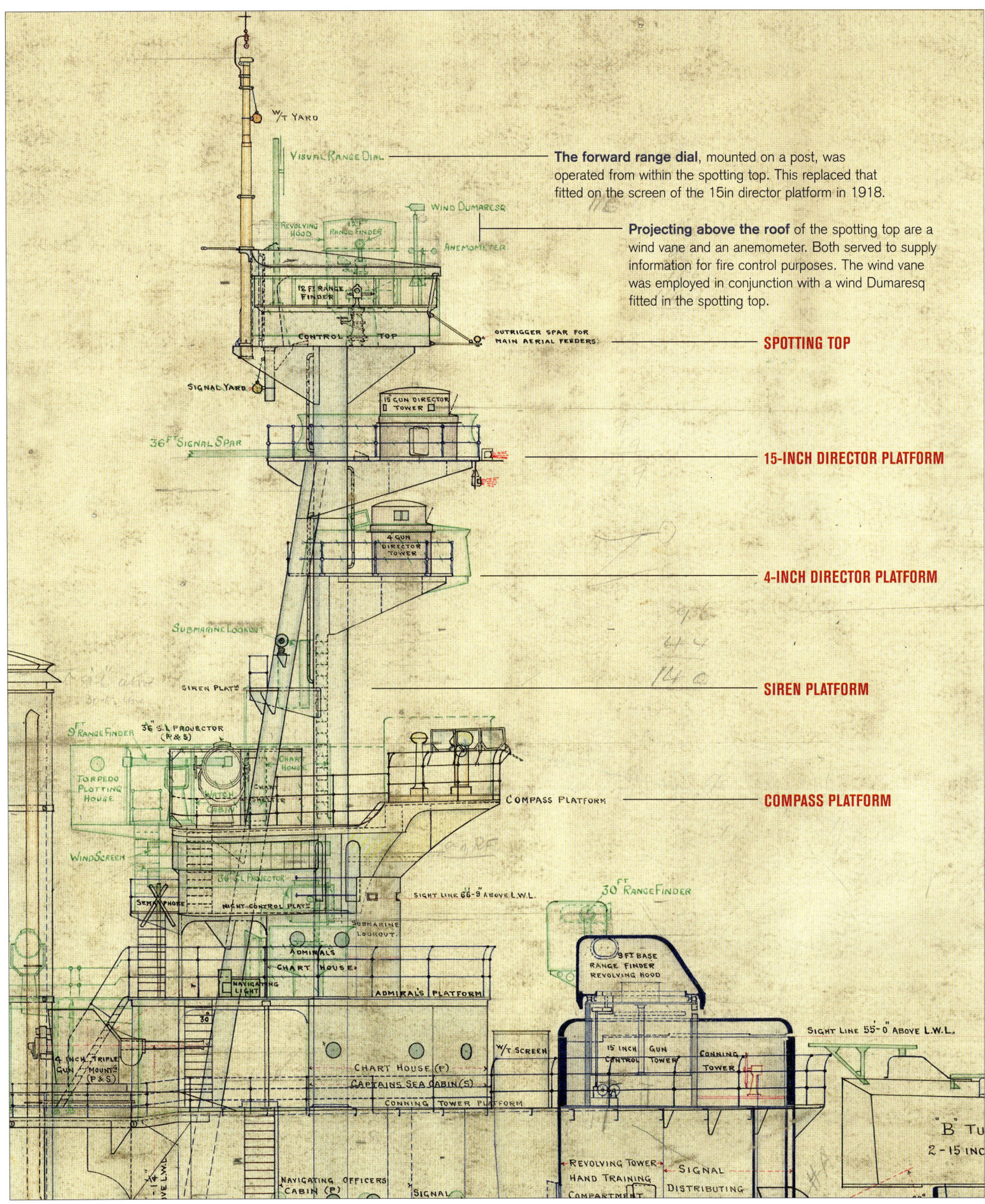

FOREMAST UPPER PLATFORMS

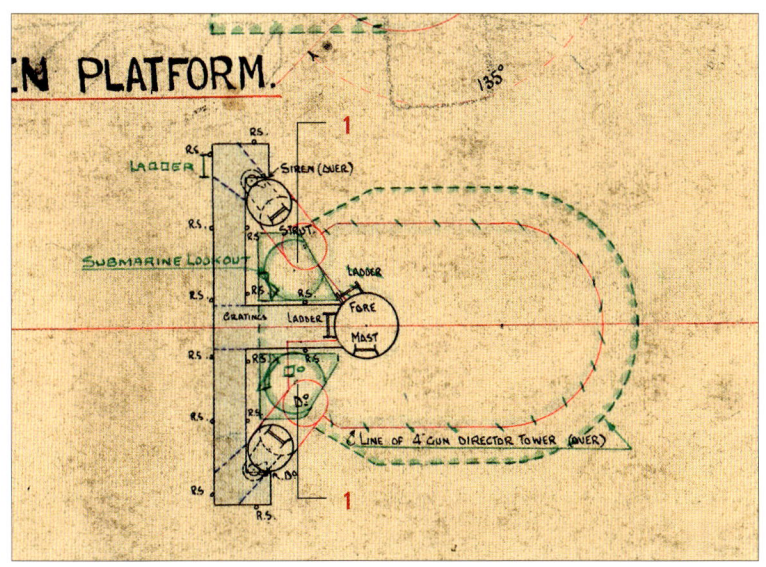

SIREN PLATFORM
1. Submarine lookouts added forward of the siren platform on each side of the foremast in late 1917. They were removed c1925–26.

4-INCH DIRECTOR PLATFORM
2. The outer green line represents the extension made to the 4in director platform during the 1916–17 refit.

15-INCH DIRECTOR PLATFORM
3. The 36ft signal spars fitted on each side of the 15in director platform during the 1916–17 refit replaced the signal yard fitted below the foretop.

SPOTTING TOP, 1916
4. As first installed the 12ft FQ2 rangefinder mounting could be moved from side to side of the top on traversing rails.
5. Vickers range clock.
6. Dumaresq instrument (p & s).
7. Evershed bearing instruments (p & s).

SPOTTING TOP, 1921
8. The spotting top, as modified in 1917, retained the original floor and screen (less the wind-deflectors) but the latter ended up hidden (apart from about 10in of the lower section) behind the enclosure into which the sliding sash windows could be lowered. The 12ft rangefinder is now raised on a fixed pedestal to project through the roof. The range clock is no longer present and the two forward Evershed instruments have been replaced with torpedo directors.

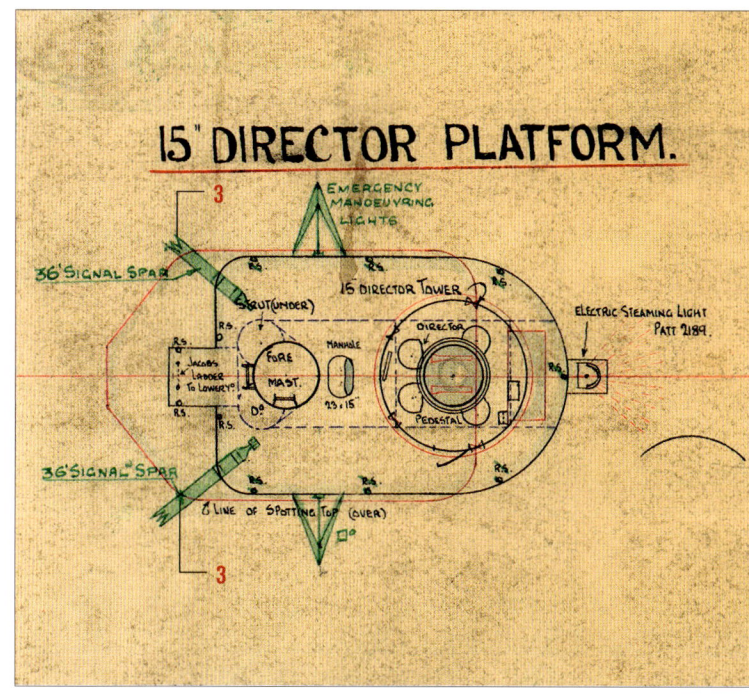

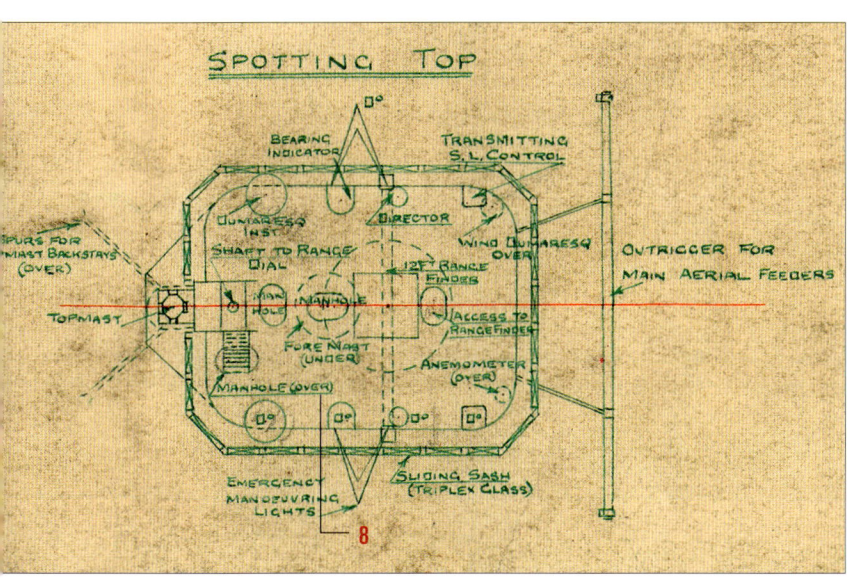

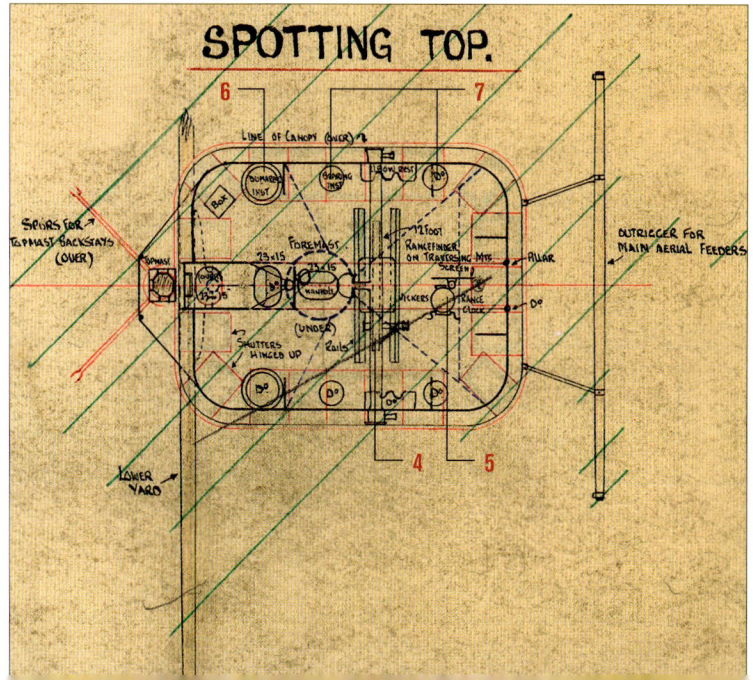

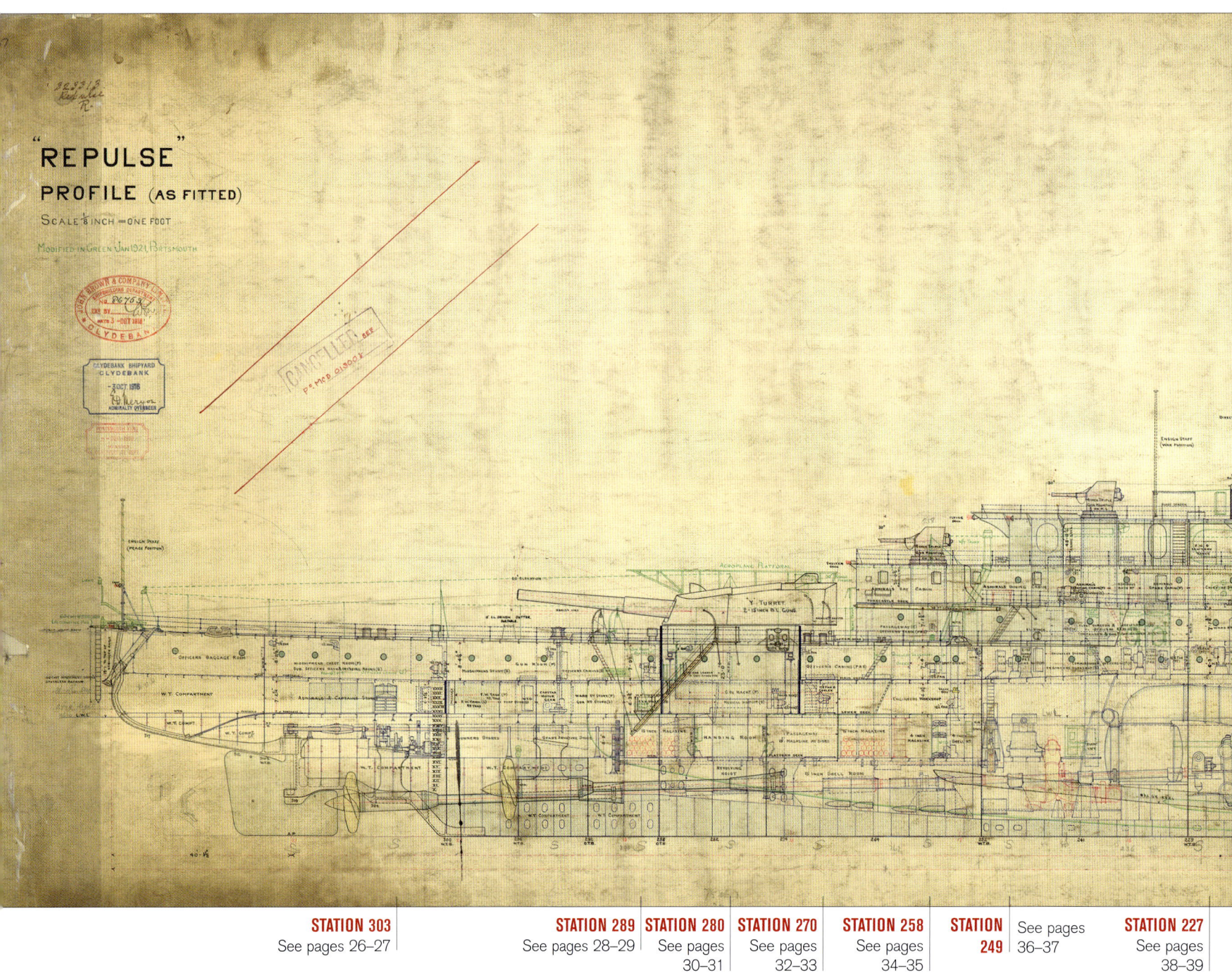

| STATION 303 See pages 26–27 | STATION 289 See pages 28–29 | STATION 280 See pages 30–31 | STATION 270 See pages 32–33 | STATION 258 See pages 34–35 | STATION 249 See pages 36–37 | STATION 227 See pages 38–39 |

PROFILE, AS FITTED 1916 (MODIFIED IN GREEN JANUARY 1921, PORTSMOUTH YARD)

The wartime capital ships produced under the direction of Tennyson D'Eyncourt showed a marked change in appearance compared with their pre-war counterparts. The *Repulse*, *Renown*, *Courageous*, *Glorious* and *Furious* were all stylish and elegant ships which looked every bit as fast as they were but also gave an impression of power somewhat greater than they actually deserved. One feature of their appearance which stands out is the form of the stem – a combination of the ram and clipper bow which was generally referred to as a plough bow. It was not unique since it had been used earlier in ships produced for foreign navies by Armstrongs (D'Eyncourt's previous employer) and Vickers, several of which were taken over on the outbreak of war and ended up in the Royal Navy (*Erin*, *Canada*, *Agincourt*, *Eagle*). The clipper shape may have been adopted for reasons of appearance or because it lent itself to the fairing off of the flare of the ship's side. While the ram shape was a standard form it was also favoured by Admiral Fisher and it is noticeable that it disappeared in the next design of British battlecruisers (the *Hood* class), which had the clipper form but no ram, at much the same time as Fisher left the Admiralty.

The ship's side above water was angled upward and outboard at 6° to the vertical with its base set 3ft inboard of the lower section of the hull. This angle, which gradually increased and curved outward towards the fore end of the ship to form a substantial flare, was intended, together with a high freeboard and the sheer, to aid the maintenance of high speed in heavy seas.

PROFILE, AS FITTED 1936

"E" PROFILE (AS FITTED).
TO ONE FOOT.

STATION 303	STATION 294	STATION 289	STATION 280	STATION 270	STATION 258	STATION 249	STATION 227	STATION 198	STATION 165
See pages 90–91	See pages 92–93	See pages 94–95	See pages 96–97	See pages 98–99	See pages 100–101	See pages 102–103	See pages 104–105	See pages 106–107	See pages 108–109

PROFILE, AS FITTED 1916 (MODIFIED IN JAN

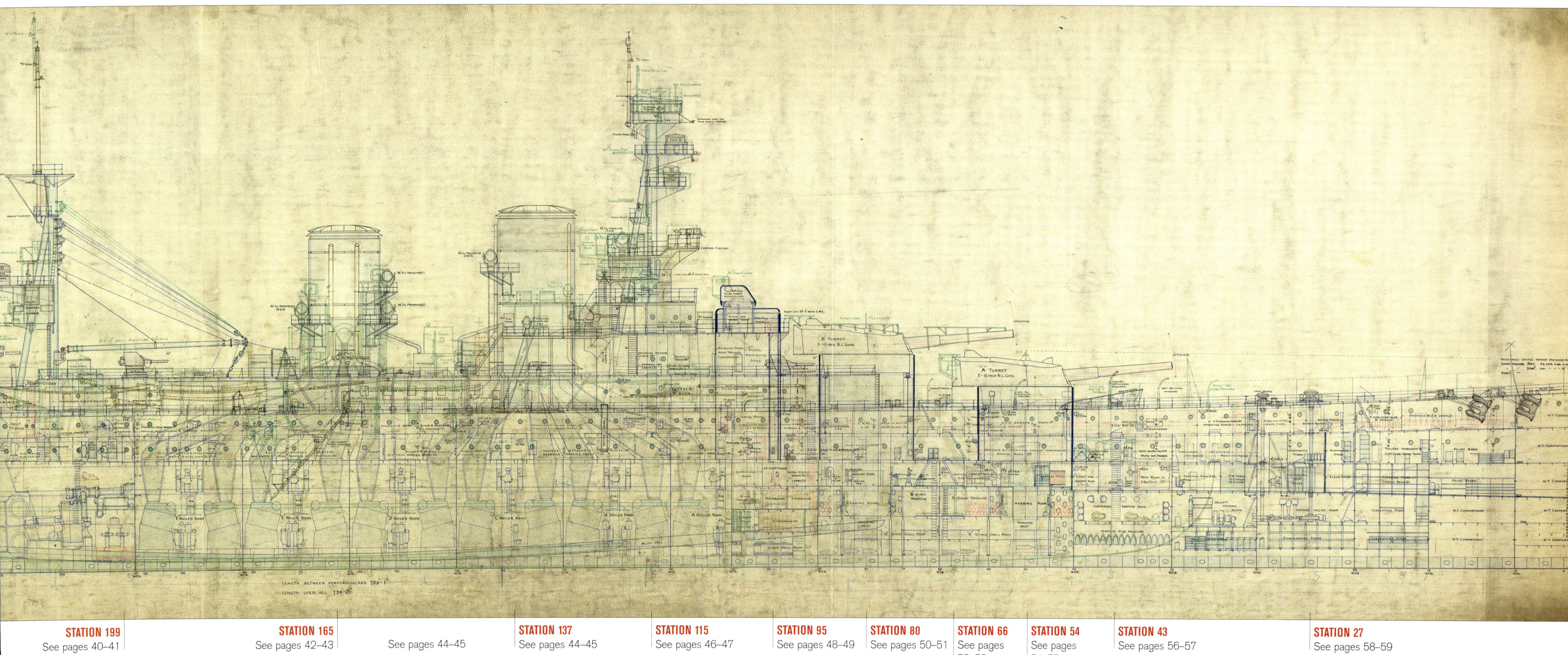

STATION 199	STATION 165		STATION 137	STATION 115	STATION 95	STATION 80	STATION 66	STATION 54	STATION 43	STATION 27
See pages 40–41	See pages 42–43	See pages 44–45	See pages 44–45	See pages 46–47	See pages 48–49	See pages 50–51	See pages 52–53	See pages 54–55	See pages 56–57	See pages 58–59

The profile serves well to illustrate the unique system of Station numbering. Along the keel line are two sets of numbers: those in black are Station (or frame) numbers, those in red the positions of the lines which define the hull shape in section employed in the body plan (see page 6). Generally, the Station numbers are given for the main watertight bulkheads but are also used where the frames are spaced at less than the standard 4ft, at a few random points between the main bulkheads and at the centre of the rudder post (the after perpendicular). The box keel extended from Station 46, the bulkhead forward of 'A' mounting, to the after bulkhead of the condenser room at Station 252. Beyond these limits it reverted to the standard form with a single central vertical keel plate. The standard 4ft frame spacing began at Station 2 (2ft abaft the fore perpendicular – the intersection of the stem with the designed load water-line – which served as Station 1) and ending at 318. There were two anomalies in this arrangement. Firstly, that the 4ft spaced frame numbers from Stations 46 to 288 dropped every other number (ie 46, 48, 50 etc). The apparently missing numbers normally applied to intermediate frames fitted between the main frames, almost entirely limited to local framing providing additional support behind the side armour. However, with a view to saving weight, various proposals (see table below) regarding the form of support behind the side armour resulted in the omission of the intermediate frames in favour of heavier main frames. Standard numbering practice was, nevertheless, followed despite the fact that there were very few intermediate frames to number. The exceptions were three positions behind the armour at Stations 253, 261 and 269 which served to support the butts of the armour plates (generally at 16ft intervals) in those positions (all the other butts coincided with main frames or bulkheads). In addition, since the required distances between main transverse bulkheads did not always lend themselves to the 4ft frame spacing, the after frame space in all but the first boiler room was reduced to 3ft to fit the 35ft length of each of the remaining five boiler rooms and, for similar reasons, the after frame space in the condenser room was reduced to 2ft. There was also a reduction to 3ft between frames 307 and 308 in order to align the after perpendicular with frame 309. In all these positions the intermediate frame number was omitted, which is why the main frame numbers occasionally change from an even to an odd number sequence.

PROPOSED ARRANGEMENTS FOR FRAMING BEHIND SIDE ARMOUR, 1

	Weight (tons)	Arrangement
1.	58	8in channel bar at 2ft intervals
2.	64	8in channel bar at 2ft intervals, with 12in 'I' bars at armour but
3.	80	8in 'I' bar at 2ft intervals, with 12in 'I' bars at armour but
4.	38	8in 'I' bar at 4ft intervals, with 12in 'I' bars at armour but
5.	58	10in 'I' bar at 4ft intervals, with 12in 'I' bars at armour b

The arrangement chosen was 5. Note that where bulkheads terminated the side armour they supplanted the frame but were reinforced locally w doubling plates and angle bars – in several cases this occurred at the bu the armour.

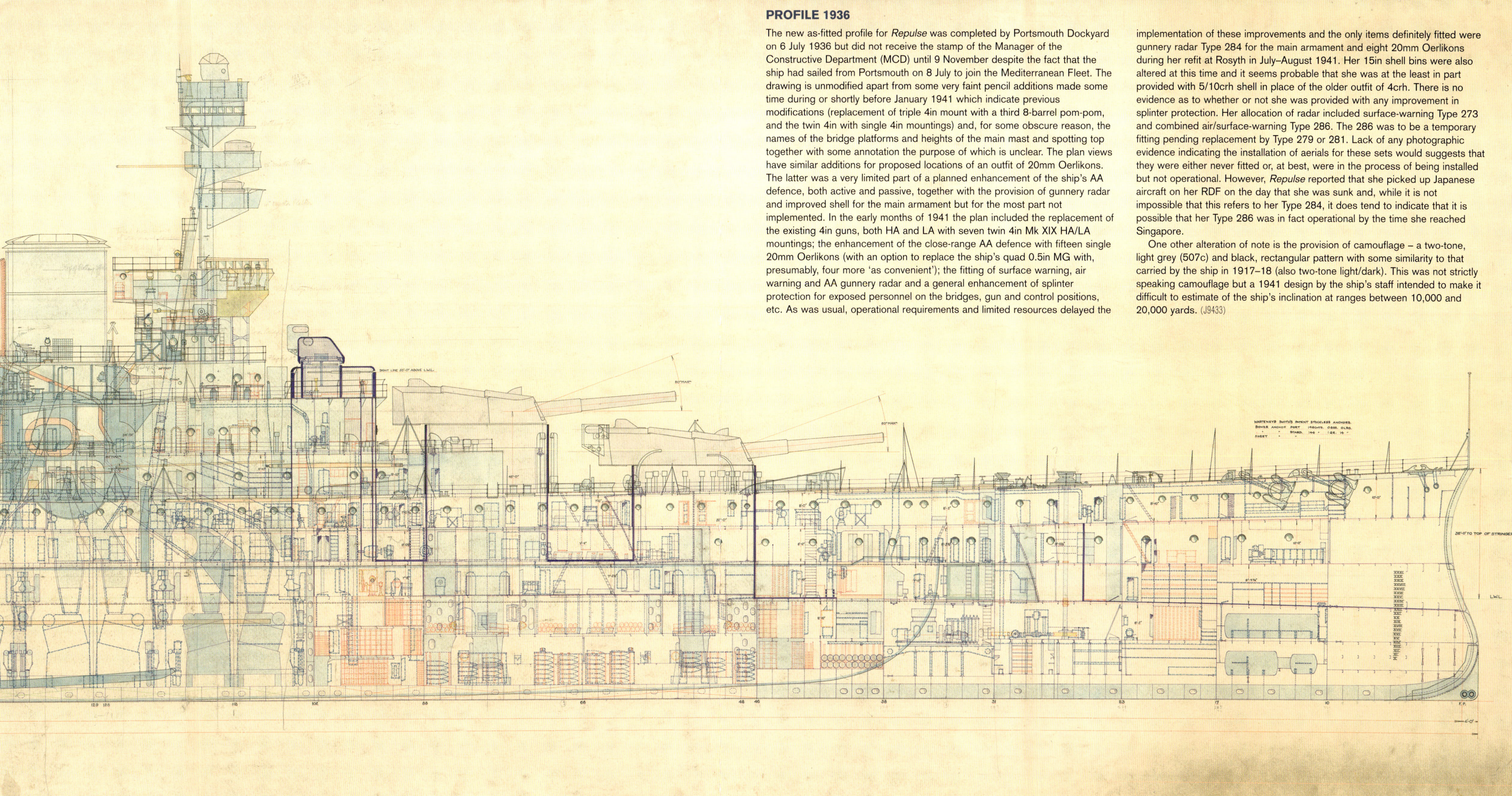

PROFILE 1936

The new as-fitted profile for *Repulse* was completed by Portsmouth Dockyard on 6 July 1936 but did not receive the stamp of the Manager of the Constructive Department (MCD) until 9 November despite the fact that the ship had sailed from Portsmouth on 8 July to join the Mediterranean Fleet. The drawing is unmodified apart from some very faint pencil additions made some time during or shortly before January 1941 which indicate previous modifications (replacement of triple 4in mount with a third 8-barrel pom-pom, and the twin 4in with single 4in mountings) and, for some obscure reason, the names of the bridge platforms and heights of the main mast and spotting top together with some annotation the purpose of which is unclear. The plan views have similar additions for proposed locations of an outfit of 20mm Oerlikons. The latter was a very limited part of a planned enhancement of the ship's AA defence, both active and passive, together with the provision of gunnery radar and improved shell for the main armament but for the most part not implemented. In the early months of 1941 the plan included the replacement of the existing 4in guns, both HA and LA with seven twin 4in Mk XIX HA/LA mountings; the enhancement of the close-range AA defence with fifteen single 20mm Oerlikons (with an option to replace the ship's quad 0.5in MG with, presumably, four more 'as convenient'); the fitting of surface warning, air warning and AA gunnery radar and a general enhancement of splinter protection for exposed personnel on the bridges, gun and control positions, etc. As was usual, operational requirements and limited resources delayed the implementation of these improvements and the only items definitely fitted were gunnery radar Type 284 for the main armament and eight 20mm Oerlikons during her refit at Rosyth in July–August 1941. Her 15in shell bins were also altered at this time and it seems probable that she was at the least in part provided with 5/10crh shell in place of the older outfit of 4crh. There is no evidence as to whether or not she was provided with any improvement in splinter protection. Her allocation of radar included surface-warning Type 273 and combined air/surface-warning Type 286. The 286 was to be a temporary fitting pending replacement by Type 279 or 281. Lack of any photographic evidence indicating the installation of aerials for these sets would suggests that they were either never fitted or, at best, were in the process of being installed but not operational. However, *Repulse* reported that she picked up Japanese aircraft on her RDF on the day that she was sunk and, while it is not impossible that this refers to her Type 284, it does tend to indicate that it is possible that her Type 286 was in fact operational by the time she reached Singapore.

One other alteration of note is the provision of camouflage – a two-tone, light grey (507c) and black, rectangular pattern with some similarity to that carried by the ship in 1917–18 (also two-tone light/dark). This was not strictly speaking camouflage but a 1941 design by the ship's staff intended to make it difficult to estimate of the ship's inclination at ranges between 10,000 and 20,000 yards. (J9433)

STATION 115 See pages 112–113

STATION 95 See pages 114–115

STATION 80 See pages 116–117

STATION 66 See pages 118–119

STATION 54 See pages 120–121

STATION 43 See pages 122–123

STATION 32 See pages 124–125

STATION 27 See pages 126–127

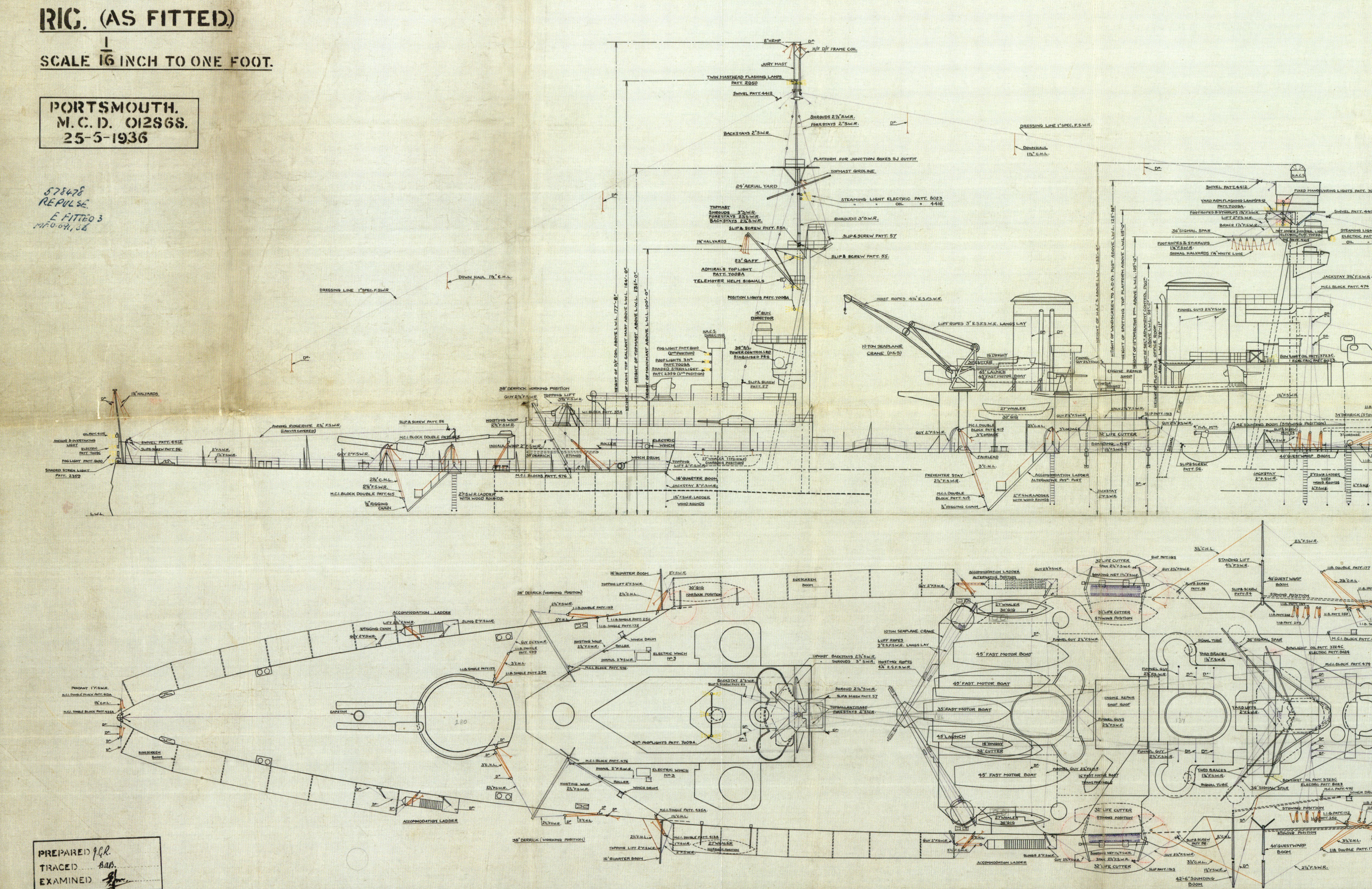

RIG, AS FITTED 1936

RIG, 1936

The rig plan has the advantage of providing a simplified view of the ship's superstructure which clarifies the general layout by the omission of the detail provided in the main as-fitted drawings. Apart from the rig in general, it identifies the ship's navigation and signalling lights. It also provides dimensions for the heights of the masts and mast platforms – still measured from the 1915 designed LWL. The lengths of the derricks, booms, signalling yard and spars are also given and all are shown in their working positions. Compared with the figures given on page 40, the main topmast, and topgallant mast have been reduced in overall length to 46ft 3in and 40ft 2in respectively. The 'jury mast' shown abaft the D/F aerial pole was not normally rigged but stowed below – its purpose is unclear given that it does not appear to fit the normal definition of a jury mast. The aircraft cranes also served to handle the ship's boats allowing the omission of the three 34ft derricks originally provided amidships (see page 36). Note the provision of side screen awnings (sun shades) forward, amidships and aft, which for the most part benefit the ship's officers and the sick bay. (J9439)

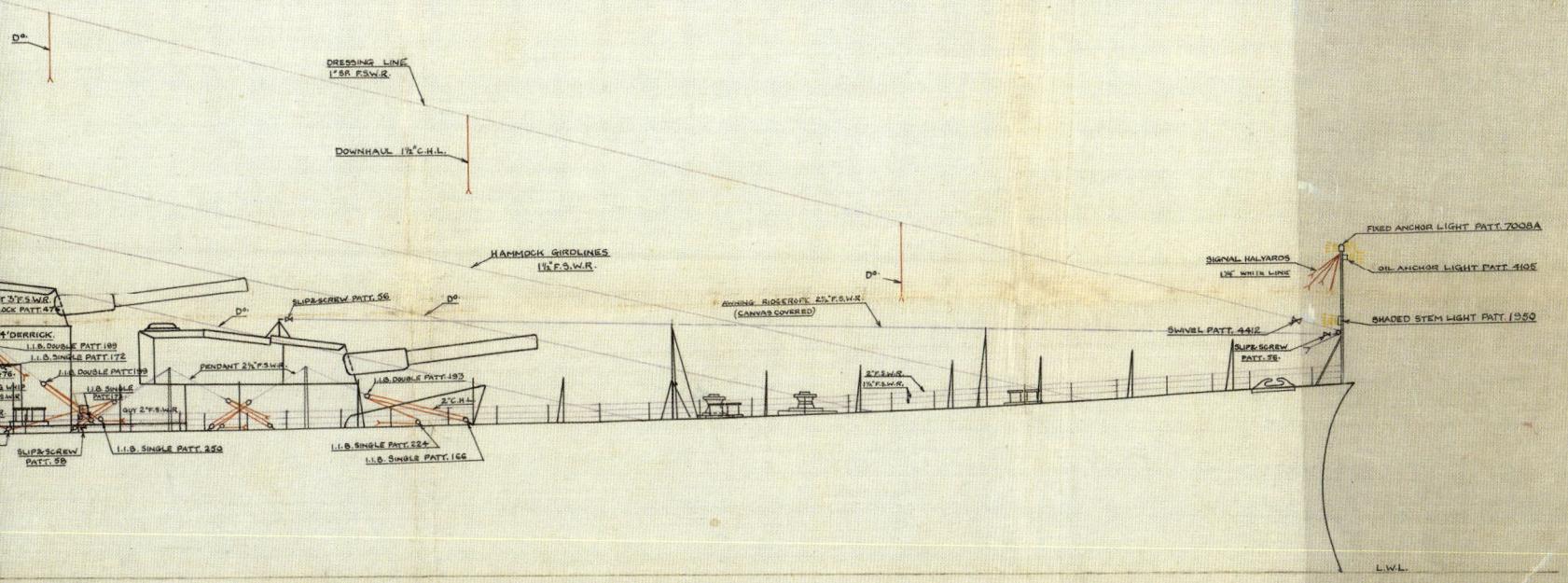

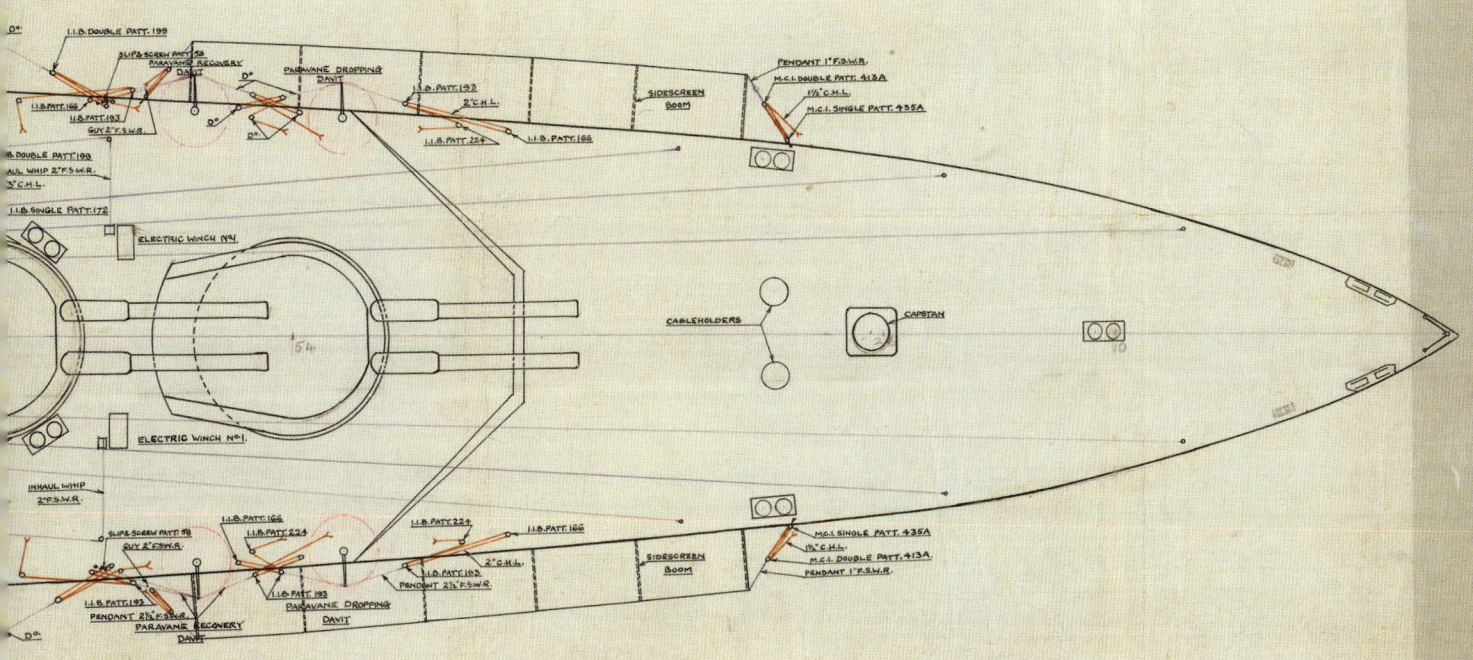

MODERNISATION 1933–1936

The *Repulse* was taken in hand at Portsmouth in April 1933 for a modernisation that was primarily intended to improve her defences against air attack. This involved the fitting of NC deck armour, which provided defence against plunging shell as well as bombs, the addition of modern close-range AA guns, an increase in her long-range AA capability and the provision of updated control systems for both. In addition, she was fitted with aircraft to provide spotting and reconnaissance duties. They could also be used offensively, being provided with torpedoes and bombs should an occasion to use them arise. This was not a major reconstruction of the type which began with *Warspite* and *Renown* since *Repulse* retained her original machinery, main armament (including its primary fire control system) and the minimal deck protection over her boiler rooms. The alterations to the superstructure substantially changed her appearance despite the fact that apart from the aircraft arrangements, it did not involve any major reconstruction. Compensation for the increased weight was obtained by removing the torpedo CT, the submerged torpedo tubes and the crushing tubes from the bulges. The ship commissioned for trials in January 1936 and completed to full complement on 14 April 1936. A four-hour full power trial was carried out on 6 March 1936 during which she developed a mean power of 112,400shp. Two runs on the Polperro measured mile resulted in a mean speed of 28.36 knots but since the ship began to reduce power during the second run this result is slightly less than might otherwise have been the case.

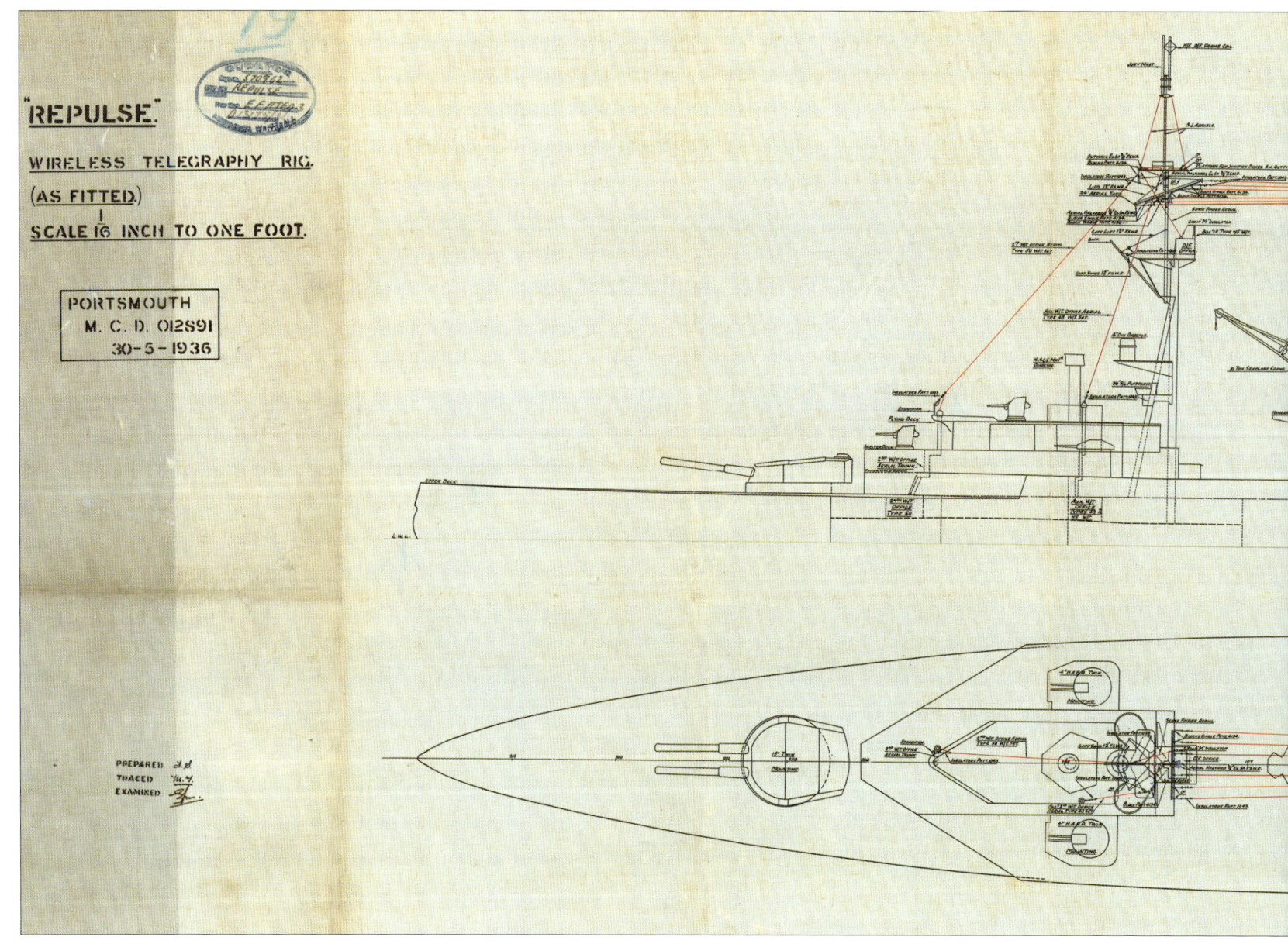

CAREER SUMMARY

After some delay, for working up and the early installation of improved deck protection, *Repulse* joined the 1st BCS of the Grand Fleet in December 1916 and served as its flagship until November 1918. During this time she took part in the Heligoland Bight Action in November 1917 in which she had a brief, but ineffective, engagement with the battleships *Kaiser* and *Kaiserin* and scored a single, superficial, hit on the cruiser *Königsberg*. Following her major refit of 1918–21 she served with the BCS in the Atlantic Fleet until laid-up at Portsmouth in 1932 pending her 1933–36 modernisation. During the 1920s she was detached to accompany *Hood* and the 1st LCS on an around-the-world Empire cruise that lasted from November 1923 to September 1924. She was detached again during February–October 1925 for a Royal Tour by the Prince of Wales to South Africa and South America. She rejoined the BCS in 1926 after a short refit. She served as temporary flagship of the BCS during April–September 1929 while *Hood* and *Renown* were refitting.

Following her modernisation, she joined the Mediterranean Fleet but was recalled in 1938 to refit prior to employment in conveying the King and Queen to Canada for a Royal Tour. The refit completed in March but owing to the international situation it was decided that *Repulse* could not be spared during a time of crisis and she rejoined

W/T RIG

The W/T outfit in 1936 consisted of a Type 36M in the main office, a Type 50 in the second office and Types 43 and 75 in the auxiliary office. The Type 43 was an experimental set, later replaced by a Type 52, while the Type 75 was a fire control set with aerials on the roof of the D/F office and at the after end of the air defence platform above the spotting top. She was due to receive additional auxiliary sets in 1939 – Types 60 (emergency battery powered set), 73, 53 (portable) and a Type 52T (portable) – but it is not known when or if these were actually provided. The D/F office on the mainmast platform contained two direction sets – an FH2 for HF and an LM1 for MF. The S16 frame coil aerial for the former is at the masthead while the SJ wire aerial array for the latter is fitted around the main topgallant mast. (J9440)

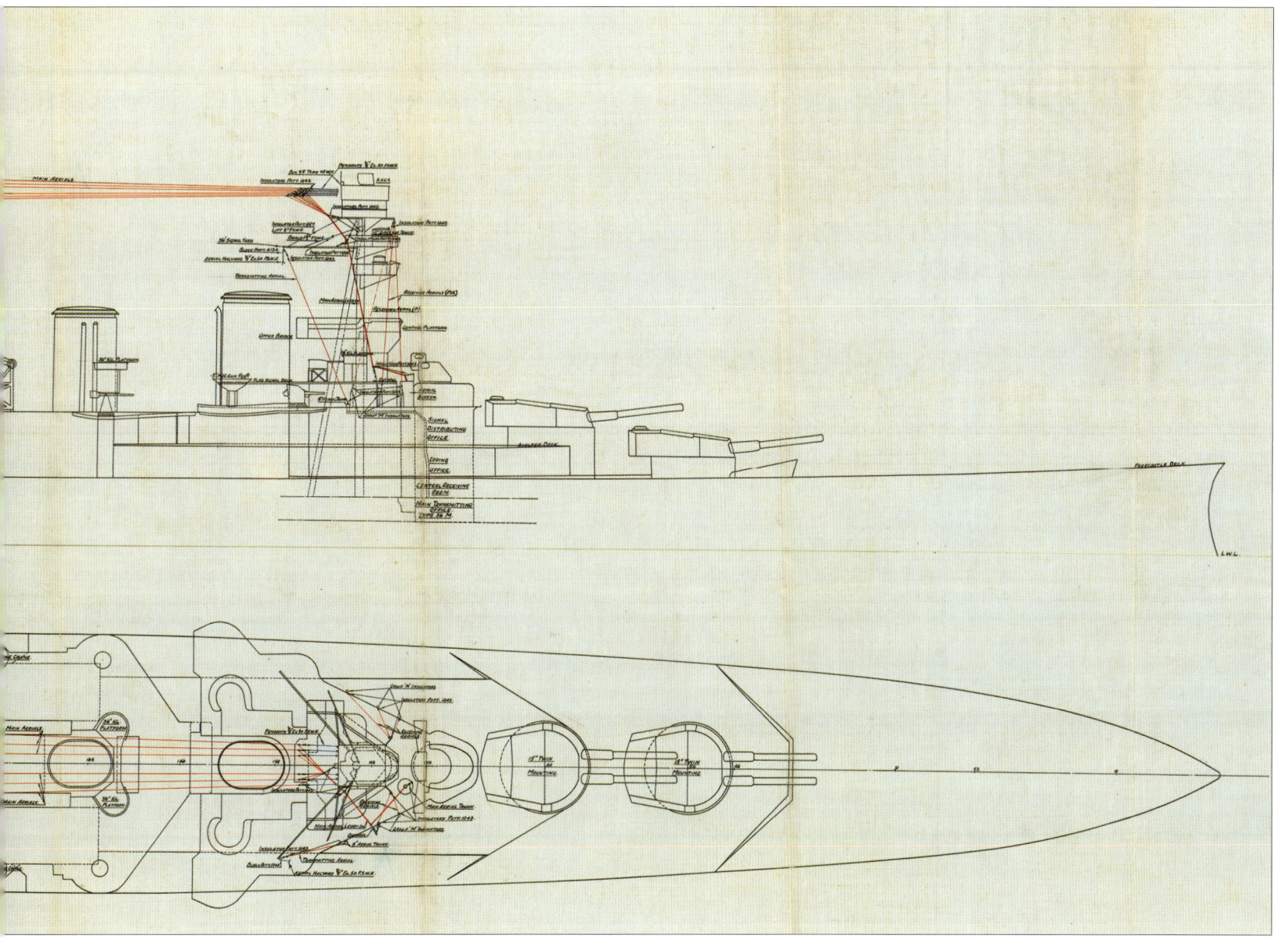

SUMMARY OF MODIFICATIONS 1933–1941

Modernisation 1933–1936

NC armour fitted to main deck over magazines, engine and condenser rooms and on lower deck forward of 'B' barbette over the HA Magazine. These changes involving removal of the upper layer of existing protective plating (see 1936 table of particulars).

Crushing tubes removed from bulges.

Fitted with fixed cross-deck aircraft catapult on the forecastle deck between the after funnel and mainmast (which involved removal of the superstructure and the triple 4in mounting in this area) and a hangar on each side of the after funnel.

Submerged torpedo tubes removed and compartment subdivided and converted into HA magazine and store rooms.

Fitted with two twin 4in BD mountings abreast the mainmast.

Four single 4in HA relocated one on each side of the forecastle deck abreast the fore funnel and one each side of the after funnel on the hangar roof.

A multiple pom-pom mounting and a quad 0.5in MG mounting were fitted on each side at the after end of the conning tower platform.

Fitted with two HACSs with the directors on the fore top roof and mounted on a tower above the after superstructure.

A pom-pom director was fitted on each side of the foretop roof.

Torpedo CT removed.

Fitted with six new 36in searchlights – two on new platforms abreast the fore side of the after funnel and four in the original 36in searchlight positions on the bridge and mainmast.

Portsmouth Oct 1938–Mar 1939

Refit for Royal Tour to Canada (subsequently cancelled).

Officer's accommodation in after superstructure converted in to Royal apartments.

Twin 4in BD mountings removed and replaced with two 4in Mk V guns on single HA Mk IV mountings.

Two additional 0.5in MG quad mountings fitted on after 4in director platform.

Feb 1940

Fitted degaussing coil at Devonport.

Rosyth Oct 1940

Fitted with third multiple pom-pom mounting in place of triple 4in mounting on flying deck.

Rosyth Jul–Aug 1941

Fitted with a least 8 x 20mm Oerlikons on single Mk IIA mountings (it is possible that the number was higher by the end of the year since she was allocated 15 but there is no evidence that all were actually fitted).

Fitted with gunnery radar Type 284 (aerial on armoured director hood above CT). She was also scheduled to be fitted with surface warning Type 273 and combined air-surface warning Type 286. The 286 was to be a temporary fitting pending replacement by a Type 279 or 281. Lack of any photographic evidence for the aerials of these sets would seem to indicate that they were either never fitted or, at best, were in the process of being installed but not operational when the ship was sunk.

PARTICULARS, 1936

Generally as in 1922 except for following:

Displacement (tons):	32,000 standard, 32,520 light, 35,990 half oil, 38,110 deep
Length:	750ft 1in pp, 794ft 2½in oa, 790ft 2½in wl
Mean Draught:	27ft 5in standard, 27ft 9¾in light, 30ft 5¼in half oil, 32ft 0¼in deep
Gun Armament:	6 x 15in/42cal BL Mk I, two twin Mk I and one twin Mk I* mounting (120 + 6 shrapnel rpg)
	12 x 4in/44.35cal BL Mk IX*, four triple TI mountings (200rpg)
	4 x 4in/45cal QF Mk XV, two twin HA Mk XVIII BD mountings (340 rpg)
	4 x 4in/45cal QF Mk V, single HA Mk III mountings (340 rpg)
	(200 x 4in star shell for ship)
	16 x 2pdr pom-poms Mk VIII, two 8-barrel Mk VI* mountings (720 rpg)
	8 x 0.5in Mk III MG, two quad Mk II* mountings (2500 rpg)
	4 x 3pdr saluting, single Mk I mountings (500 rpg)
	Note: rpg does not include practice ammunition
Torpedo Tubes:	Submerged tubes removed
Small Arms:	2 Vickers MG (field and boat mountings), 20 Lewis MG (12 for seamen and 8 for marines – ship, field and boat mountings – those for the marines were replaced with Bren guns c1939) and 432 rifles (330 for seamen and 102 for marines)
Armour:	Torpedo CT removed
	Main Deck: 3¾in NC (+ 2in HT) over magazines: 3½in NC (+ ¾in HT) abaft 'Y' barbette; 2½in NC (+1in HT) on flat of the Main Deck and 3½in NC between flat and ships sides over the engine and condenser rooms
	Lower Deck: 3½in NC (+¾in HT) forward of 'B' barbette over HA magazine
Endurance (approx):	1600nm at 28 knots; 2000nm at 25 knots; 2860nm at 20 knots; 3230nm at 18 knots; 3640nm at 12 knots
	Above on basis of sea-going conditions, 6 months out of dock and 5 per cent of maximum oil fuel remaining in tanks.
Complement:	1240

AIRCRAFT ARRANGEMENTS

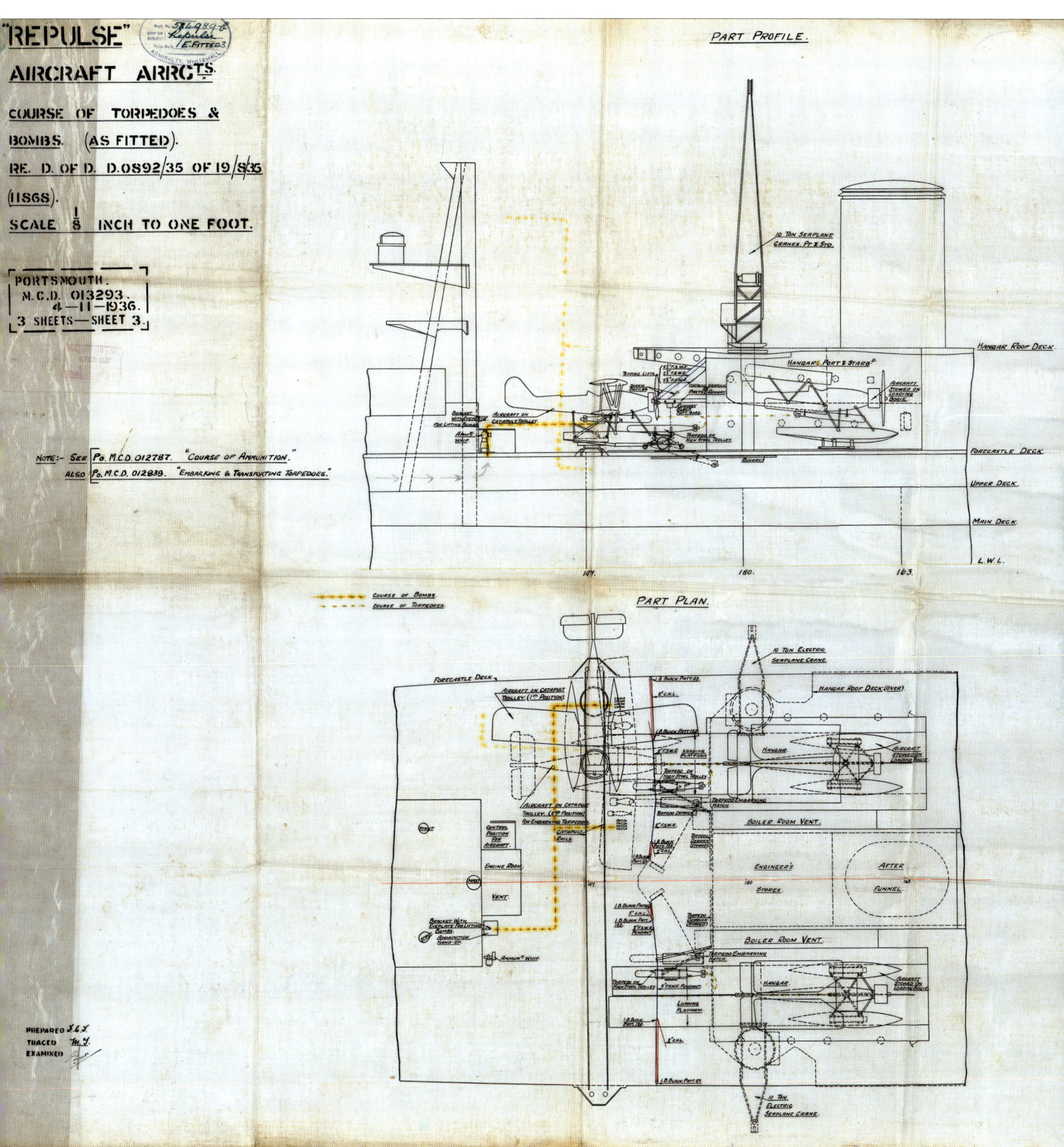

the Home Fleet. During her early war service, she was detached on a number of occasions to the North Atlantic to search for raiders and guard convoy routes and also took part in the Norwegian Campaign during April–June 1940. In August 1941 she sailed for the East Indies to serve, together with the battleship *Prince of Wales*, as the prime units of the Eastern Fleet in the hope of deterring any aggressive intent by the Japanese. They arrived at Singapore on 2 December 1941 a few days before the outbreak of war in the Pacific and Far East. On 8 December the *Repulse*, *Prince of Wales* and four destroyers sailed to intercept a Japanese invasion force reported to be heading for the east coast of Malaya. Two days later they were attacked by Japanese aircraft and both ships were sunk by aerial torpedoes. The *Prince of Wales* was disabled early in the action but *Repulse* did reasonably well in using her speed to out-manoeuvre her attackers until they approached from two different directions simultaneously. In three separate attacks, she was hit by one bomb which passed through the port hangar and burst on the main deck and by two torpedoes on the port side and then one on the port side and one on the starboard side. One of these torpedoes jammed her rudder. Unable to manoeuvre, she was abandoned and sank 1 hour and 20 minutes after the first attack.

AIRCRAFT ARRANGEMENTS – ARMING AIRCRAFT
(previous page)

The bomb room was on the platform deck, at Stations 290–292, so it was necessary to bring them up three decks and about 190ft forward to a position below the bomb hatch. The latter was located at the start of the yellow tinted line indicating the route of the bombs to the aircraft. The torpedoes had a somewhat shorter journey since they were stowed on the upper deck above the AW torpedo tubes with their warheads protected by the upper section of the armour mantle box. They were brought up though the torpedo hatches just abaft the inboard sides of the hangars. The profile shows both the transport/lifting torpedo trolley and a torpedo fitted to an aircraft. (M0942)

AIRCRAFT ARRANGEMENTS – STOWAGE

The plan opposite illustrates the original stowage arrangements for the aircraft: two on the catapult, referred to here as the 'sea position' (given as 'harbour position' on the as-fitted plans), and one each in the hangars.

Below on the left is the stowage arrangement for the spare floats located on the roof of the boat engine workshop (one pair of floats each for a Swordfish and a Shark). On the right is the arrangement of the aircraft stores located abaft the after funnel, between the hangars. The table lists the aircraft spares they contain. (M0940)

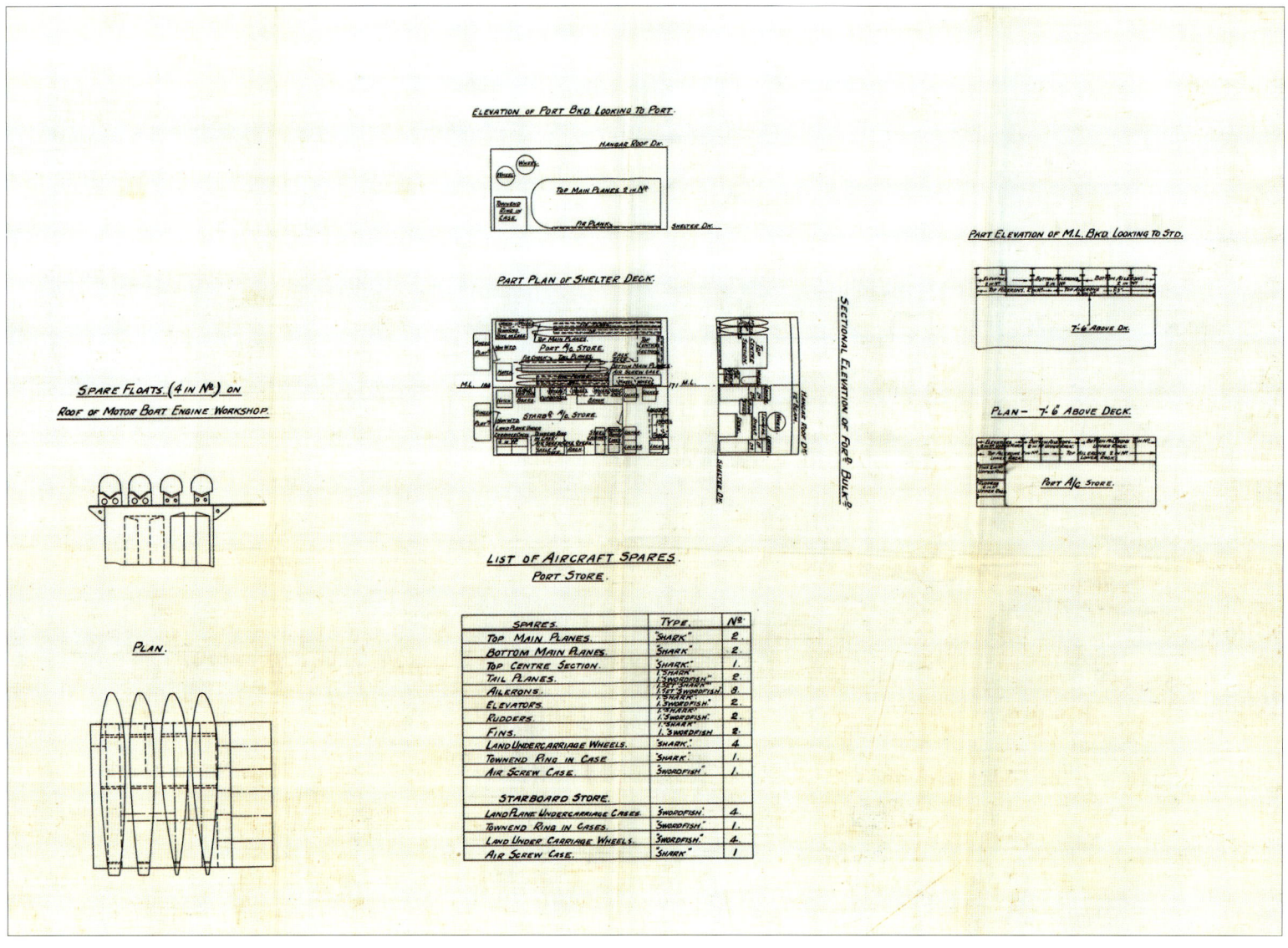

AIRCRAFT ARRANGEMENTS

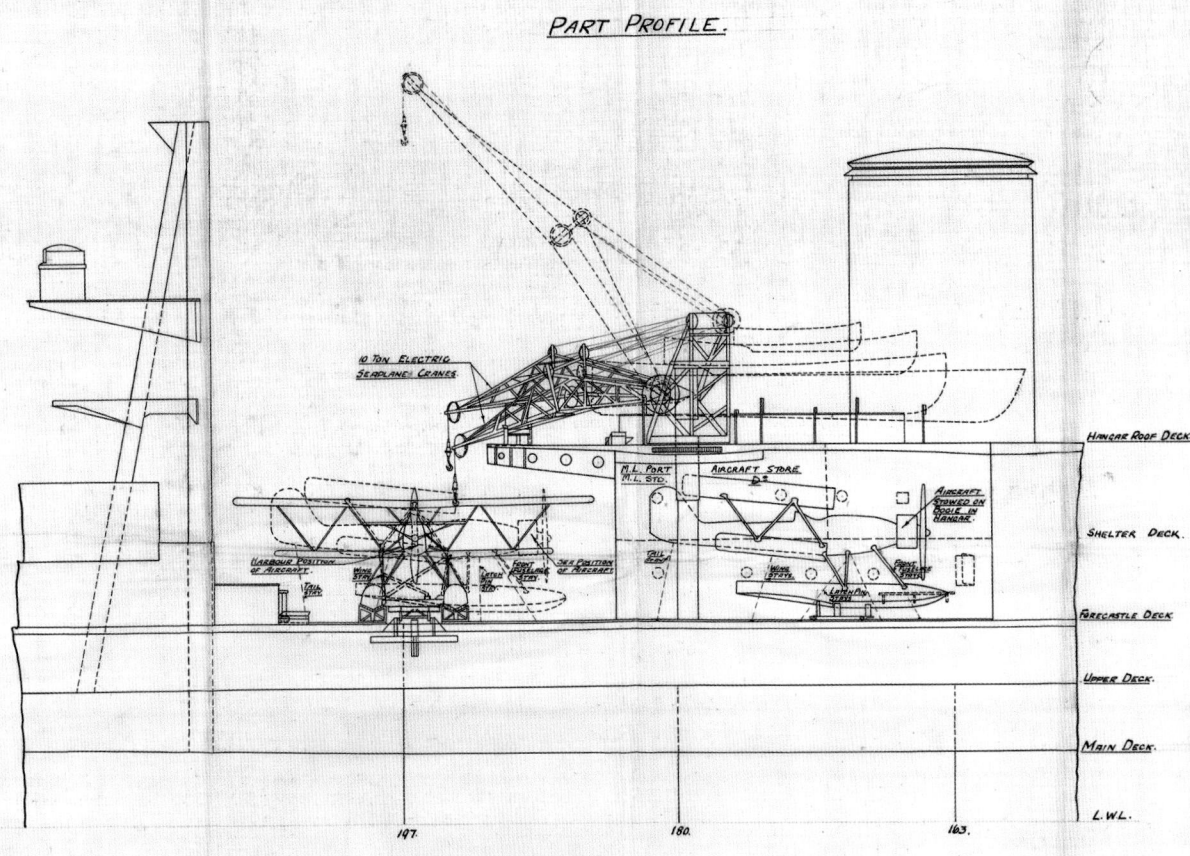

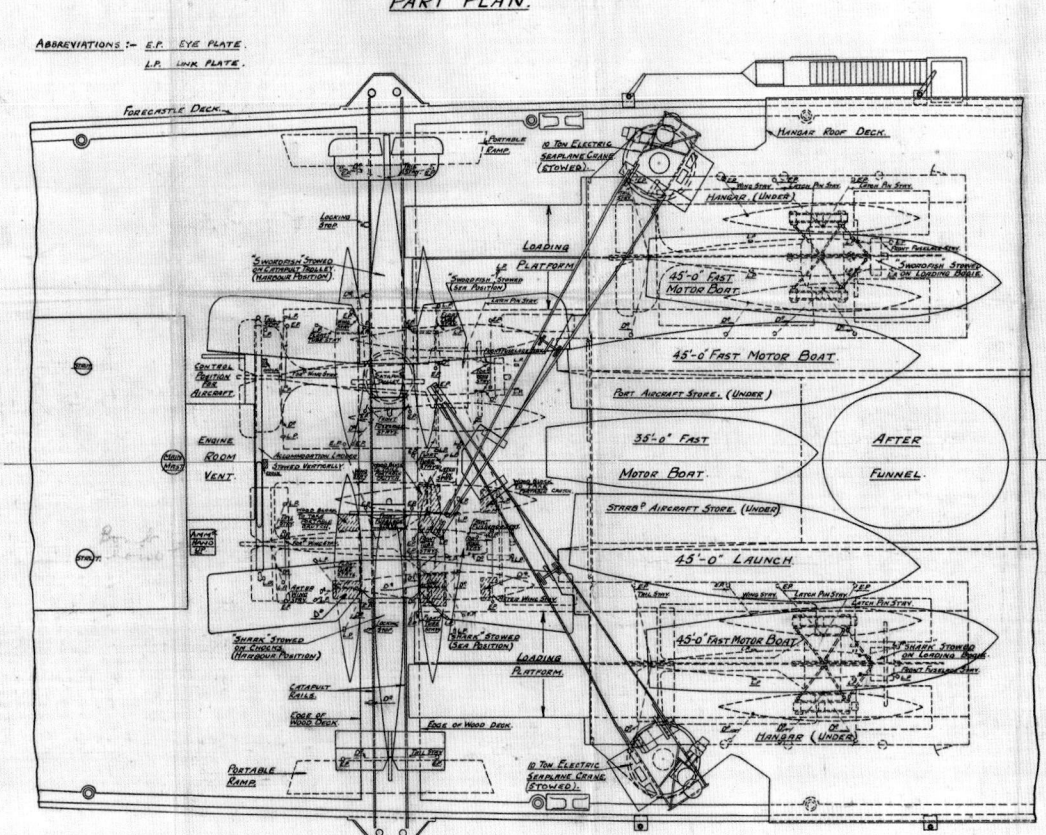

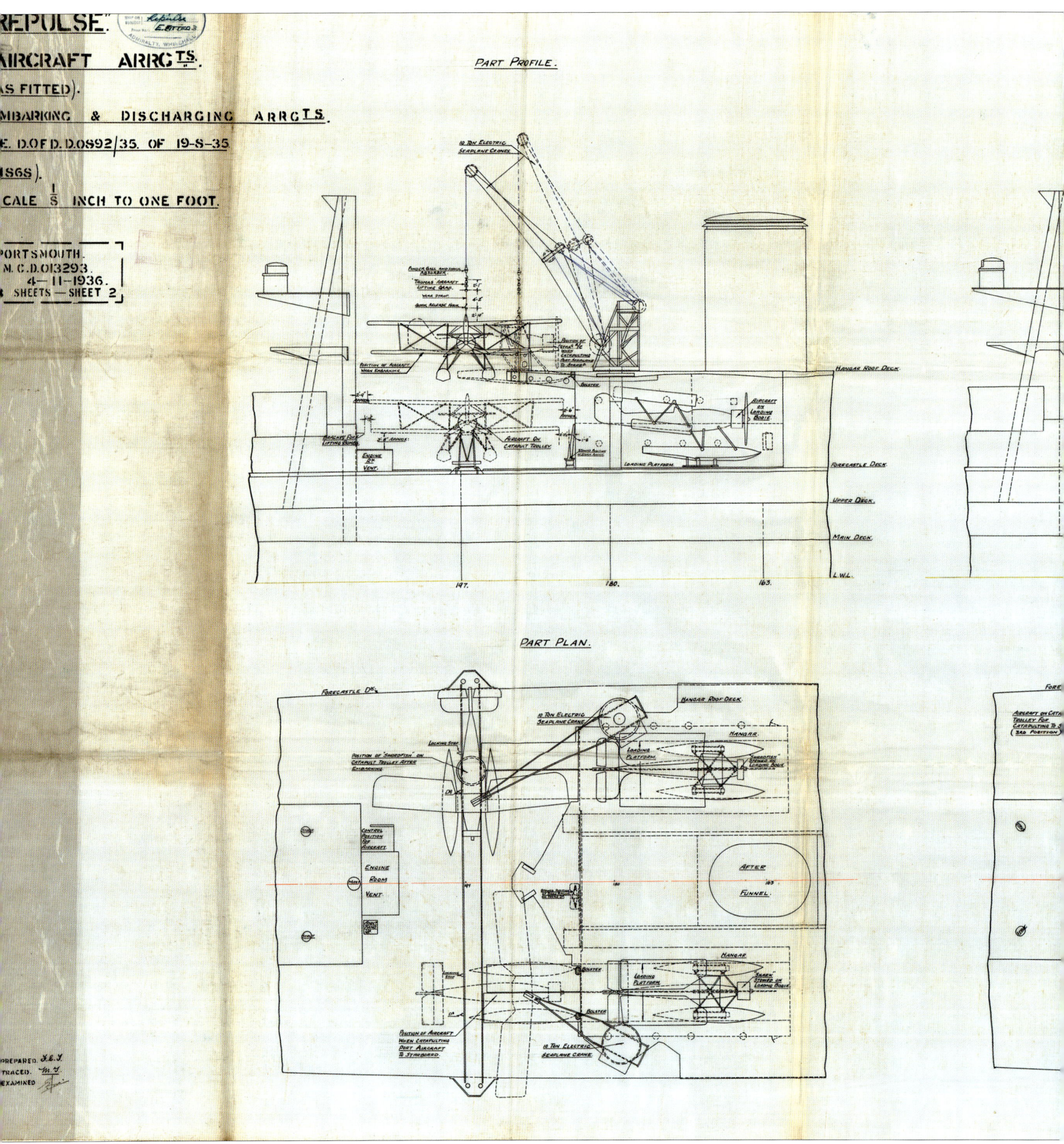

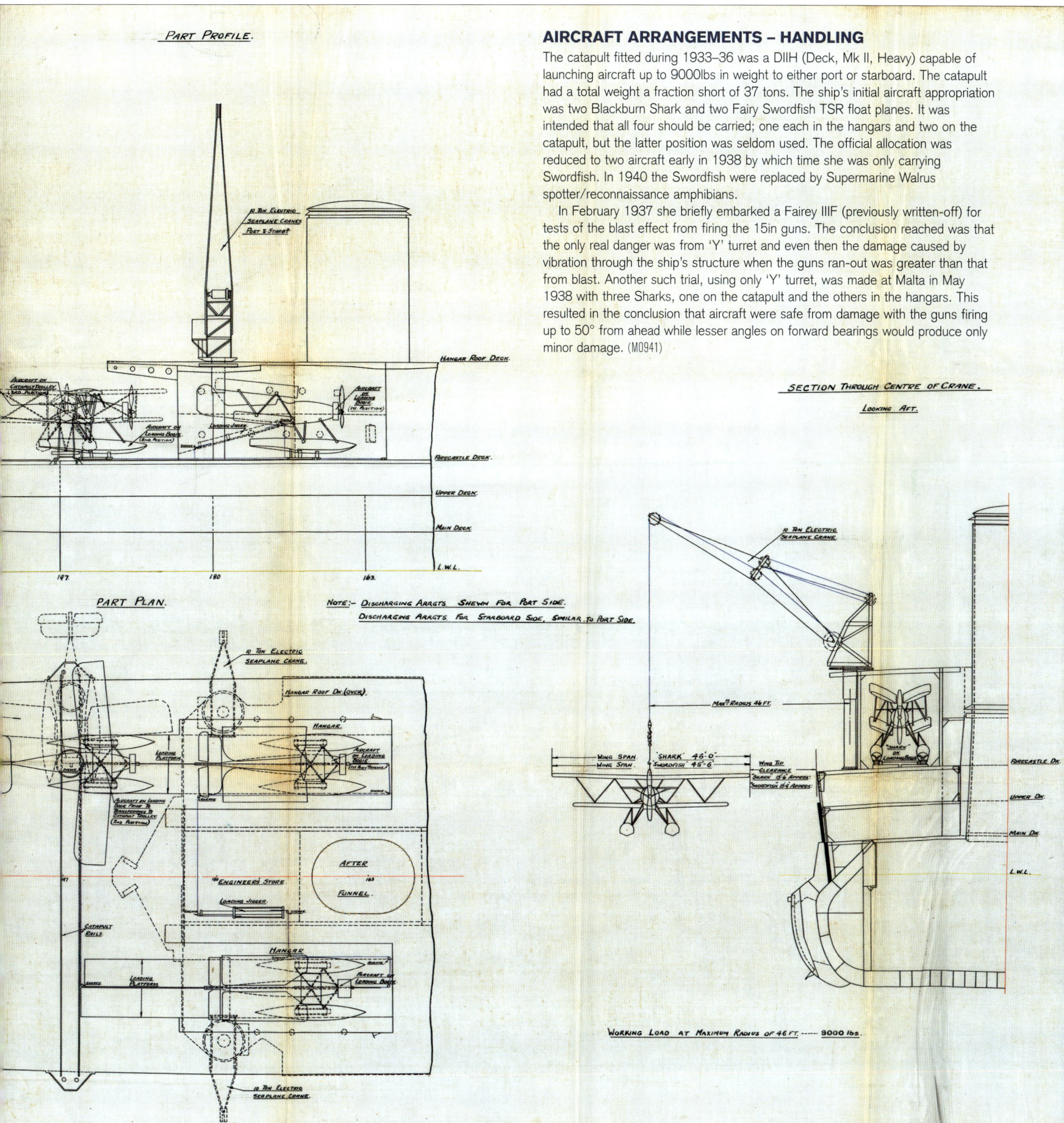

AIRCRAFT ARRANGEMENTS – HANDLING

The catapult fitted during 1933–36 was a DIIH (Deck, Mk II, Heavy) capable of launching aircraft up to 9000lbs in weight to either port or starboard. The catapult had a total weight a fraction short of 37 tons. The ship's initial aircraft appropriation was two Blackburn Shark and two Fairy Swordfish TSR float planes. It was intended that all four should be carried; one each in the hangars and two on the catapult, but the latter position was seldom used. The official allocation was reduced to two aircraft early in 1938 by which time she was only carrying Swordfish. In 1940 the Swordfish were replaced by Supermarine Walrus spotter/reconnaissance amphibians.

In February 1937 she briefly embarked a Fairey IIIF (previously written-off) for tests of the blast effect from firing the 15in guns. The conclusion reached was that the only real danger was from 'Y' turret and even then the damage caused by vibration through the ship's structure when the guns ran-out was greater than that from blast. Another such trial, using only 'Y' turret, was made at Malta in May 1938 with three Sharks, one on the catapult and the others in the hangars. This resulted in the conclusion that aircraft were safe from damage with the guns firing up to 50° from ahead while lesser angles on forward bearings would produce only minor damage. (M0941)

ENLARGED PROFILE AND SECTIONS, AS FITTED 1936

STERN TO STATION 303

The following pages follow the same layout as provided on pages 25–59 for the ship in 1916. As before, all the sections reproduced derive from a single plan (J9438) and the accompanying profiles from the main 1936 profile (J9433, which like that for 1916, is reproduced in full in the gatefold). The 1936 sections differ from those of 1916 in that the transverse half sections all show the starboard side rather than starboard forward/port aft.

- **A roller fairlead** to guide cables that run over the stern. The item mounted above it is a fog light.

- **New after awning stanchion** arranged to support the ensign staff at an angle rather than vertically. The vertical arm at the end of the support bracket is for the anchor and overtaking light – electric light at the bottom and, in case of power failure, alternative oil light at the top.

- **The hawse pipe** for the stream anchor is unoccupied because the anchor is now stowed amidships on the forecastle deck on the superstructure bulkhead forward of the catapult deck. This appears to have been the standard arrangement, although there are photographs of *Repulse* at Malta c1937 with the anchor stowed in the hawse pipe.

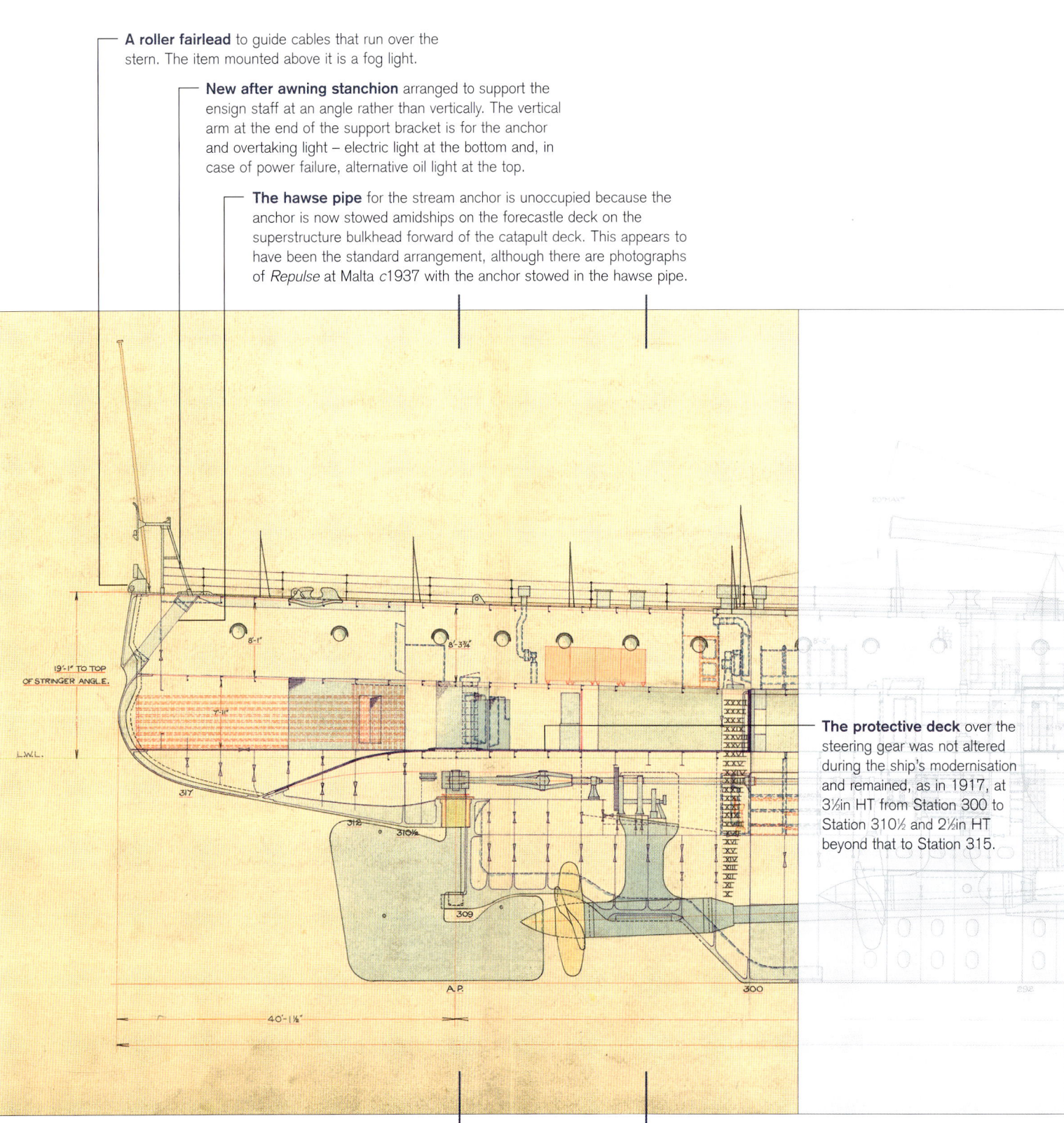

- **The protective deck** over the steering gear was not altered during the ship's modernisation and remained, as in 1917, at 3½in HT from Station 300 to Station 310½ and 2½in HT beyond that to Station 315.

309 STATION   **303 STATION**

SECTIONS AT STATIONS 309 AND 303, STARBOARD SIDE, LOOKING AFT

Alterations to the ship's internal arrangements at the after end during her modernisation are few, and mainly re-allocation of some accommodation and storage spaces which are more adequately covered by reference to the plan views (pages 140–159). It should be noted that some of these changes, and other internal alterations to the ship, may well have taken place during 1921–33.

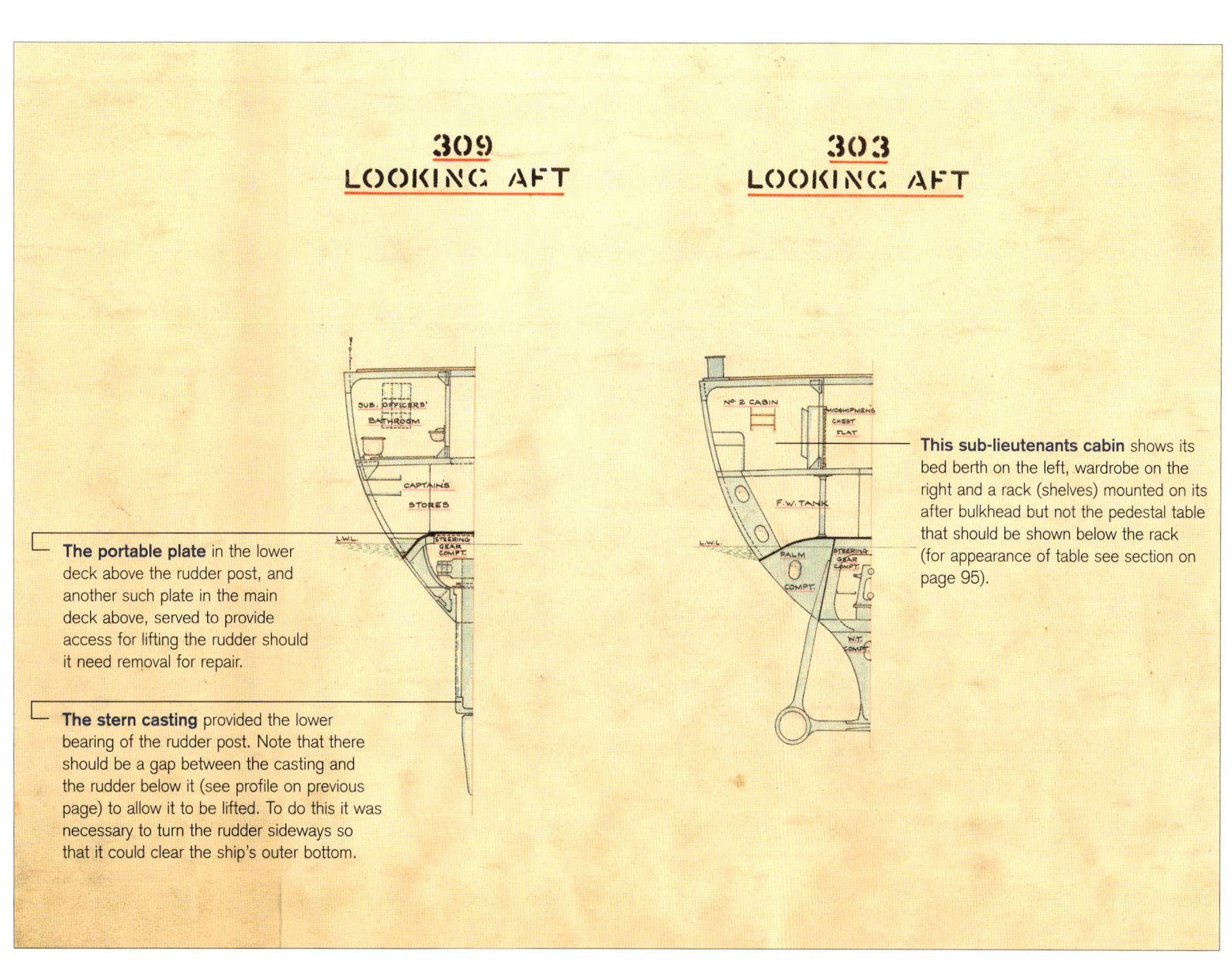

The portable plate in the lower deck above the rudder post, and another such plate in the main deck above, served to provide access for lifting the rudder should it need removal for repair.

The stern casting provided the lower bearing of the rudder post. Note that there should be a gap between the casting and the rudder below it (see profile on previous page) to allow it to be lifted. To do this it was necessary to turn the rudder sideways so that it could clear the ship's outer bottom.

This sub-lieutenants cabin shows its bed berth on the left, wardrobe on the right and a rack (shelves) mounted on its after bulkhead but not the pedestal table that should be shown below the rack (for appearance of table see section on page 95).

STATIONS 303 TO 294

This part of the profile clearly demonstrates that the new as-fitted drawings produced in 1936 were based directly on the original 1916 as-fitted set. Apart from the repetition of the dimensions based on the designed LWL of 1915, it still shows the (incorrect) 4-bladed propellers in the profile and the (correct) 3-bladed propellers in the plan view and still omits the figure for the depression of the 15in guns (5°).

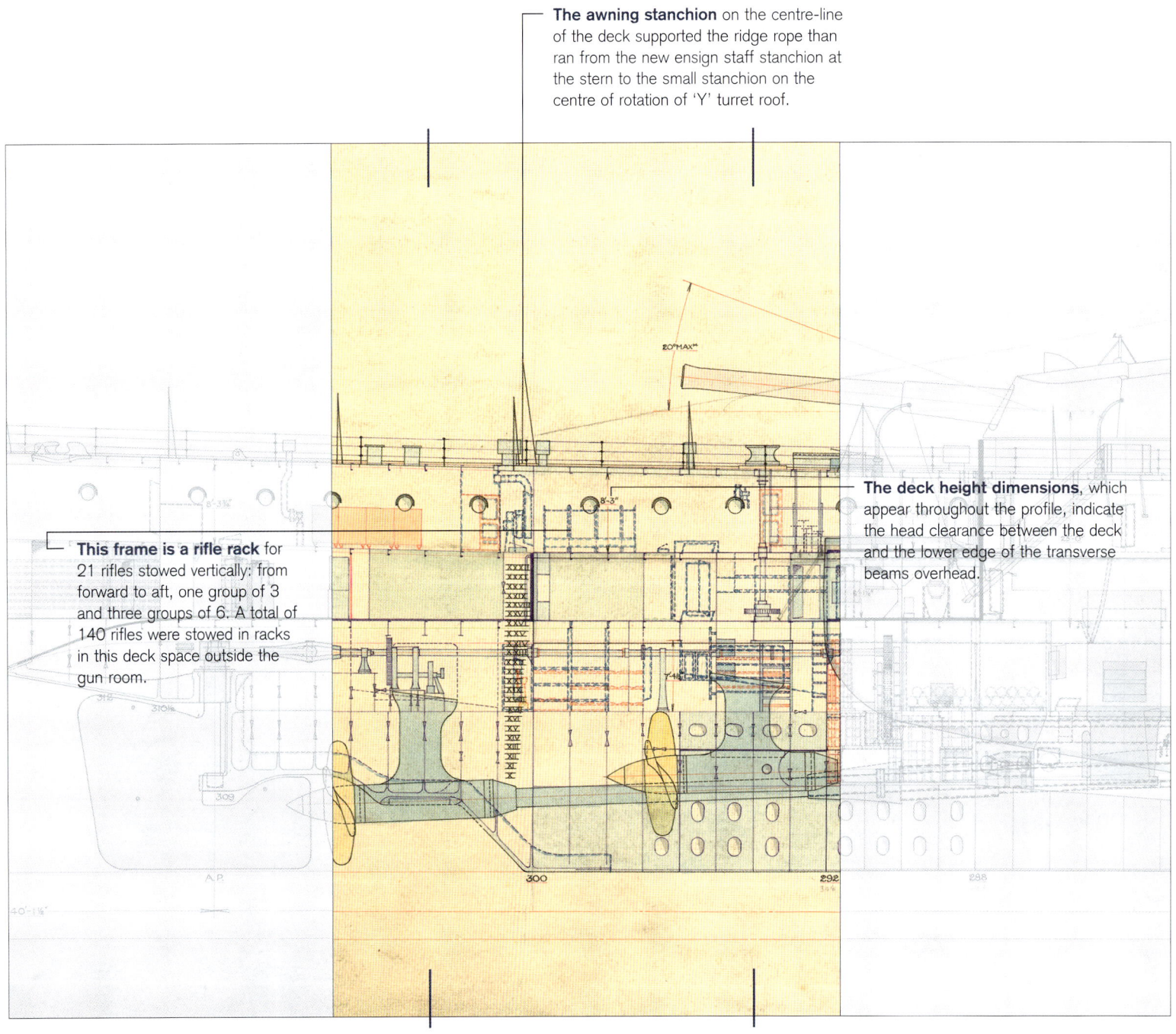

The awning stanchion on the centre-line of the deck supported the ridge rope than ran from the new ensign staff stanchion at the stern to the small stanchion on the centre of rotation of 'Y' turret roof.

This frame is a rifle rack for 21 rifles stowed vertically: from forward to aft, one group of 3 and three groups of 6. A total of 140 rifles were stowed in racks in this deck space outside the gun room.

The deck height dimensions, which appear throughout the profile, indicate the head clearance between the deck and the lower edge of the transverse beams overhead.

303 STATION   **294 STATION**

STATIONS 303 TO 294

SECTION AT STATION 294, STARBOARD SIDE, LOOKING AFT

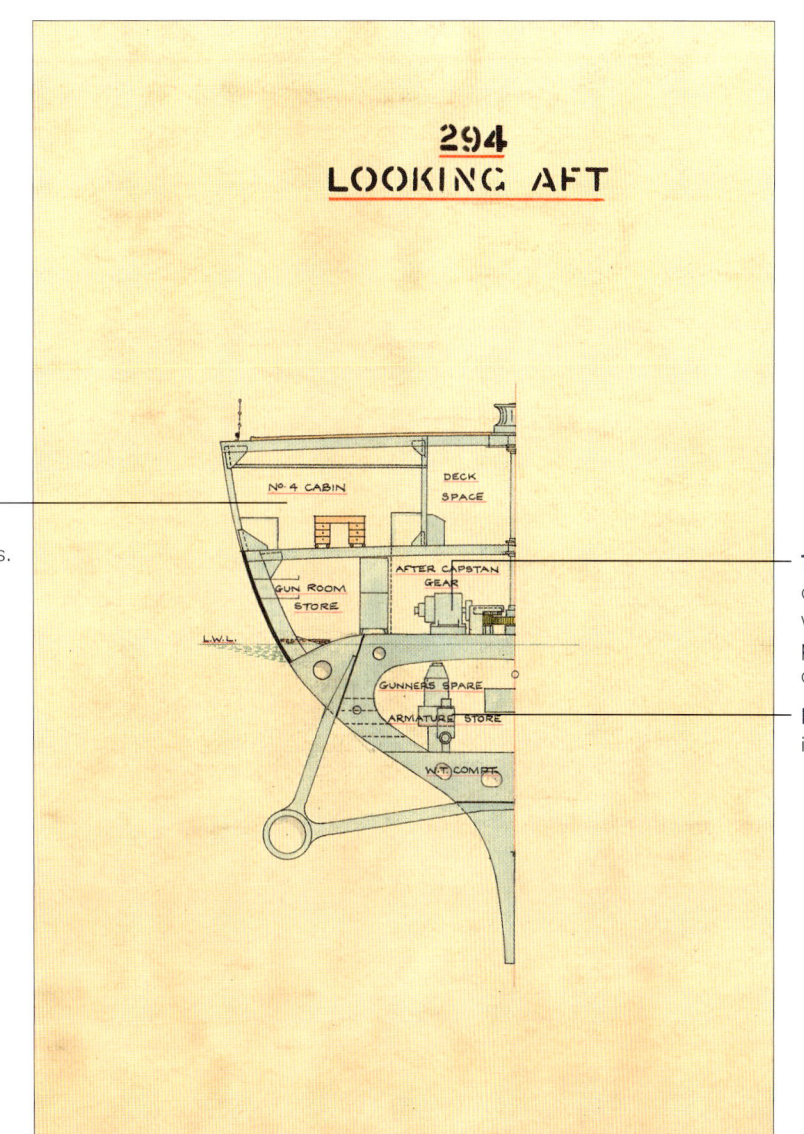

Cabin 4 is double berth accommodation for sub-lieutenants. It illustrates well the form of a knee-hole table which in modern terms would be called a desk.

The electric drive motor for the after capstan is clearly illustrated in this view which, if combined with the section on page 29, provides a full profile of the capstan machinery.

No 5 350-ton salvage pump, located in the gunner's spare armature store.

ENLARGED PROFILE AND SECTIONS, AS FITTED 1936

STATIONS 294 TO 289

During modernisation the top layer of 1in HT plating on the main deck abaft 'Y' barbette was removed and replaced by 3½in NC armour over the full width of the ship from Station 286 to 292. This armour was fitted on top of the original ¾in deck plating. The protective plating on the lower deck immediately below this area remained at its existing 3½in HT on the flat and 2½in HT on the slope. This substantially improved the protection to the after magazines from direct bomb attack but they still remained vulnerable to shellfire from after bearings and to bomb hits between 292 and 300 Stations where both the main and lower decks remained at ¾in HT (the upper deck in this area was ½in MS with ½in HT stringer plates).

The upper edge of the bulge over a length of about 8ft from its after end has been extended about 2ft higher than that originally fitted in 1918–21. The fore end of the bulge, for a length of around 11ft, was similarly arranged. The reminder of the top edge of the bulge terminated, as before, at the edge of the main deck. This addition is shown clearly in the section on the next page.

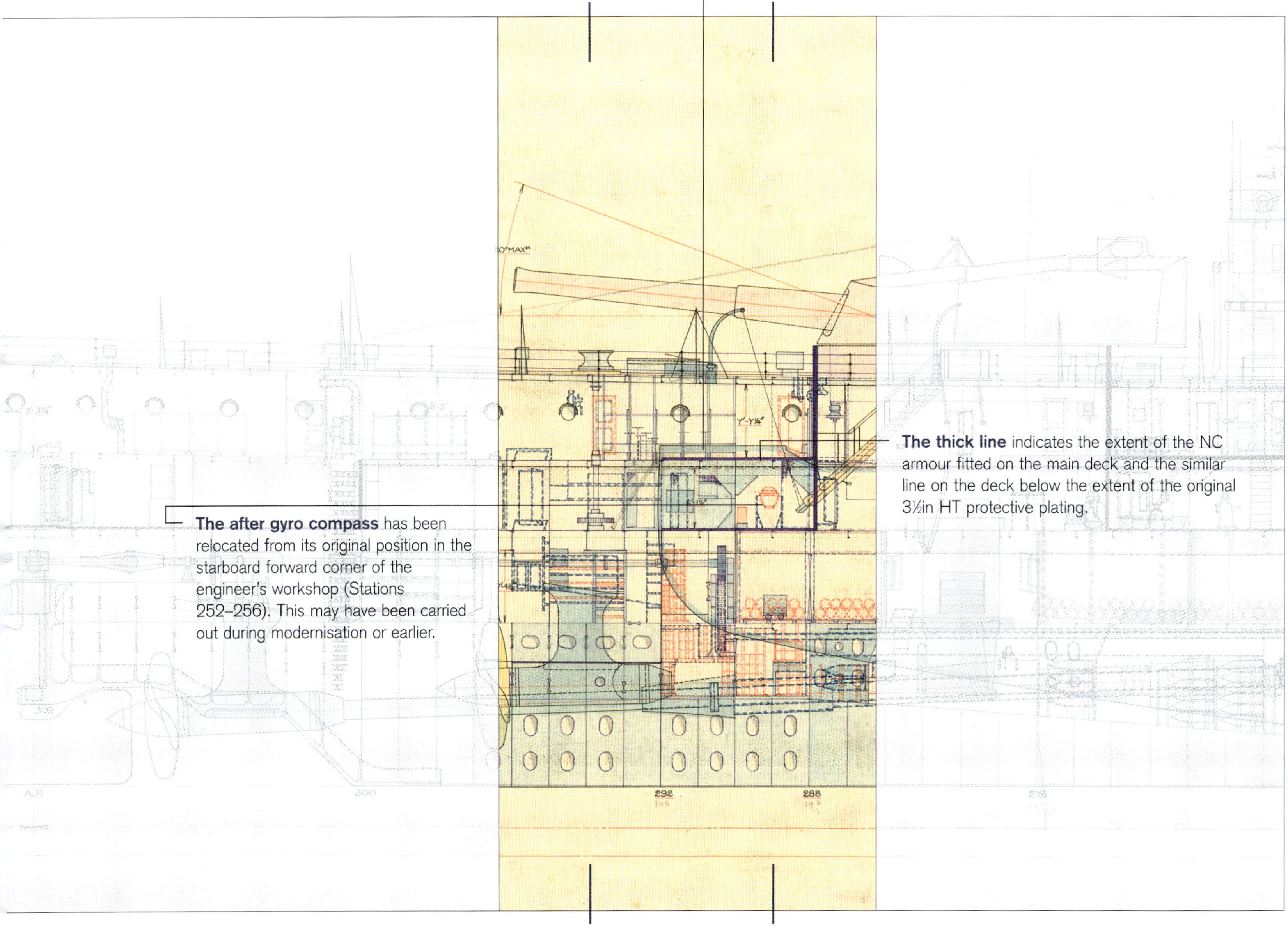

The thick line indicates the extent of the NC armour fitted on the main deck and the similar line on the deck below the extent of the original 3½in HT protective plating.

The after gyro compass has been relocated from its original position in the starboard forward corner of the engineer's workshop (Stations 252–256). This may have been carried out during modernisation or earlier.

294 STATION   **289 STATION**

STATIONS 294 TO 289

SECTION AT STATION 289, STARBOARD SIDE, LOOKING AFT

While this section shows the thick black line indicating the 3½in HT plating on the lower deck, it omits those required to show the 2½in HT plating on the slope of the lower deck and the NC armour on the main deck. There is a faint pencil annotation stating that the main deck is fitted with '140 lbs NC on 30 lbs HT' [*ie* 3½in NC on ¾in HT].

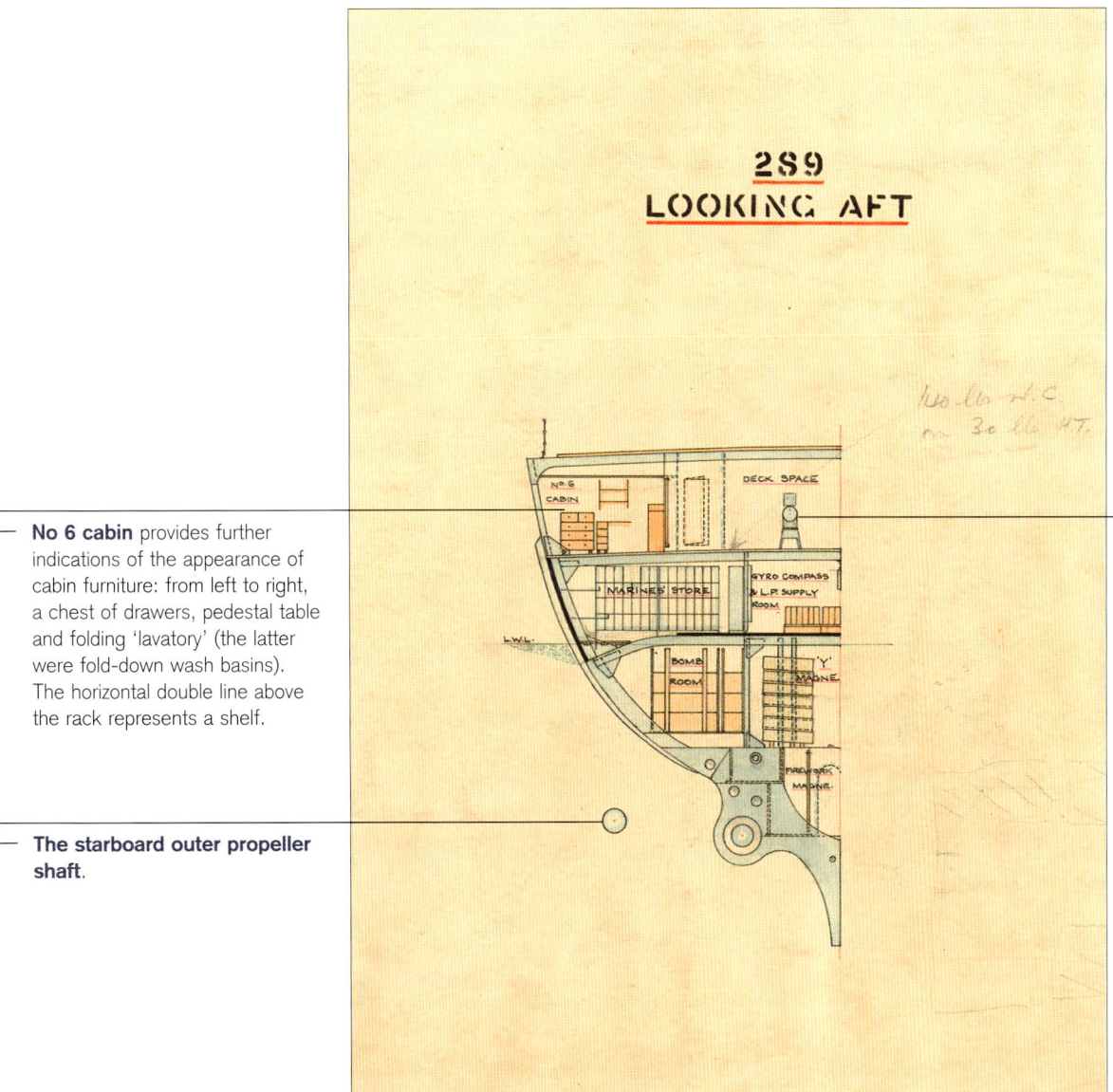

No 6 cabin provides further indications of the appearance of cabin furniture: from left to right, a chest of drawers, pedestal table and folding 'lavatory' (the latter were fold-down wash basins). The horizontal double line above the rack represents a shelf.

The starboard outer propeller shaft.

The electric motor and its stand for a 17½in ventilation fan; the fan casing is not shown since it is forward of Station 289.

STATIONS 289 TO 280

Of the three 15in gun mountings, 'Y' turret had the shortest ammunition trunk. This was primarily due to the turret's lower position but was further reduced by the shorter height from the weather deck to the top of the barbette. The trunk was 20ft 10⅛in in length compared with 33ft 7⅛in and 43ft 7⅛in for 'A' and 'B' turrets respectively. The revolving weights recorded for turrets were generally nominal with little account taken of differences in trunk length or added weights (such as the 30ft rangefinders added to 'A' and 'Y' turrets). However, these variations would have been relatively small considering the total weight involved.

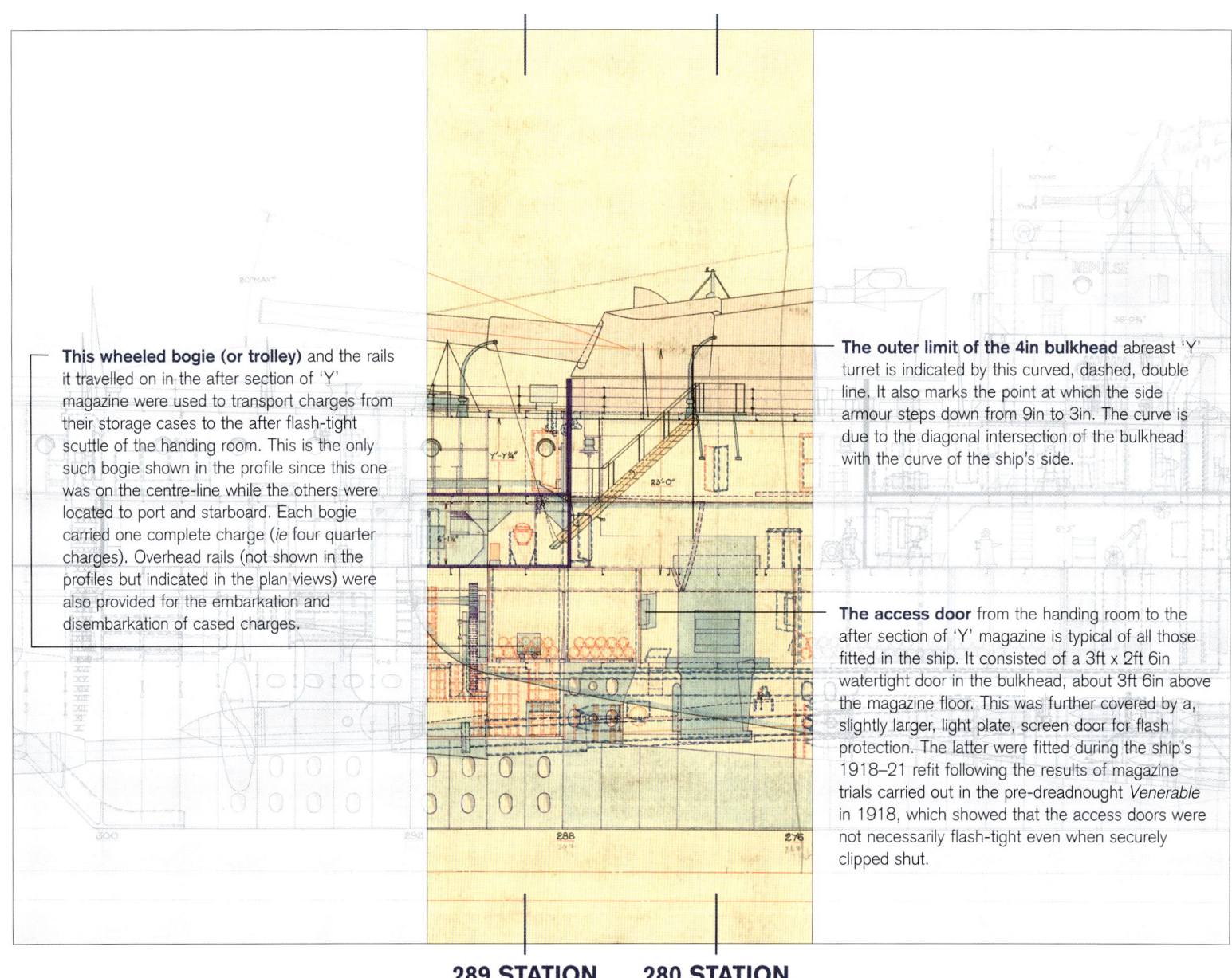

This wheeled bogie (or trolley) and the rails it travelled on in the after section of 'Y' magazine were used to transport charges from their storage cases to the after flash-tight scuttle of the handing room. This is the only such bogie shown in the profile since this one was on the centre-line while the others were located to port and starboard. Each bogie carried one complete charge (*ie* four quarter charges). Overhead rails (not shown in the profiles but indicated in the plan views) were also provided for the embarkation and disembarkation of cased charges.

The outer limit of the 4in bulkhead abreast 'Y' turret is indicated by this curved, dashed, double line. It also marks the point at which the side armour steps down from 9in to 3in. The curve is due to the diagonal intersection of the bulkhead with the curve of the ship's side.

The access door from the handing room to the after section of 'Y' magazine is typical of all those fitted in the ship. It consisted of a 3ft x 2ft 6in watertight door in the bulkhead, about 3ft 6in above the magazine floor. This was further covered by a slightly larger, light plate, screen door for flash protection. The latter were fitted during the ship's 1918–21 refit following the results of magazine trials carried out in the pre-dreadnought *Venerable* in 1918, which showed that the access doors were not necessarily flash-tight even when securely clipped shut.

289 STATION   280 STATION

STATIONS 289 TO 280

SECTION AT STATION 280, STARBOARD SIDE, LOOKING AFT

The fitting of 9in in place of the 6in side armour should have resulted in a 3in outboard step between its lower edge and the outer bottom plating at the side armour's forward and after ends. This step is missing on this section and on the forward sections at Stations 54 and 66. There is a slight indication of a step on Section 270 but this scales at substantially less than 3in. However, the 3in offset between the top of the 9in side armour and the 6in side above it is clearly represented on all the sections affected. Excepting the rather unlikely possibility that the armour recess had been locally set-back it would appear that this is a simple drawing error.

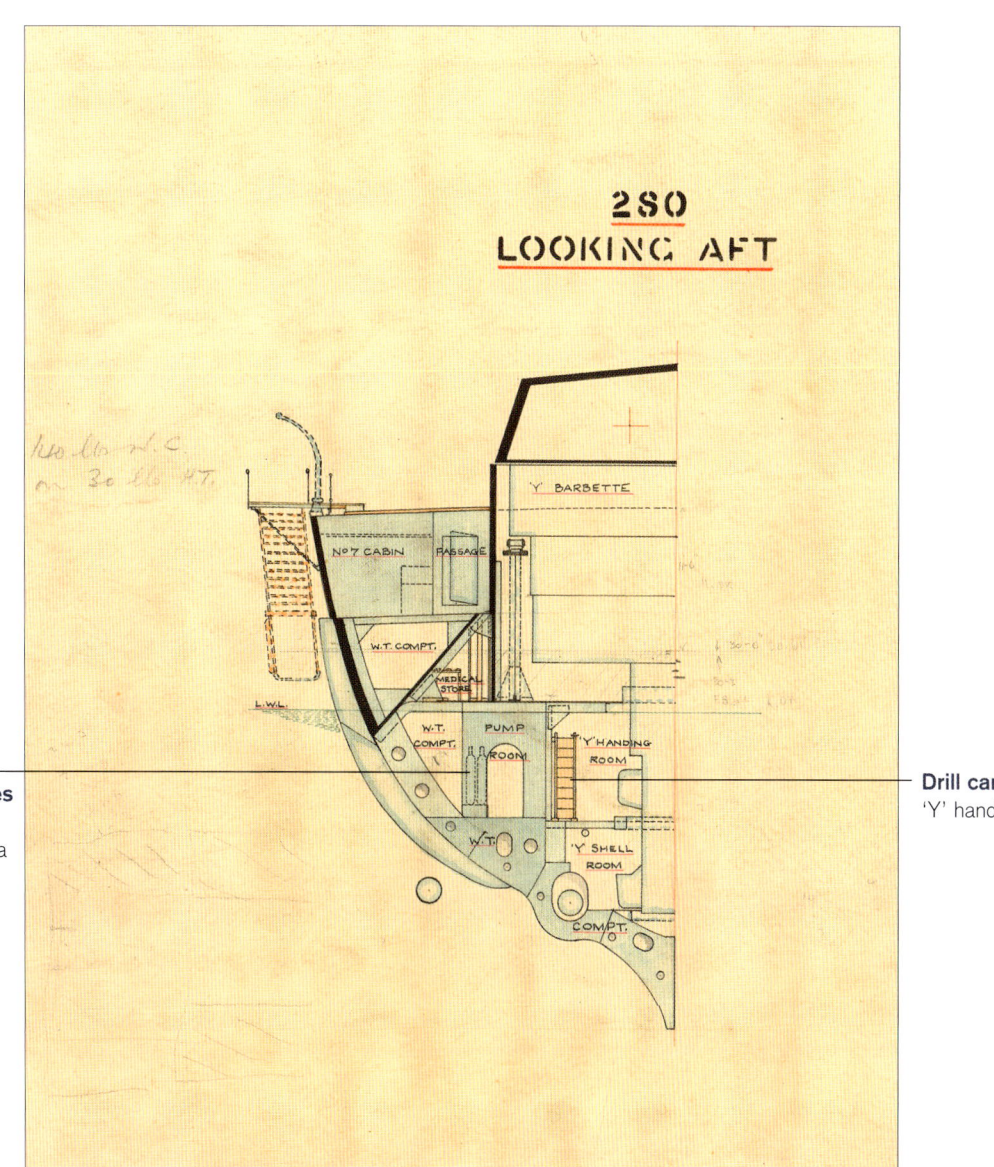

Two compressed air bottles located behind a bulkhead (with arched opening) inside a 50-ton pump room.

Drill cartridge rack in 'Y' handing room.

98 ENLARGED PROFILE AND SECTIONS, AS FITTED 1936

STATIONS 280 TO 270

Nominally the internal detail in the profile is shown as if the ship were cut down the centre-line. Items along the middle line are generally shown in solid outline while those to port, if behind other structure, are shown as hidden detail (dashed line). Occasionally starboard detail, if considered important, is also included, again as hidden detail. Both are employed in this section of the profile – for example the CO_2 machinery on the port side of the lower deck, beyond 'Y' barbette, and the steering gear shaft on the starboard side below the platform deck.

The gangway along the front of the 30ft rangefinder was supported at its outer end by this triangular bracket attached to the rangefinder casing support bracket. The vertical and horizontal lines joining the outer edge of the platform to the top of the rangefinder casing are the platform's guardrails. The gangway served as access to the rangefinder windows and their outer covers.

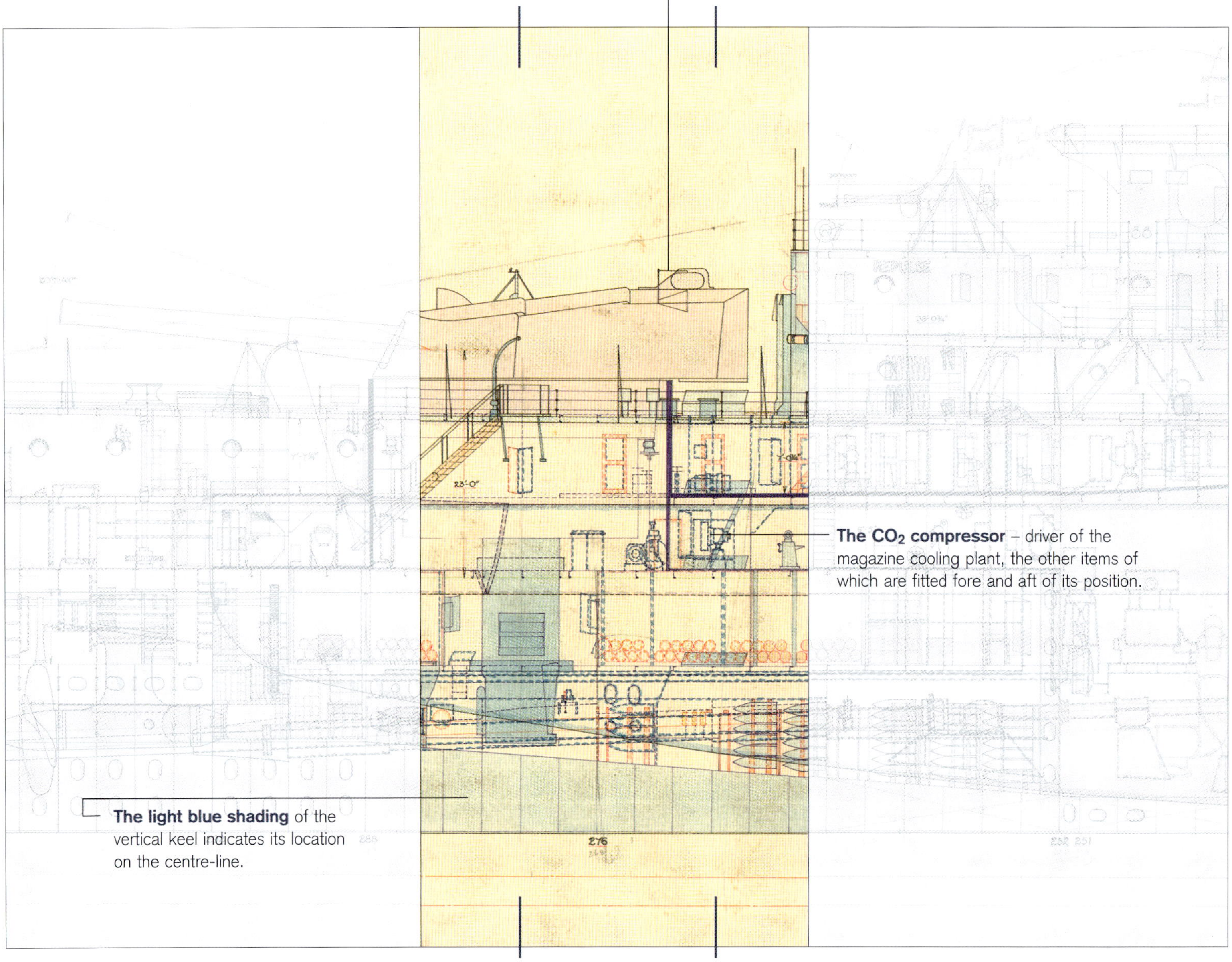

The CO_2 compressor – driver of the magazine cooling plant, the other items of which are fitted fore and aft of its position.

The light blue shading of the vertical keel indicates its location on the centre-line.

280 STATION   **270 STATION**

STATIONS 280 TO 270

SECTION AT STATION 270, STARBOARD SIDE, LOOKING AFT

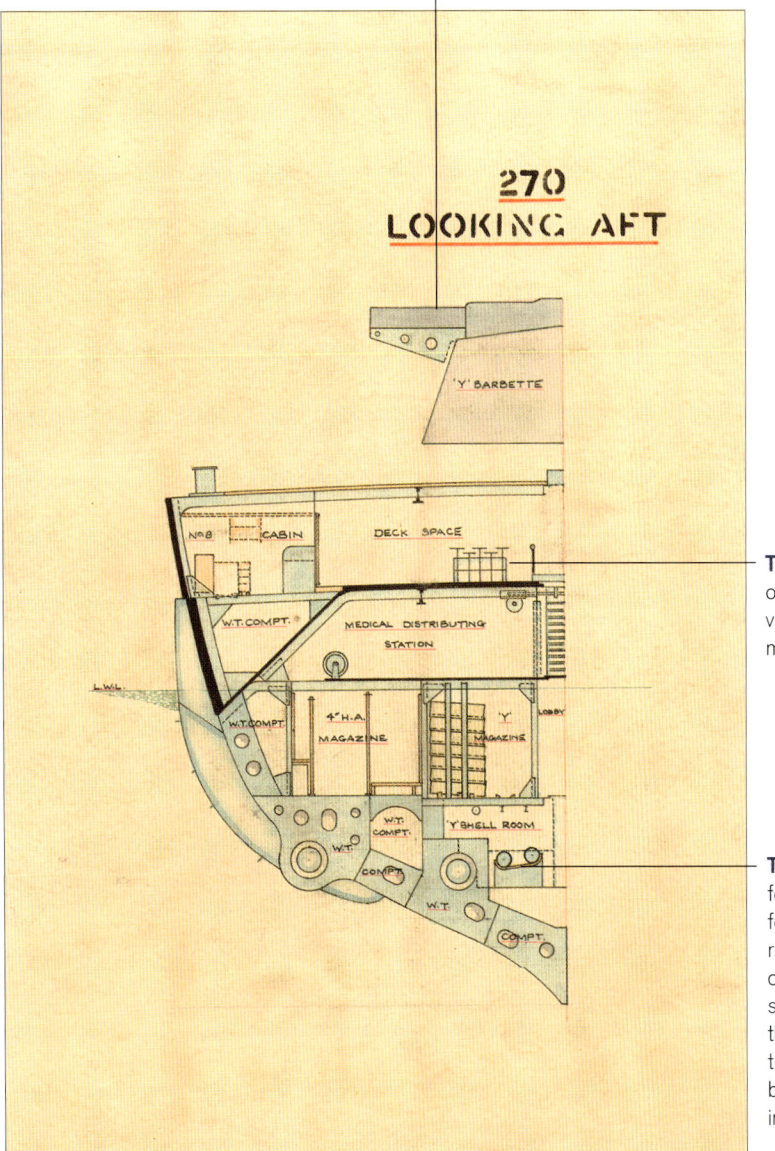

The 30ft rangefinder, which replaced the 15ft rangefinder on the roof of 'Y' turret during the ship's 1918–21 refit, required these extensions to the rangefinder housing together with the support brackets fitted on their underside. Note that there was not a gap between the bracket and the turret wall – that shown here seems to result from the fact that the rangefinder bracket is about 3ft aft of the point at which Station 270 cuts through the turret.

The hand-wheels were used to remotely open or close, via rod gearing, distant valves in the areas below – principally the magazine flood valves.

The sloping chute served as a transfer point for 15in shell brought aft from the bins in the forward part of the magazine using a lifting grab run on an overhead rail. The shell was lowered onto the chute, rolled sideways, picked up by a second grab and overhead rail, for transport to the central hoist. The whole arrangement for transfer and lift was powered by hydraulic rams but hand-operated winches were also provided in case of power failure.

100 ENLARGED PROFILE AND SECTIONS, AS FITTED 1936

STATIONS 270 TO 258

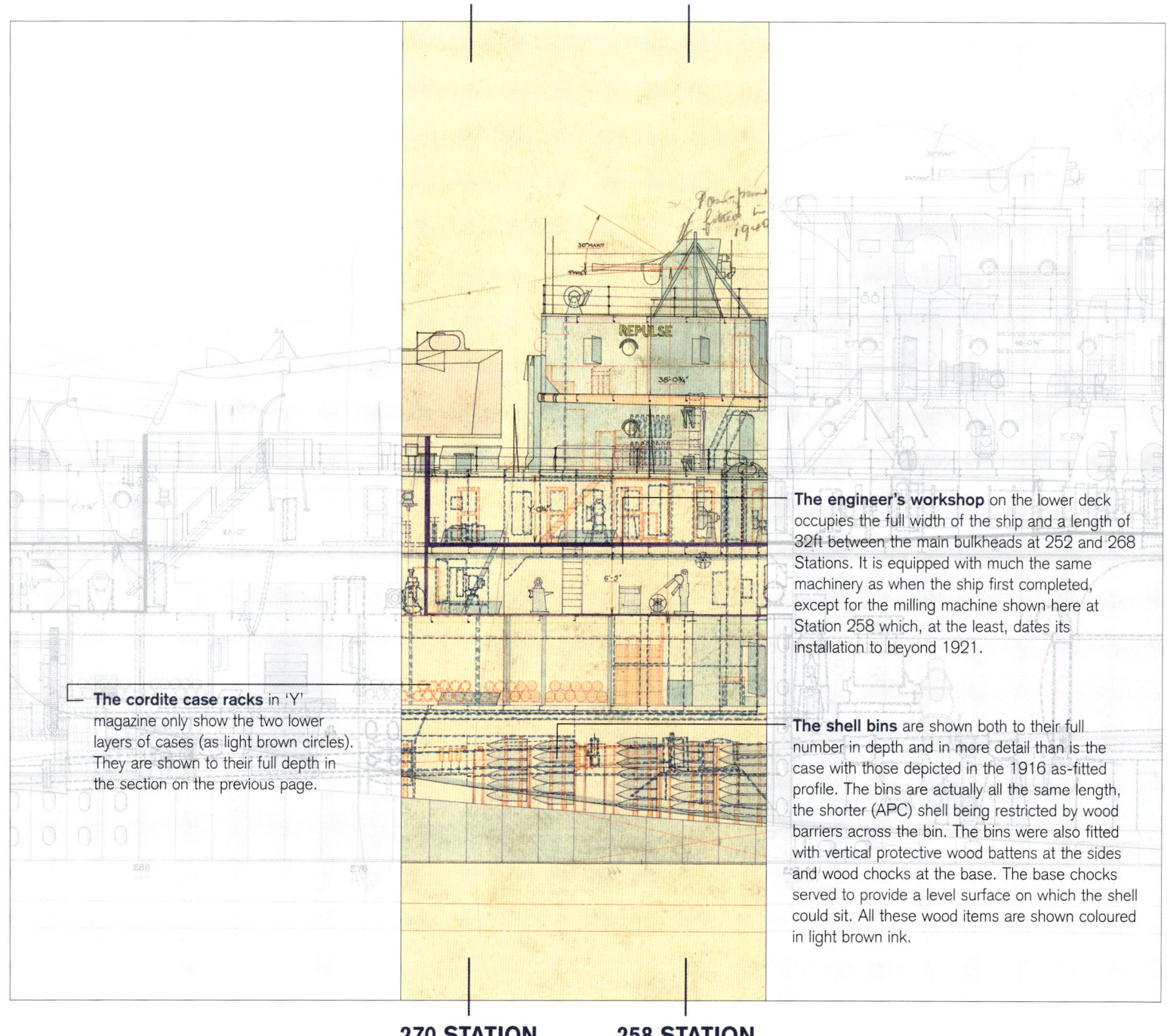

The engineer's workshop on the lower deck occupies the full width of the ship and a length of 32ft between the main bulkheads at 252 and 268 Stations. It is equipped with much the same machinery as when the ship first completed, except for the milling machine shown here at Station 258 which, at the least, dates its installation to beyond 1921.

The cordite case racks in 'Y' magazine only show the two lower layers of cases (as light brown circles). They are shown to their full depth in the section on the previous page.

The shell bins are shown both to their full number in depth and in more detail than is the case with those depicted in the 1916 as-fitted profile. The bins are actually all the same length, the shorter (APC) shell being restricted by wood barriers across the bin. The bins were also fitted with vertical protective wood battens at the sides and wood chocks at the base. The base chocks served to provide a level surface on which the shell could sit. All these wood items are shown coloured in light brown ink.

270 STATION   **258 STATION**

SECTION AT STATION 258, STARBOARD SIDE, LOOKING AFT

The thick line across the flat of the main deck represents the 3¾in NC armour fitted over the magazines from 'Y' barbette to the after bulkhead of the condenser room during modernisation. This was fitted on top of 2in (1in+1in) of the original HT plating, the top 1in layer having been removed. The slope of the main deck retained its existing protection of 4in (1in+1in+2in) HT plating as did the lower deck over the crown of the magazine – 2in HT (1in+1in) to a point 8ft outboard of the longitudinal bulkheads of 'Y' magazine.

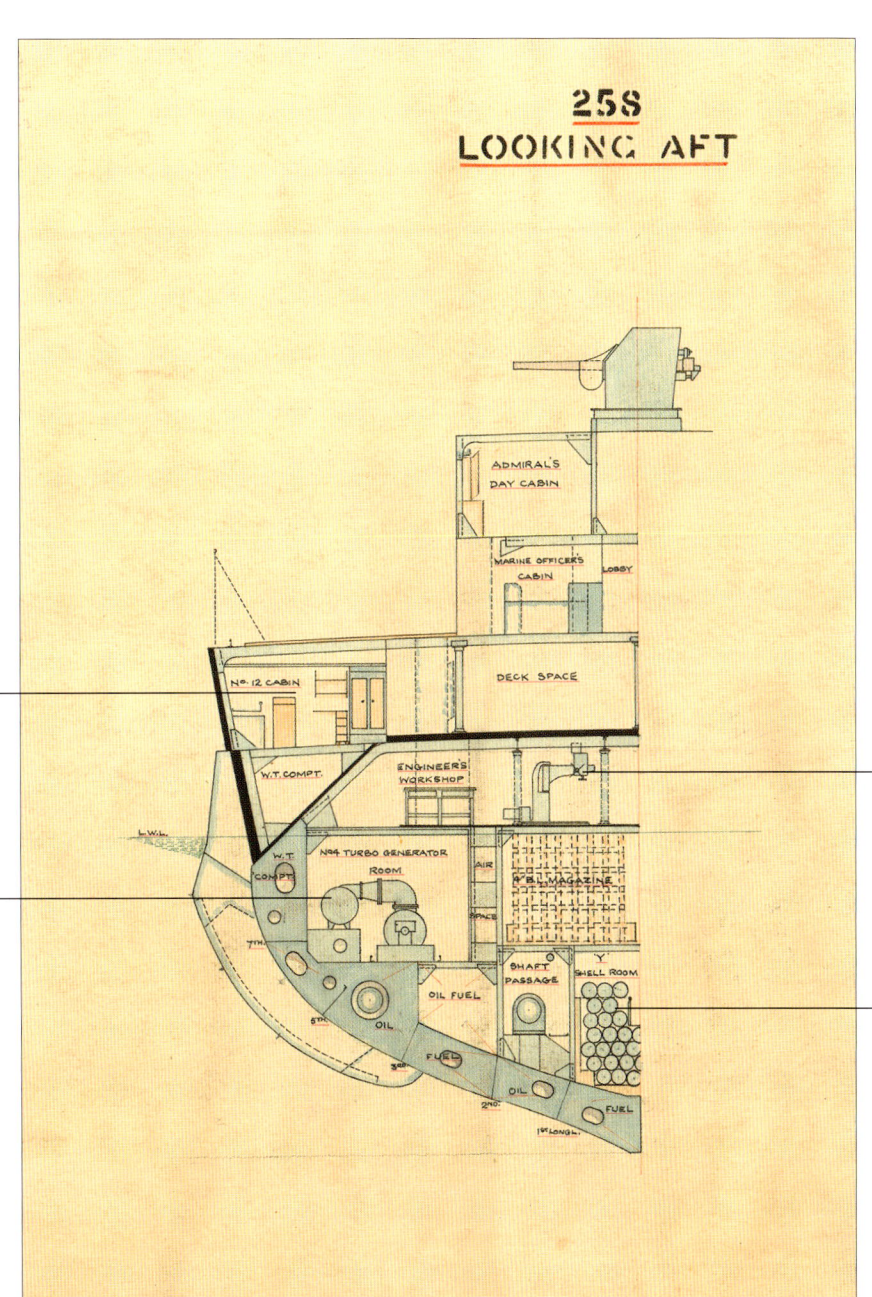

No 12 cabin shows similar furniture to that already described on previous pages but does add a rather neat front view of a typical wardrobe.

No 4 turbo generator room is misnamed since there were not four turbo generators. It is more accurately given as No 4 dynamo room in the plan view of the platform deck. The turbo generator is on the right and its condenser on the left.

The engineer's workshop provides a profile view of the ship's radial drilling machine and, to starboard, a workbench with two drawers.

'Y' shell room showing the full depth of shell stowage and the wooden battens and chocks that supported them. Note that the bins run under the raised walkway down the centre of the shell room.

STATIONS 258 TO 249

The *Repulse* was fitted with a third Mk VI 8-barrel pom-pom mounting at Rosyth in October 1941. It was fitted in place of the triple 4in mounting on the flying deck. This fact is noted in pencil on the profile but this has arrows pointing to both the correct position and to the lower triple 4in mounting on the shelter deck. This could indicate a change of mind or a misunderstanding – the latter seems the more likely.

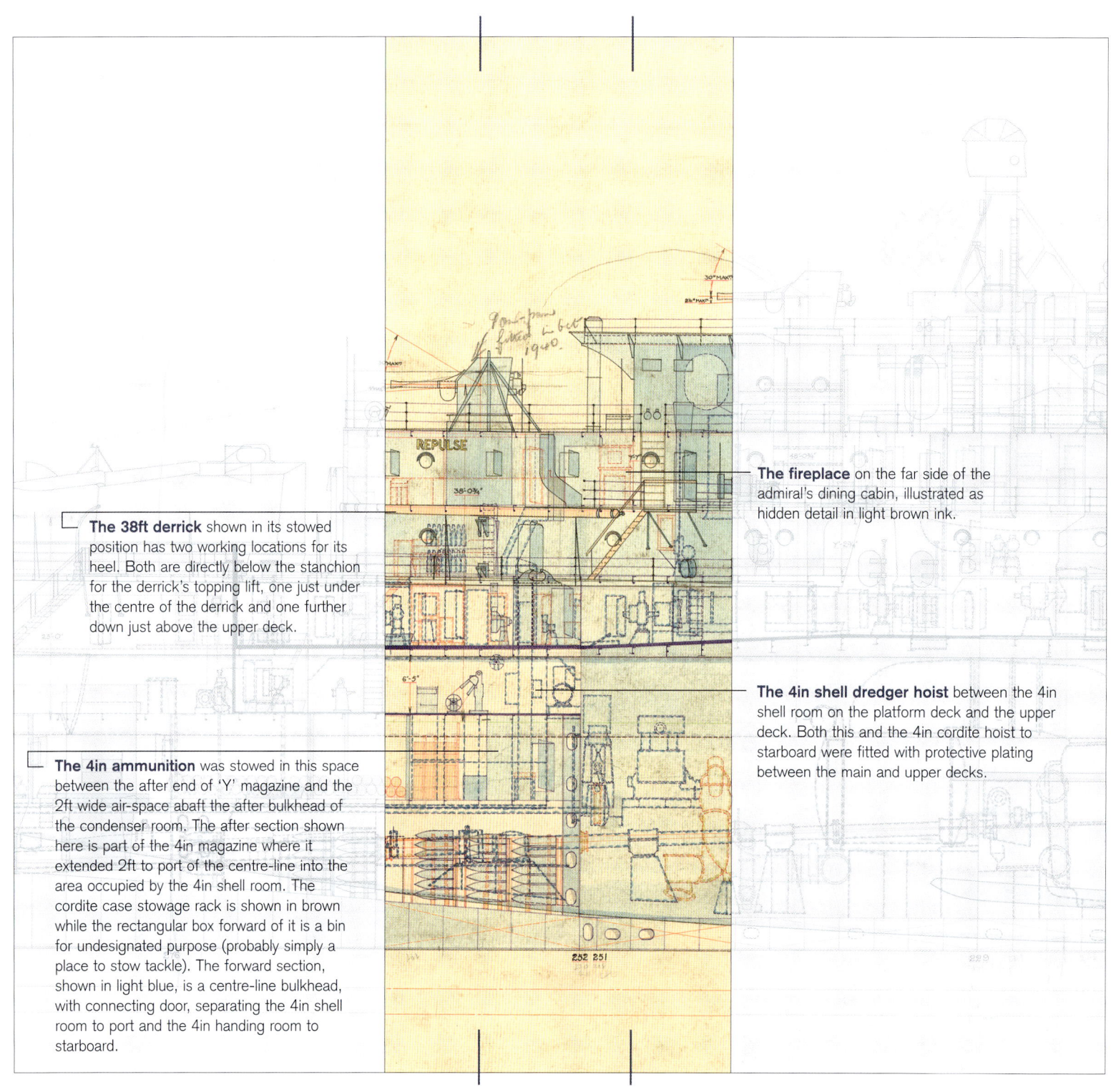

The 38ft derrick shown in its stowed position has two working locations for its heel. Both are directly below the stanchion for the derrick's topping lift, one just under the centre of the derrick and one further down just above the upper deck.

The 4in ammunition was stowed in this space between the after end of 'Y' magazine and the 2ft wide air-space abaft the after bulkhead of the condenser room. The after section shown here is part of the 4in magazine where it extended 2ft to port of the centre-line into the area occupied by the 4in shell room. The cordite case stowage rack is shown in brown while the rectangular box forward of it is a bin for undesignated purpose (probably simply a place to stow tackle). The forward section, shown in light blue, is a centre-line bulkhead, with connecting door, separating the 4in shell room to port and the 4in handing room to starboard.

The fireplace on the far side of the admiral's dining cabin, illustrated as hidden detail in light brown ink.

The 4in shell dredger hoist between the 4in shell room on the platform deck and the upper deck. Both this and the 4in cordite hoist to starboard were fitted with protective plating between the main and upper decks.

258 STATION   249 STATION

STATIONS 258 TO 249

SECTION AT STATION 249, STARBOARD SIDE, LOOKING AFT

Section at after end of starboard condenser room showing one of its three evaporators and the starboard steering engine mounted on the after bulkhead together with the cross-connecting shaft that linked it to the alternative port steering engine via a changeover clutch.

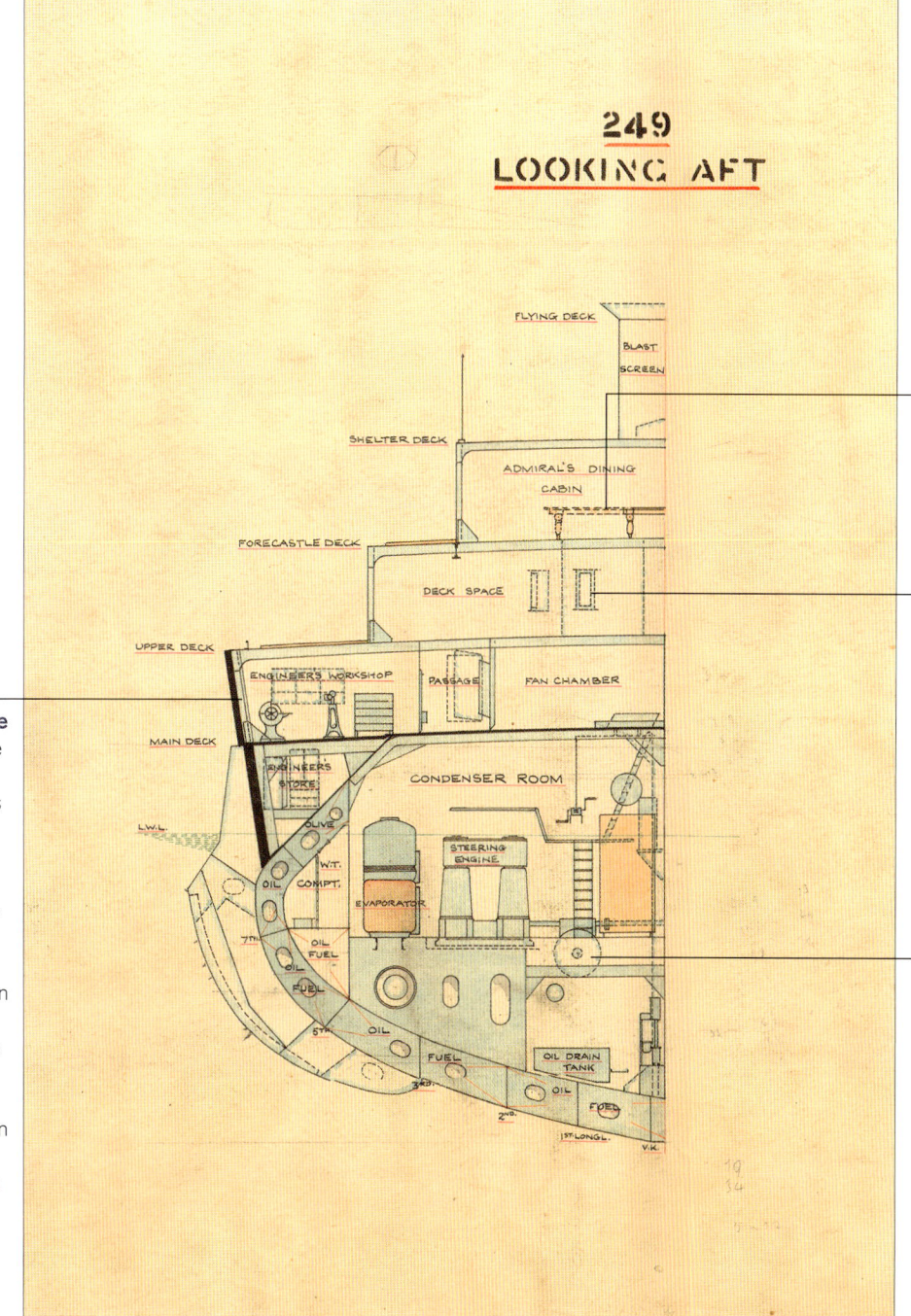

Framing behind 6in side armour. The fitting of the 6in side armour between the main and upper decks during the 1918–21 refit included the stiffening of the original framing. No record of the detail of this additional support has been located but the second line shown here on the inboard side of this and other frames over the length of the 6in armour, indicate that they were at least made wider (from 6in to c9in). The additions would certainly have been flanged in some way on their inner edges.

The admiral's dining cabin shows only the dining table but does add the detail of how much the table could be extended. It could be extended by the same amount on the port side giving an overall length of about 20ft.

The flash-tight scuttles in the after side of the 4in cordite handing lobby are represented by these rectangles (see page 140).

The worm and worm wheel driven by the steering engines turned the steering gear drive through 90°.

ENLARGED PROFILE AND SECTIONS, AS FITTED 1936

STATIONS 249 TO 227

This section of the profile covers the length of the condenser room. Colour shading is employed to identify some specific areas on the profile drawing. For example, light blue indicates the area of the centre-line bulkhead in the condenser and engine rooms. Note that the machinery shown is on the port side, beyond the bulkhead and therefore shown as hidden detail by dashed lines. The same colour is used for the entire superstructure with slightly darker shades employed to identify such items vent trunks and fittings which overlap the base colour.

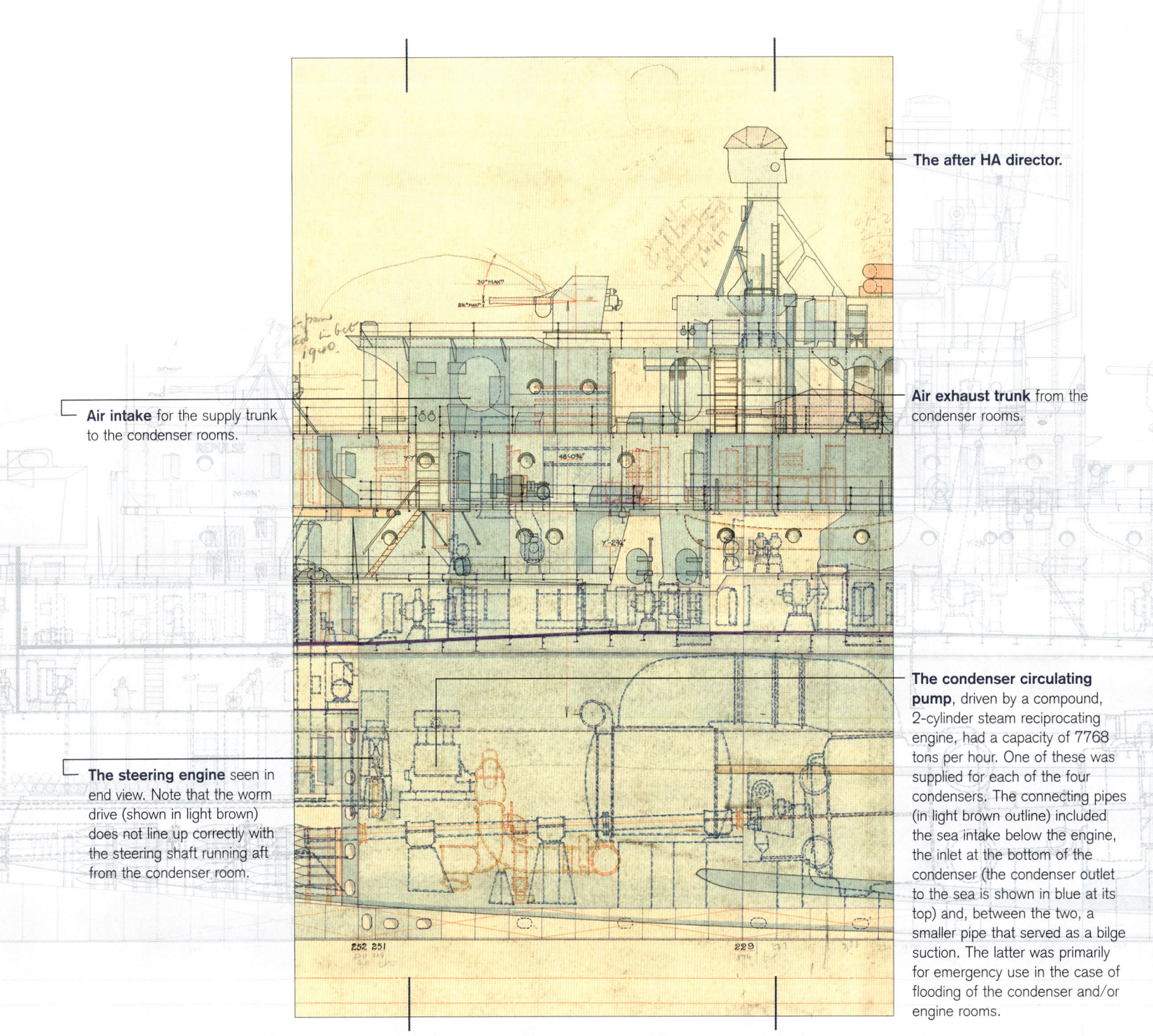

The after HA director.

Air intake for the supply trunk to the condenser rooms.

Air exhaust trunk from the condenser rooms.

The steering engine seen in end view. Note that the worm drive (shown in light brown) does not line up correctly with the steering shaft running aft from the condenser room.

The condenser circulating pump, driven by a compound, 2-cylinder steam reciprocating engine, had a capacity of 7768 tons per hour. One of these was supplied for each of the four condensers. The connecting pipes (in light brown outline) included the sea intake below the engine, the inlet at the bottom of the condenser (the condenser outlet to the sea is shown in blue at its top) and, between the two, a smaller pipe that served as a bilge suction. The latter was primarily for emergency use in the case of flooding of the condenser and/or engine rooms.

249 STATION   **227 STATION**

SECTION AT STATION 227, STARBOARD SIDE, LOOKING AFT

The armour added to the flat of the main deck over the engine and condenser rooms during modernisation consisted of 2½in NC replacing the two upper layers of 1in HT (the lower 1in HT layer remained). In addition, 3½in NC armour was fitted horizontally between the tops of the 9in side armour and the top of the slope of the deck. Note that the raised section at the top of the slope in this section is due to the local rise of the main deck above the engine rooms.

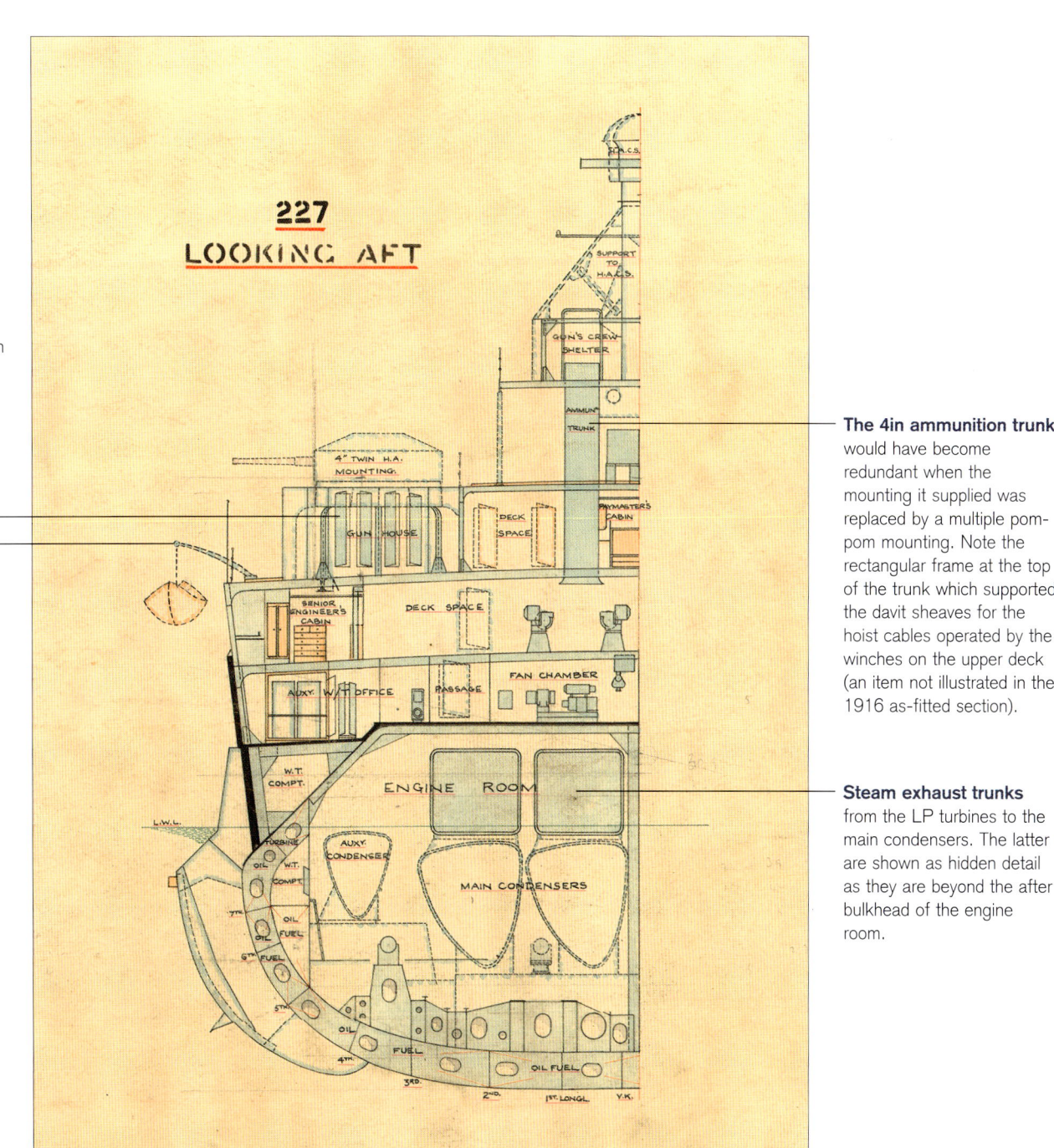

Access doors to the 4in ready-use ammunition lockers for the twin 4in BD mounting.

Harbour davits for a 27ft whaler.

The 4in ammunition trunk would have become redundant when the mounting it supplied was replaced by a multiple pom-pom mounting. Note the rectangular frame at the top of the trunk which supported the davit sheaves for the hoist cables operated by the winches on the upper deck (an item not illustrated in the 1916 as-fitted section).

Steam exhaust trunks from the LP turbines to the main condensers. The latter are shown as hidden detail as they are beyond the after bulkhead of the engine room.

106

STATIONS 227 TO 198

This section of the profile covers the length of the engine rooms. The turbines shown beyond the centreline bulkhead are those for the port inner shaft – the HP ahead at the forward end and the combined LP ahead and astern at the after end. The main steam pipe runs from the forward bulkhead of the engine room to the top of the HP turbine. The machine below the steam pipe is one of the ship's air pumps which extracted air (to maintain vacuum) and water (for transfer to the feed tanks) from the condensers.

An anemometer (port) and wind vane (starboard) fitted on poles fixed to the upper sides of the D/F office.

The stove pipe from the admiral's galley on the shelter deck runs up the starboard side of the mainmast to a point just below the fid platform – approximately 48ft above where it started.

The outlet of the engine room exhaust vent trunk.

The inlet of the engine room supply vent trunk.

The wood fender fitted along the side of the bulge is indicated by this horizontal, light brown stripe

227 STATION

198 STATION

SECTION AT STATION 198, STARBOARD SIDE, LOOKING AFT

The *Repulse* was the first ship to be fitted with a fixed cross-deck catapult. Built by McTaggart Scott, it could launch aircraft to port or starboard, via a telescopic ram powered by a cordite charge. The force generated was utilised to drive a cable and pulley arrangement to transmit the required acceleration to the aircraft launching trolley. Note that deeper transverse beams have been added under the upper deck to support the additional weight of the catapult machinery and that it was intended that the aircraft, when stowed on the catapult, should face fore-and-aft (with wings folded) when at sea and athwartships when in harbour.

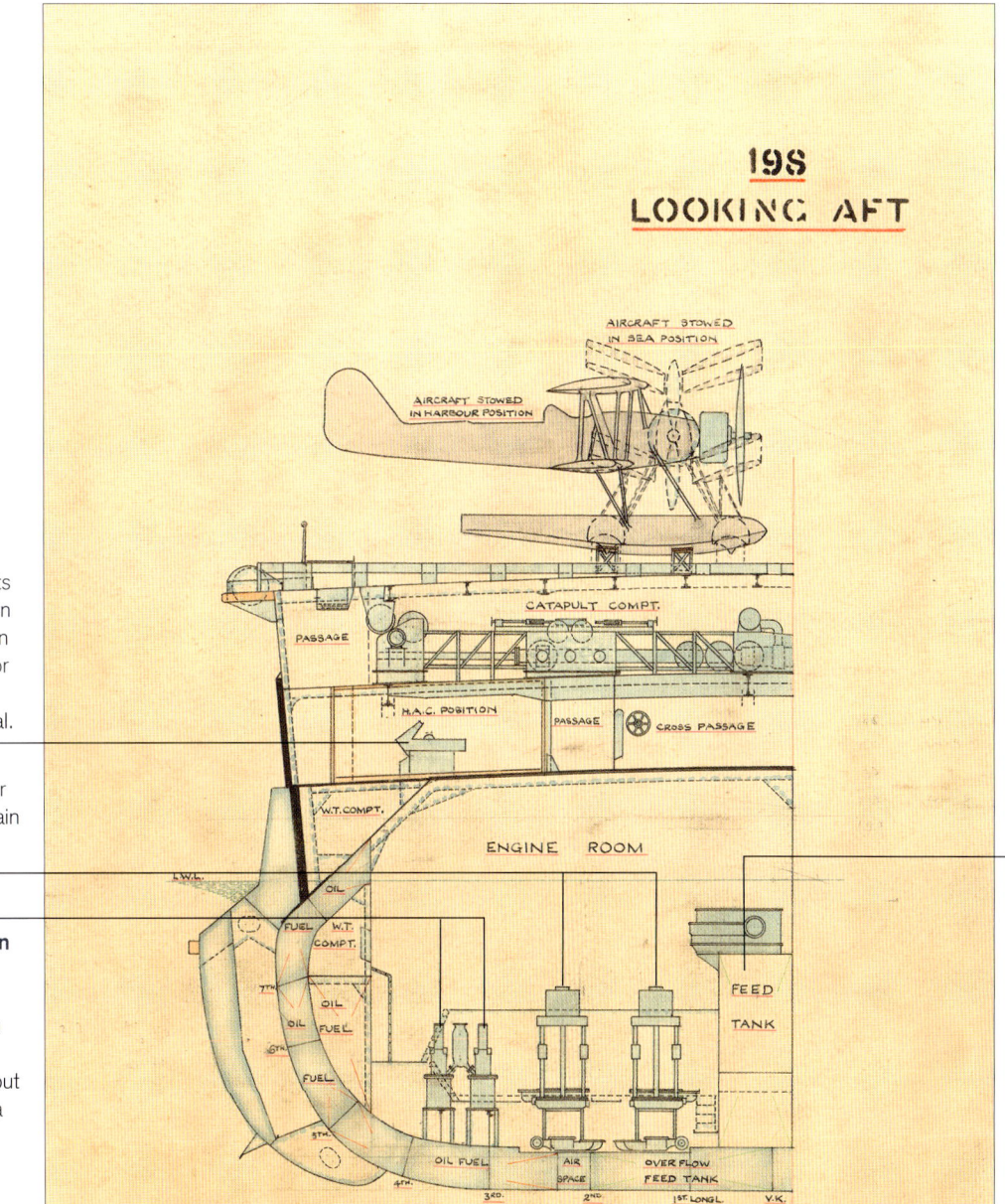

The after HACP with its HACS Mk I* table shown but little else. The brown edging to the walls, floor and deck-head indicate sound insulation material.

The two air pumps for the starboard pair of main condensers.

Two forced lubrication pumps. The item between them and connected to both is an air vessel intended to smooth the pumps output (liable to oscillate with a reciprocating pump).

The feed tank stored distilled water for the boilers. The overflow tank in the double bottom below the feed tank was provided to collect any overflow from the main tank since the boiler water was a valuable commodity that could only be replaced at sea from the distillation plant.

108   ENLARGED PROFILE AND SECTIONS, AS FITTED 1936

STATIONS 198 TO 165

The changes to this area of the ship's profile resulted in substantial alteration to her overall appearance despite the fact that the areas from the mainmast aft and from the fore funnel to the stem showed very limited modification. The modification that made the most impact was the installation of the new aircraft arrangements, which required the removal of a little over 50ft of the shelter deck, to clear the forecastle deck for the installation of the catapult, and the addition of hangars abreast the after funnel. The impact of the latter was enhanced by the added height effect of the cranes and boats fitted above them and the extension of the roof forward to join the CT platform, the whole giving an impression of a large central block which was in fact a relatively open superstructure. The aircraft shown on the catapult and in the hangar are Blackburn Sharks.

The two 10-ton electrically powered cranes served to handle both the aircraft and the ship's boats. They are shown in their stowed position resting on crutches fitted at the ends of the extension to the boat deck that overhangs the catapult deck and, in dashed line, in their operating position. When stowed, the jib of the port crane crosses above that of the starboard crane, the crutches being arranged to suit. Note that the pedestal, around which the crane rotated, extends down to the forecastle deck.

The vent trunk intakes for 'E' and 'F' boiler rooms fitted inboard of each hangar. The partial cross shading indicates the wire screens over the openings.

The slope marks the division between the funnel hatch and the triangular (in profile) compartment above it which served as one of the engineer's stores.

The armour doors for the midship pair of 21in AW torpedo tubes. Note that the top edge of the 6in side armour has been lowered locally by about 18in to clear the doors (also applies in the case of the after pairs of tubes).

198 STATION   **165 STATION**

STATIONS 198 TO 165

SECTION AT STATION 165, STARBOARD SIDE, LOOKING AFT

The bulges were expected to provide defence against a 500lbs charge, but this obviously decreased fore and aft where the width of the bulge reduced and the inner hull compartments were less defensively arranged. There were also qualifications, since the ideal situation was considered to be with the bulge compartment empty, the oil fuel in the double bottom inboard of the bulge compartment full, and the wing oil fuel tanks empty. It was therefore recommended that the oil in the wing tanks be used as soon as possible while that in the double bottom tanks inboard of the bulge be maintained full for as long as possible. It was also recommended that the other double bottom compartments should be 50 per cent (+/- 25 per cent) full whenever practical. Unlike other ships, *Repulse* was not fitted with water protection compartments to enhance her defence against underwater attack but the wing double bottom oil fuel tanks could be flooded with sea water if the oil in them had been used.

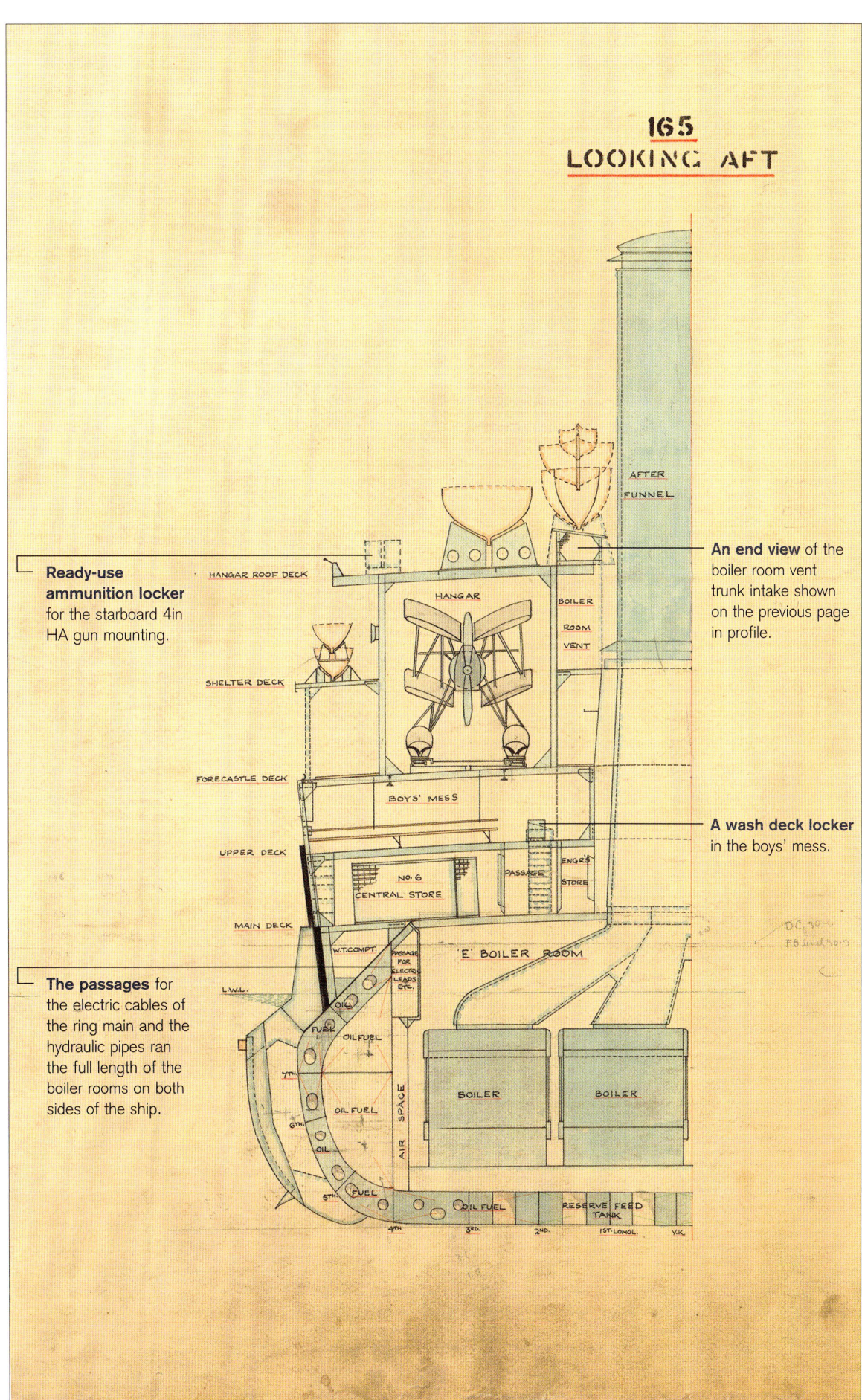

Ready-use ammunition locker for the starboard 4in HA gun mounting.

The passages for the electric cables of the ring main and the hydraulic pipes ran the full length of the boiler rooms on both sides of the ship.

An end view of the boiler room vent trunk intake shown on the previous page in profile.

A wash deck locker in the boys' mess.

STATIONS 165 TO 115

During modernisation the *Repulse* was re-equipped with a new searchlight outfit of six 36in searchlights, stabilized in both azimuth and elevation. These could be controlled remotely, by Evershed transmitters, from the upper bridge or locally. The forward pair was fitted on platforms at the sides of, and just below, the lower bridge; the second pair on a new platform across the fore side of the second funnel; the after pair on the mainmast in much the same location as those they replaced. At the same time the 24in signalling projectors were replaced by four 18in projectors in the forward wings of the signal deck (the after pair on raised platforms) and a 10in signalling projector on each side of the signal deck abreast the funnel.

The 12ft rangefinders on the upper bridge and the 9ft rangefinders on the wings of the lower bridge remained in the positions they had occupied since 1926.

The steam pipes originally fitted on the forward side of the funnel were rerouted during the ship's modernisation to the after side. The purpose of this change is unknown but it seems likely that when in their original location they were too close to the bridge for comfort.

The ammunition shoot (*sic*) for supplying ammunition to the 4in HA gun from the shelter deck is indicated here by these vertical black lines.

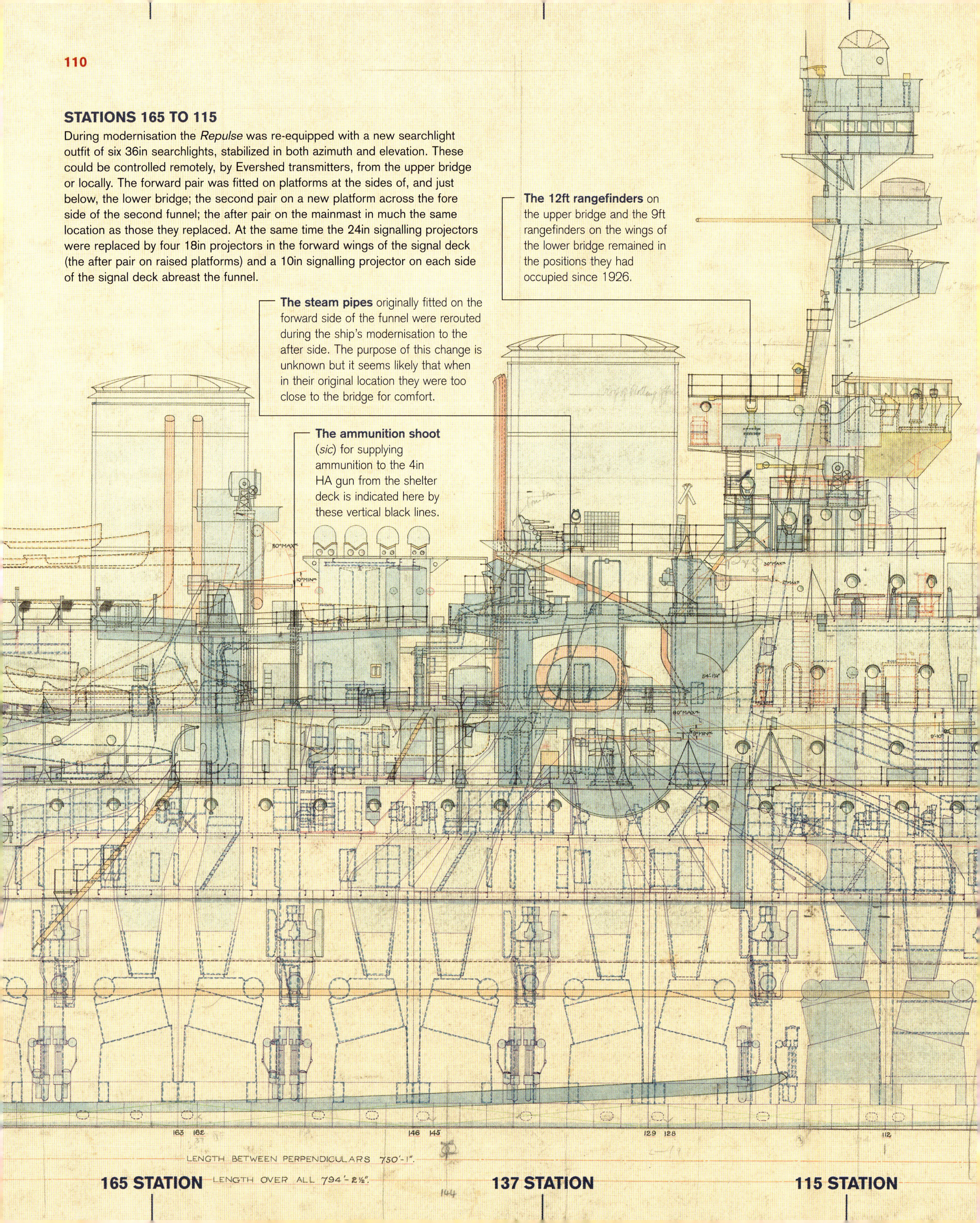

165 STATION LENGTH OVER ALL 794'-2½".

137 STATION

115 STATION

LENGTH BETWEEN PERPENDICULARS 750'-1".

STATIONS 165 TO 115

SECTION AT STATION 137, STARBOARD SIDE, LOOKING AFT

Section at the centre of 'C' boiler room and the after part of the fore funnel showing the starboard group of the close-range AA armament fitted on the CT platform during modernisation – the 8-barrel Mk VI 2pdr pom-pom mounting at the after end of the CT platform and the quad 0.5in Mk II* mounting on an extension to the flag deck.

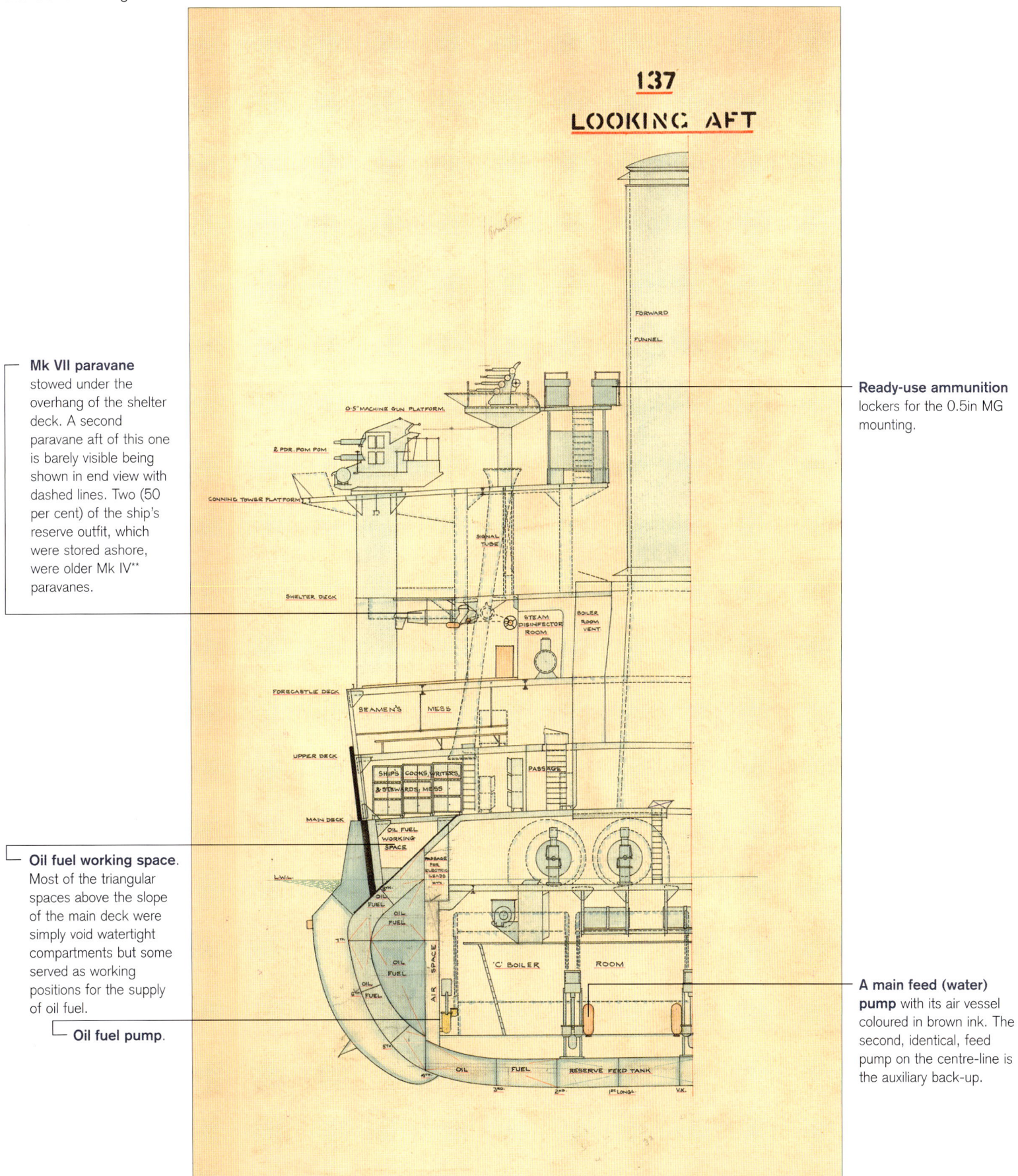

Mk VII paravane stowed under the overhang of the shelter deck. A second paravane aft of this one is barely visible being shown in end view with dashed lines. Two (50 per cent) of the ship's reserve outfit, which were stored ashore, were older Mk IV** paravanes.

Oil fuel working space. Most of the triangular spaces above the slope of the main deck were simply void watertight compartments but some served as working positions for the supply of oil fuel.

Oil fuel pump.

Ready-use ammunition lockers for the 0.5in MG mounting.

A main feed (water) pump with its air vessel coloured in brown ink. The second, identical, feed pump on the centre-line is the auxiliary back-up.

SECTION AT STATION 115, STARBOARD SIDE, LOOKING FORWARD

A section down the centre of the foremast which cuts through the boiler uptakes for both 'A' boiler room (between the upper and forecastle decks) and that for 'B' boiler room below the upper deck.

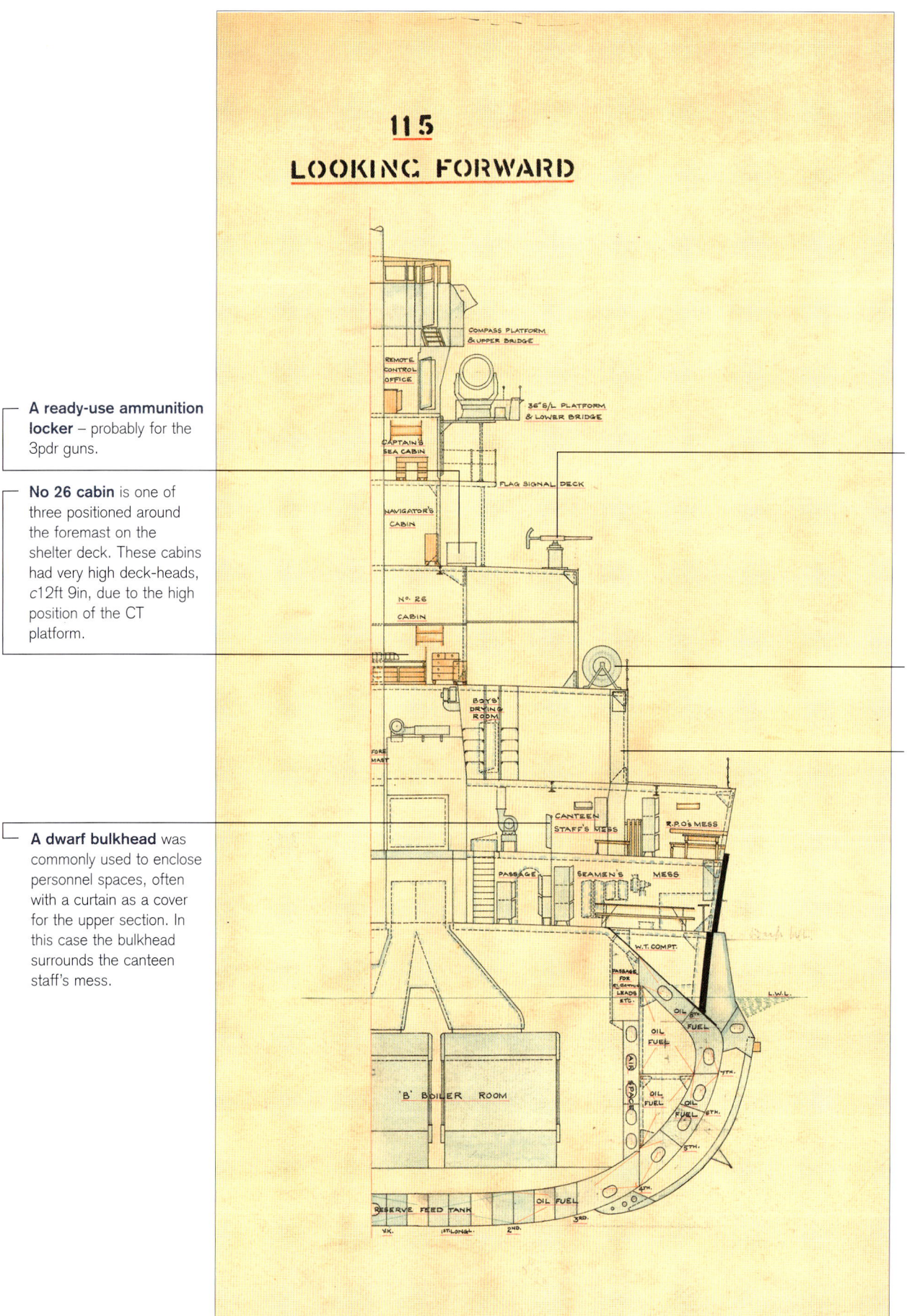

- **A ready-use ammunition locker** – probably for the 3pdr guns.

- **No 26 cabin** is one of three positioned around the foremast on the shelter deck. These cabins had very high deck-heads, c12ft 9in, due to the high position of the CT platform.

- **A dwarf bulkhead** was commonly used to enclose personnel spaces, often with a curtain as a cover for the upper section. In this case the bulkhead surrounds the canteen staff's mess.

- **One of the ship's four Hotchkiss 3pdr saluting guns.** One of the longest serving guns in the RN since it was adopted as an anti-torpedo boat weapon in the 1880s and later became the Navy's standard saluting gun, in which role served for the following century.

- **A hawser reel** fitted on the shelter deck.

- **This vent trunk** supplied air to the seamen's mess on the main deck. It appears to be misidentified as a 'diving pump' on the plan view of the forecastle deck.

STATIONS 115 TO 95

The initial sea trials of *Repulse* on 31 January 1936 revealed problems for personnel on the open compass platform created by strong air-currents and funnel smoke. The problem was so severe that the platform's suitability as a conning position in anything but calm weather was seriously questioned. The platform was therefore fitted with a wood roof, windows and rear screens with doors by Portsmouth dockyard which, during trials in March 1936, proved completely successful. The alterations were made on the recommendation of officers who had served in the ship during 1929–32 at which time she had a similar arrangement that had been installed by the ship's staff.

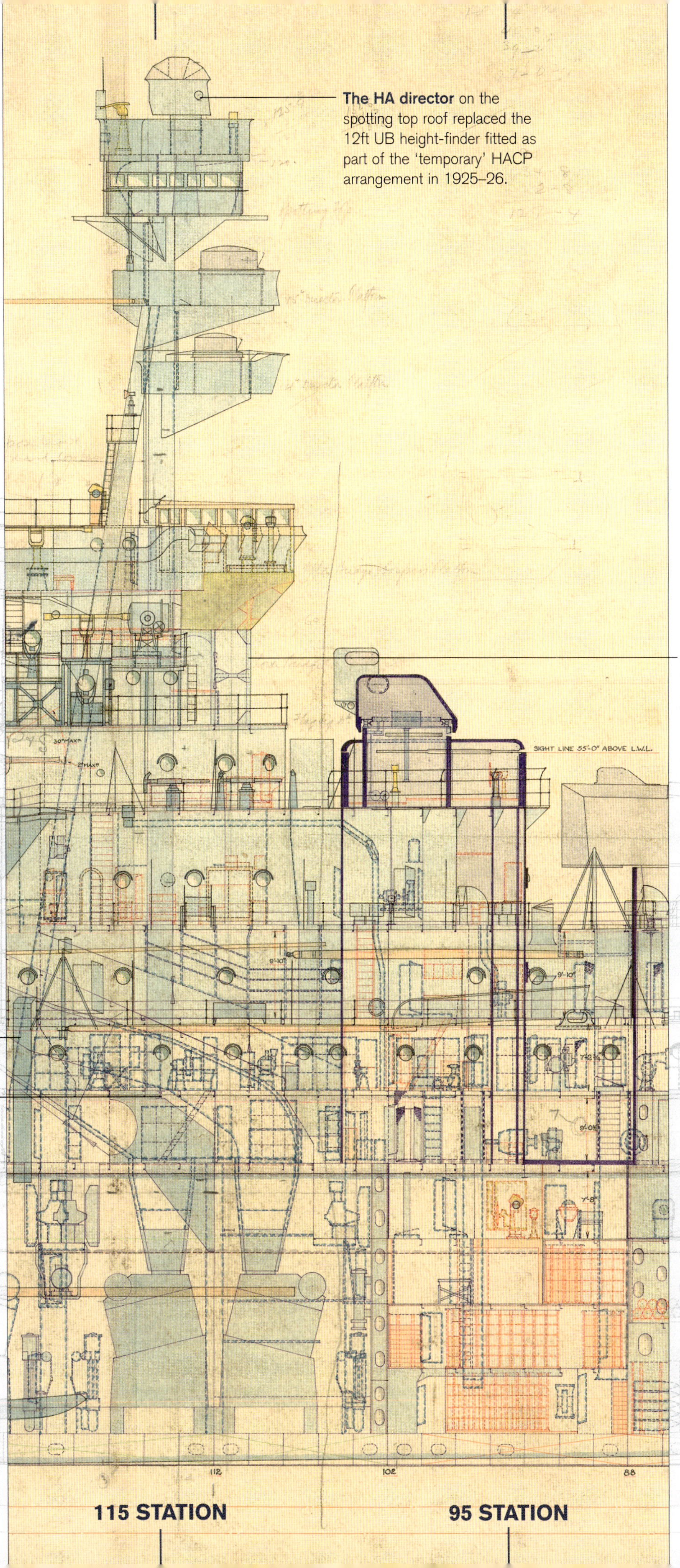

The HA director on the spotting top roof replaced the 12ft UB height-finder fitted as part of the 'temporary' HACP arrangement in 1925–26.

Additional support has been fitted to the compass platform and although the support beams are visible in the drawing, the whole, including that under the compass platform overhang, was plated over. The lower part of this addition was fitted across the fore side of the, now redundant, submarine lookout and both the old and new compartments became storage spaces, both being accessible from the starboard side of the lower bridge. The brown horizontal line in the former submarine lookout is the floor of the compartment.

The refuse shoot [chute]. One was also fitted on the port side.

The heel of the foremast was supported by an intermediate beam fitted across the width of the funnel hatch and the deep brackets shown in blue immediately below.

115 STATION

95 STATION

SECTION AT STATION 95, STARBOARD SIDE, LOOKING FORWARD

The section at Station 90 has changed little from that of 1916 although it has added the steering wheel and engine room telegraph in the CT and a little detail of the furnishings in the CT support; the earlier version was devoid of detail in these respects. The more noticeable changes are the installation of a central receiving office at upper deck level in place of the coding office, which has been moved up one deck into what used to be the intelligence office. There are also changes to the magazine spaces and 15in TS but most of these were carried out during the 1918–21 refit. There were also some changes to the arrangement of the 4in magazines which can be more easily followed by reference to the plan views.

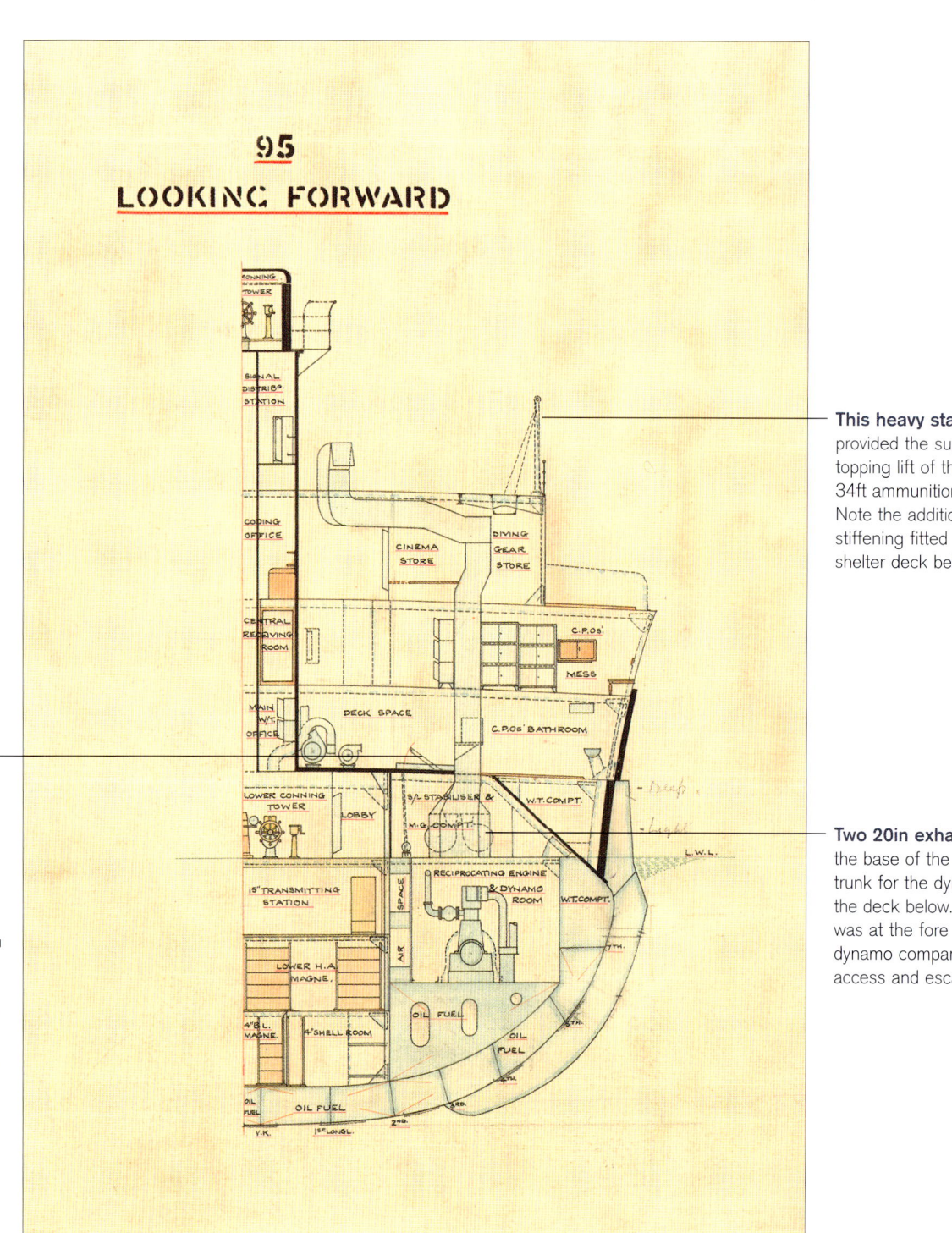

One of the armoured hatches in the main deck. These were added during modernisation to match the material and thickness of the newly fitted NC armour decks. They were fitted flush with the deck and surrounded with a coaming intended to stop water flowing into the hatchway in the case of minor flooding or when decks were washed.

This heavy stanchion provided the support for the topping lift of the forward 34ft ammunition derrick. Note the additional stiffening fitted under the shelter deck below it.

Two 20in exhaust fans at the base of the vent exhaust trunk for the dynamo room on the deck below. Air supply was at the fore end of the dynamo compartment via its access and escape trunk.

STATIONS 95 TO 80

The NC armour fitted on the flat of the main deck from the 3in bulkhead abreast 'A' barbette to the fore bulkhead of 'A' boiler room followed the same arrangement as that provided above the after magazine group (for description see page 101). Apart from the magazines it also covered the lower conning tower and its surrounding compartments and the 15in and 4in transmitting stations. The deck immediately below the base of the armoured support structure of the CT was not armoured. The profile also shows, in thick line, the forward and after 2in HT bulkheads (at Stations 88 and 102, lower to main deck) of those fitted around the lower CT in 1916–17 (see also plan view on page 150). This change was not included in the modified version of the 1916 as-fitted set.

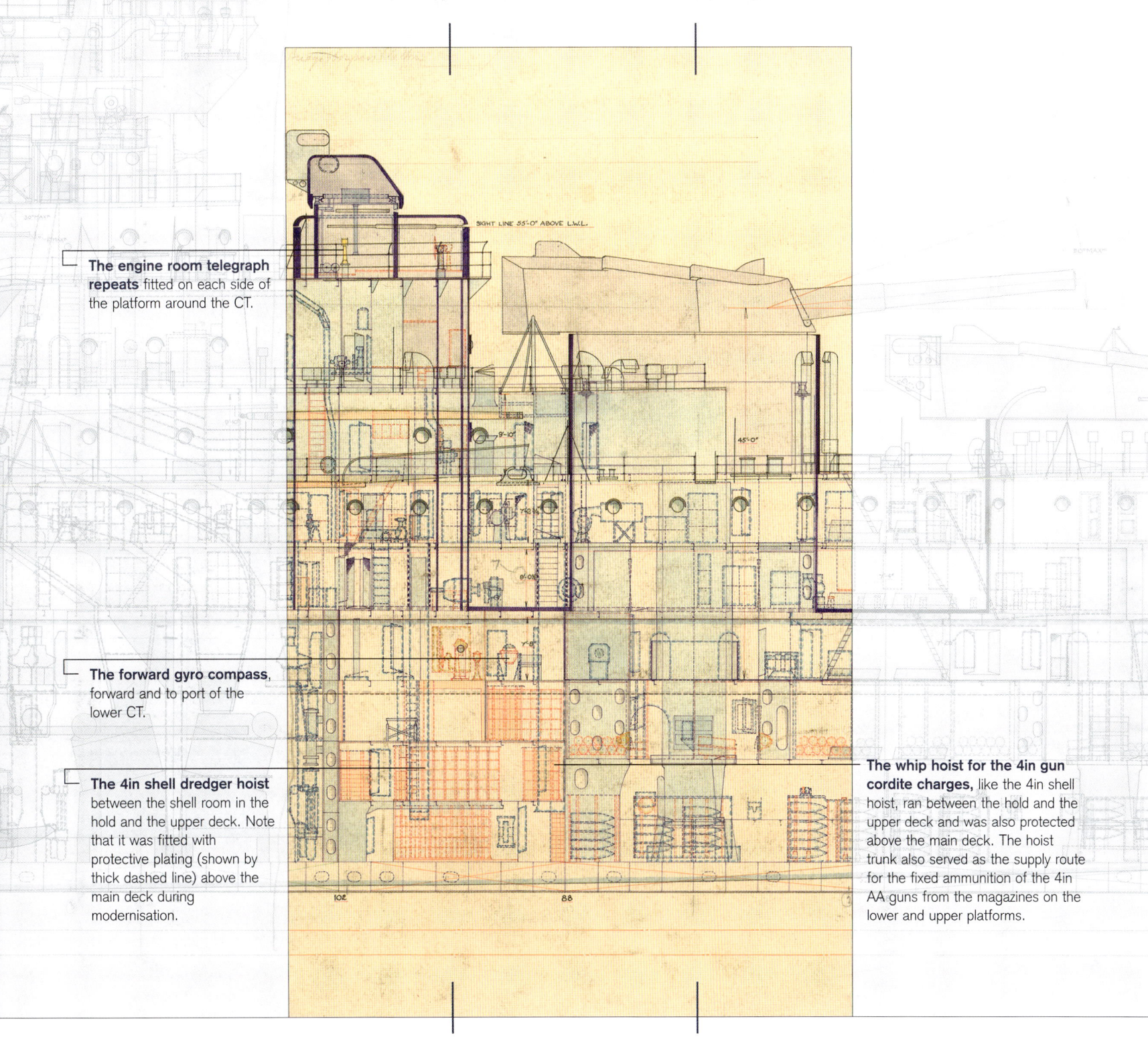

The engine room telegraph repeats fitted on each side of the platform around the CT.

The forward gyro compass, forward and to port of the lower CT.

The 4in shell dredger hoist between the shell room in the hold and the upper deck. Note that it was fitted with protective plating (shown by thick dashed line) above the main deck during modernisation.

The whip hoist for the 4in gun cordite charges, like the 4in shell hoist, ran between the hold and the upper deck and was also protected above the main deck. The hoist trunk also served as the supply route for the fixed ammunition of the 4in AA guns from the magazines on the lower and upper platforms.

95 STATION **80 STATION**

SECTION AT STATION 80, STARBOARD SIDE, LOOKING FORWARD

The lack of any changes of substance to this section through the centre of 'B' barbette compared with those for 1916 leaves little worthy of comment.

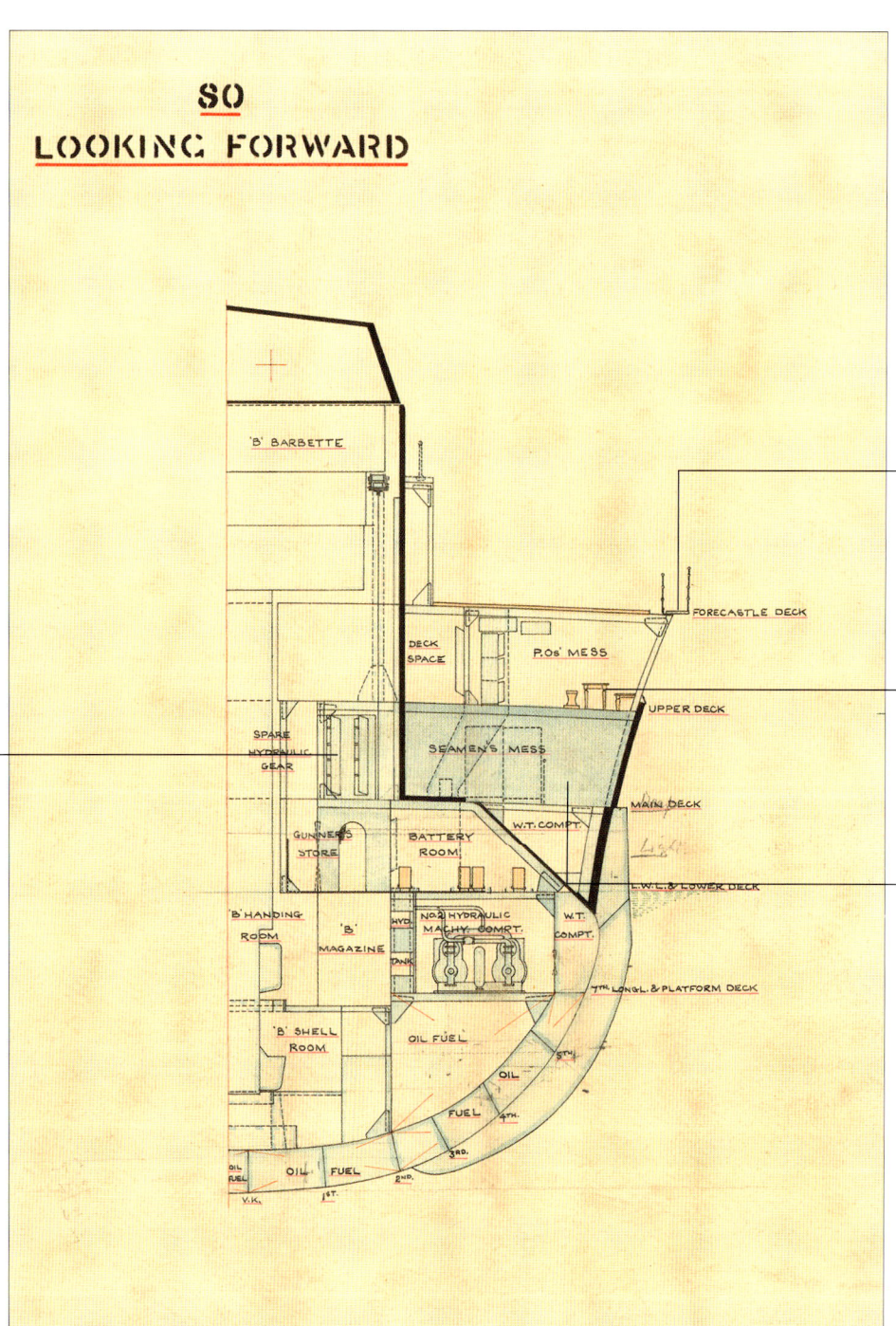

Storage cupboards in the spare hydraulic gear store at the base of 'B' barbette.

The leadsman's platform has been moved about 30ft further forward of its earlier position. This allowed the provision of a shorter platform since the deck edge at this point substantially overlapped the bulge below.

The furniture in the POs' mess has been updated from the mess table and tools originally provided. However, the latter remained the standard provision for lower ranks.

This blue shaded area indicates a transverse bulkhead at Station 80. The seamen's mess is forward of this bulkhead – in the 1916 as-fitted set this is given as the POs' wash place which is actually aft of the bulkhead.

STATIONS 80 TO 66

In 1941 proposals were made to increase the range and power of the 15in gun armament of those ships that had not had their mountings modernised (*ie*, maximum elevation increased to 30° and provision of new projectiles). This was to be achieved by supplying the guns with a limited number (20rpg) of 490lbs supercharges in place of the standard 428lbs charge and more streamlined shell (5/10crh in place of 4crh) which was expected to increase the maximum range by about 3000yds. There was some concern about the additional force of recoil on the ageing structure of the ships, especially in the case of 'B' mounting of *Repulse* but, after test firings in the *Malaya*, it was concluded that the forces involved would be acceptable provided both guns in the turret were not fired together and even then a few such salvoes might be fired without undue risk. The proposed arrangement required alterations in the shell rooms and magazines and the fitting of new flash-tight scuttles for the charges. It was intended that this should be done in *Repulse* in 1942 – in fact it was initially suggested she should be the last of the seven ships involved to be so fitted – but some preliminary work on the shell bins seems to have been carried out during her Aug–Sep 1941 refit. It is certain that she never received supercharges but it is faintly possible she was supplied with new shell given that she was about to be dispatched to the Far East.

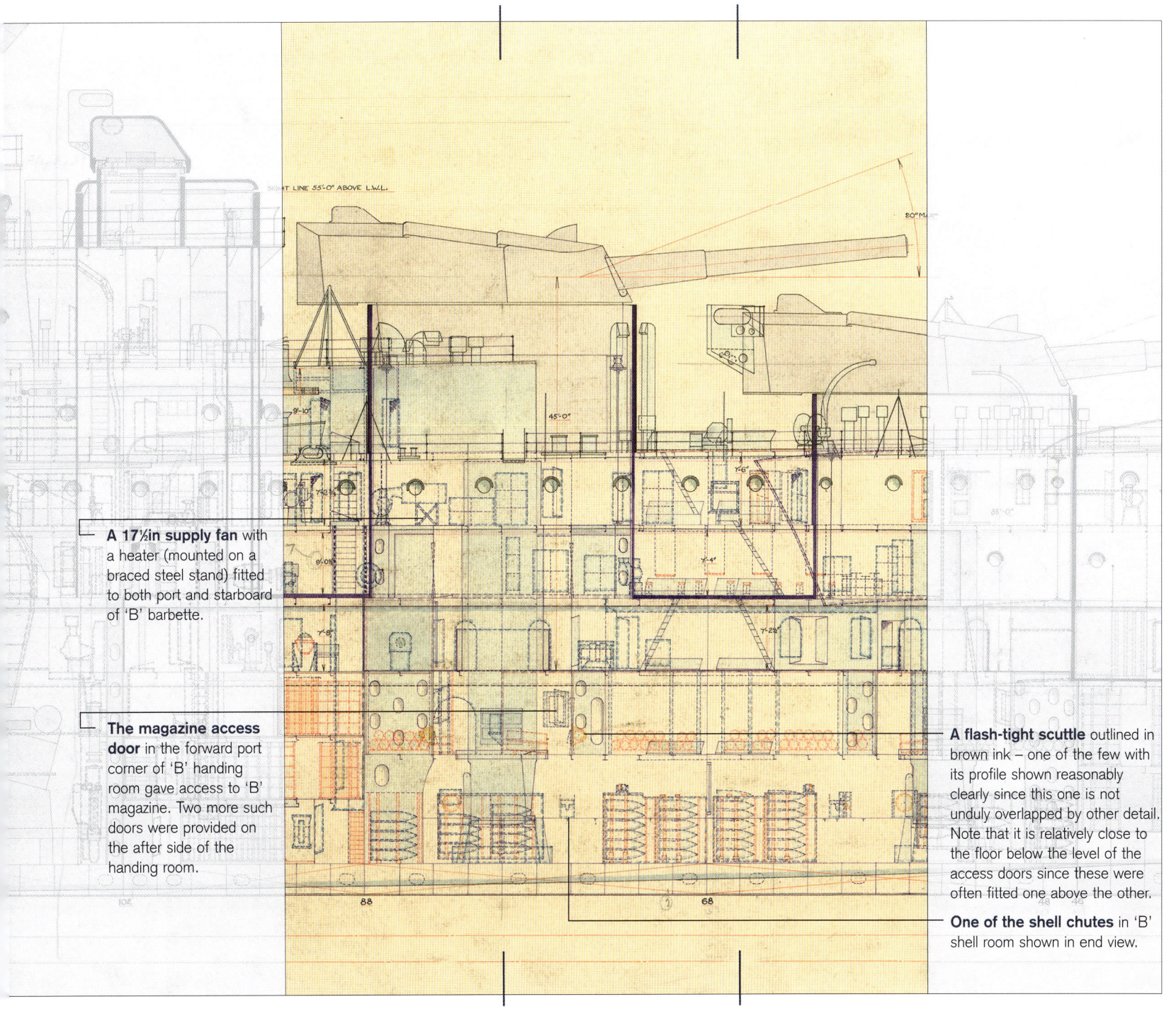

A 17½in supply fan with a heater (mounted on a braced steel stand) fitted to both port and starboard of 'B' barbette.

The magazine access door in the forward port corner of 'B' handing room gave access to 'B' magazine. Two more such doors were provided on the after side of the handing room.

A flash-tight scuttle outlined in brown ink – one of the few with its profile shown reasonably clearly since this one is not unduly overlapped by other detail. Note that it is relatively close to the floor below the level of the access doors since these were often fitted one above the other.

One of the shell chutes in 'B' shell room shown in end view.

80 STATION **66 STATION**

SECTION AT STATION 66, STARBOARD SIDE, LOOKING FORWARD

This Section is taken half way between 'A' and 'B' barbettes. The most noticeable differences between this and the same section in the 1916 as-fitted is that it has added a rear view of 'A' turret and includes the upper and lower pom-pom magazines fitted during the modernisation.

The 30ft FX2 rangefinder on an MG18 mounting was fitted to the rear face of 'A' turret during the ship's 1918–21 refit. The enclosure in the centre was accessed via vertical ladder hung from its underside and a hinged manhole in the right side of the floor.

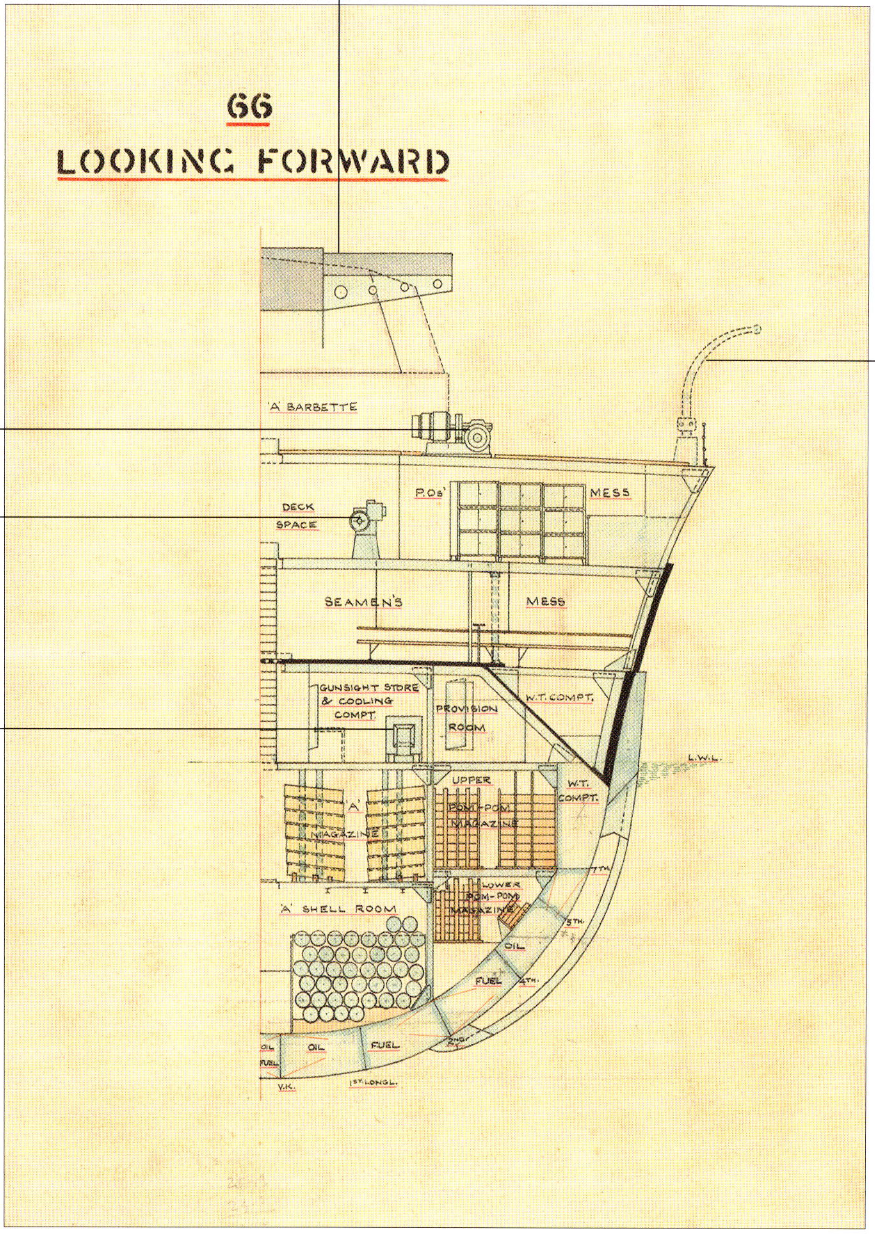

The starboard electric winch provided the power for the hoist whips of both the forward 34ft ammunition derrick and the paravanes.

One of the two paravane derricks fitted on each side of the forecastle deck.

The hoist for the ammunition whips for embarking and disembarking 15in shell and cordite via the series of hatches on the middle line of the ship.

The cooler for 'A' magazine in end view.

STATIONS 66 TO 54

Two things stand out in this profile compared with that of 1916. First, the considerable number of mushroom-top vents surrounding 'A' barbette which, although the majority were also present in the ship when completed, are mostly missing from the earlier profile (but fortunately not the plan view). Second, both profiles omit the side sighting hoods on the turret roofs but not the centre hood. The latter protected the trainer's periscope sights while the, omitted, side hoods covered the periscope sights for the gunlayers. These positions were entirely for local control of the mounting since under director control direct observation of the target from the turrets was not necessary.

The 15in guns were first fitted in the ship in 1916, those in 'A' and 'B' turrets in April and those in 'Y' turret in May. Two of these (the left guns in 'A' and 'B' turrets) were replaced in 1917 presumably due to having developed faults. The entire outfit was replaced during modernisation, the new guns being fitted in January 1935.

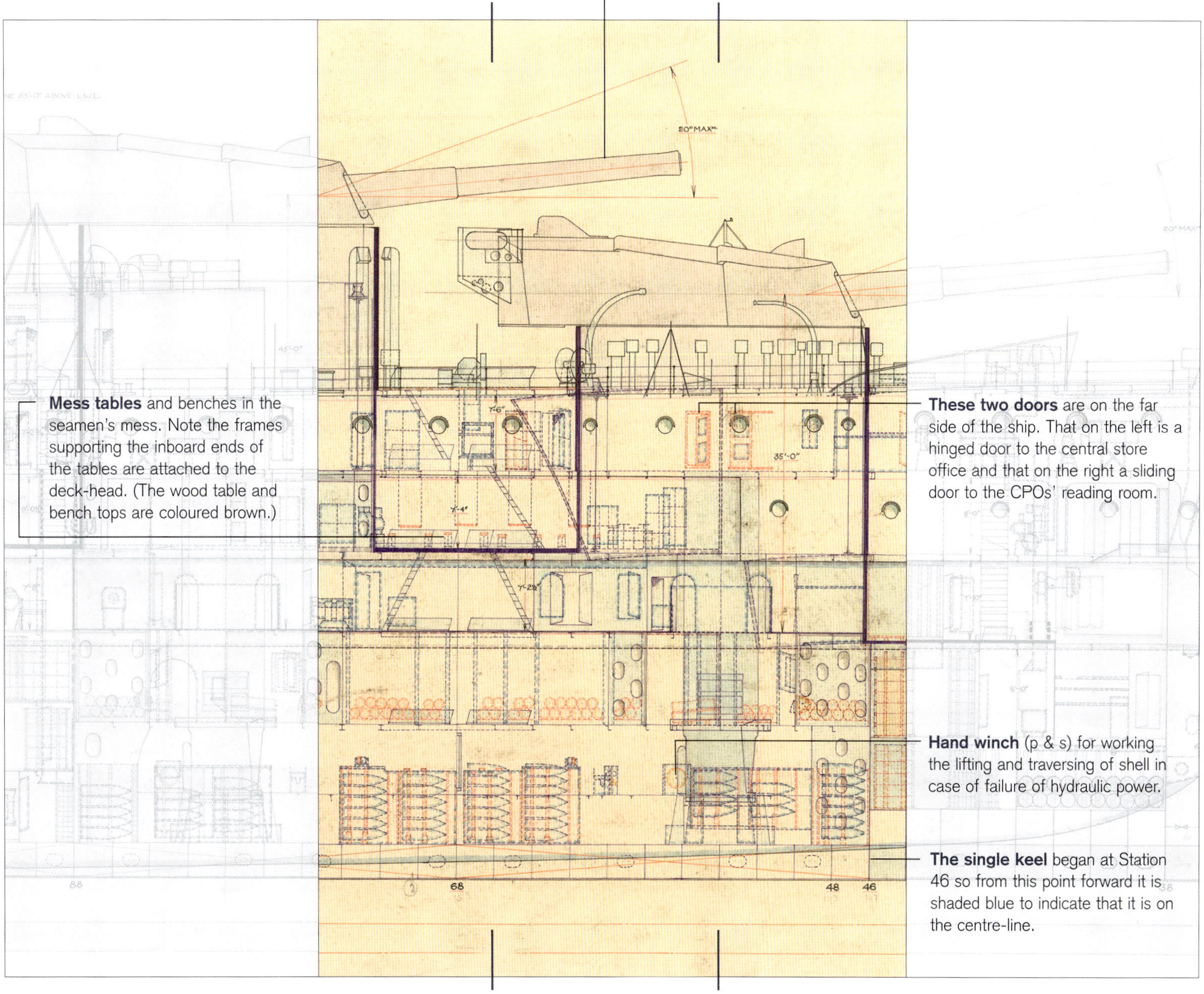

Mess tables and benches in the seamen's mess. Note the frames supporting the inboard ends of the tables are attached to the deck-head. (The wood table and bench tops are coloured brown.)

These two doors are on the far side of the ship. That on the left is a hinged door to the central store office and that on the right a sliding door to the CPOs' reading room.

Hand winch (p & s) for working the lifting and traversing of shell in case of failure of hydraulic power.

The single keel began at Station 46 so from this point forward it is shaded blue to indicate that it is on the centre-line.

66 STATION   **54 STATION**

SECTION AT STATION 54, STARBOARD SIDE, LOOKING FORWARD

This section reflects not how much but how little was done during the modernisation of *Repulse*. Compared with the same section in the 1916 as-fitted it shows only minor changes, no modernising features and some minor variations due to draughtsman's preferences. The limits on the modernisation of *Repulse* were imposed by the financial restrictions of the early 1930s and the fact that these 'large repairs' were merely an attempt to keep old ships as frontline units until such time as new ships could be constructed. The latter were constantly delayed by a series of international naval limitation treaties. Improvements to the battle fleet in the 1920s concentrated on fitting bulges, a necessary precursor to deck armour for reasons of stability and draught (cost limited the provision of both at the same time), and interim measures to improve AA defence (pending the rather slow development of new AA weapons and fire control equipment). The delayed fitting of deck armour began in 1931 with the battleship *Barham* which was followed by *Repulse* and then the battleship *Malaya*. All three gained improved AA defence, both long- and short-range, but retained their original machinery, main armament and primary fire control system. The major modernisations taking place in foreign navies, particularly those of Japan and Italy, initiated a much more extensive reconstruction programme that began with *Warspite* and later included *Renown*, *Queen Elizabeth* and *Valiant*. These were much more substantial and included new machinery and modernisation of the 15in armament and its fire control.

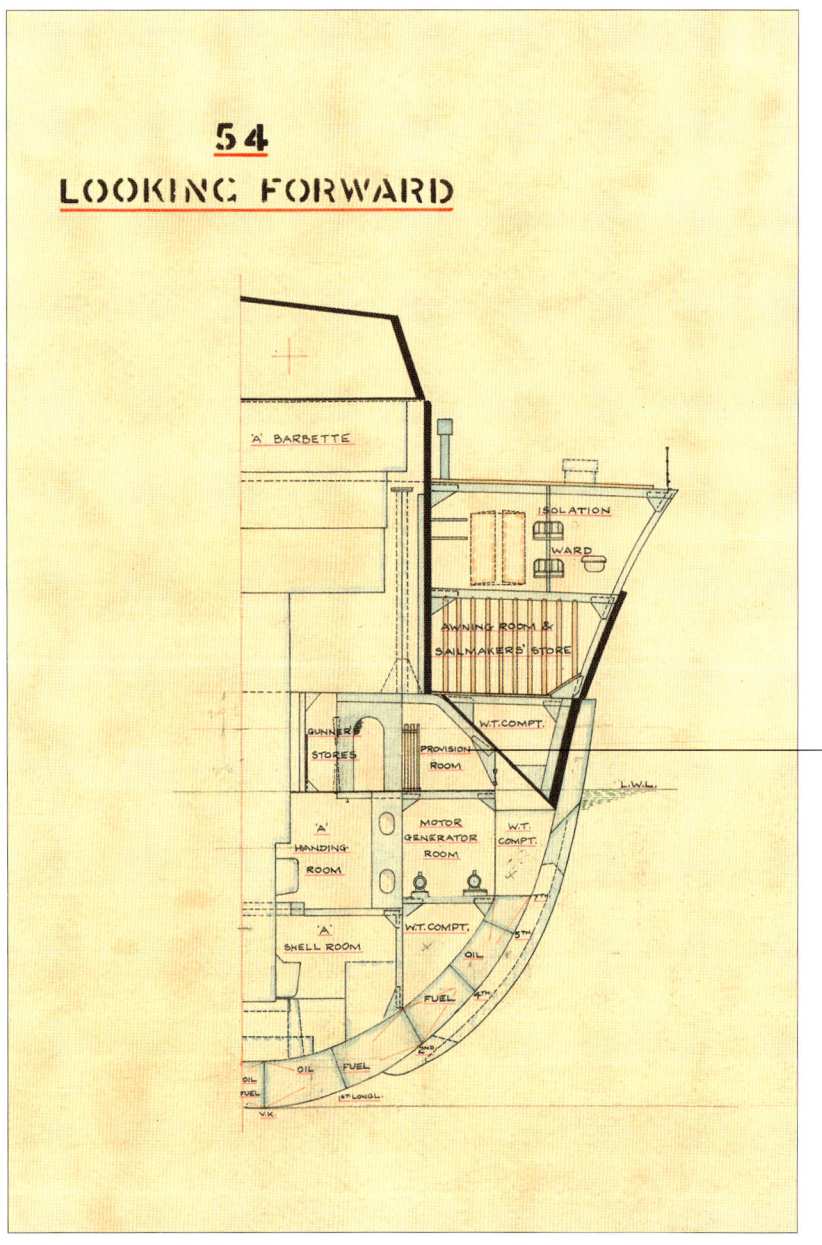

The provision room is the only change of substance in this section as it was originally the flexible voice pipe store; the alteration of function could have been implemented any time from 1921 onward.

STATIONS 54 TO 43

During modernisation the lower deck from Station 41 to the top of the 4in bulkhead across the fore sides of 'A' barbette for a width of about 24ft was fitted with 3½in NC armour. This was added above the original ¾in HT plating of the deck, the additional 1¾in HT plating added in 1916–17 being removed.

In mid-1941 it was proposed to correct some of the vulnerabilities of the ships protection by adding the following NC armour:

1. 2in bulkheads to the fore end of the 4in handing room at Station 41, the fore end of the 4in magazine in the hold at Station 42 and to the short strip of deck between them on the platform deck
2. 4in on main deck over 'A' boiler room.
3. 3in on lower deck between Stations 292 and 300.

So far as is known none of these changes were implemented.

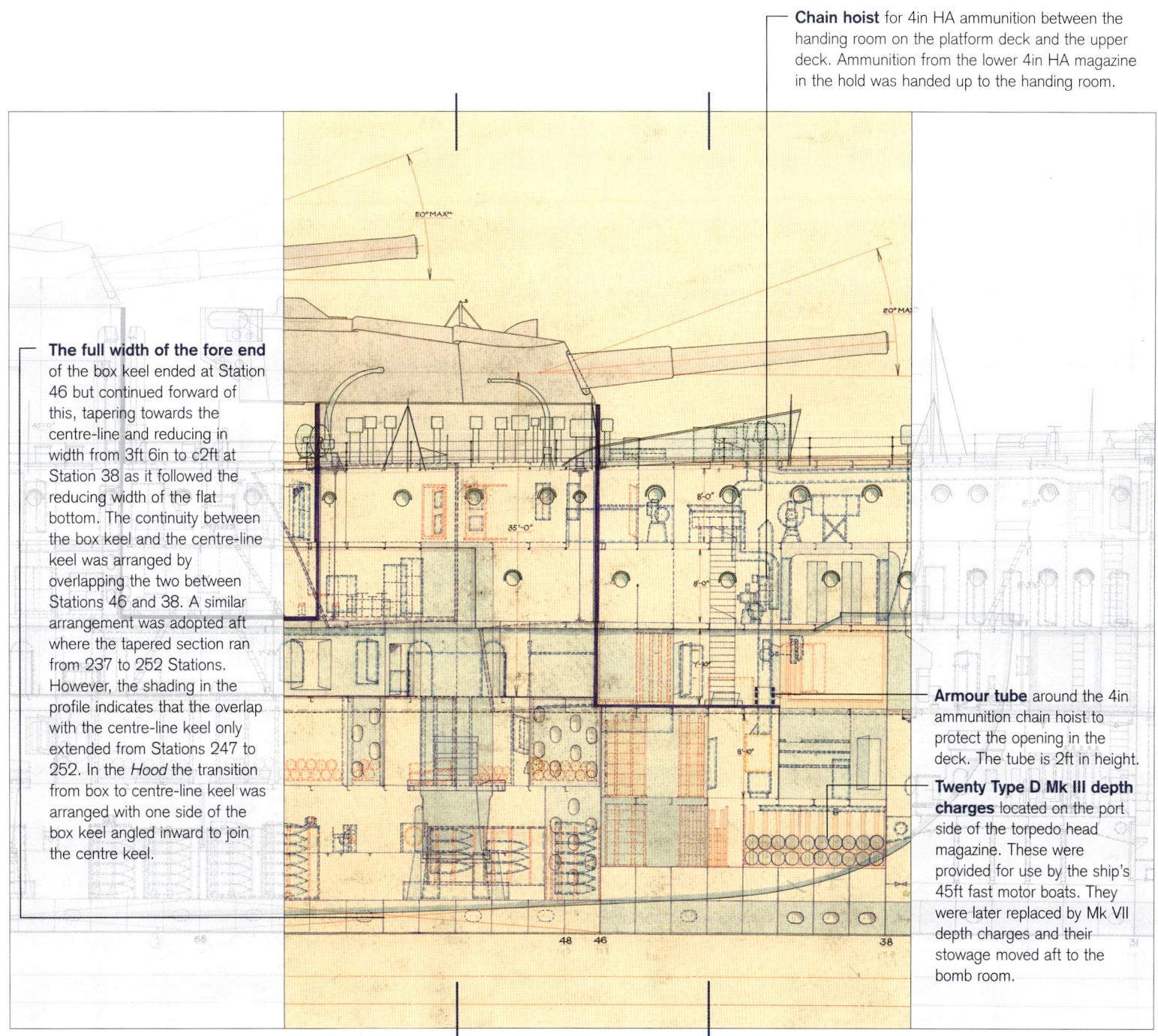

Chain hoist for 4in HA ammunition between the handing room on the platform deck and the upper deck. Ammunition from the lower 4in HA magazine in the hold was handed up to the handing room.

The full width of the fore end of the box keel ended at Station 46 but continued forward of this, tapering towards the centre-line and reducing in width from 3ft 6in to c2ft at Station 38 as it followed the reducing width of the flat bottom. The continuity between the box keel and the centre-line keel was arranged by overlapping the two between Stations 46 and 38. A similar arrangement was adopted aft where the tapered section ran from 237 to 252 Stations. However, the shading in the profile indicates that the overlap with the centre-line keel only extended from Stations 247 to 252. In the *Hood* the transition from box to centre-line keel was arranged with one side of the box keel angled inward to join the centre keel.

Armour tube around the 4in ammunition chain hoist to protect the opening in the deck. The tube is 2ft in height.

Twenty Type D Mk III depth charges located on the port side of the torpedo head magazine. These were provided for use by the ship's 45ft fast motor boats. They were later replaced by Mk VII depth charges and their stowage moved aft to the bomb room.

54 STATION   **43 STATION**

SECTION AT STATION 43, STARBOARD SIDE, LOOKING FORWARD

During modernisation the submerged torpedo tubes were removed and the compartment subdivided, which served to improve the ship's watertight integrity. In addition, the drawing implies that the space below the hold platform, which had served as the torpedo tube drain tank, was structurally modified although this may again be a case of features being omitted from the original 1916 drawings.

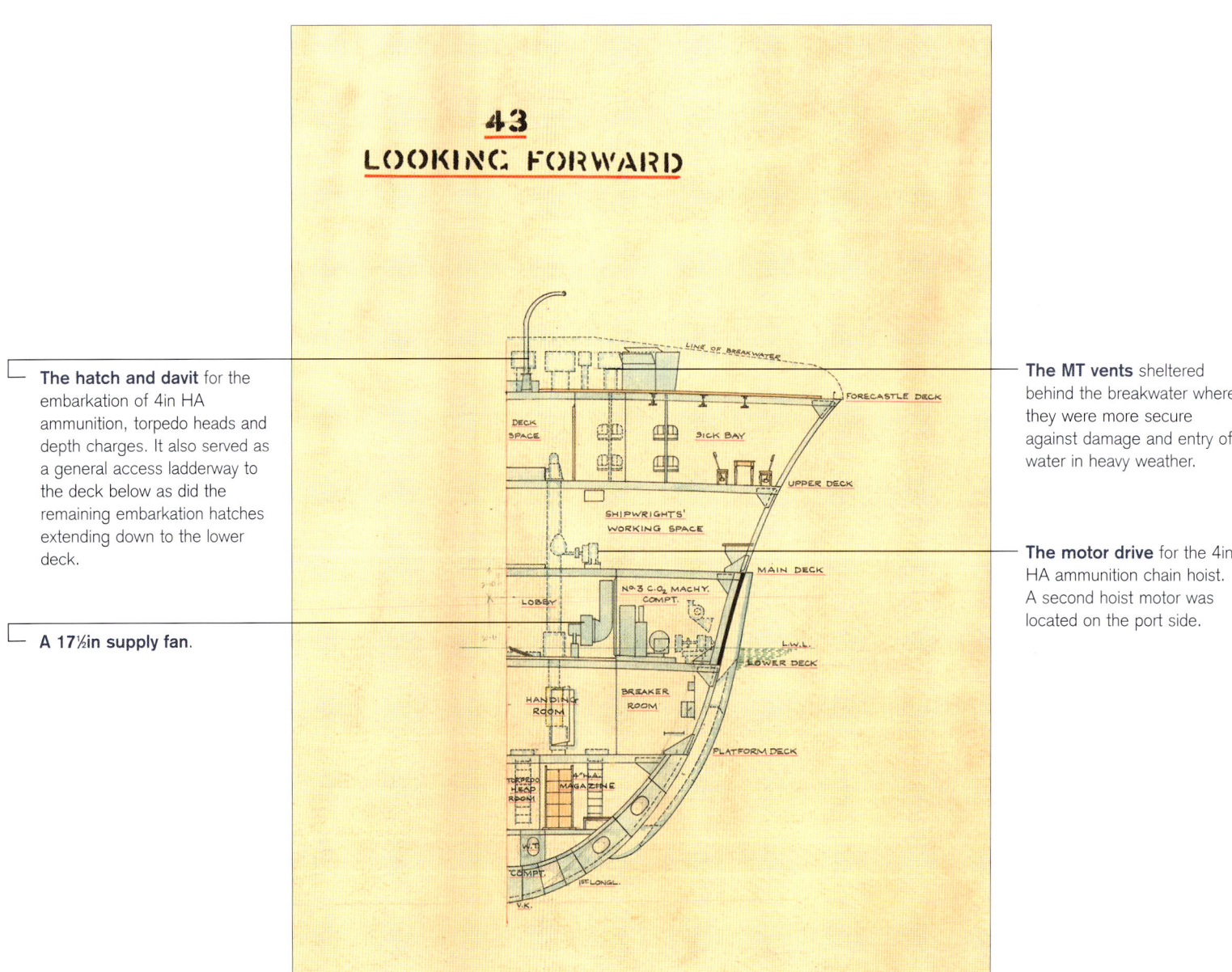

The hatch and davit for the embarkation of 4in HA ammunition, torpedo heads and depth charges. It also served as a general access ladderway to the deck below as did the remaining embarkation hatches extending down to the lower deck.

A 17½in supply fan.

The MT vents sheltered behind the breakwater where they were more secure against damage and entry of water in heavy weather.

The motor drive for the 4in HA ammunition chain hoist. A second hoist motor was located on the port side.

STATIONS 43 TO 32

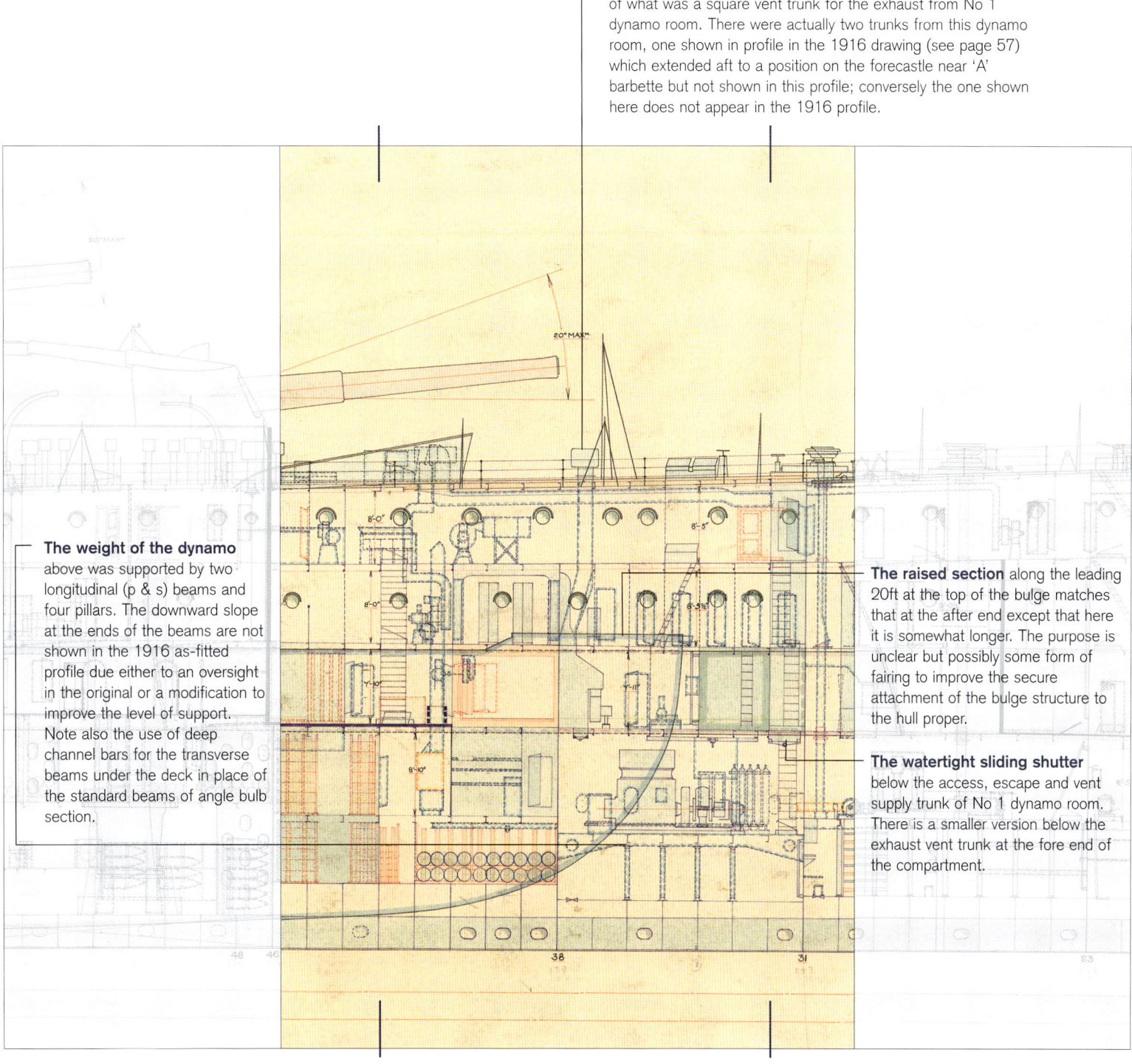

A mushroom top added sometime during 1916–18 to the top of what was a square vent trunk for the exhaust from No 1 dynamo room. There were actually two trunks from this dynamo room, one shown in profile in the 1916 drawing (see page 57) which extended aft to a position on the forecastle near 'A' barbette but not shown in this profile; conversely the one shown here does not appear in the 1916 profile.

The weight of the dynamo above was supported by two longitudinal (p & s) beams and four pillars. The downward slope at the ends of the beams are not shown in the 1916 as-fitted profile due either to an oversight in the original or a modification to improve the level of support. Note also the use of deep channel bars for the transverse beams under the deck in place of the standard beams of angle bulb section.

The raised section along the leading 20ft at the top of the bulge matches that at the after end except that here it is somewhat longer. The purpose is unclear but possibly some form of fairing to improve the secure attachment of the bulge structure to the hull proper.

The watertight sliding shutter below the access, escape and vent supply trunk of No 1 dynamo room. There is a smaller version below the exhaust vent trunk at the fore end of the compartment.

43 STATION   **32 STATION**

SECTION AT STATION 32, STARBOARD SIDE, LOOKING FORWARD

The ship's double bottom extended from just aft of 'Y' barbette to just forward of 'A' barbette at 46 Station. Forward of this the deep frames were continued to Station 38, the hold flat, which was watertight, substituting for the inner bottom. Beyond 38 the framing reduced generally to 6in x 3½in x 3in 'Z' bars (except behind side armour and at bulkheads). This size of framing was also employed above the main deck over the length of the main side armour excepting the additional stiffening fitted between the main and upper decks in 1918–21. The pattern of framing employed forward was in general also followed at the after end of the ship except that the rudder, propellers and the generally more complex lower hull required more substantial framing below the lower deck.

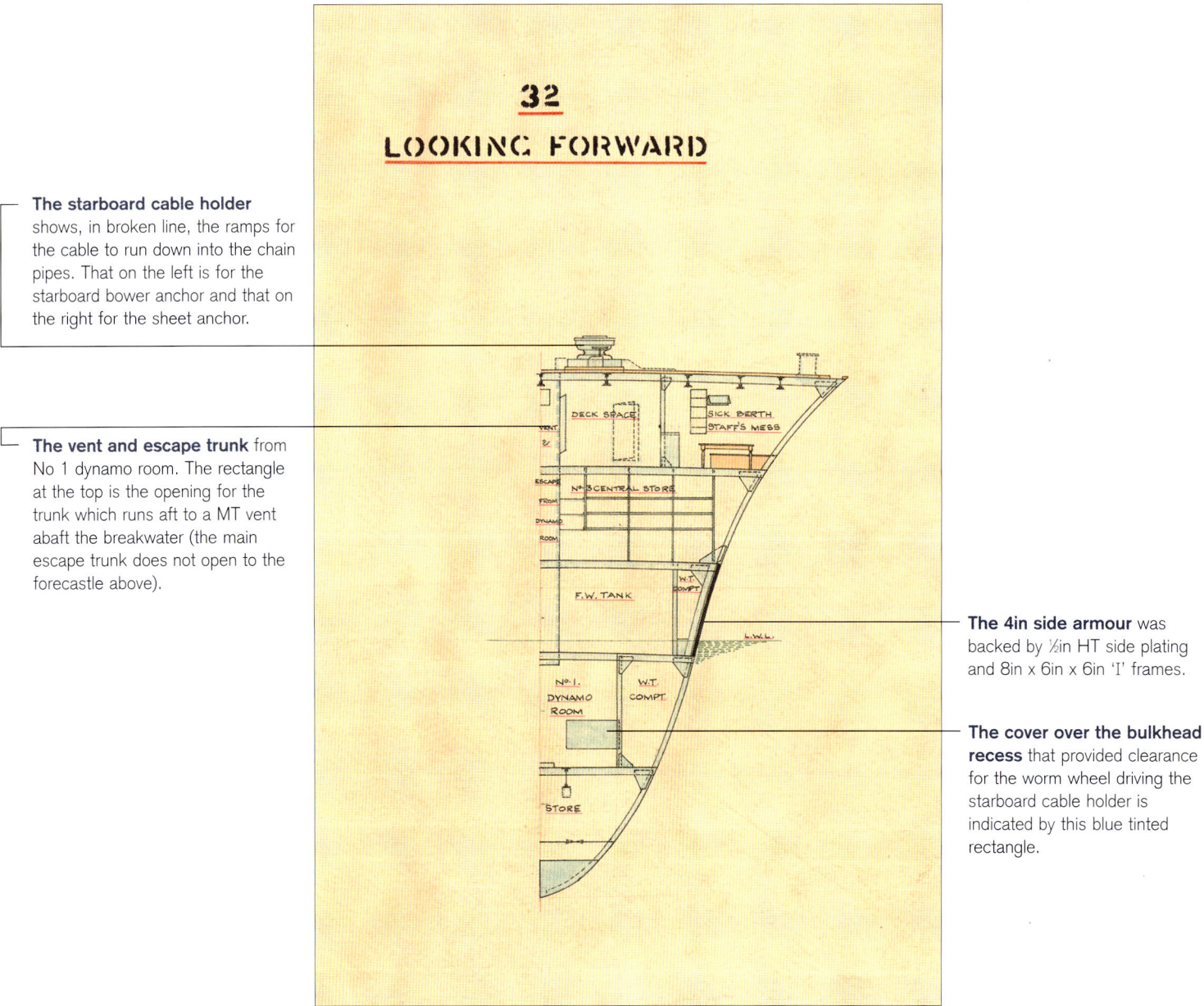

The starboard cable holder shows, in broken line, the ramps for the cable to run down into the chain pipes. That on the left is for the starboard bower anchor and that on the right for the sheet anchor.

The vent and escape trunk from No 1 dynamo room. The rectangle at the top is the opening for the trunk which runs aft to a MT vent abaft the breakwater (the main escape trunk does not open to the forecastle above).

The 4in side armour was backed by ½in HT side plating and 8in x 6in x 6in 'I' frames.

The cover over the bulkhead recess that provided clearance for the worm wheel driving the starboard cable holder is indicated by this blue tinted rectangle.

STATIONS 32 TO 27

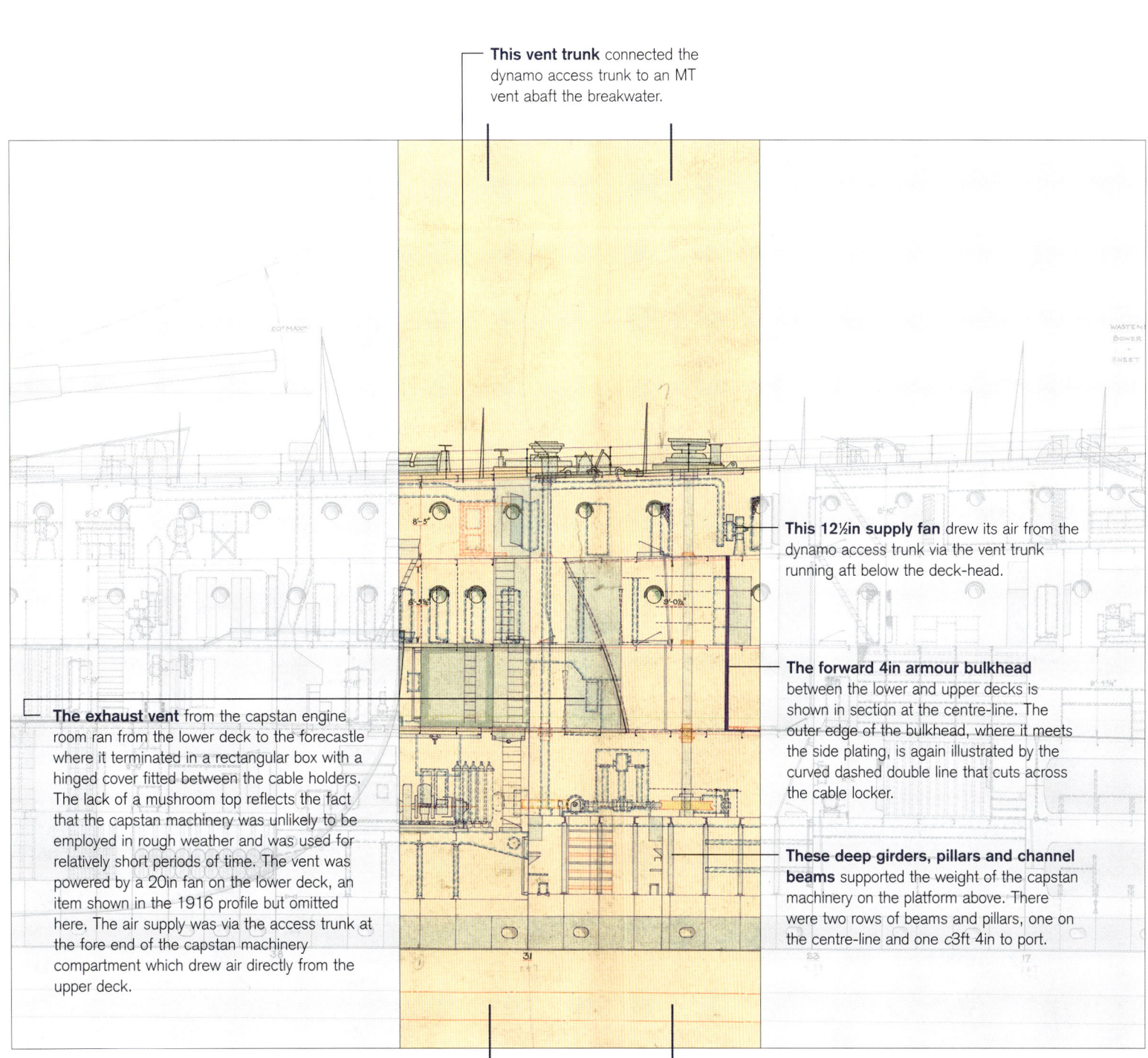

This vent trunk connected the dynamo access trunk to an MT vent abaft the breakwater.

This 12½in supply fan drew its air from the dynamo access trunk via the vent trunk running aft below the deck-head.

The forward 4in armour bulkhead between the lower and upper decks is shown in section at the centre-line. The outer edge of the bulkhead, where it meets the side plating, is again illustrated by the curved dashed double line that cuts across the cable locker.

The exhaust vent from the capstan engine room ran from the lower deck to the forecastle where it terminated in a rectangular box with a hinged cover fitted between the cable holders. The lack of a mushroom top reflects the fact that the capstan machinery was unlikely to be employed in rough weather and was used for relatively short periods of time. The vent was powered by a 20in fan on the lower deck, an item shown in the 1916 profile but omitted here. The air supply was via the access trunk at the fore end of the capstan machinery compartment which drew air directly from the upper deck.

These deep girders, pillars and channel beams supported the weight of the capstan machinery on the platform above. There were two rows of beams and pillars, one on the centre-line and one c3ft 4in to port.

32 STATION **27 STATION**

SECTIONS AT STATIONS 27 AND 19, STARBOARD SIDE, LOOKING FORWARD

There is very little worthy of comment in these two sections beyond those made for the 1916 as-fitted (see page 58). There have been several changes in the use of the store rooms since 1921 (best seen in the plan views) but the general structural arrangement is unaltered except for the addition of a watertight transverse bulkhead in the hold at Station 23, and new pillars (p & s) between the upper and forecastle decks at Station 27. Note that the 'bosun's store' shown on the starboard side of the upper deck in Section 27 is still the 'bosun's oil skin store' as it was when the ship completed. There is one noticeable alteration to the seamen's WCs on the upper deck – those WCs shown inboard in the section at 19 Station are a group of three added on both sides at the after end of the compartment. Although some of these changes were no doubt applied during modernisation, it is also probable that several were made at an earlier date.

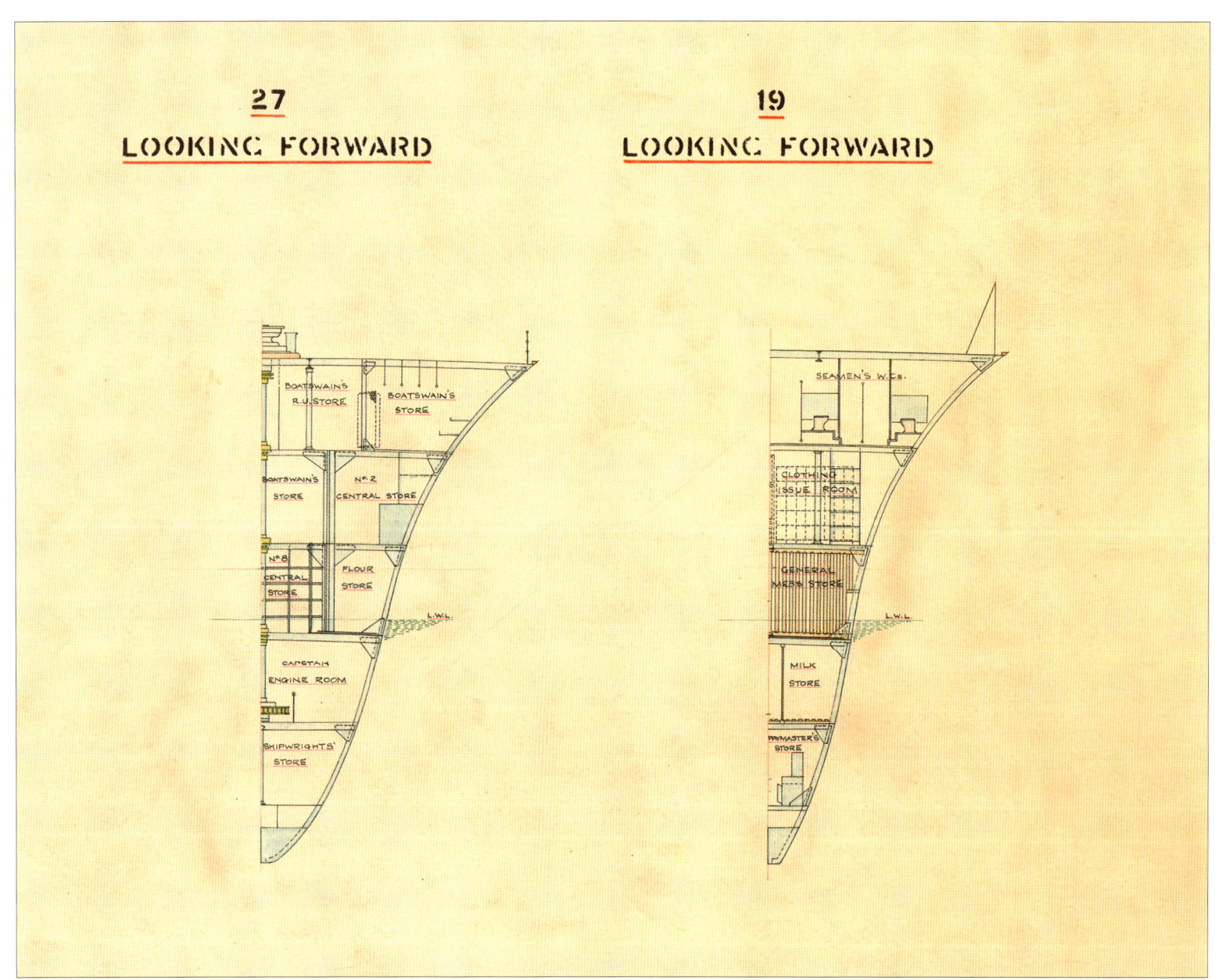

STATION 27 TO STEM

Despite the assumption that 'official records' are the ultimate in accurate information, this is not always the case. This section of the profile repeats the exact figures for the weight of the bower anchors as those printed on the 1916 profile. In 1925 it was approved to increase the weight of the bower and sheet anchors from 145cwt to 160cwt and to increase the cable from $2^{15}/_{16}$in to $3^{1}/_{8}$in in both *Renown* and *Repulse* to compensate for their substantial increases in displacement. This alteration is confirmed by figures given in the 1937 Admiralty Manual of Seamanship. Unfortunately, the 1939 as-fitted profile of the modernised *Renown* also gives the weights of her anchors as 145cwt. The conflict of whether or not this proposal was actually implemented awaits a more definitive answer (*ie*, 'this was done' as opposed to 'this was approved to be done').

The motor boat petrol tank, with the mineral vaporising oil (MVO) tank forward of it. The latter was for paraffin-based fuel used in those boats with paraffin engines. This was not as efficient as using petrol but was less inflammable and cheaper.

The aviation spirit tank was placed, like the motor boat tanks in the hold below, well forward to keep its highly inflammable contents as far distant as was reasonably possible. All the tank spaces could be flooded to reduce the danger of ignition by action damage.

The paravane fairleads were fitted before the ship's 1918–21 refit but the chain pipes they replaced remained in position – perhaps for some secondary use or because their removal was not regarded as sufficiently important.

The screens for the heads and WCs are indicated in outline by these dashed, blue shaded, lines.

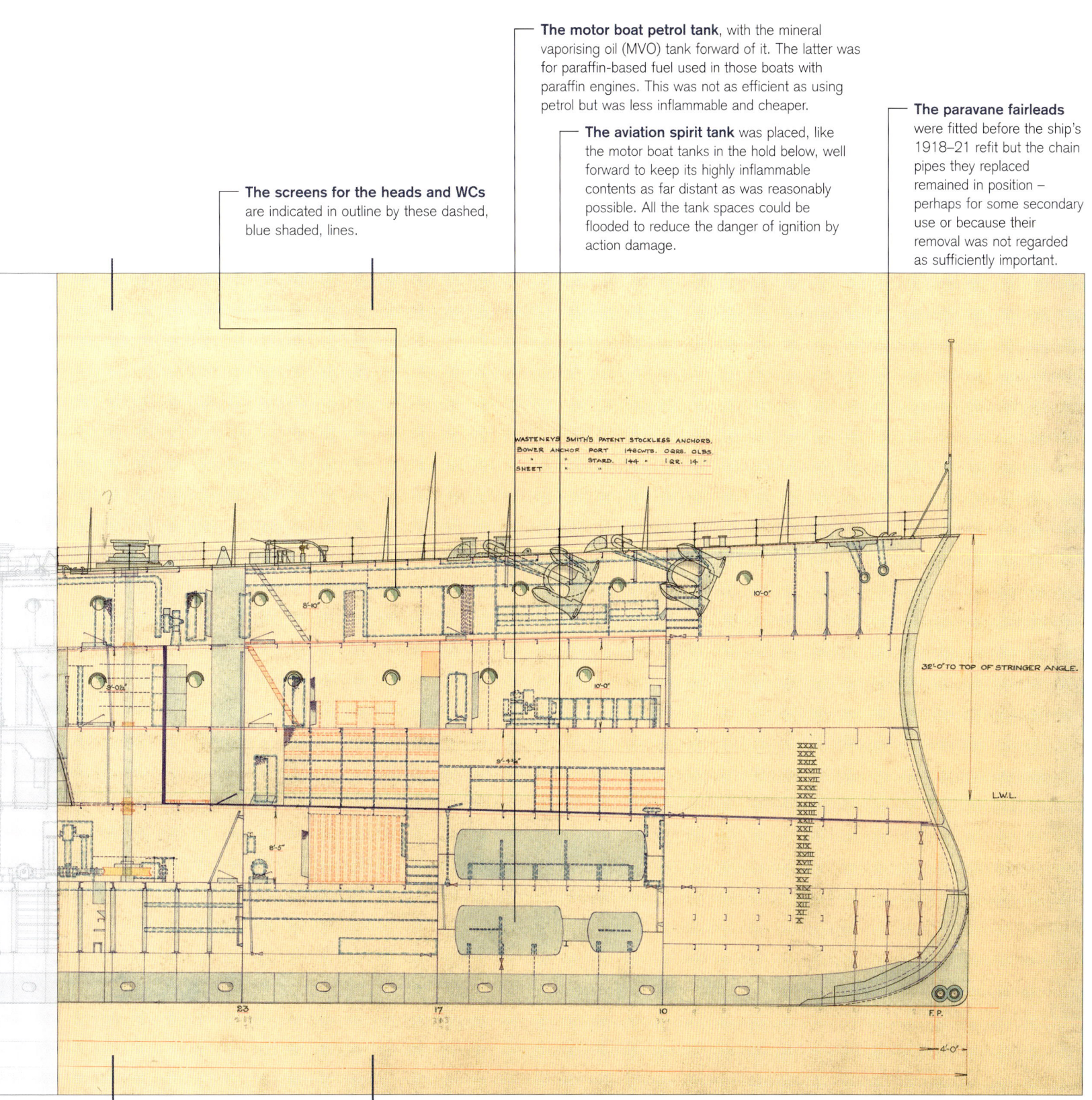

27 STATION   **19 STATION**

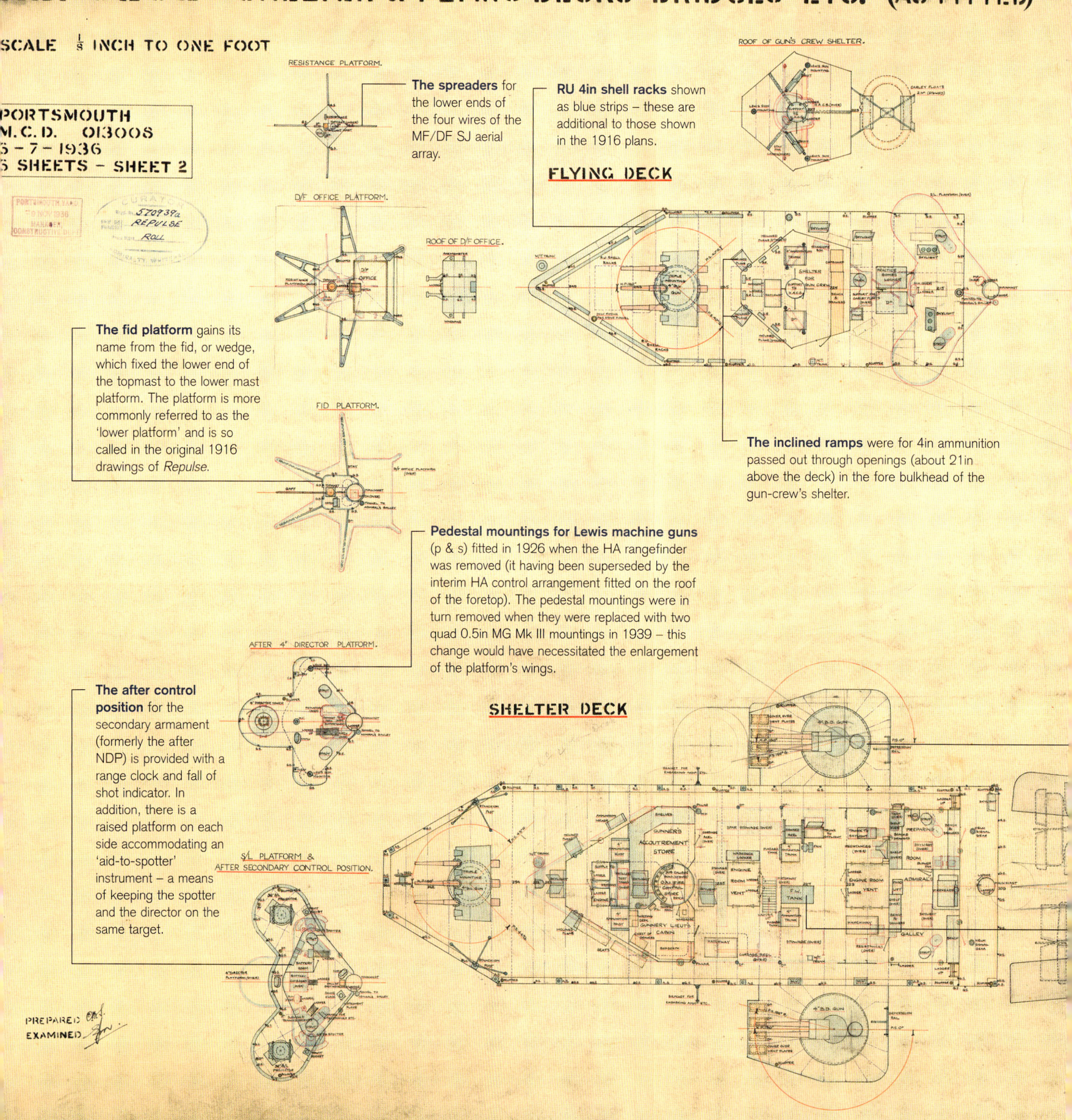

AFTER SUPERSTRUCTURE DECKS

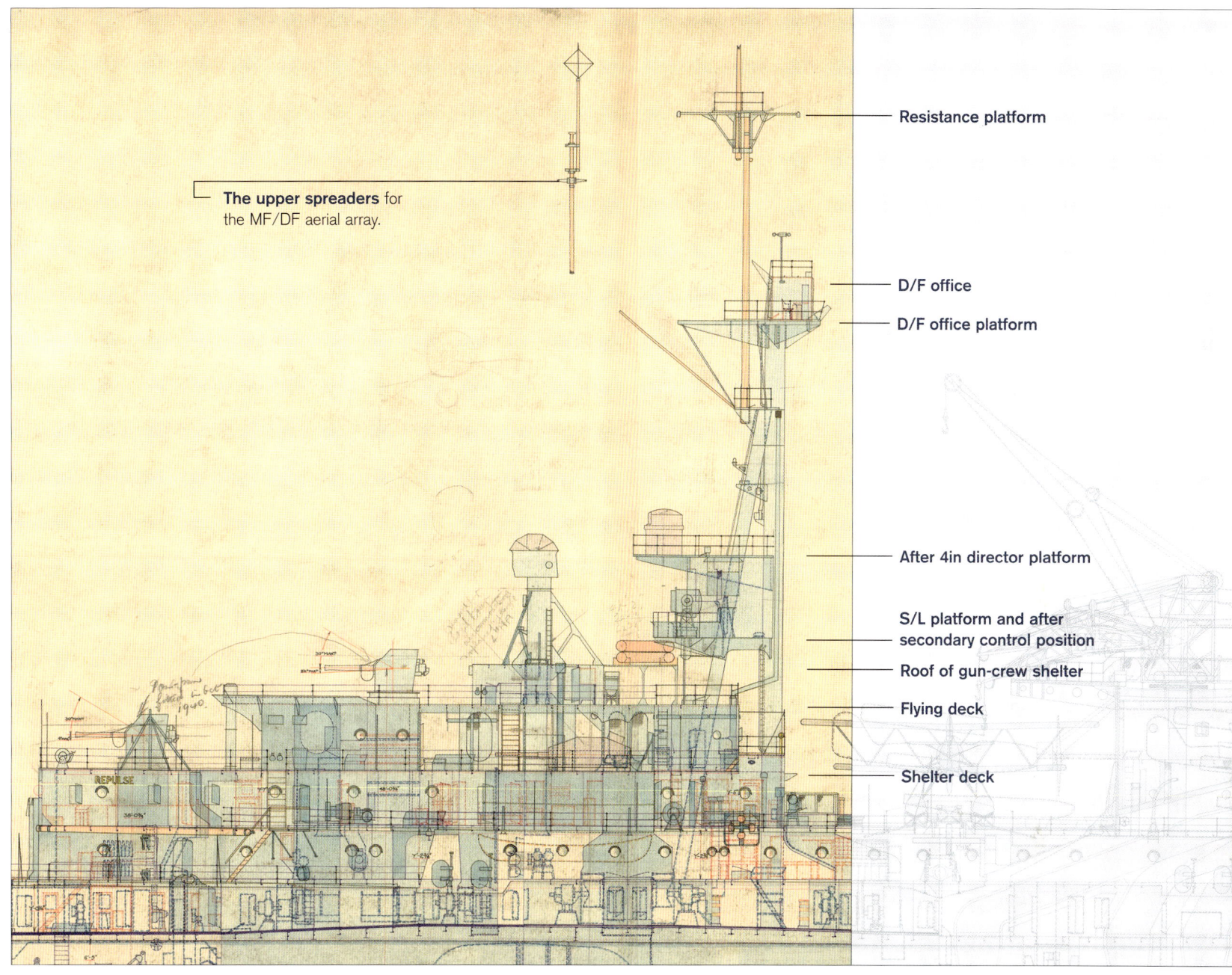

- **Twin 4in BD HA/LA mountings** (p & s). The experimental Mk XVII version of this mounting, fitted with two Mk V guns, was fitted in the battleship *Resolution* in 1931. The production version (Mk XVIII with Mk XV guns) was fitted in *Repulse* during modernisation. It was not a success, as it lacked a sufficient rate of fire for effective AA defence, and was not fitted in any other ship. They were replaced by single 4in Mk V guns on HA Mk III mountings during 1938–39 (that in *Resolution* was removed in 1938). Despite this failure, the general design reappeared later in the much more successful twin 4.5in BD mounting employed in the *Renown*, *Queen Elizabeth*, *Valiant* and the fleet aircraft carriers of the *Formidable* and later classes.

- **The fresh water gravity tank** in the position previously occupied by the sanitary tank, the latter being no longer present. By this time the use of gravity tanks for the salt water system had given way to reliance on the fire and bilge pumps. Nevertheless, there is still a sanitary tank shown on the CT deck (to starboard of the fore funnel). It is possible that this is an error and should be a second fresh water tank – the normal number for the fresh water system.

AFTER SUPERSTRUCTURE

The modernisation left this area more or less intact. The most noticeable changes are the removal of the TCT and the additions of the HA Mk I director and the D/F office. Less obvious are the new 36in searchlights fitted in the same positions as those they replaced but mounted on larger platforms with a linking walkway between them. Also new is the admiral's galley and [food] preparing room at the fore end of the shelter deck – displaced from the forecastle deck by the fitting of the aircraft catapult (note that the 'preparing room' was previously designated the 'admiral's kitchen'). (J9434)

ENLARGED DECKS, AS FITTED 1936

The after waste steam pipe (p & s) on the after funnel has been moved forward c4ft to clear the bows of the inboard 45ft FMB and 45ft motor launch.

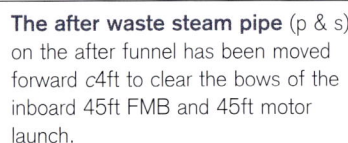

Two of the six 36in Mk III** searchlights fitted in *Repulse* during modernisation were located on new platforms fitted on the fore side of the after funnel. Primary direction for the searchlights was from the Evershed sights on the upper bridge. The searchlight remote control was provided from the manipulating platforms fitted below them (note that it is only this searchlight control position that retains the original 'manipulating' terminology). The *Repulse* was among the last ships to be equipped with 36in searchlights as these were superseded by 44in searchlights shortly after the completion of her modernisation.

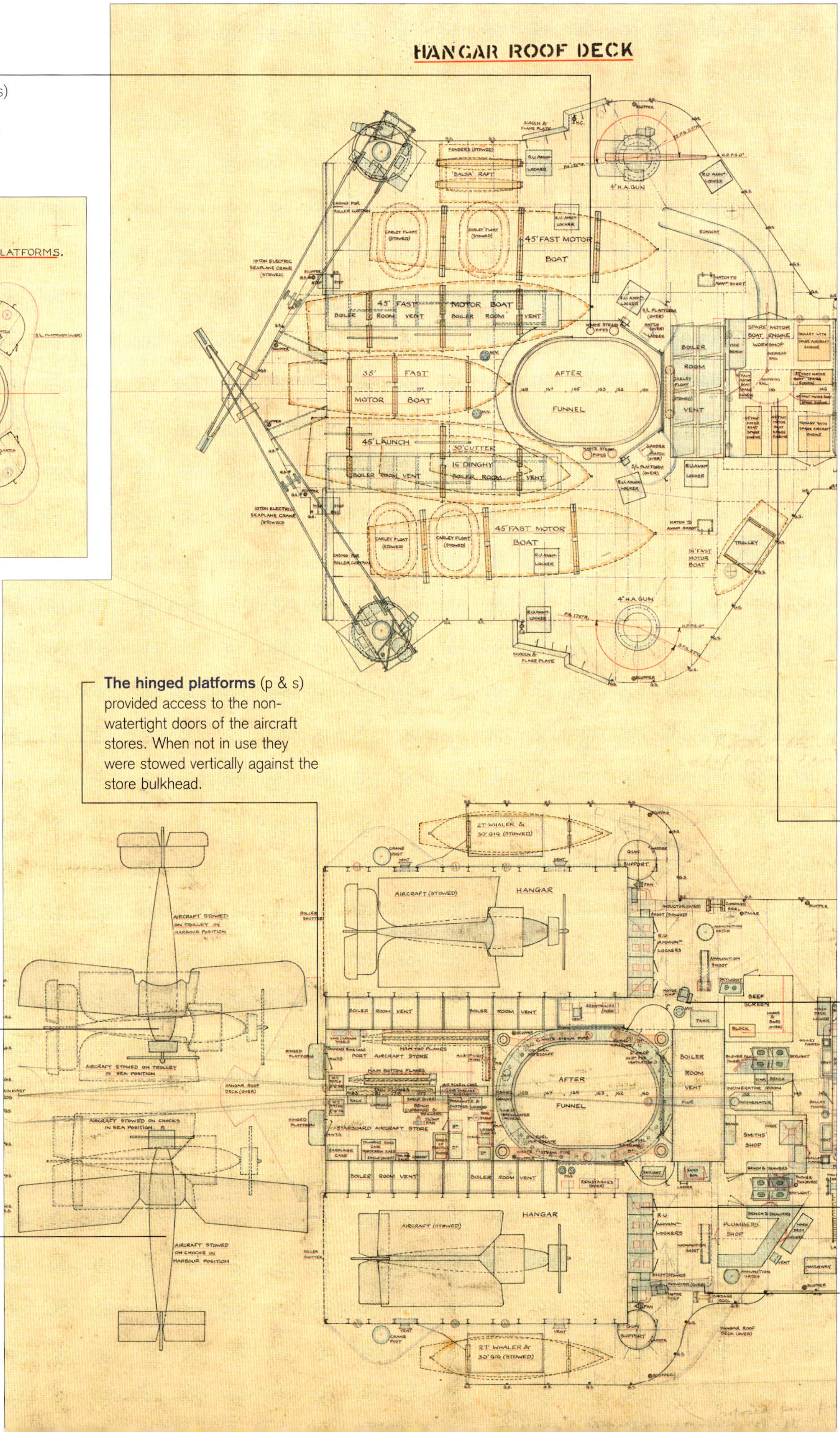

The hinged platforms (p & s) provided access to the non-watertight doors of the aircraft stores. When not in use they were stowed vertically against the store bulkhead.

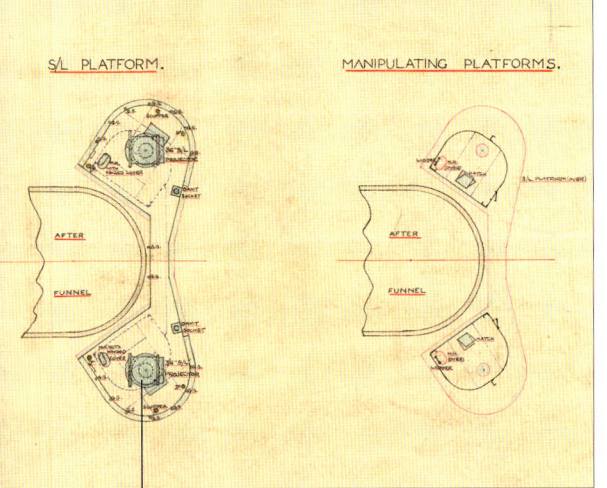

The aircraft, although drawn in very basic outline, are nevertheless recognisable as Fairey Swordfish to port and Blackburn Sharks to starboard.

MIDSHIPS SUPERSTRUCTURE DECKS

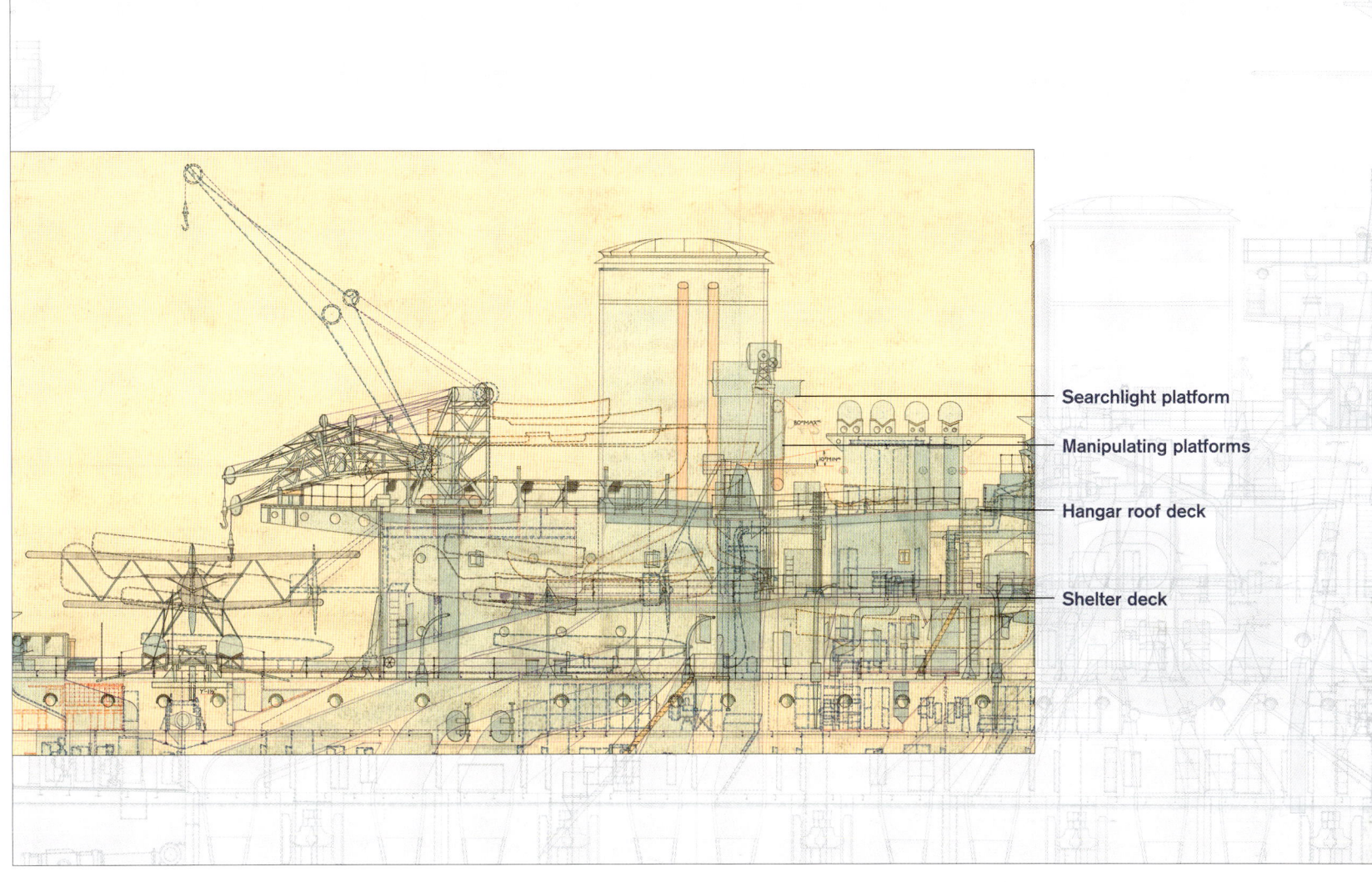

- **The spare motor boat engine workshop** stores one engine for each of the five FMBs and two spare engines for the aircraft.

- **The whip motor [winch]** for handling the 4in HA ammunition. That to starboard is positioned further outboard and aft compared with that to port.

- **Ready-use ammunition lockers** (p & s) for the 4in HA guns on the hanger roof deck. The red squares represent vent plates in the tops of the lockers. Similar lockers are fitted on the forecastle deck abaft the two twin 4in BD mountings (see page 137).

- **The trunks of the hangar ventilation inductors** (p & s) ran from the bottom of the hangars to the underside of the hangar roof platform.

MIDSHIPS SUPERSTRUCTURE

This area covers the most extensive changes to the ship's superstructure – principally the aircraft and main boat stowage arrangements – which required some relocation of various parts of the superstructure around the after funnel. The intake vents for 'E' and 'F' boiler rooms, which previously terminated just below the shelter deck, were extended upward, inboard of the hangars, to intakes on its roof. The intake for 'D' boiler room, on the shelter deck forward of the after funnel, was also extended up to the hangar roof platform. In addition, the [black]smith's shop, beef screen and plumber's shop on the shelter deck were relocated from abaft the after funnel to positions forward of 'D' boiler room vent. This in turn required a new incinerator house to be constructed on the middle line between the beef screen and the [black]smith's shop. (J9434)

SHIP'S BOATS

July 1936

3 x 45ft FMB	2 x 30ft gigs
1 x 35ft FMB	2 x 27ft whalers
1 x 16ft FMB	1 x 16ft dinghy
1 x 45ft motor launch	1 x 13ft 6in balsa raft
2 x 32ft (life) cutters	9 x Carley life floats
1 x 30ft cutter	(5 pattern 17, 4 pattern 18)

The hull form of the FMBs was hard chine and that of the motor launch round bilge. Two further Carley floats had been fitted abreast the forward superstructure by 1937 (probably pattern 20)

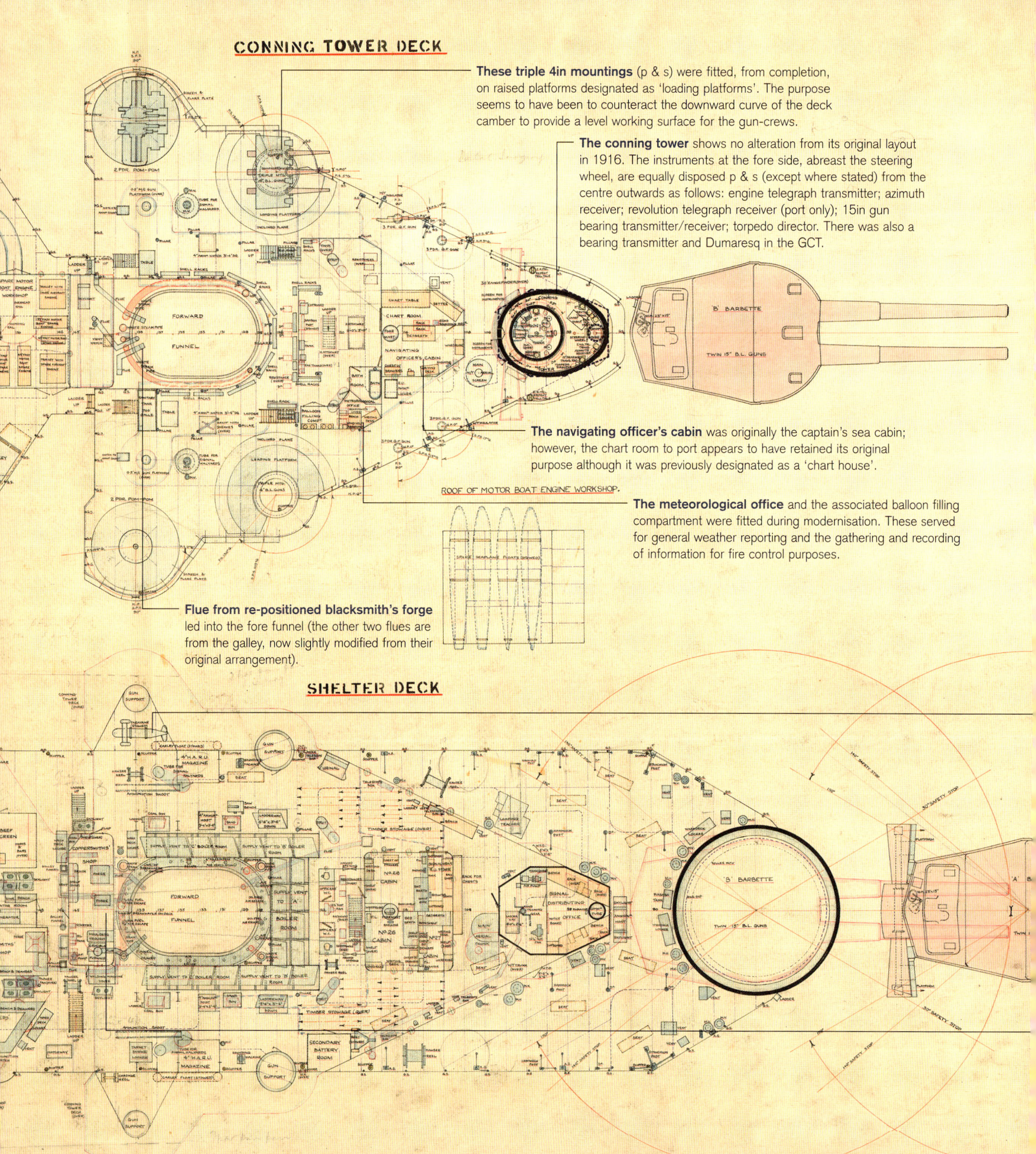

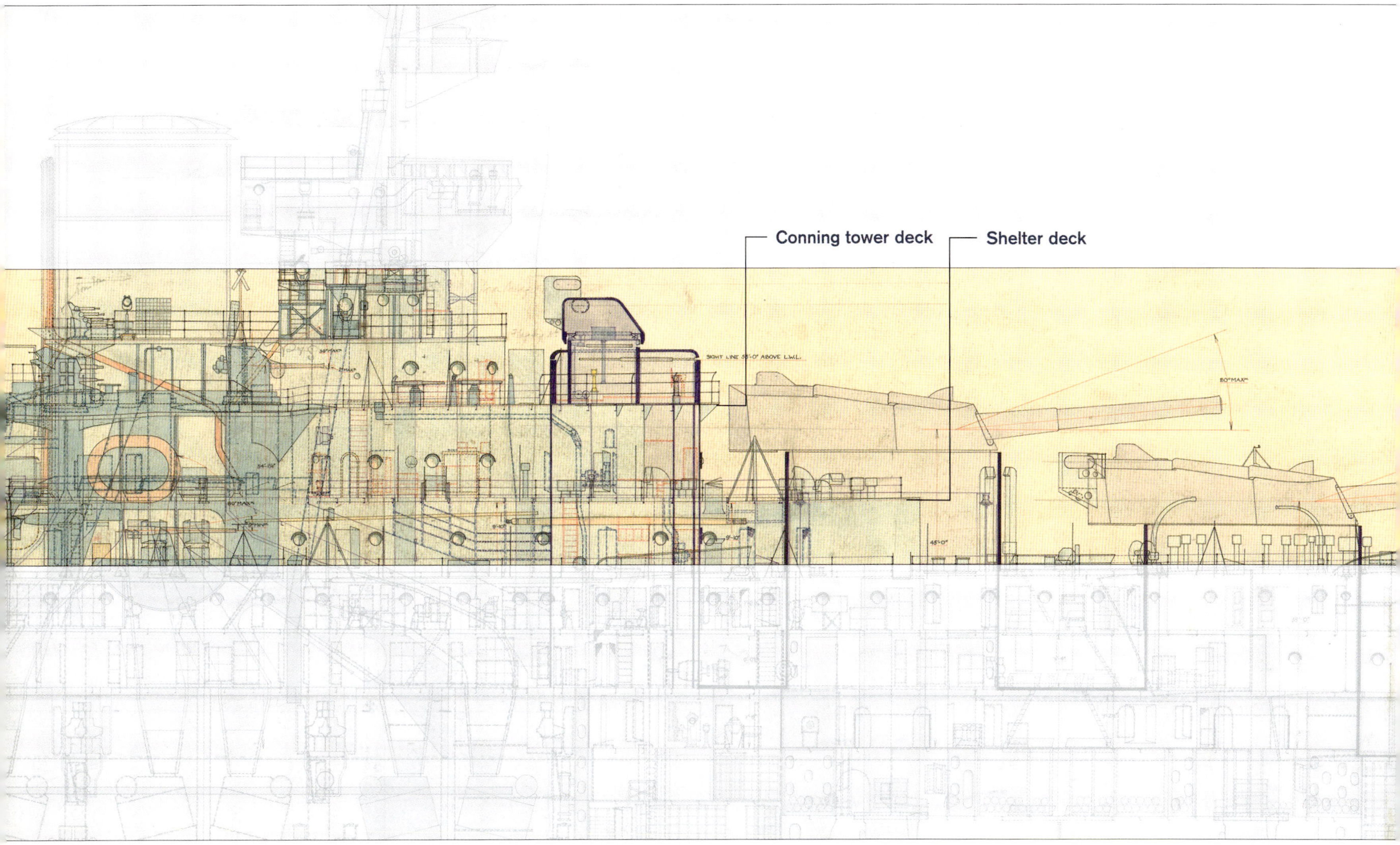

FORWARD SUPERSTRUCTURE DECKS

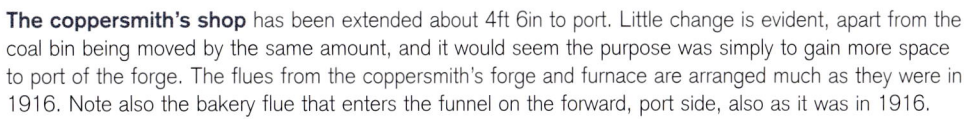

Conning tower deck — Shelter deck

FORWARD SUPERSTRUCTURE

There are few signs of alterations made during modernisation on the CT platform (now designated 'conning tower deck') or the forward section of the shelter deck. The more obvious change is the extension of the after corners of the CT deck to accommodate the ship's two 8-barrel Mk VI pom-pom mountings and their support structure. On the shelter deck the intake vents for 'A', 'B' and 'C' boiler rooms are unchanged as is the structure below the CT and the cabins grouped around the foremast. However, the latter have changed designation becoming simply numbered cabins (previously 26 was the admiral's sea cabin, 27 the signal officer's cabin and 28 the navigating officer's cabin). (J9434)

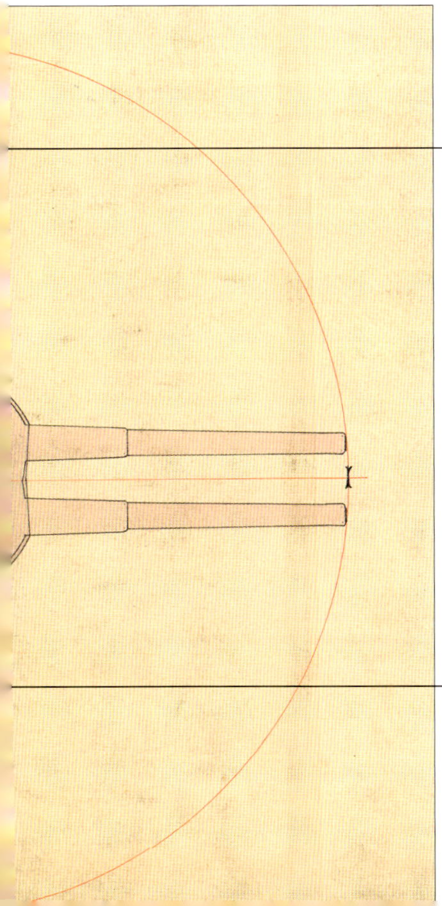

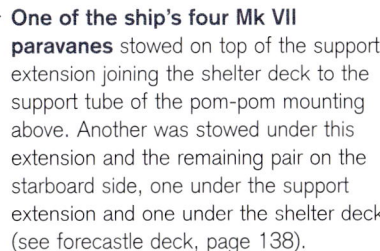

One of the ship's four Mk VII paravanes stowed on top of the support extension joining the shelter deck to the support tube of the pom-pom mounting above. Another was stowed under this extension and the remaining pair on the starboard side, one under the support extension and one under the shelter deck (see forecastle deck, page 138).

The coppersmith's shop has been extended about 4ft 6in to port. Little change is evident, apart from the coal bin being moved by the same amount, and it would seem the purpose was simply to gain more space to port of the forge. The flues from the coppersmith's forge and furnace are arranged much as they were in 1916. Note also the bakery flue that enters the funnel on the forward, port side, also as it was in 1916.

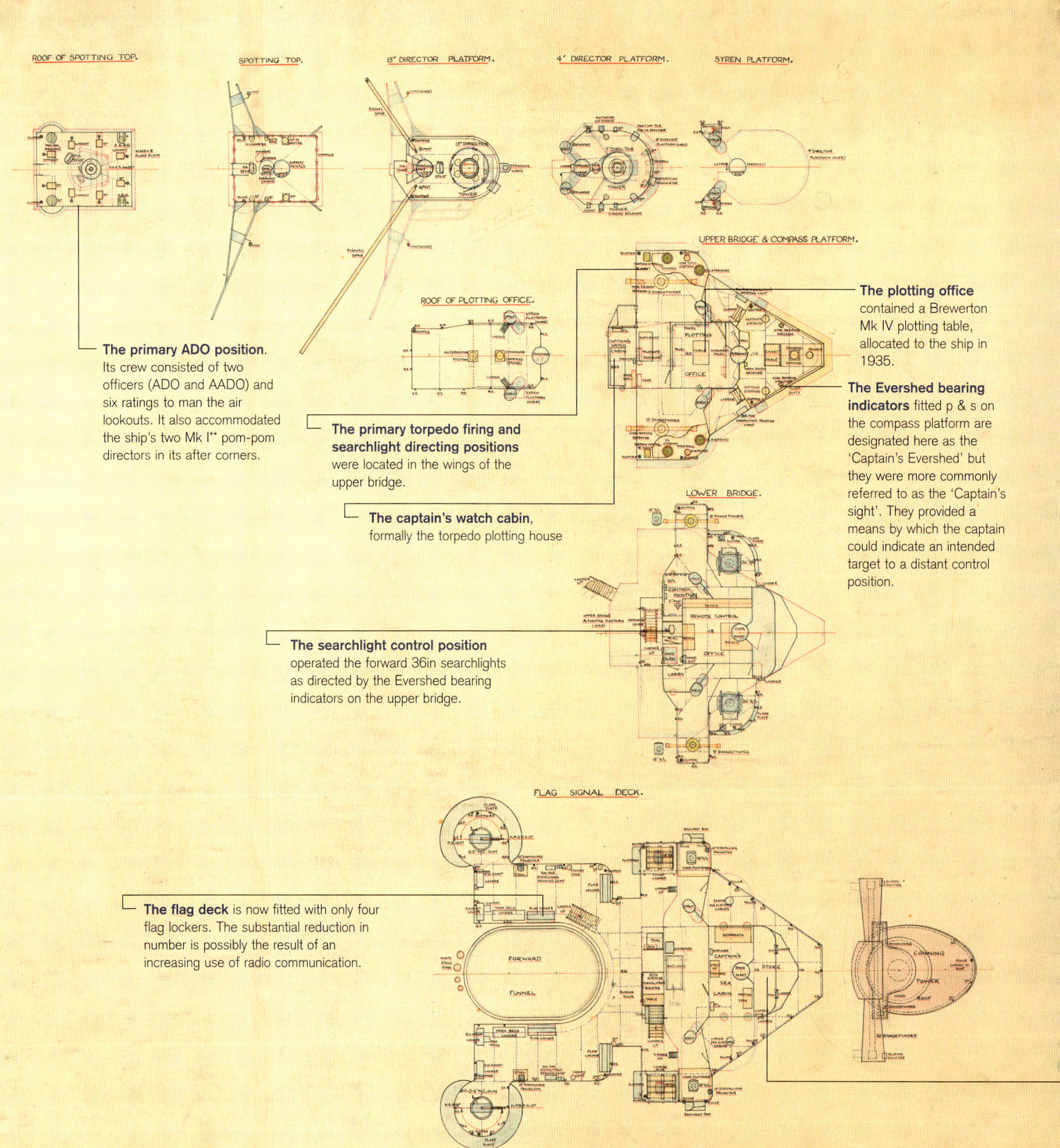

BRIDGE PLATFORMS

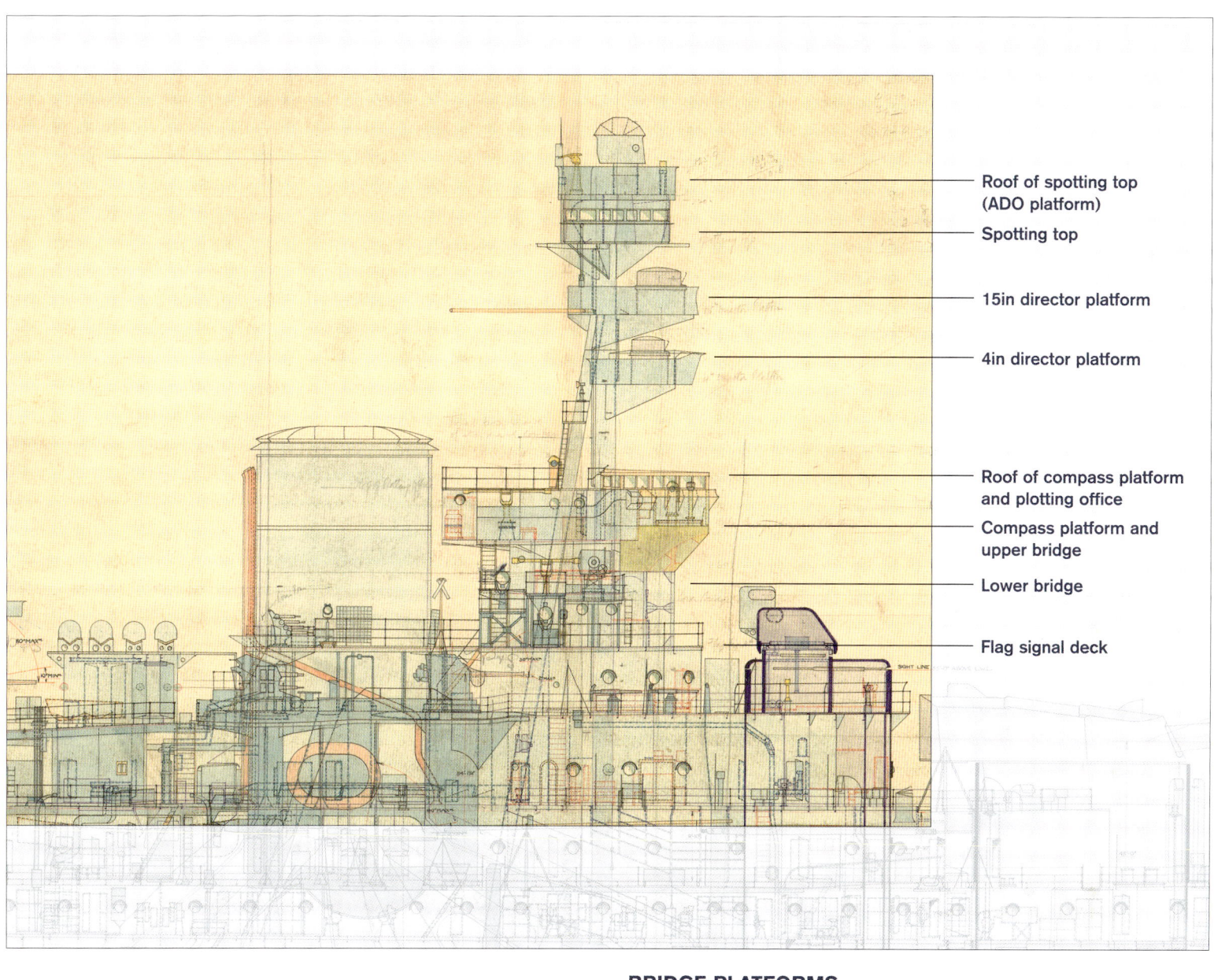

- Roof of spotting top (ADO platform)
- Spotting top
- 15in director platform
- 4in director platform
- Roof of compass platform and plotting office
- Compass platform and upper bridge
- Lower bridge
- Flag signal deck

The former submarine lookout, together with the extension constructed forward of it during modernisation, has been re-designated as a store. Access to the ex-lookout space was still from the starboard side of the lower bridge (access to the new extension was via manholes in the forward screen of the ex-lookout).

BRIDGE PLATFORMS

The bridge platforms have been modified in detail but these involved relatively minor changes to the external appearance of the bridge structure. The most noticeable results of modernisation are the HA director above the spotting top, the two quad 0.5in MG mountings and the new arrangement of searchlight and signalling projectors. The other noticeable differences from the earlier as-fitted drawings are the new fore top and the 9ft rangefinders on the wing platforms of the lower bridge – both installed during her 1925–26 refit. The lower bridge was originally the forward NDP but its plan outline has been substantially altered. Since the internal area of this platform is almost impossible to see in photographs the exact sequence of the interior alterations which transformed the platform from NDP to remote control office/searchlight platform cannot be determined.

The HA director was Mk II but the only important difference between this and the after Mk I director was that it was fitted with AV (anti-vibration) mountings for its 12ft UD3 height-finder (despite the official designation the latter were in effect rangefinders). While the early HACS was approaching obsolescence by 1939 it was not as dated as the ship's AA armament of six 4in Mk V guns on HA Mk III mountings, the design of which dated from the First World War. A proposed armament statement prepared for *Repulse* in 1941 indicates that it was planned to replace both the 4in triple mountings and the single 4in HA mountings with fourteen 4in QF Mk XVI guns on twin HA/LA Mk XIX mountings. (J9434)

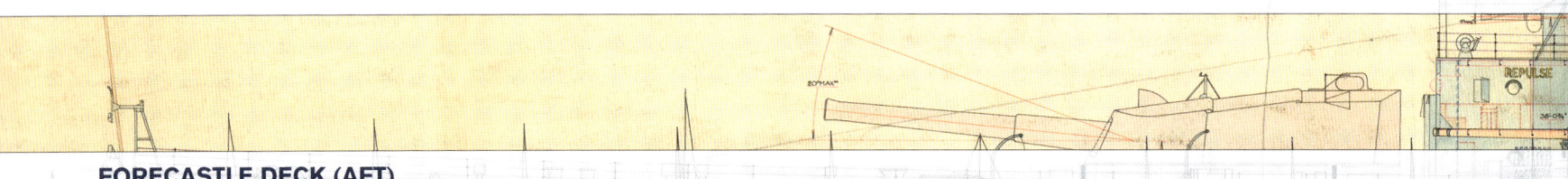

FORECASTLE DECK (AFT)

The admiral's accommodation at the after end of the forecastle deck shows no significant changes since the ship completed. However, the area forward of this, from Stations 209 to 229, which formally accommodated the admiral's chief of staff, flag lieutenant and secretary, have been reallocated to the captain and paymaster. The single cabin to starboard, for the surgeon commander, was previously occupied by the navigating officer. Given that modernisation created some problems with accommodating personnel, stores and magazine space, it seem odd that the admiral's quarters were so little affected. This is especially so since after modernisation the *Repulse* only served as a flagship once – temporarily in September 1940 for the Rear Admiral Home Fleet Destroyers, R H C Hallifax. (J9435)

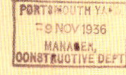 

"REPULSE" FORECASTLE & UPPER DECKS (AS FITTED)

SCALE 1/8 INCH TO ONE FOOT

PORTSMOUTH
C.D. 01300S
6 – 7 – 1936
SHEETS — SHEET 3

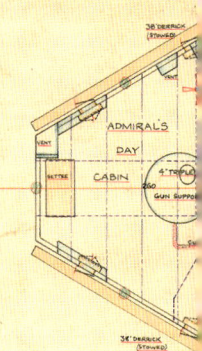

The platforms for access to the quarterdeck have been re-orientated fore and aft and now have double rather than single ladders. This alteration was made during, or very shortly after, the ship's 1918–21 refit but was not included in the modifications applied to the 1916 as-fitted drawings.

The pencil circles on this deck and others appear to be proposed locations for the outfit of 20mm Oerlikons planned for the ship in 1941. The positions shown are p & s on the forecastle deck at Stations *239*, 213, *114*, *78* and 45; on the shelter deck at Station *108*; on the CT deck at Station 110; on the quarterdeck at Station 264; and a single on the centre-line at Station 312. This may give some clues as to the arrangement finally adopted but is far from definitive since it totals 17 mountings as opposed to the 15 allocated. In addition, it is probable that only 8 were actually fitted and 2 of these were definitely mounted on the roof of 'Y' turret. Photographs of the ship in late 1941 provide a barely discernible indication that four of the other mountings were located at the station numbers given above in italics.

The ammunition lockers, in the base structure that housed the twin 4in BD mountings, provided ready use storage for the guns' ammunition. The single 4in HA guns used the same ammunition, which was 'fixed' in the sense that shell and its charge, in a brass case, were provided as a single assembly. The ammunition hoists in the inboard forward corner of the base structure were small hatches for the top ends of portable ammunition 'shoots' [chutes].

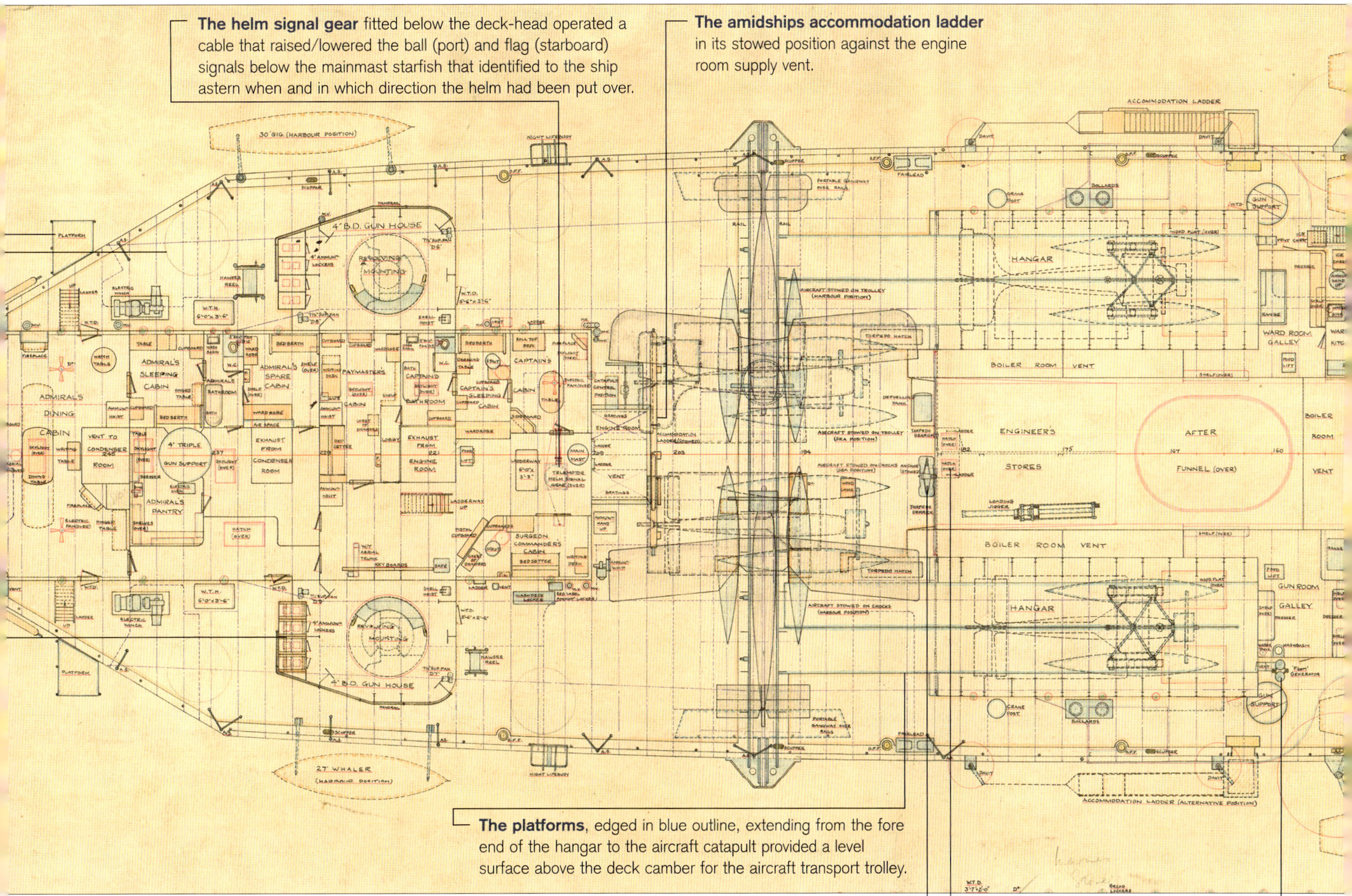

FORECASTLE DECK

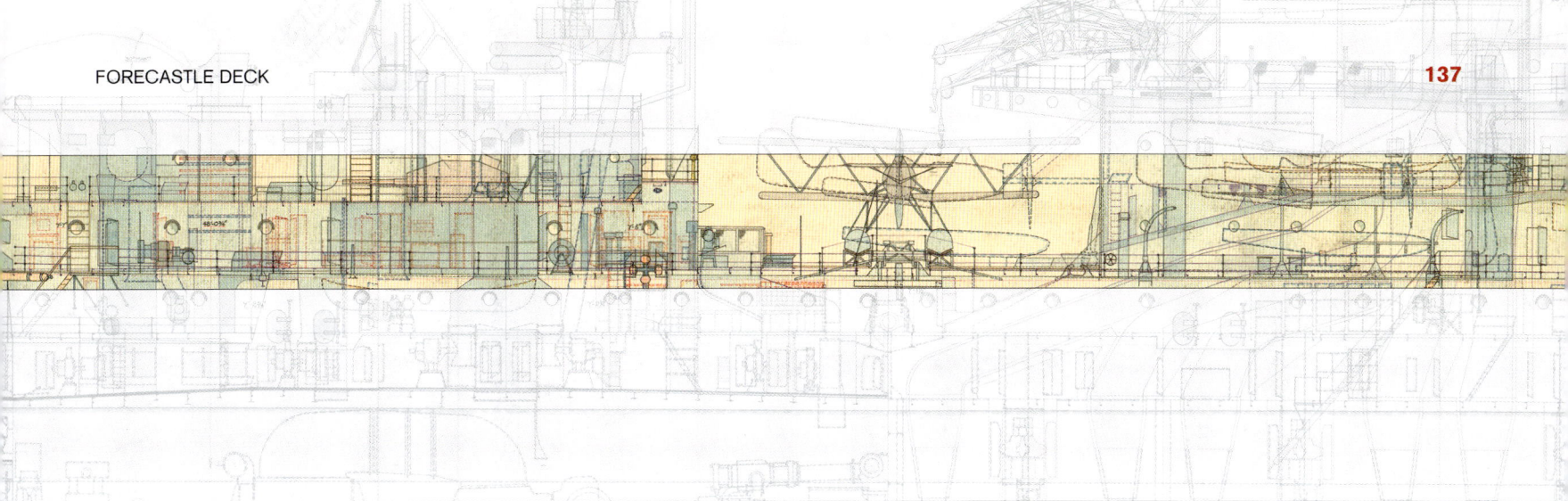

The helm signal gear fitted below the deck-head operated a cable that raised/lowered the ball (port) and flag (starboard) signals below the mainmast starfish that identified to the ship astern when and in which direction the helm had been put over.

The amidships accommodation ladder in its stowed position against the engine room supply vent.

The platforms, edged in blue outline, extending from the fore end of the hangar to the aircraft catapult provided a level surface above the deck camber for the aircraft transport trolley.

The 60cwt stream (stern) anchor in its stowed position.

Access to the engineers' stores was via ladders from hatches in the aircraft stores above. Judging by the dashed outline the access space was enclosed by a wire mesh screen.

The foam generator for dealing with inflammable liquid fires located close to the areas where petrol and aviation spirit was in use.

ENLARGED DECKS, AS FITTED 1936

FORECASTLE DECK (FORWARD)

While the modification of the forward part of the forecastle show only minor alterations, the area does show two differences from the 1916 as-fitted plans that are worthy of comment. Firstly, the enclosed area under the shelter deck from the fore end of the fore funnel to the aft side of 'B' barbette contains a large number of positions for hammocks (the red dashed lines with a black arrowhead at each end). These are not present in the 1916 drawings. The same comment applies to the upper deck below the after end of the forecastle. The complement of the ship increased by nearly 30 per cent between 1916

The ship's primary cooking facilities fitted between and abreast the funnels are little changed from 1916 apart from the ward room and gun room galleys which, although in the same general position (to p & s of the after funnel, page 137), have been rearranged to clear the area required for the fore ends of the hangars. The lack of coal bins suggests that the galley ranges had been converted to electric heating.

The vegetable store, soda fountain and lobby were probably fitted during modernisation but could, at least in part, be modifications of earlier (post-1921) alterations. The scullery, outboard of the cooks' kitchen, port side, was fitted prior to 1921. There are no equivalent additions on the starboard side.

The former carpenter's ready use store has been divided into two, the after section serving as a bacon store and the forward section as the gymnastic gear store. This change could have occurred any time after 1921.

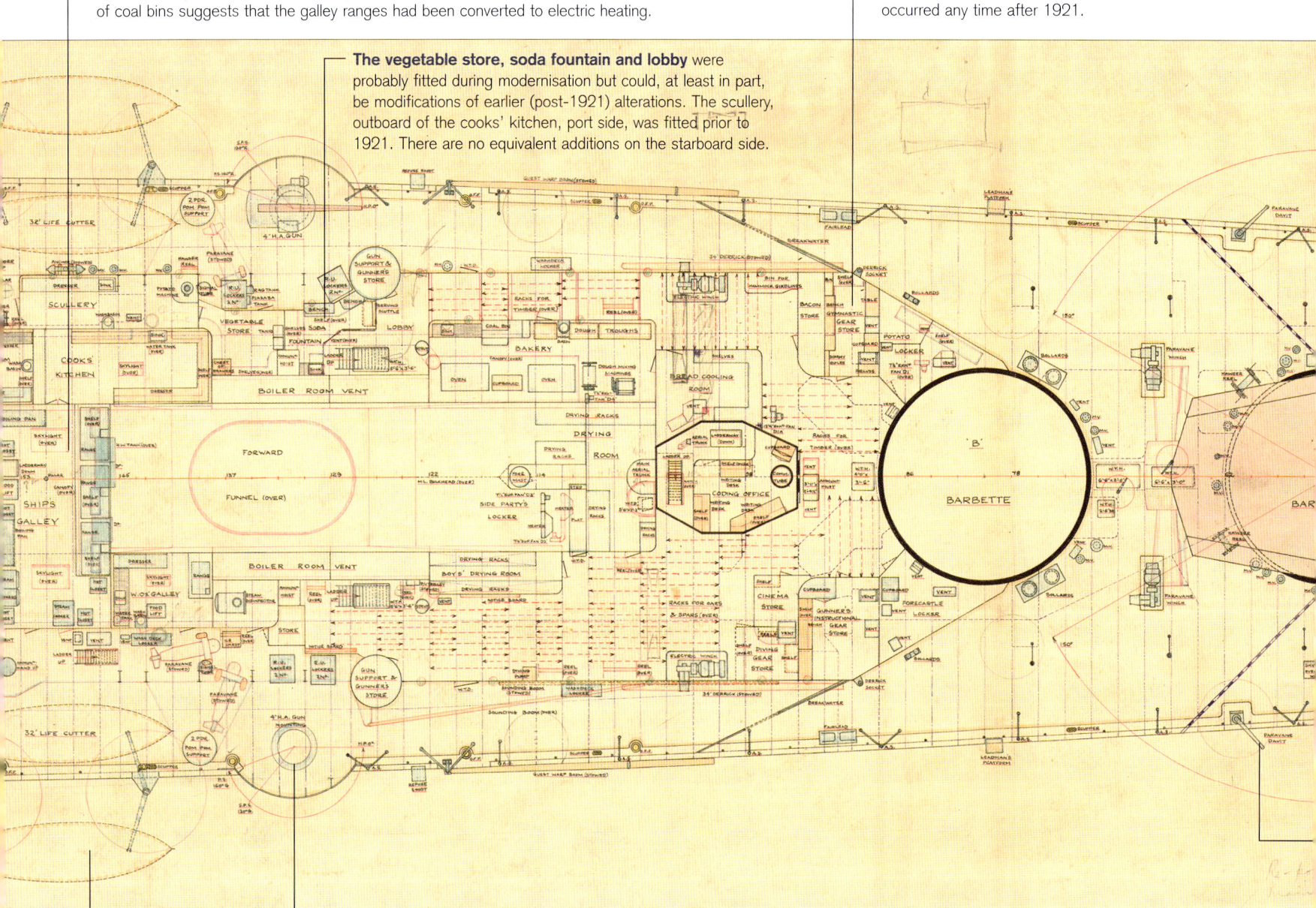

The 32ft life cutters and their davits (p & s) have been moved forward 7ft during the modernisation to clear the gun support of the 4in HA gun mounting on the hangar roof deck.

The 4in HA mountings are fitted close to the edge of the forecastle deck to provide a clear arc of fire forward and, apart from limits set by the support to the 2pdr pom-pom mounting and the life cutter (if swung outboard), to maximise that on after bearings. The provision of sufficient working area outboard of the mountings required the addition of a screened sponson overhanging the deck edge by c3ft 6in.

FORECASTLE DECK

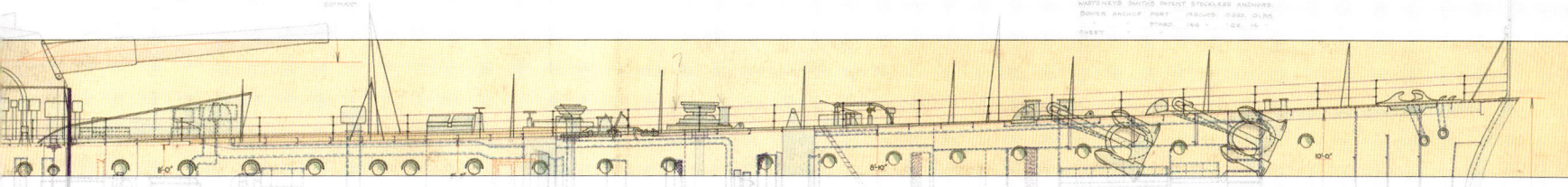

and 1921, which may well account for the increase but they do not appear in the modifications made to the plans in 1920–21 (unfortunately, this is not a guarantee that these had not been provided earlier). The second item is a mystery, at least to this author. From abreast 'B' barbette to Station 18 the forecastle has a large number of stanchions described as 'stanchions for weather deck billets'. These are not the standard awning stanchions arranged along the deck edge. I have never before come across the term 'weather deck billets' nor seen anything similar on other ship drawings. (J9435)

The former torpedo embarkation hatch now served to provide for the embarkation of HA ammunition, torpedo heads and depth charges to the magazines spaces below.

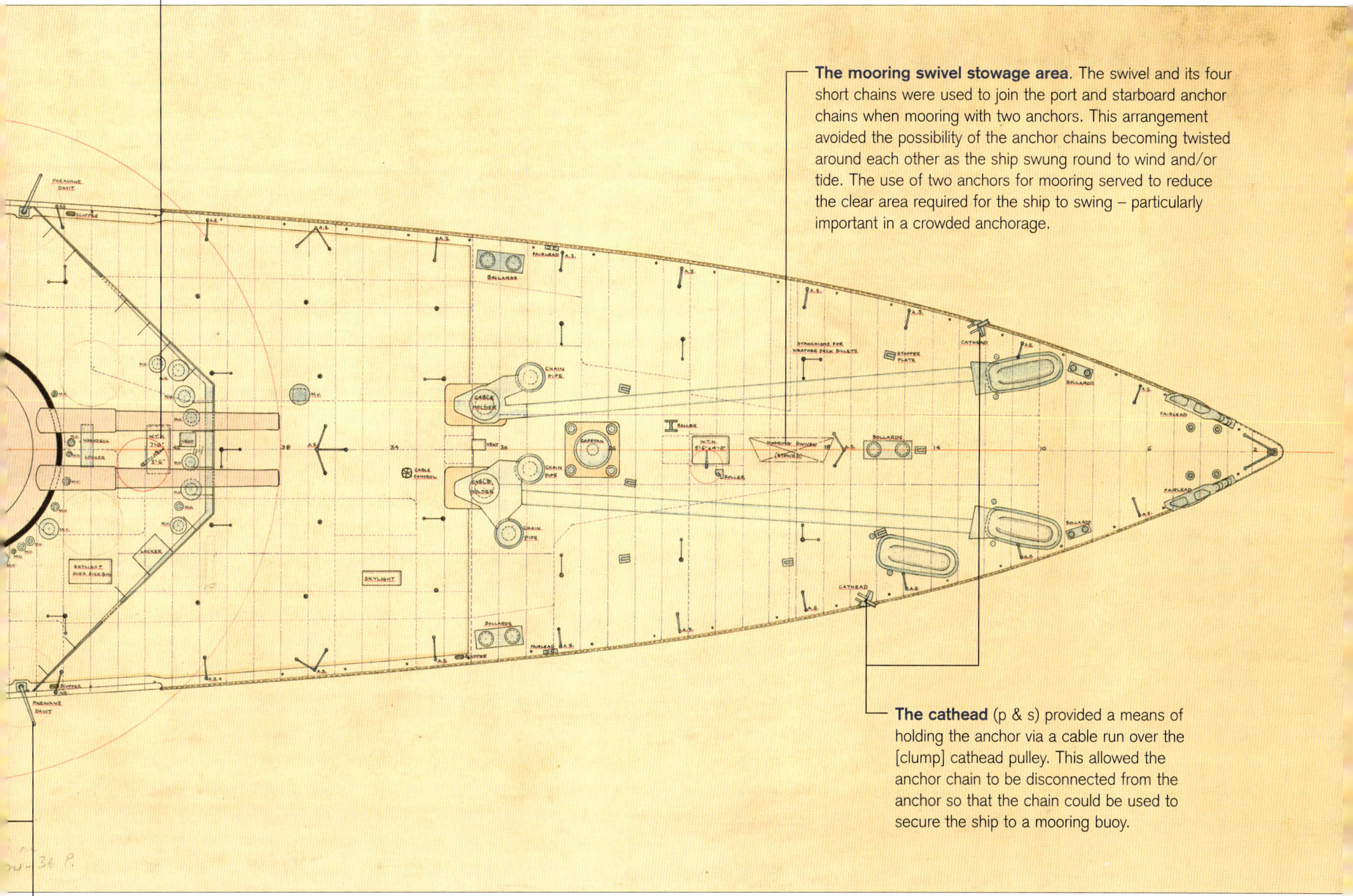

The mooring swivel stowage area. The swivel and its four short chains were used to join the port and starboard anchor chains when mooring with two anchors. This arrangement avoided the possibility of the anchor chains becoming twisted around each other as the ship swung round to wind and/or tide. The use of two anchors for mooring served to reduce the clear area required for the ship to swing – particularly important in a crowded anchorage.

The cathead (p & s) provided a means of holding the anchor via a cable run over the [clump] cathead pulley. This allowed the anchor chain to be disconnected from the anchor so that the chain could be used to secure the ship to a mooring buoy.

The two pairs of paravane davits (p & s) have been relocated further aft and, following the removal of the submerged torpedo tubes, the torpedo davits have been removed.

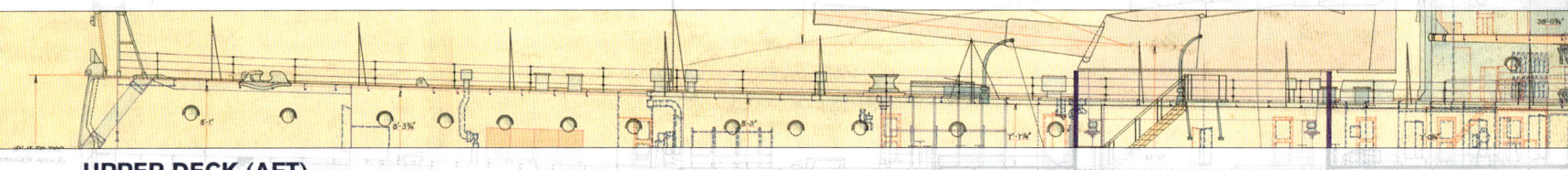

UPPER DECK (AFT)

While there has been a general re-designation and some modification of the cabins and offices located between the break of the forecastle and the forward AW torpedo tubes, the ward room, together with its ante-room and pantry, have only had the furniture re-arranged or replaced. The original coal-fired heating stoves provided here and in other officer accommodation, have been replaced by electric heaters. In the ward room and ward room ante-room these were fitted in fireplaces – an arrangement also provided on the forecastle deck for the admiral's dining and day cabins and the captain's cabin. Note that the

The sloped outward extension of the deck edge marks the after end of the 6in upper belt which effectively increased the width of the quarterdeck by 6in on each side. The slope follows the line of the fairing plate at the end of the belt. Note that the awning stanchions are shown with their heels above the side armour.

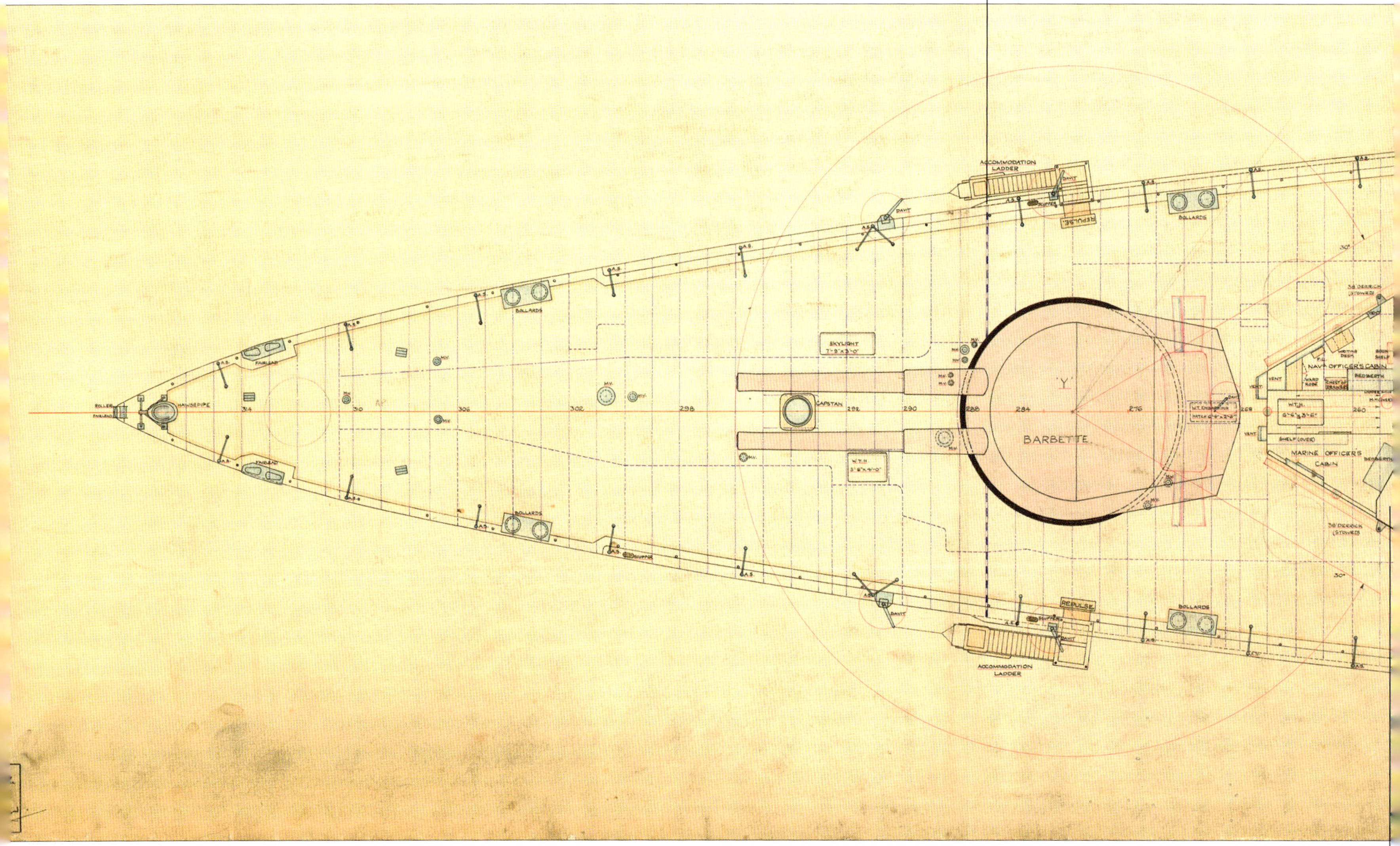

The handing lobby for the charges of the triple 4in gun mountings has been considerably enlarged during modernisation. The thick outline to the compartment indicates that it has been enclosed with protective plating (probably also fitted to its roof and floor). The room has three F/T scuttles in its walls, contains the top of the original ammunition hoist and has a new whip hoist winch. From here the charges were transported forward to the original hoists to be taken up to the gun-crew's shelters on the superstructure before being passed to the guns. Note that the original dredger hoist for the 4in shell is a short distance to port of the handing lobby.

UPPER DECK

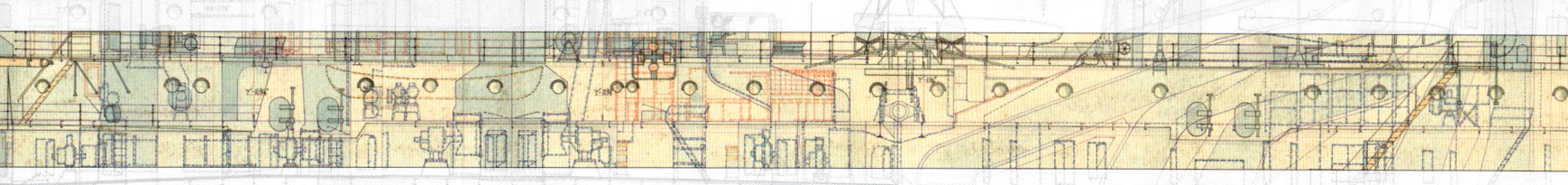

ship was built with electric radiators for officer accommodation, offices and important compartments – only a few positions were provided with coal stoves. Alterations in general include changes made over an extended period up to and including modernisation, some of which result from the fitting of the AW tubes during 1918–21 and some others from the installation of the aircraft catapult. (J9435)

The after pairs of AW 21in torpedo tubes were not altered during modernisation but the means of loading their torpedoes was. The original arrangement brought torpedoes to the tubes by double overhead rails to each tube. The new arrangement employed a single overhead rail to each pair of tubes, the section immediately above the tubes being pivoted so that it could be swung over either tube.

The forward pairs of AW 21in torpedo tubes, unlike those aft, retained their original double overhead loading rails. They did, however, have an additional fore and aft single rail fitted for the transport of torpedoes to and from the aircraft torpedo hatches in the catapult deck. As early as 1925 it was decided to replace the ship's outfit of 21in Mk IV torpedoes with Mk V. This re-appropriation was never made as it was found the greater length of the Mk V prevented loading into the existing tubes.

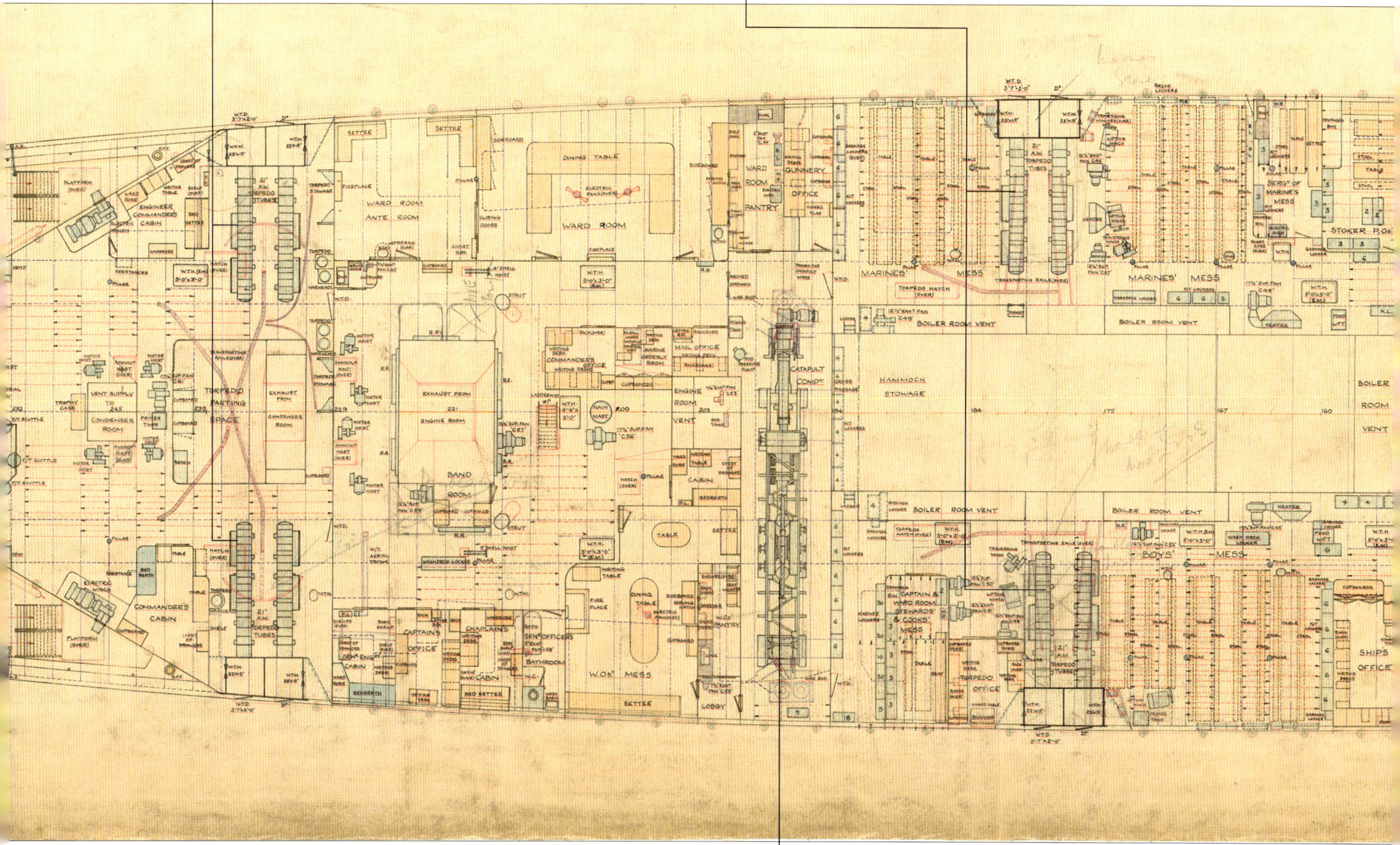

The catapult machinery is offset to starboard allowing sufficient room on the port side to retain the original ward room pantry and fit a new gunnery office (previously on the starboard side). The catapult machinery is mounted directly above the main WT bulkhead at 197 Station between the after boiler room and the engine rooms. This point was chosen, no doubt, because the bulkhead was already heavily supported by deep 'I' bars which nevertheless required further support immediately below the upper deck (visible in both the profile and sections). The arrangement made it necessary to remove that section of 197 bulkhead between the upper and forecastle decks. This was replaced by a new WT bulkhead at Station 194 while a non-WT bulkhead on the aft side of the machinery completed the enclosed 'catapult compartment'.

ENLARGED DECKS, AS FITTED 1936

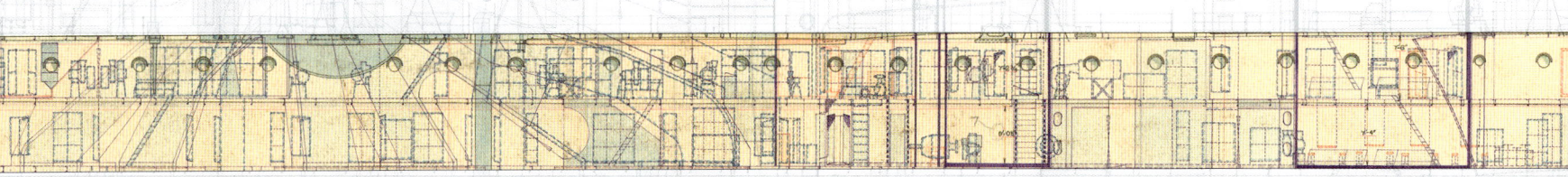

UPPER DECK (FORWARD)

Apart from the funnel uptakes and the forward barbettes this area is primarily occupied with crew accommodation. Alterations since the ship's completion are relatively minor, the primary mess decks not having been subjected to any major changes, although a few of the smaller compartments have been re-allocated, re-arranged or modified. For example, the MAA's mess has been moved from a position on the starboard side (Stations 152–156), to a position on the port side (Stations 143–147), its original location now occupied by a much larger compartment serving as the ship's office. Several such adjustments can be found by comparing the 1916 as-fitted plans with those for 1936. (J9435)

— **The forward 4in HA and BL handing lobbies** (p & s). Like that aft these replaced the original, smaller, enclosures and were constructed of protective plating, and accommodated an ammunition whip hoist and three F/T scuttles for the charges of the 4in BL, low-angle guns. Unlike that in the after lobby the hoist was also used for the 4in fixed HA ammunition brought up from the new HA magazines on the lower deck and lower platform. Since the fixed HA ammunition would not have required the F/T scuttles, these would have been passed straight out from the tops of the hoists through the adjacent access doors. The arrangement suggests that it was seen as unlikely that both HA and LA 4in guns would be in use at the same time. The BL shell came up outside the enclosure via the original dredger hoists fitted abreast the CT support.

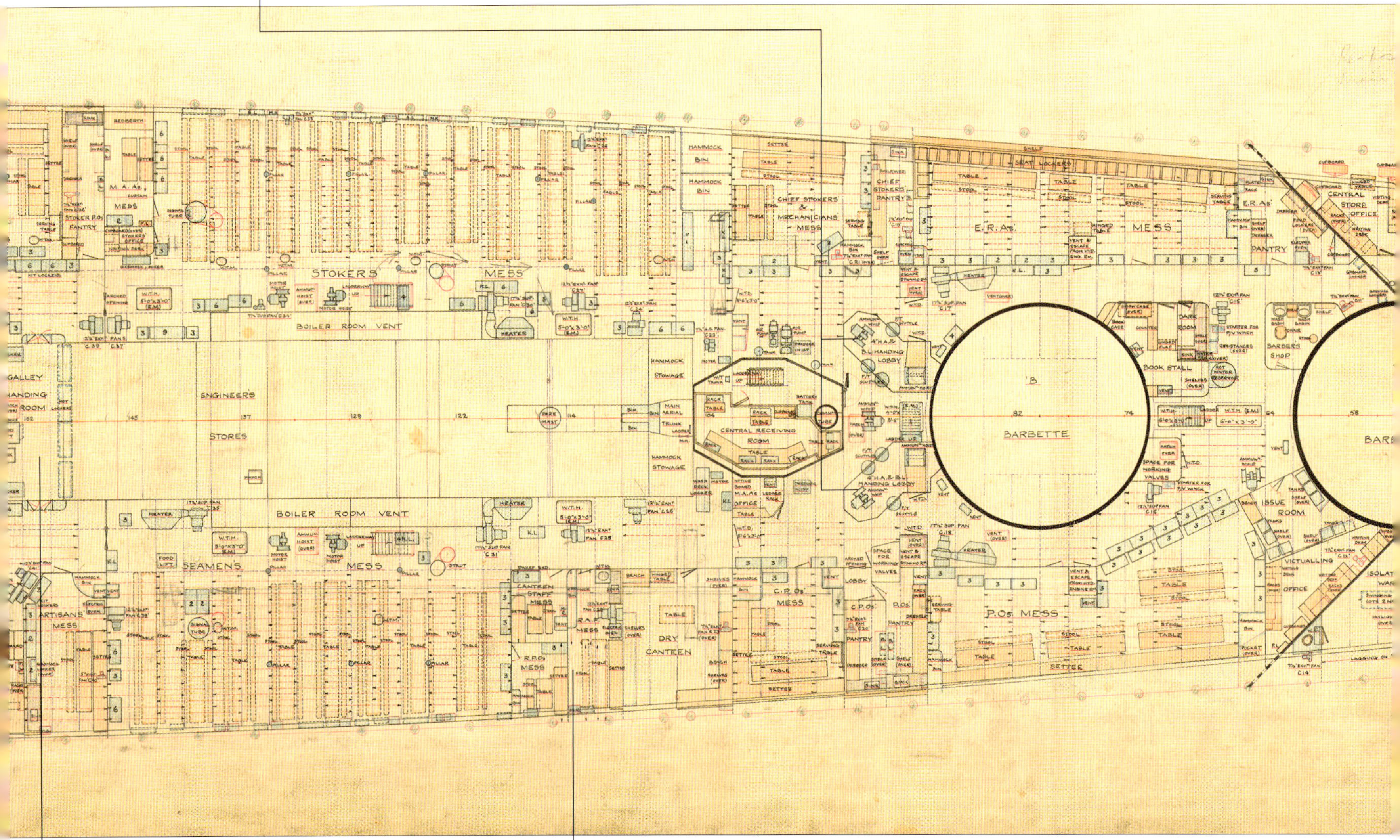

— **The galley handing room** provided for the distribution of meals to the mess decks. Food was brought down from the ship's galley on the deck above via the food lift and, if necessary, kept in the hot lockers to port and starboard until collected.

— **The RAF mess**, a necessity for the ship's aircraft personnel so long as the Fleet Air Arm was under the control of the Royal Air Force. Presumably it became the FAA mess when the Admiralty regained control of its aircraft in 1939.

UPPER DECK

143

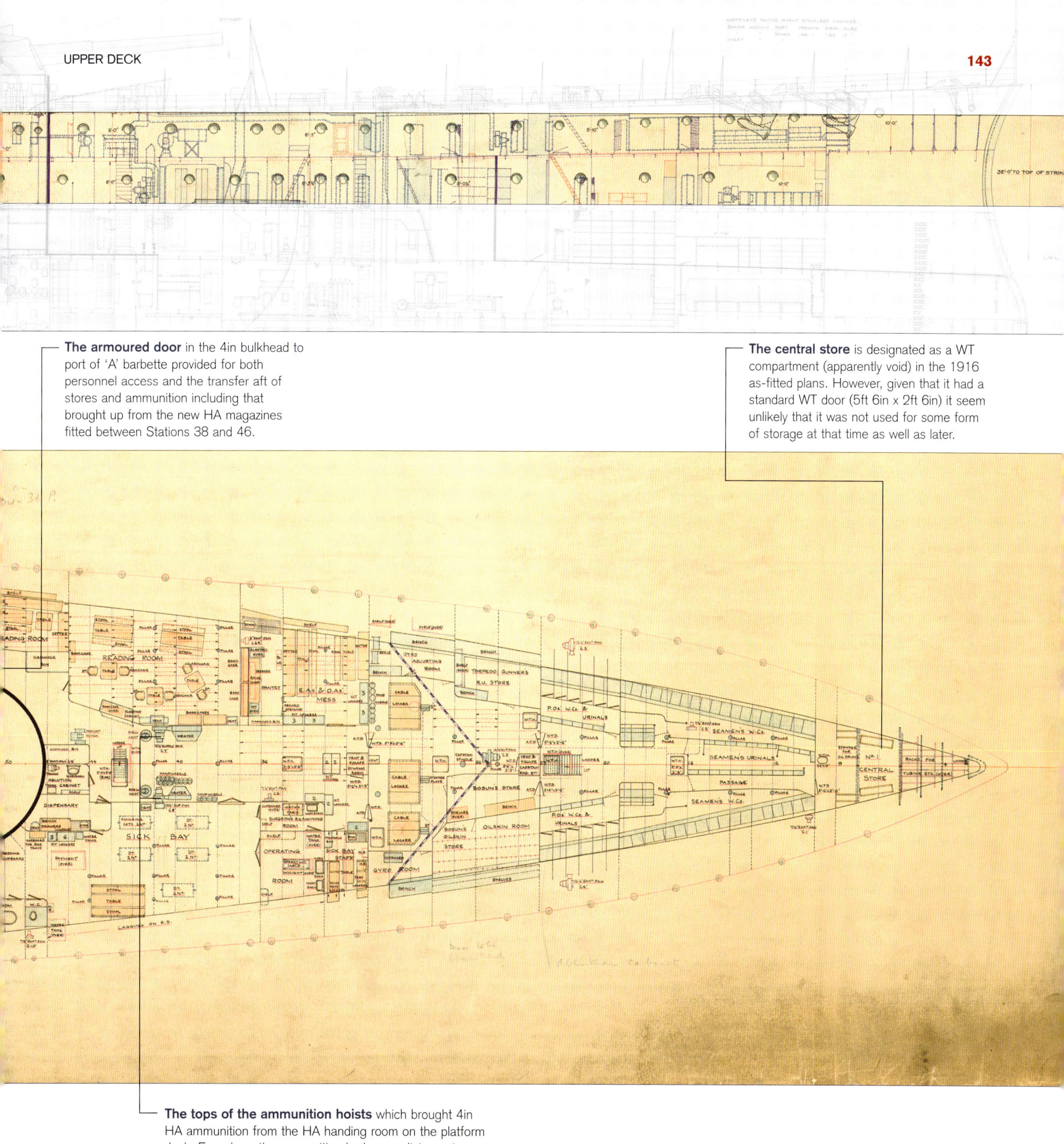

The armoured door in the 4in bulkhead to port of 'A' barbette provided for both personnel access and the transfer aft of stores and ammunition including that brought up from the new HA magazines fitted between Stations 38 and 46.

The central store is designated as a WT compartment (apparently void) in the 1916 as-fitted plans. However, given that it had a standard WT door (5ft 6in x 2ft 6in) it seem unlikely that it was not used for some form of storage at that time as well as later.

The tops of the ammunition hoists which brought 4in HA ammunition from the HA handing room on the platform deck. From here the ammunition had some distance to travel to reach the hand-up scuttles provided in the forecastle deck, abaft (port side) and before (starboard side) Station 155. Given that this was not the end of the journey, the need for ready-use ammunition close to the 4in HA guns can be clearly understood.

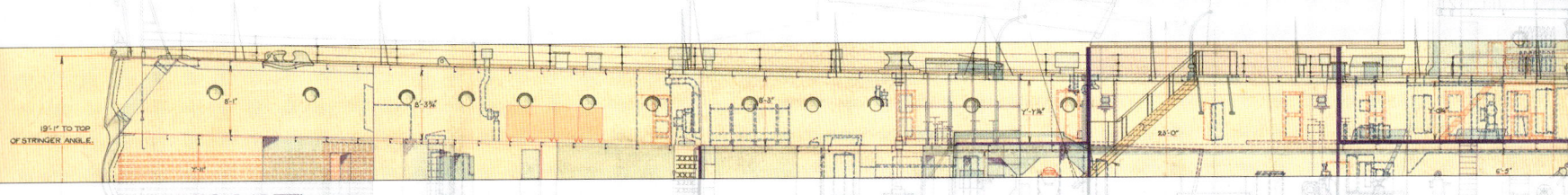

MAIN DECK (AFT)

Following the general pattern of the other accommodation and main machinery areas, there are only minor alterations to this section of the main deck. Among these is the complete renumbering of the officer cabins abaft Station 229. Oddly, what were designated in the 1916 as-fitted plans as the WOs' cabins between Stations 180 and 229 have been allocated numbers on the port side and letters on the starboard side when they previously had neither – possibly the lettered versions indicated they were for WOs while the numbers applied to commissioned officers. (J9436)

The 2nd W/T office for the ship's Type 50 set is slightly reduced in size compared with that originally fitted in the ship. The thick wall enclosing its 'silent cabinet' represents, as with other such cabinets, the thickness of its sound insulation material.

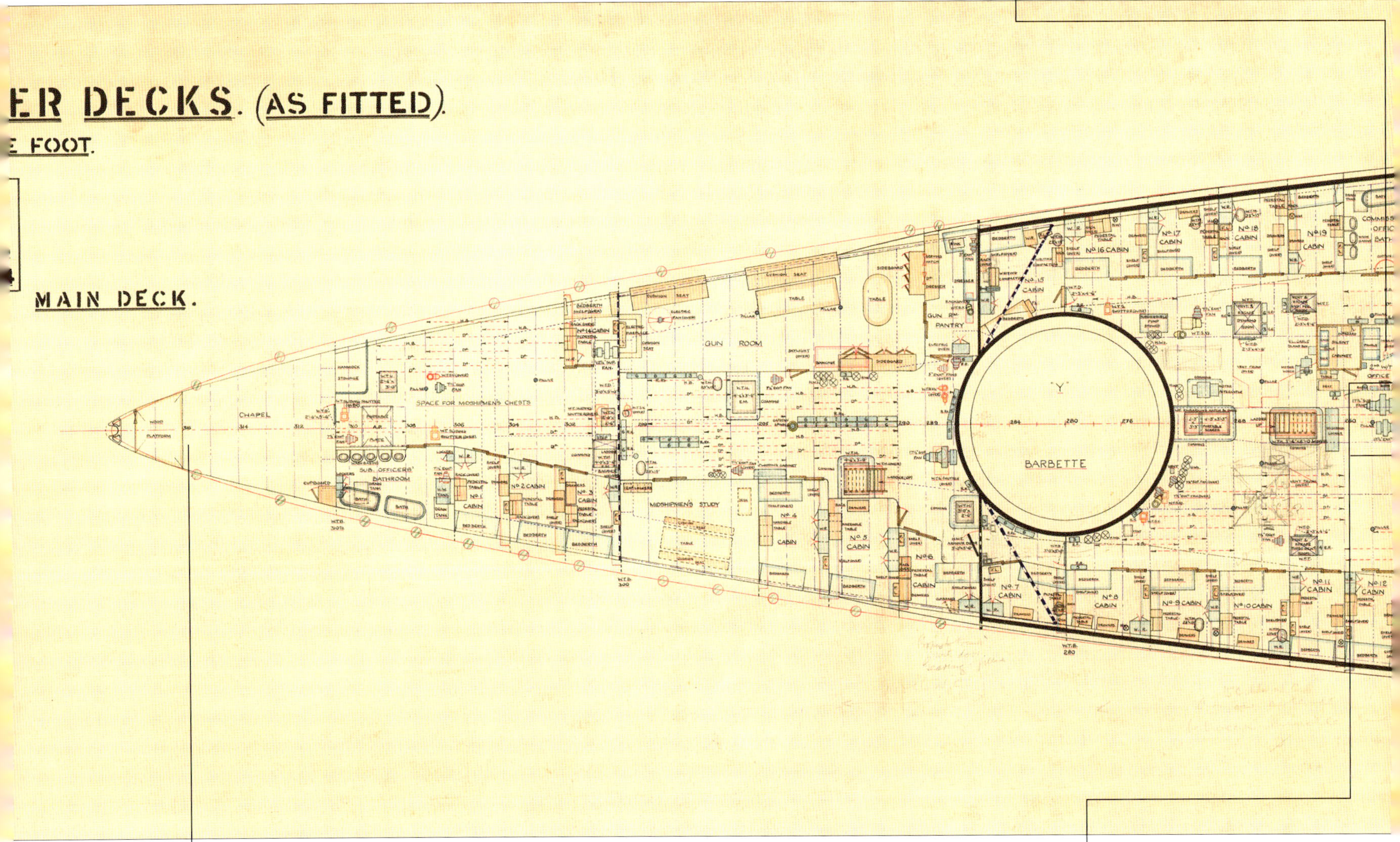

The chapel was, at least up to 1921, the officer's baggage room. The provision of this space for religious services may explain the loss of the chaplin's office that originally occupied a position adjacent to 'B' barbette on the upper deck.

The thick black squares enclosing the dredger and whip hoists from the after 4in BL magazine and shell room represent the addition of splinter protection to the hoist trunks between the main and upper decks.

MAIN DECK

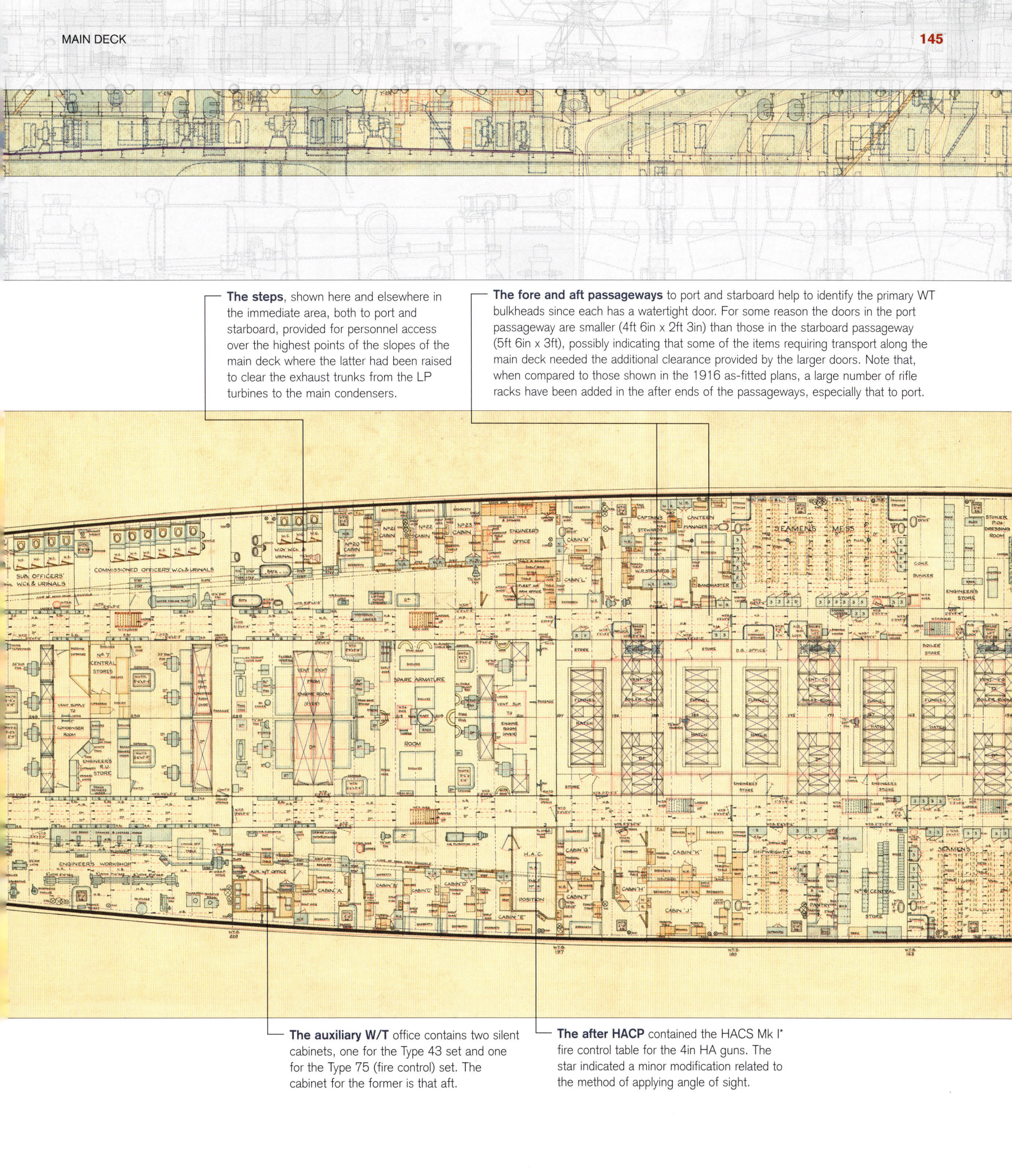

The steps, shown here and elsewhere in the immediate area, both to port and starboard, provided for personnel access over the highest points of the slopes of the main deck where the latter had been raised to clear the exhaust trunks from the LP turbines to the main condensers.

The fore and aft passageways to port and starboard help to identify the primary WT bulkheads since each has a watertight door. For some reason the doors in the port passageway are smaller (4ft 6in x 2ft 3in) than those in the starboard passageway (5ft 6in x 3ft), possibly indicating that some of the items requiring transport along the main deck needed the additional clearance provided by the larger doors. Note that, when compared to those shown in the 1916 as-fitted plans, a large number of rifle racks have been added in the after ends of the passageways, especially that to port.

The auxiliary W/T office contains two silent cabinets, one for the Type 43 set and one for the Type 75 (fire control) set. The cabinet for the former is that aft.

The after HACP contained the HACS Mk I* fire control table for the 4in HA guns. The star indicated a minor modification related to the method of applying angle of sight.

MAIN DECK (FORWARD)

As with the after part of this deck, few changes have occurred in the accommodation and washing areas from amidships to 'A' barbette, although the term 'washplace' has been dropped in favour of 'bathroom'. In the workshops and stores forward of 'A' barbette there have been a considerable number of changes since 1921 in both the functions and naming of compartments. There have, however, been few structural alterations, those that have occurred relating to non-WT sub-division between Station 38 and 'A' barbette. (J9436)

The (war) signal stations (p & s) have been partially reinstated during the ship's modernisation. Both the compartments concerned have primary peacetime functions and are provided with only one flag locker each which, in the case of the starboard compartment, is actually outside it.

The thick black squares (p & s) represent the splinter protection fitted between the main and upper decks around the dredger hoists for the 4in BL shell and (further forward) the whip hoists for the 4in BL and HA ammunition.

The calorifier was a steam heat exchanger for supplying hot water to the adjacent bathrooms.

The spare armature (stowed) is, judging by its size, probably for one of the ship's main dynamos.

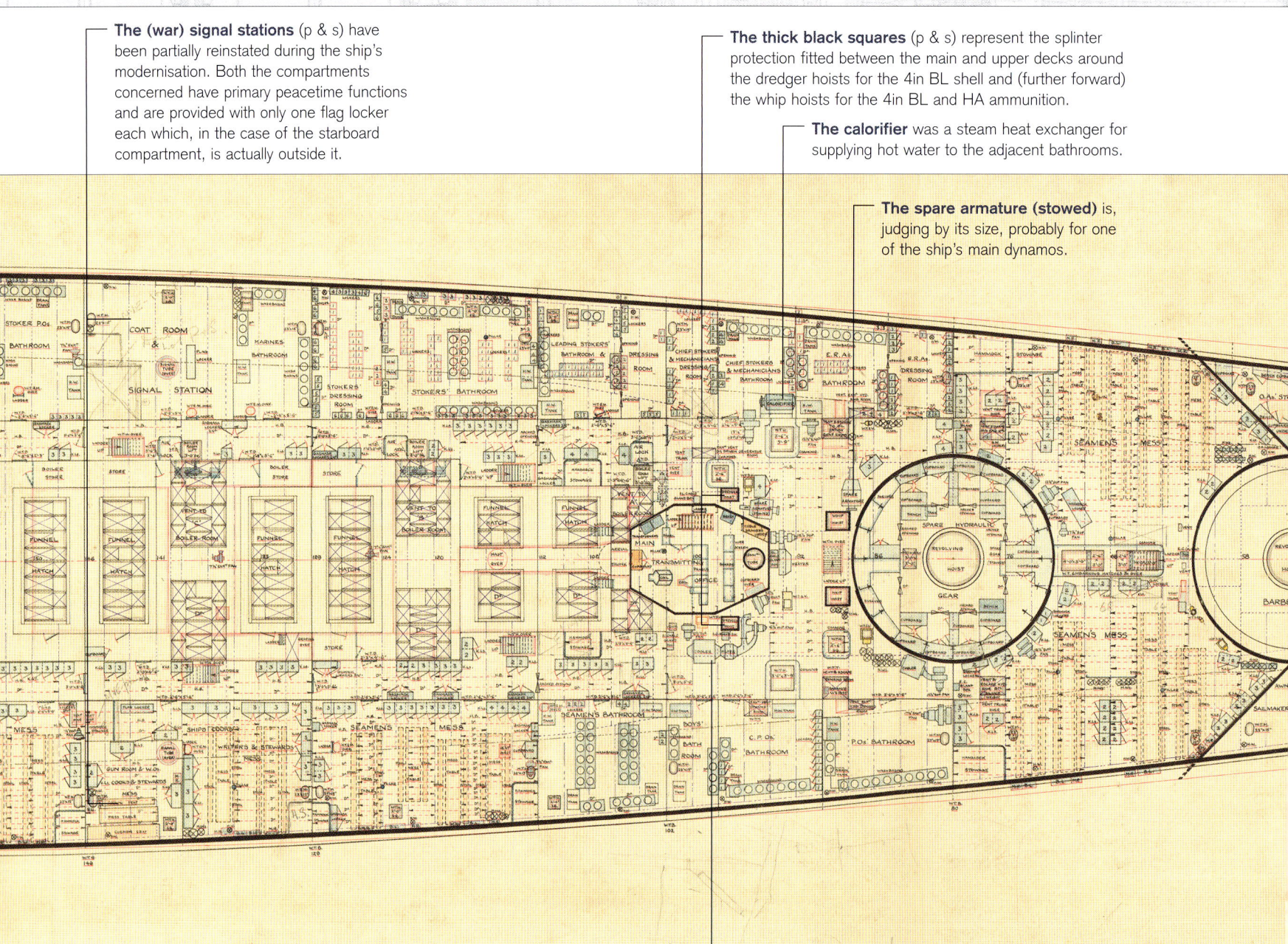

This combination of fan, filter and cooler was part of the ship's collective protection (defence against poison gas fitted in 1925–26), arrangements which involved making the relevant compartments gas-tight and re-circulating the air within them. The compartments concerned were the primary centres of control in action – the lower CT (and possibly its surrounding compartments) on the lower deck and the TS on the platform deck. Elsewhere it was intended that officers and crew should rely on gas masks.

MAIN DECK

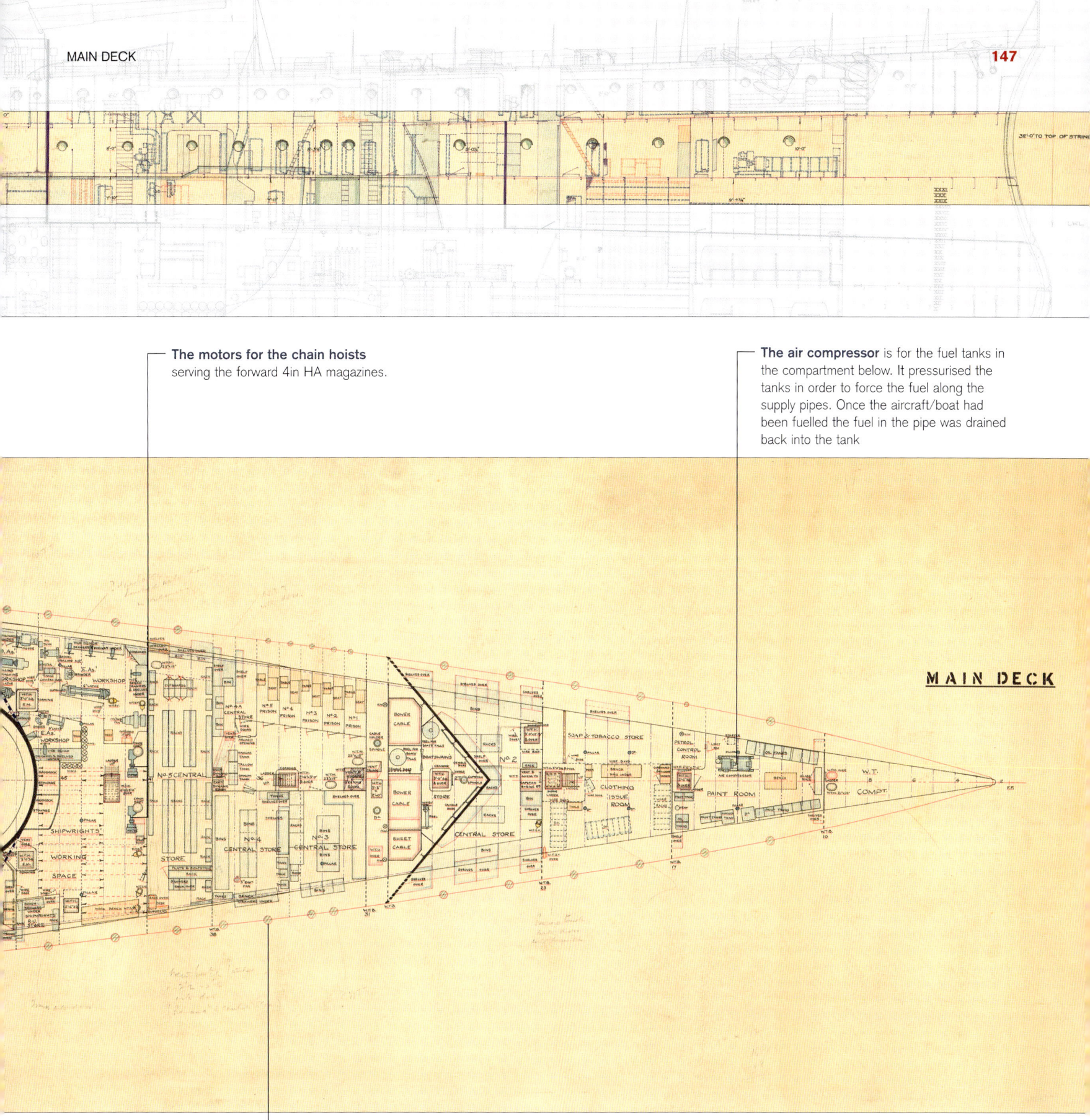

The motors for the chain hoists serving the forward 4in HA magazines.

The air compressor is for the fuel tanks in the compartment below. It pressurised the tanks in order to force the fuel along the supply pipes. Once the aircraft/boat had been fuelled the fuel in the pipe was drained back into the tank

The positions of side scuttles were represented in plan view by circles located on the outline of the deck above. Although this was accurate for their longitudinal position, it was not for their location athwartships (unless the side was vertical) or their shape. No doubt this was an acceptable convention given the work involved in a more accurate but relatively pointless representation.

ENLARGED DECKS, AS FITTED 1936

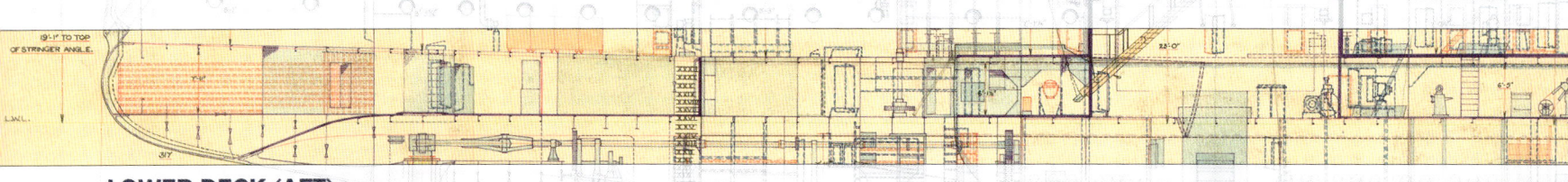

LOWER DECK (AFT)

Apart from the removal of the tubes from the bulge compartments and the alterations to the secondary, AA and torpedo armament magazines, very little was altered below the main deck during modernisation. However, the 1936 as-fitted plans do provide more detail than in the originals – especially in relation to the main machinery compartments. (J9436)

The fresh water tank is an addition probably made during modernisation, but possibly earlier, which increased the available fresh water stowage from 146.6 to 214.6 tons. The likely reasons for this addition are the increase in the complement and the adoption of fresh water showers in place of the salt water showers originally provided.

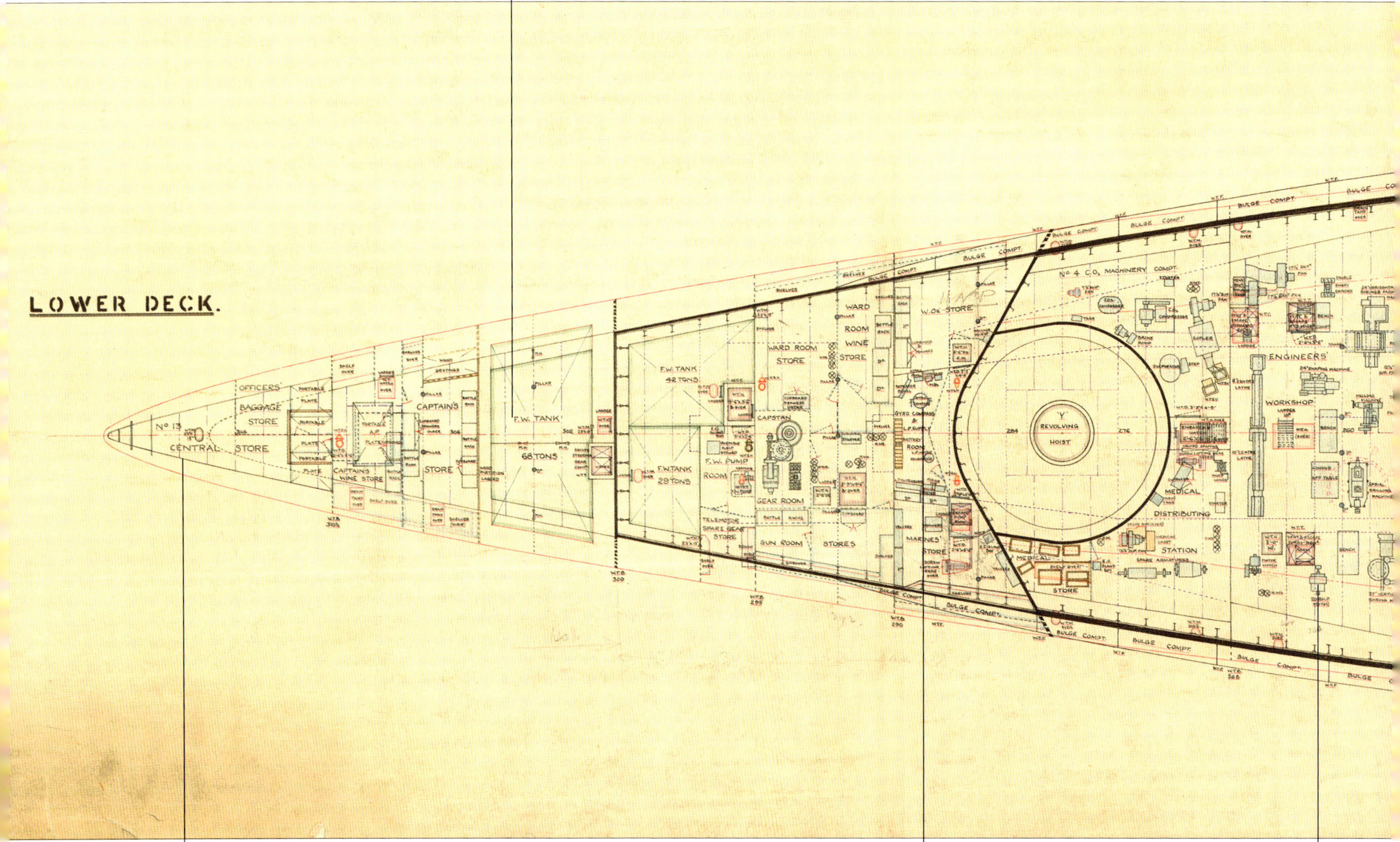

The outline of the lower deck at the extreme after end is not shown in the 1916 as-fitted plan, which provides instead the outline of the protective deck which curves downward towards the stern below the lower deck. The latter is still shown here but in dashed line, indicating its status as hidden detail.

The after gyro compass has been moved here from its previous location in the starboard forward corner of the engineers' workshop, an alteration made sometime between 1921 and 1936.

The two 20hp electric motors provided the power for overhead belts that drove the machinery in the engineers' workshop.

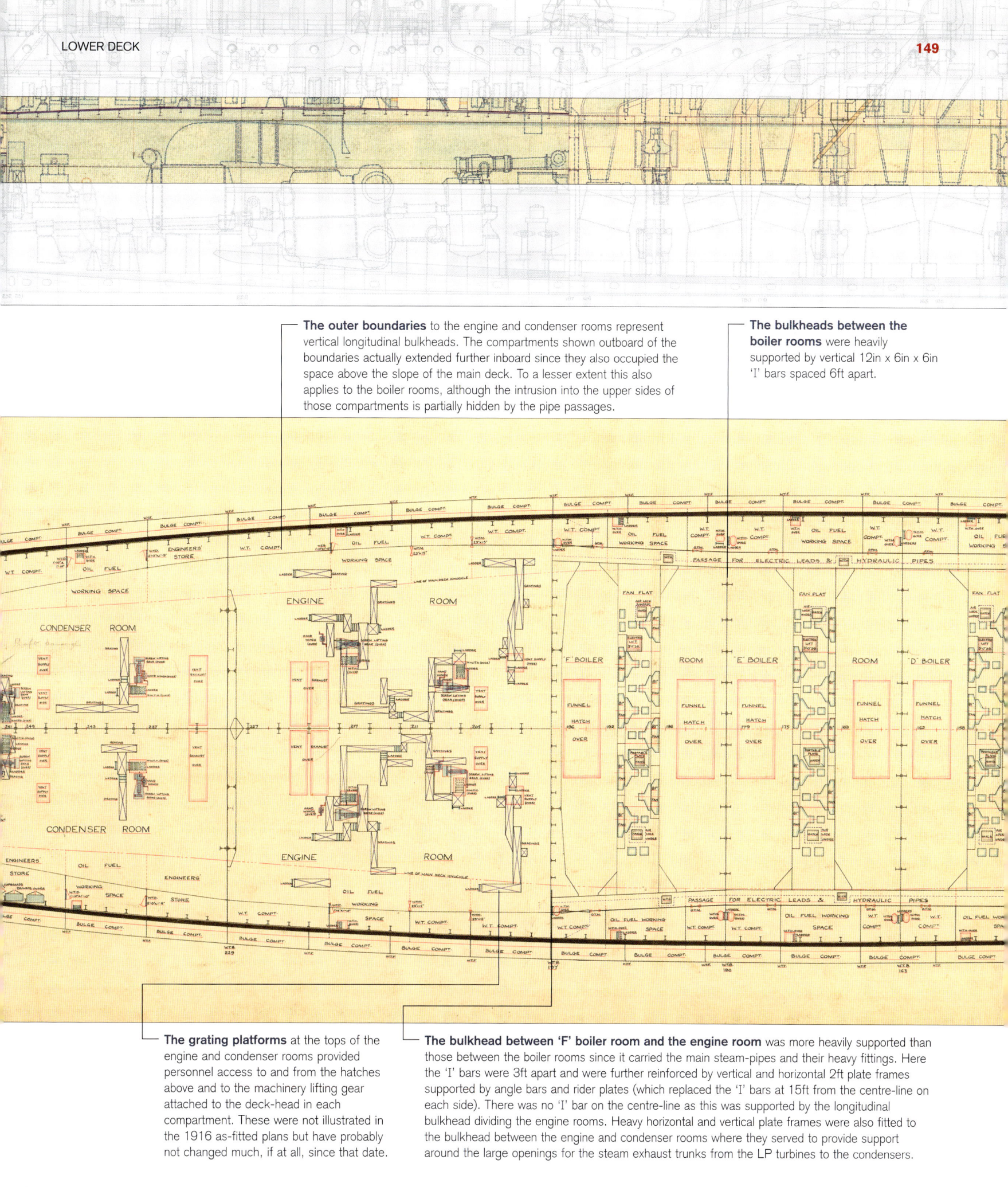

LOWER DECK

The outer boundaries to the engine and condenser rooms represent vertical longitudinal bulkheads. The compartments shown outboard of the boundaries actually extended further inboard since they also occupied the space above the slope of the main deck. To a lesser extent this also applies to the boiler rooms, although the intrusion into the upper sides of those compartments is partially hidden by the pipe passages.

The bulkheads between the boiler rooms were heavily supported by vertical 12in x 6in x 6in 'I' bars spaced 6ft apart.

The grating platforms at the tops of the engine and condenser rooms provided personnel access to and from the hatches above and to the machinery lifting gear attached to the deck-head in each compartment. These were not illustrated in the 1916 as-fitted plans but have probably not changed much, if at all, since that date.

The bulkhead between 'F' boiler room and the engine room was more heavily supported than those between the boiler rooms since it carried the main steam-pipes and their heavy fittings. Here the 'I' bars were 3ft apart and were further reinforced by vertical and horizontal 2ft plate frames supported by angle bars and rider plates (which replaced the 'I' bars at 15ft from the centre-line on each side). There was no 'I' bar on the centre-line as this was supported by the longitudinal bulkhead dividing the engine rooms. Heavy horizontal and vertical plate frames were also fitted to the bulkhead between the engine and condenser rooms where they served to provide support around the large openings for the steam exhaust trunks from the LP turbines to the condensers.

150 ENLARGED DECKS, AS FITTED 1936

LOWER DECK (FORWARD)

The area around the lower CT shows, by its thick outer line, the 2in protective enclosure fitted in 1916–17 (something missing from the corrections made to the 1916 as-fitteds). The spaces are much as they were when the ship completed, with additions limited to a stand for a plotting table in the lobby and some lifting gear on the port side of the switchboard room. Note the covers over the ring main in the lobby and on each side of the CT enclosure; how the three disconnected sections join up is not evident. (J9436)

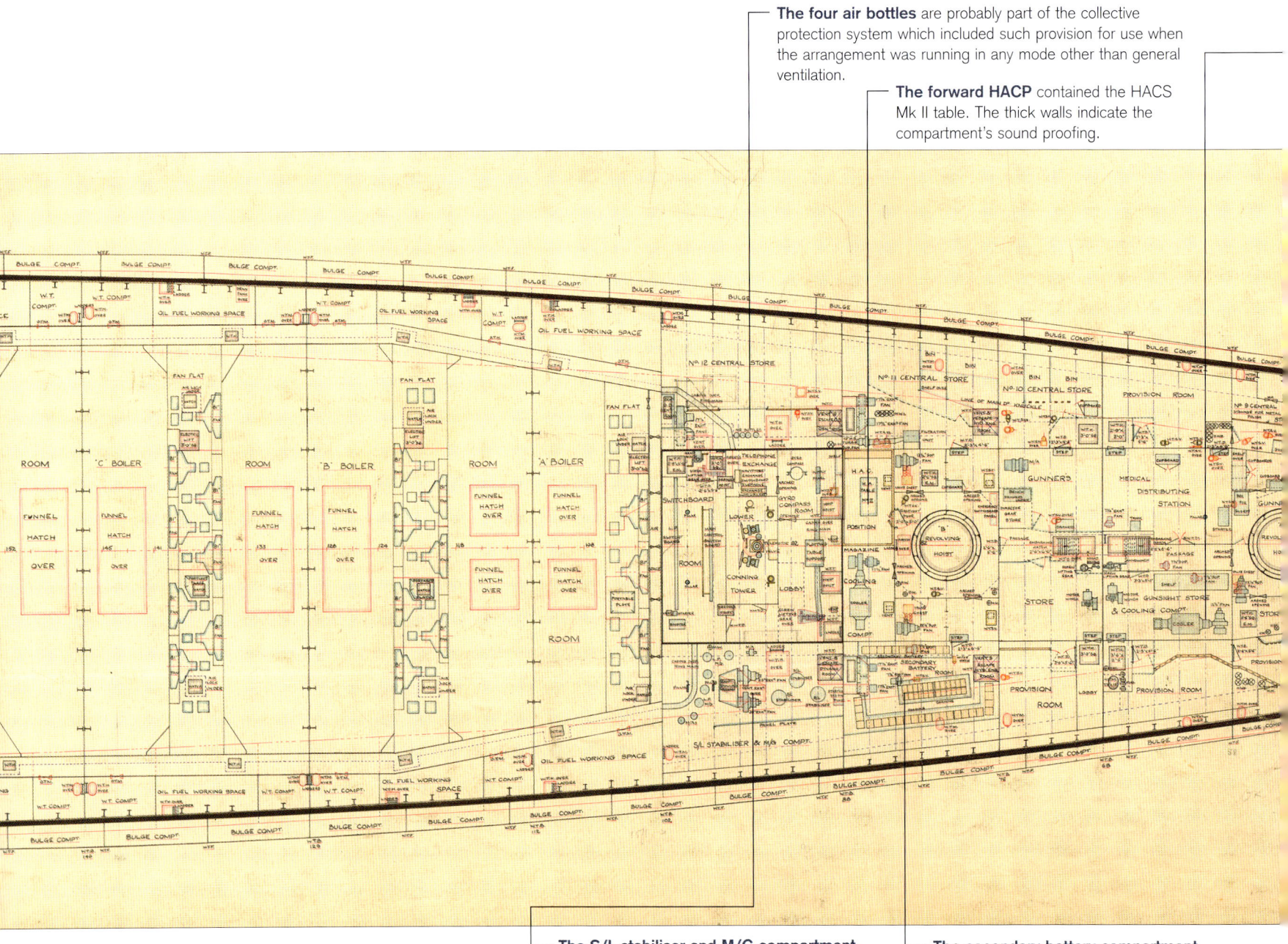

The four air bottles are probably part of the collective protection system which included such provision for use when the arrangement was running in any mode other than general ventilation.

The forward HACP contained the HACS Mk II table. The thick walls indicate the compartment's sound proofing.

The S/L stabiliser and M/G compartment converted from store rooms during modernisation. The compartment accommodates three gyro stabilising units, five LP motor generators and two motor alternators. Two fans formally fitted in the after inboard corner have been removed – presumably superseded by the collective protection ventilation.

The secondary battery compartment, formally the spare searchlight store. Batteries served as emergency back-ups for lighting and low power systems (telephones, fire control instruments, etc)

LOWER DECK

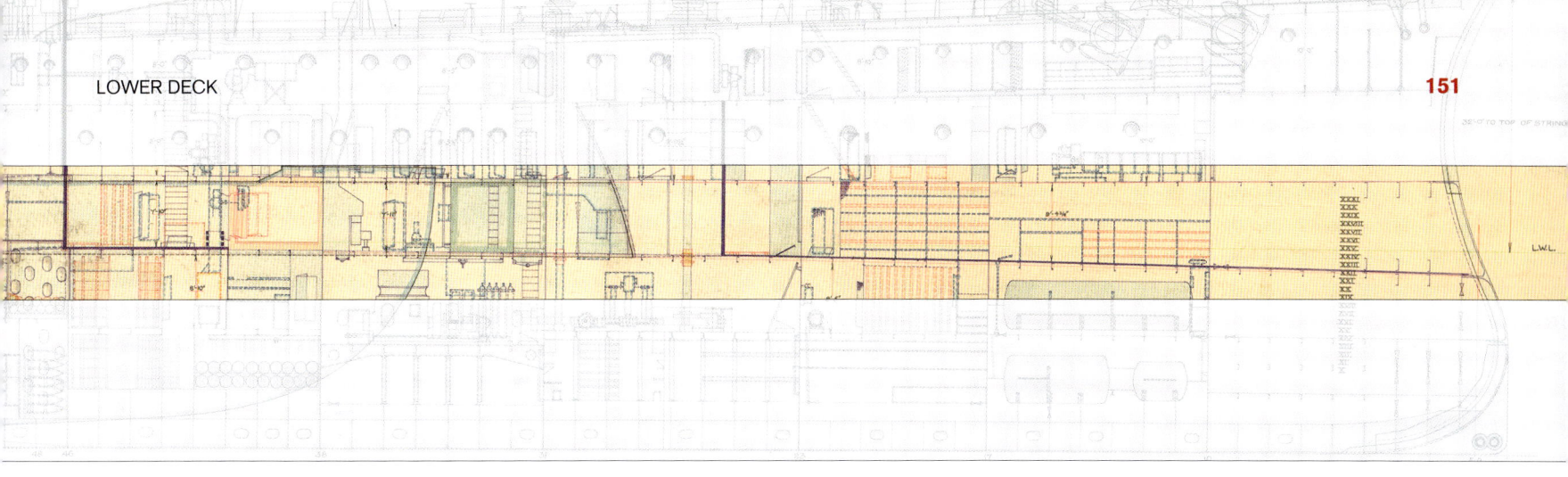

The magazine cooler no longer has local CO_2 machinery, which suggests the cooling medium was now supplied from the CO_2 machines for the cool rooms located forward of 'A' barbette.

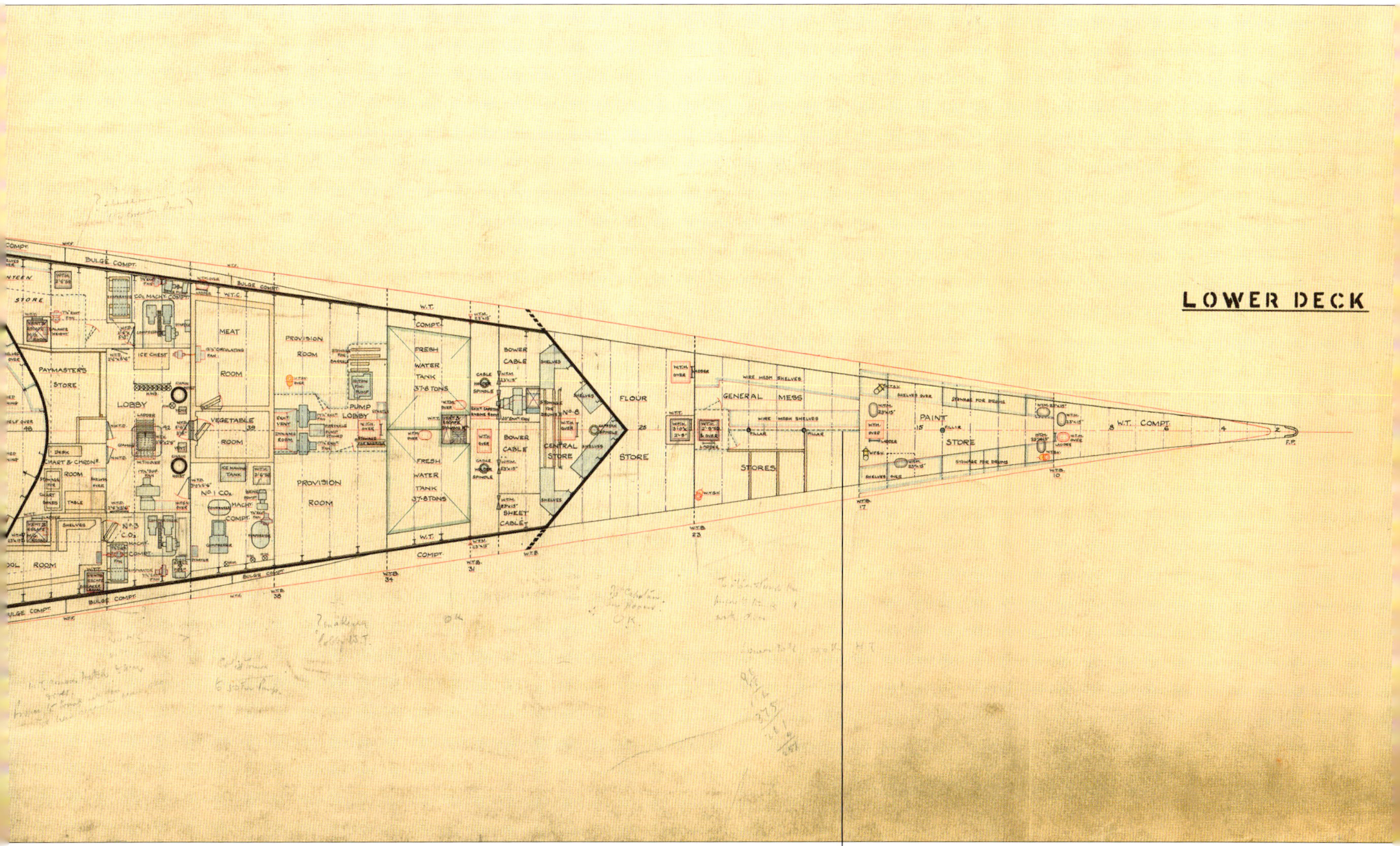

Wire mesh bulkheads are represented by dashed lines as shown here. Most commonly found as subdivisions in store rooms

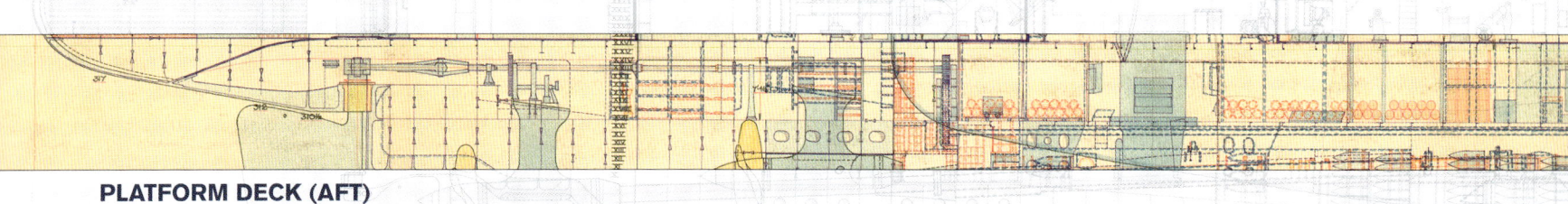

PLATFORM DECK (AFT)

Within the engine and boiler rooms bilge and flood water was dealt with by steam-powered machinery. Outside these spaces, fore and aft, the main groups of WT compartments were provided with 50-ton electrically powered pumps. The arrangement was intended to limit the piercing of main transverse WT bulkheads by water and steam pipes. *Repulse* was constructed with eight 50-ton pumps all fitted on the platform deck: they are located at Stations 296, 278, 98 (p & s), 66, 39 and 22–24 (p & s). Both these and the fire and bilge pumps in the engine and boiler rooms also supplied the fire-main salt water

Two sets of Weir evaporators are fitted in each of the condenser rooms. The pair on the outboard sides is part of a compound set and those inboard single. These used steam to boil and convert sea water into fresh feed water for the boilers when at sea (in harbour, if available, water was supplied from water boats). The complete evaporator plant also included a distiller to condense the steam boiled out of the sea water and a circulating pump. The distilled water could also be used to supply the ship's domestic fresh water service. The distilling plant had a total capacity of 480 tons of fresh water per day.

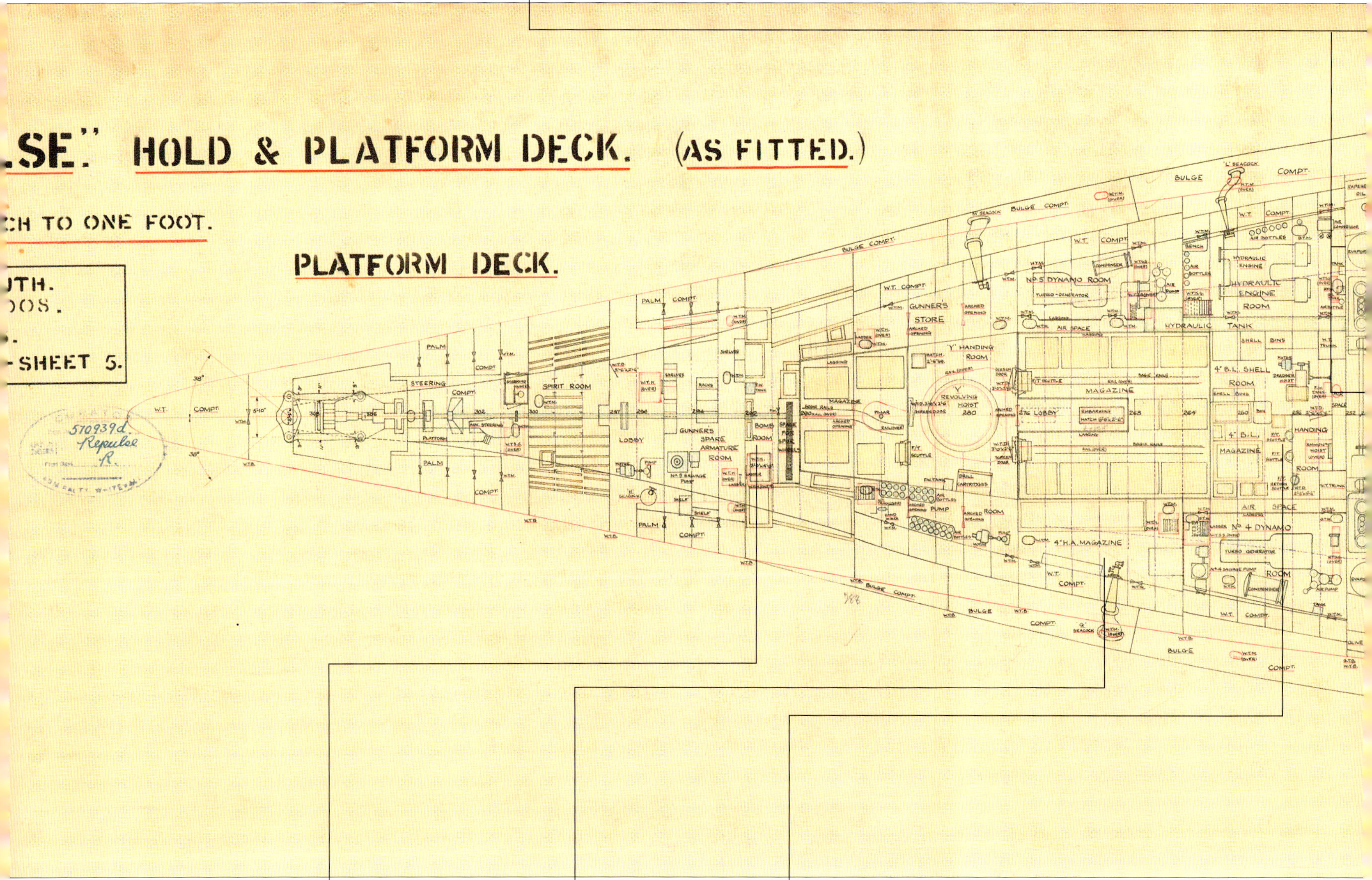

The bomb room for aircraft munitions, including the four warheads for her 18in Mk XI aerial torpedoes, was fitted around the after end of 'Y' magazine and the steering shaft transfer gears.

The 4in HA magazine, formally one of the engineers' stores, provided during modernisation to supply the twin 4in BD mountings and later the 4in singles that replaced them.

The 4in magazine and shell room for the after triple mountings has been re-arranged, probably during modernisation but possibly earlier. The two compartments are now port and starboard instead of fore and aft, and a handing room has been added to the fore end of the magazine space. The latter has three vertical F/T scuttles – two for supply, in the wall of the handing room, and one for return charges in the handing room door.

PLATFORM DECK

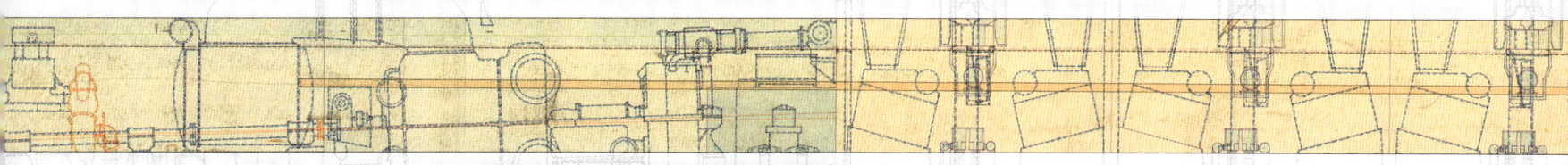

service. As the 50-ton pumps were viewed as inadequate for dealing with any major flooding at the ends of the ship, she was fitted with four 350-ton, submersible, salvage pumps during modernisation. Three were located on the platform deck at Stations 262–264, 100 and 33–35 and one in the hold at Stations 62–64 (all were fitted to starboard). The ship was also supplied with portable electric, submersible, pumps for use in emergency. As built she also had five 200-ton steam ejectors, two in the engine rooms and three in auxiliary machinery compartments, but these were extremely wasteful of feed water and it is possible some, if not all, had been removed by 1936. Note that the designation in tons refers to a pump's capacity per hour. (J9437)

Local steering wheels for the main steering engines, the latter mounted on the after bulkhead of the condenser rooms.

Two main condensers took the exhaust steam from each LP turbine, via the large rectangular-section exhaust trunk, where it was cooled by sea water pumped through the condenser by the large circulating pumps located abaft them. The air pumps at the fore end of the engine room extracted the condensate and air from the condensers returning the water to the feed tanks and the air to atmosphere. The air pumps also served to maintain the vacuum in the condenser (nominally 28in, but variable with sea temperature and atmospheric pressure). The auxiliary condensers to port and starboard served the same functions for the auxiliary steam engines and had separate circulating and air pumps.

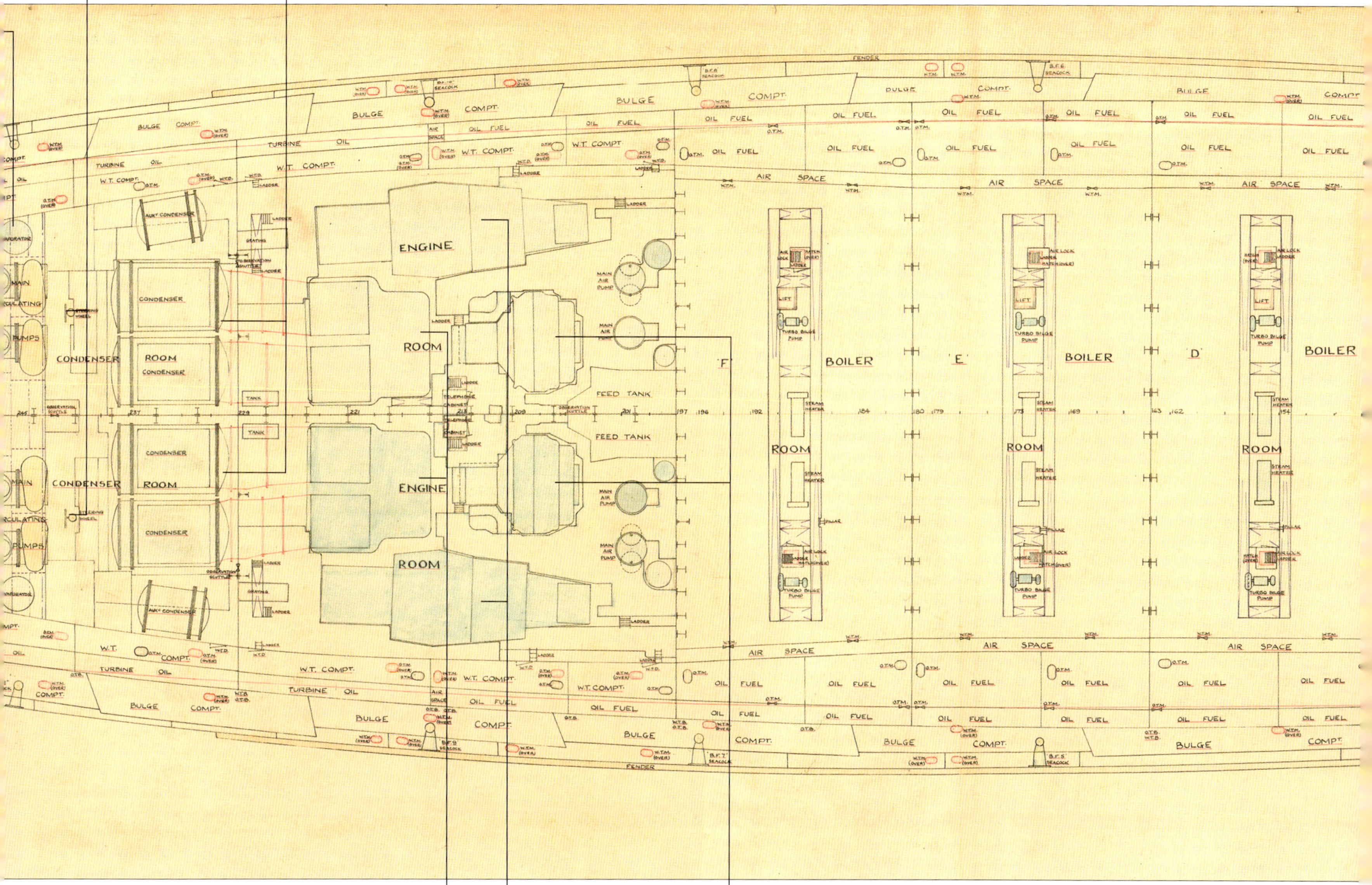

The high pressure ahead turbine exhausted its steam into the IP ahead turbine; from there it passed to the LP ahead turbine.

The IP ahead and HP astern turbine, in the same casing; the astern turbine was at the after end.

The LP ahead and astern turbine in the same casing, the latter being at the after end.

ENLARGED DECKS, AS FITTED 1936

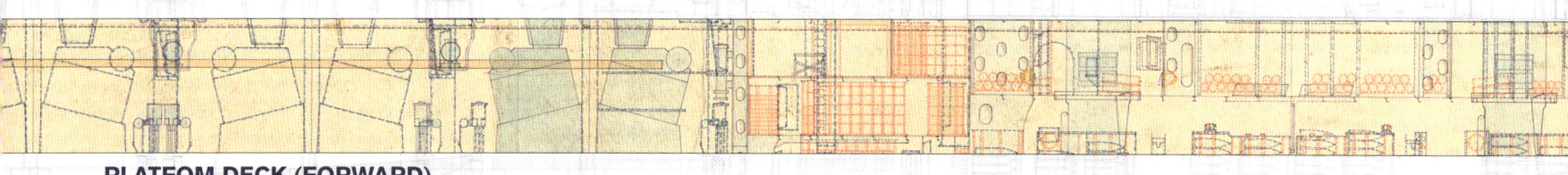

PLATFOM DECK (FORWARD)

There was a considerable re-arrangement of the 4in and HA magazines in the forward part of the ship, which was complicated by the need for space and the provision for both the fixed 4in HA ammunition, 4in BL ammunition and the pom-pom ammunition. An upper HA magazine replaced the small arms magazine on the platform deck forward of the TS. The small arms magazine was relocated on the lower platform along with a new lower HA magazine. The 4in BL magazine which previously occupied the lower platform was relocated to a new enclosure in the centre of the 4in BL shell room immediately below. In addition, another 4in HA magazine was fitted in the after part of what had been the submerged torpedo room. Upper and lower pom-pom magazines replaced

The turbo bilge pumps, were fitted at the time of the ship's construction but originally there was only one per boiler room. The number here has been increased to two per room except for the smaller 'A' boiler room which remained with only one. These were in fact salvage pumps intended to deal with large quantities of water, each having a capacity of 425 tons per hour.

The main TS still contains its First World War Dreyer Mk IV* fire control table and the secondary armament TS in the port forward corner. The Type 31 F/C wireless cabinet has, however, gone, its function having been replaced by Type 75.

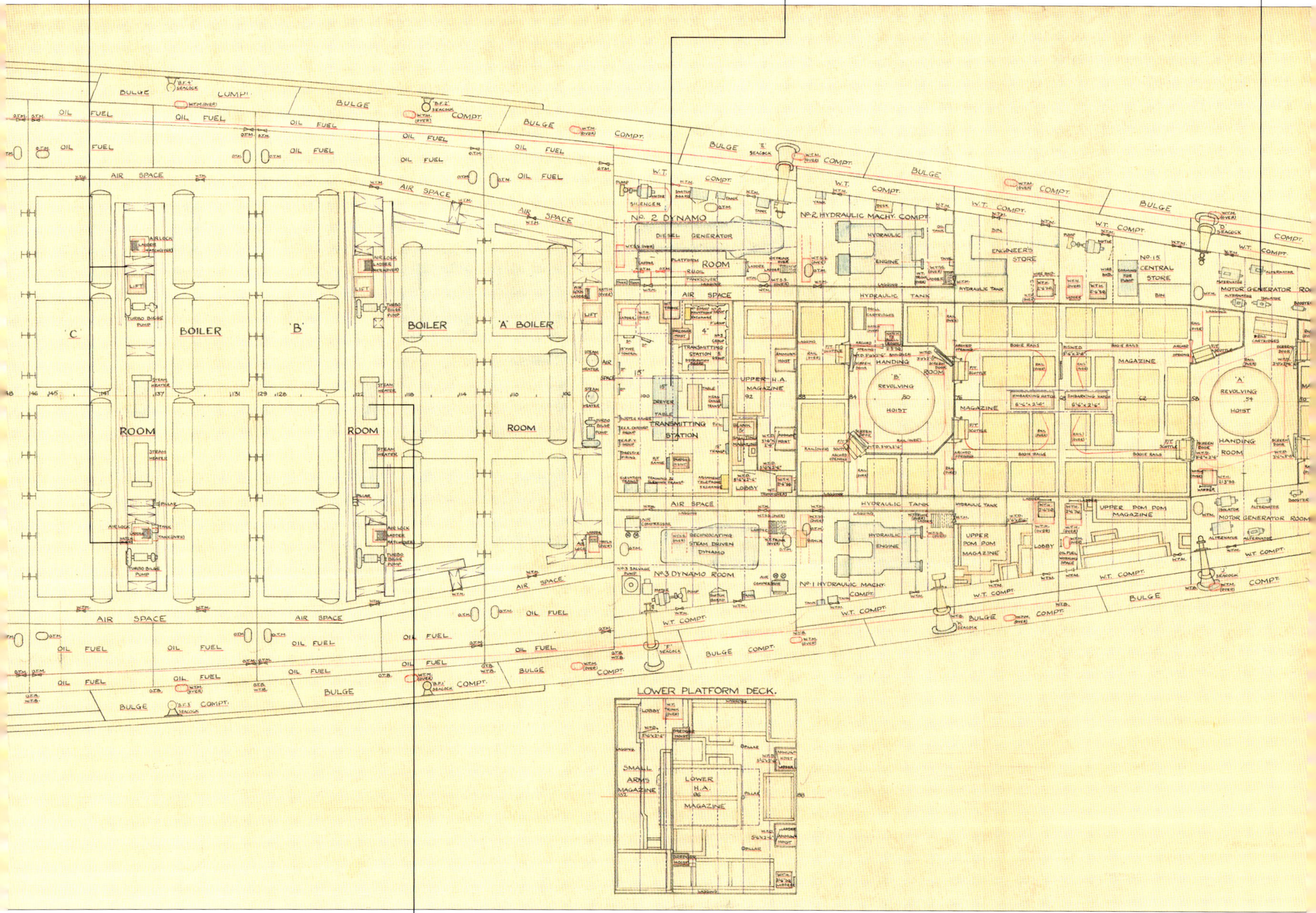

The steam heaters served to pre-heat the boiler feed water using exhaust steam from the auxiliary machinery.

PLATFORM DECK

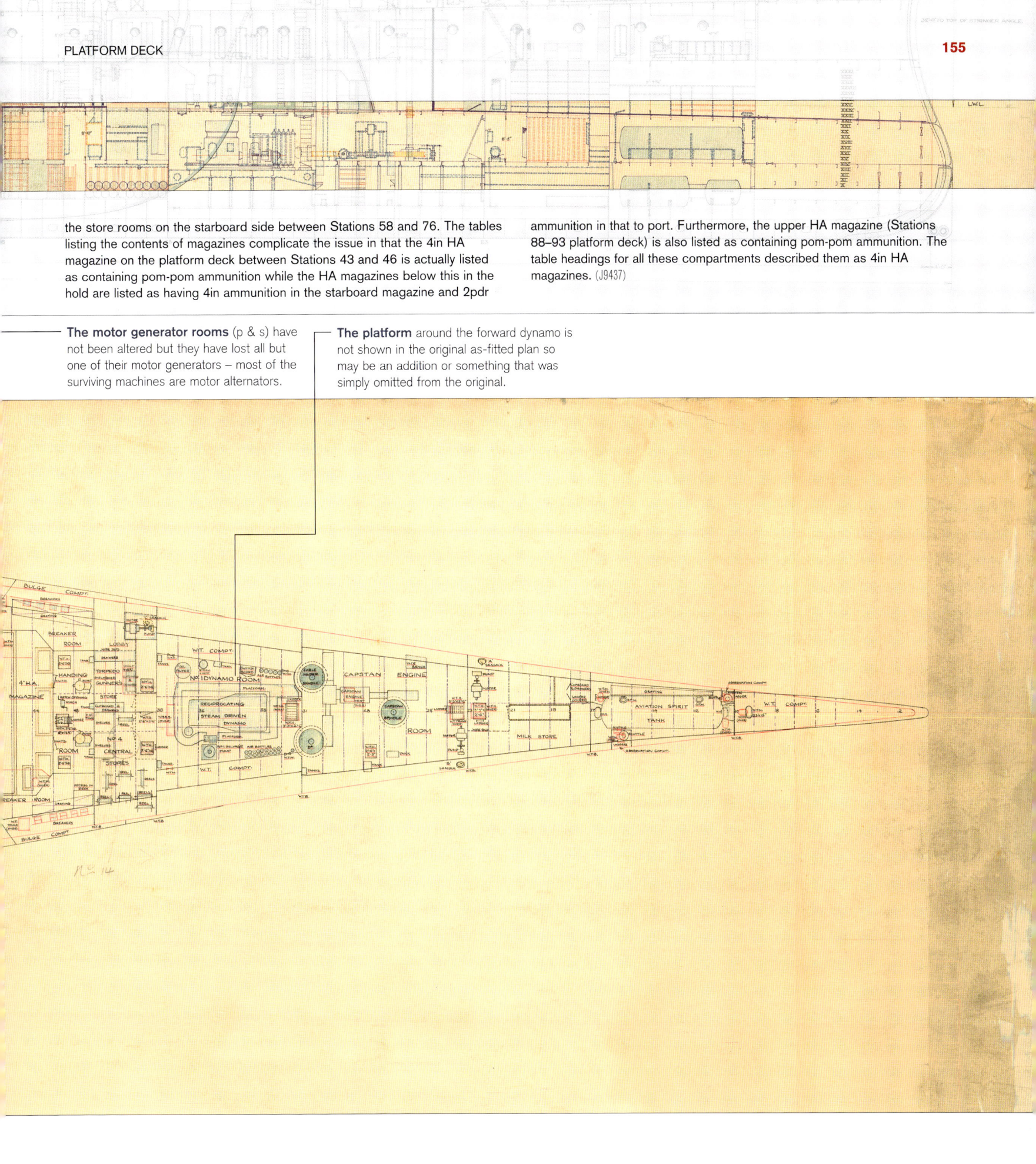

the store rooms on the starboard side between Stations 58 and 76. The tables listing the contents of magazines complicate the issue in that the 4in HA magazine on the platform deck between Stations 43 and 46 is actually listed as containing pom-pom ammunition while the HA magazines below this in the hold are listed as having 4in ammunition in the starboard magazine and 2pdr ammunition in that to port. Furthermore, the upper HA magazine (Stations 88–93 platform deck) is also listed as containing pom-pom ammunition. The table headings for all these compartments described them as 4in HA magazines. (J9437)

The motor generator rooms (p & s) have not been altered but they have lost all but one of their motor generators – most of the surviving machines are motor alternators.

The platform around the forward dynamo is not shown in the original as-fitted plan so may be an addition or something that was simply omitted from the original.

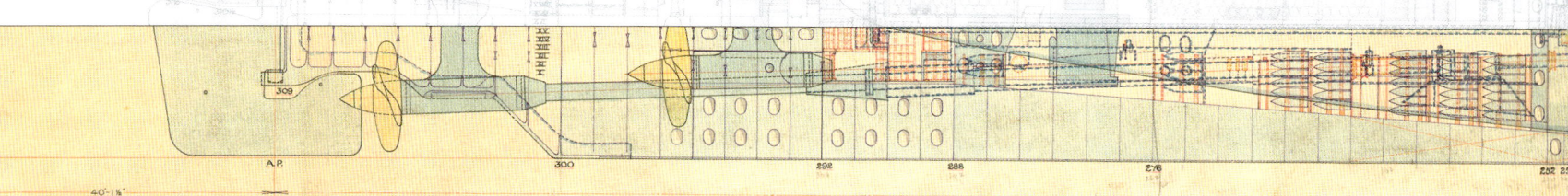

HOLD (AFT)

The contents of all magazines, shell rooms and other munitions compartments in the hold and on the platform deck are listed in the tables on this and the following pages. The provision per gun for 15in shell in 1936 was 96 APC (filled shellite), 24 CPC (filled trotyl) and 6 shrapnel, plus a total of 38 practice for the ship. These were evenly distributed to the three shell rooms, except for the practice projectiles – 8 were stowed in 'Y' shell room and 15 each in 'B' and 'A' shell rooms. The 4in BL guns were provided with 200rpg – 120 SAP and 80 HEDA (16 with night tracer) and the 4in QF HA guns with 340rpg

CONTENTS OF FIREWORKS MAGAZINE.	
BOXES FLARE LANDING AIRCRAFT WING TIP	2 Nº.
" SIGNAL DISTRESS MARINE	3 "
" CARTRIDGES SIGNAL 1½ RED ML¼	3 "
" " " " GREEN " "	3 "
" " " " WHITE " "	3 "
" FLARES AIRCRAFT RECONNAISSANCE 5·5"	20 "
" " " " 4·125"	6 "
" SMOKE FLOAT AIRCRAFT NAVIGATION	48 "
" SIGNAL IDENTIFICATION A/C ML ¼	6 "
" " UNDERWATER EXPLODING	1 "
" CARTRIDGES 1½" SMOKE PUFF ML¼	4 "
" FIREWORKS LARGE	1 "
" CARTRIDGES SIGNAL	7 "
" ROCKETS LINECARRYING SCHERMULLY	2 "
THERMOMETERS PATT. 65	1 "
HYGROMETERS " 60A	1 "
BOARD FOR THERMOGRAPH BRACKET	1 "

CONTENTS OF BOMB ROOM.	
BOXES BOMBS S.A.P. 500LBS.	24 Nº.
" " " 250 "	24 "
" " A.S. 100 "	24 "
" " COOPER 20 "	48 "
" FUZES BOMB 500 & 250LBS.	6 "
" " " 100LBS.	3 "
" " TIME AIRCRAFT NOSE Nº 28	7 "
" PISTOL AIRCRAFT SMOKE FLOAT TAIL Nº 23	10 "
" GRENADES 2½" H.E. WITHOUT DETONATORS	4 "
" FOR WARHEAD TORPEDO 18" Mk XI	4 "
" PISTOL Nº 16 BOX 206I OR A.S.A.G.S.I	1 "
SLINGS 4 LEGGED FOR 500 & 250LBS. BOMBS	2 "
BAR SLINGS FOR WARHEAD BOXES	1 "
MORRIS ½ TON BLOCKS PATT. 4005	2 "
THERMOMETERS PATT. 65	1 "
HYGROMETERS " 60A	1 "

CONTENTS OF 4" B.L. MAGAZINE AFT	
CASES POWDER RECTANGULAR "O"	78 Nº.
" CATAPULT AMMUNITION	28 "
BOXES CARTRIDGE AIRCRAFT CATAPULT C101	3 "
HYGROMETER PATT. 60A	1 "
THERMOMETER " 65	1 "
BOARD FOR THERMOGRAPH BRACKET	1 "
KEY FOR "O" CASES	
CLARKSON CASES	
STOOLS	2 "

CONTENTS OF 4" B.L. SHELL ROOM AFT.	
SHELLS FILLED B.L. 4" S.A.P.	720 Nº.
" " " " HE	384 "
" " " " H.E.N.T.	96 "
CASES W.P. FUZES	1 "
KEY BASE FUZE PLUG	1 "
HYGROMETER PATT. 60A	1 "
THERMOMETER " 65	1 "

CONTENTS OF 15" MAGAZINE "Y" BARBETTE.	
CASES CYLINDRICAL "M"	484 Nº.
CARTRIDGES DRILL	24 "
HYGROMETERS PATT. 60A	2 "
THERMOMETERS " 65	4 "
KEY CASES DOUBLE HANDED	4 "
" " SINGLE "	2 "
BOARD FOR THERMOGRAPH BRACKET	2 "
SLINGS FOR POWDER CASES	8 "
HAMMERS METAL	2 "

CONTENTS OF 15" SHELL ROOM "Y" BARBETTE.	
SHELL B.L. 15" COMMON POINTED CAPPED	48 Nº.
" " " A.P. CAPPED	192 "
" " " SHRAPNEL	12 "
" " " PRACTICE	8 "
CASES W.P. FUZES T&P 15" SHRAPNEL	1 "
THERMOMETER PATT. 65	1 "
HYGROMETER " 60A	1 "

CONTENTS OF 4" H.A MAG…
CASES 4" H.A. AMMUNITION C155
ROLLERS SWIVEL FOR STOWING CASES
THERMOMETER PATT. 65
HYGROMETER " 60A
BOARD FOR THERMOGRAPH BRACKET
STOOL

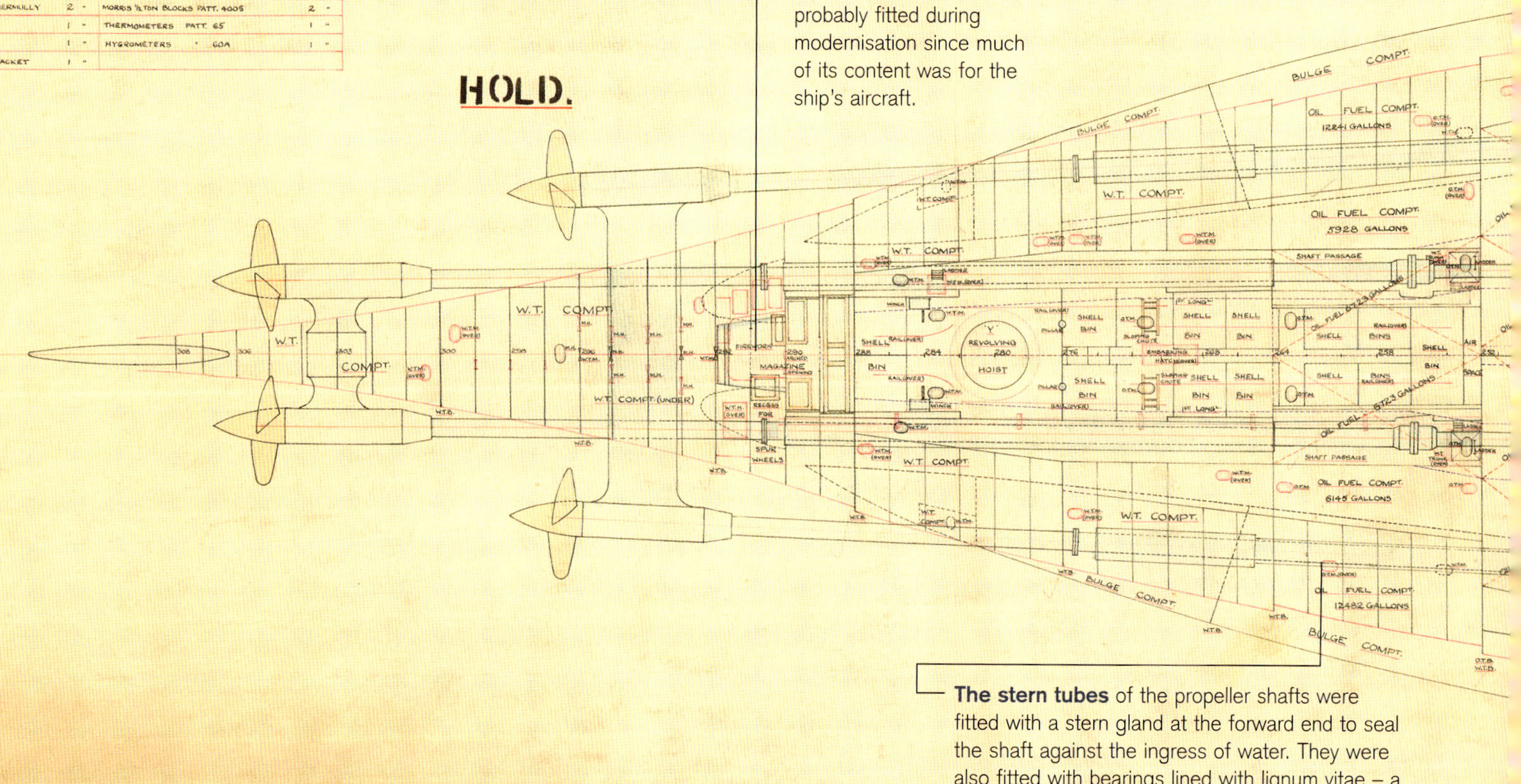

The fireworks magazine a post-1921 addition but probably fitted during modernisation since much of its content was for the ship's aircraft.

The stern tubes of the propeller shafts were fitted with a stern gland at the forward end to seal the shaft against the ingress of water. They were also fitted with bearings lined with lignum vitae – a very hard wood with self-lubricating properties. A similar arrangement was also fitted in the bearings of the 'A' bracket propeller shaft supports.

HOLD

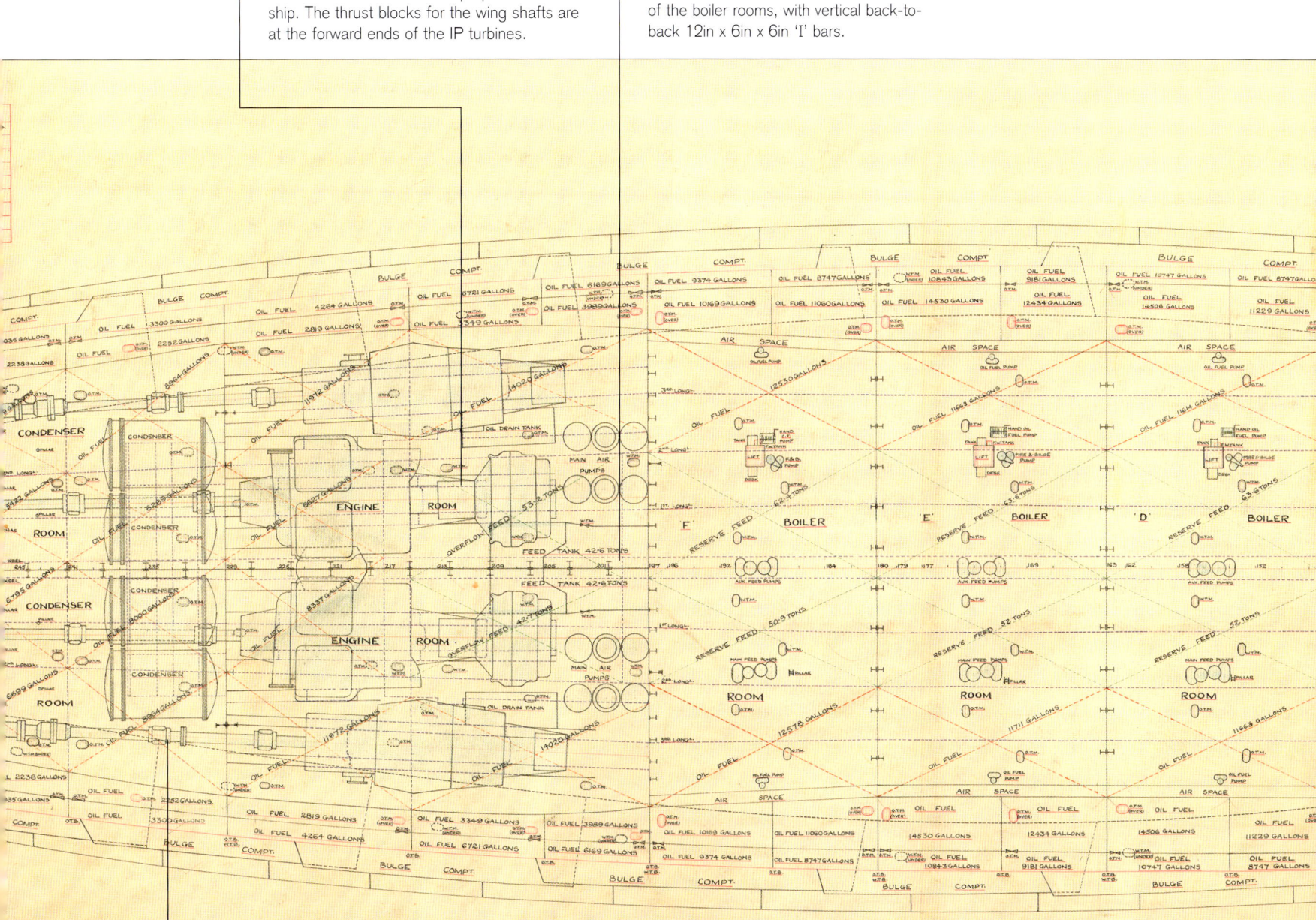

HETF plus, for the ship, 24 target smoke, 200 star shell and 500 practice projectiles. The pom-poms had 1800rpg plus 1344 practice rounds for the ship and the 0.5in MG 2500rpg.

Among the ship's allocated armament was a 3.7in howitzer and land carriage, an item that had superseded the 12pdr field gun. This was normally stored ashore and only embarked if some need for land service was anticipated. In 1940 it was transferred to the army. (J9437)

The thrust block of the inner shafts positioned between the LP and HP ahead turbines transferred the thrust of the propeller to the ship. The thrust blocks for the wing shafts are at the forward ends of the IP turbines.

The middle line bulkhead dividing the port and starboard engine rooms is supported, like the transverse bulkheads of the boiler rooms, with vertical back-to-back 12in x 6in x 6in 'I' bars.

The plummer block support bearings, two for the outer and three for the inner propeller shafts.

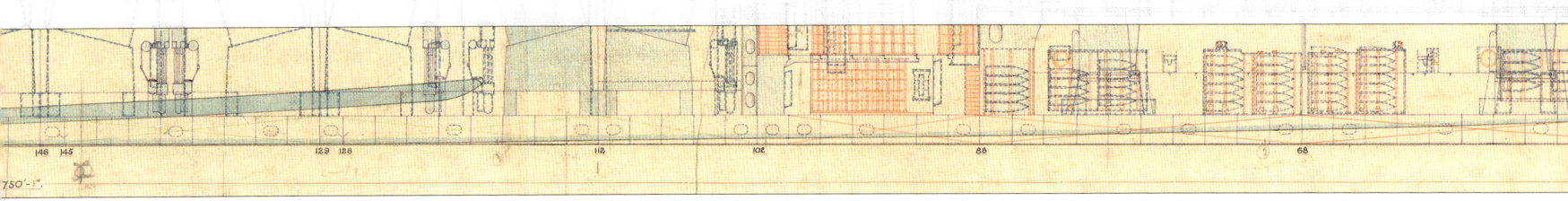

HOLD (FORWARD)

The boiler rooms accommodated 42 Babcock and Wilcox water tube boilers, 3 in 'A' boiler room, 7 in 'B' boiler room and 8 each in the remainder. Each had a total heating surface of 3743sq ft. The primary auxiliary machinery in each boiler room consisted of one fan per boiler, two (one in 'A' boiler room) turbo pumps, two main and two auxiliary feed pumps (only one of each in 'A' boiler room), two oil fuel pumps and a 75-ton (50-ton in 'A' boiler room) fire and bilge pump. All except the turbo pumps were driven by single-cylinder steam piston engines. (J9437)

The combined 4in BL shell room and magazine. As built this space was the 4in shell room, its magazine being located on the lower platform deck above. The charges were passed down into the shell room via three circular scuttles in the deck and then passed up, by whip hoist, via the ammunition trunks to the upper deck. At some point before 1921 (probably in 1917–18) the space below the scuttles was enclosed by three small handing rooms with F/T scuttles. As re-arranged during modernisation the handing rooms were removed and the 4in BL magazine repositioned in the centre of the shell room. This was fitted with three vertical F/T scuttles, the charges from which then followed the original route via the ammunition trunks to the new ammunition lobbies on the upper deck. The original whip hoists located in the hold were replaced with new hoists in the upper deck lobbies. The shell supply via the dredger hoists remained unchanged but the plan has provided an outline of their drive motors in the hold (items omitted from the 1916 as-fitted plan).

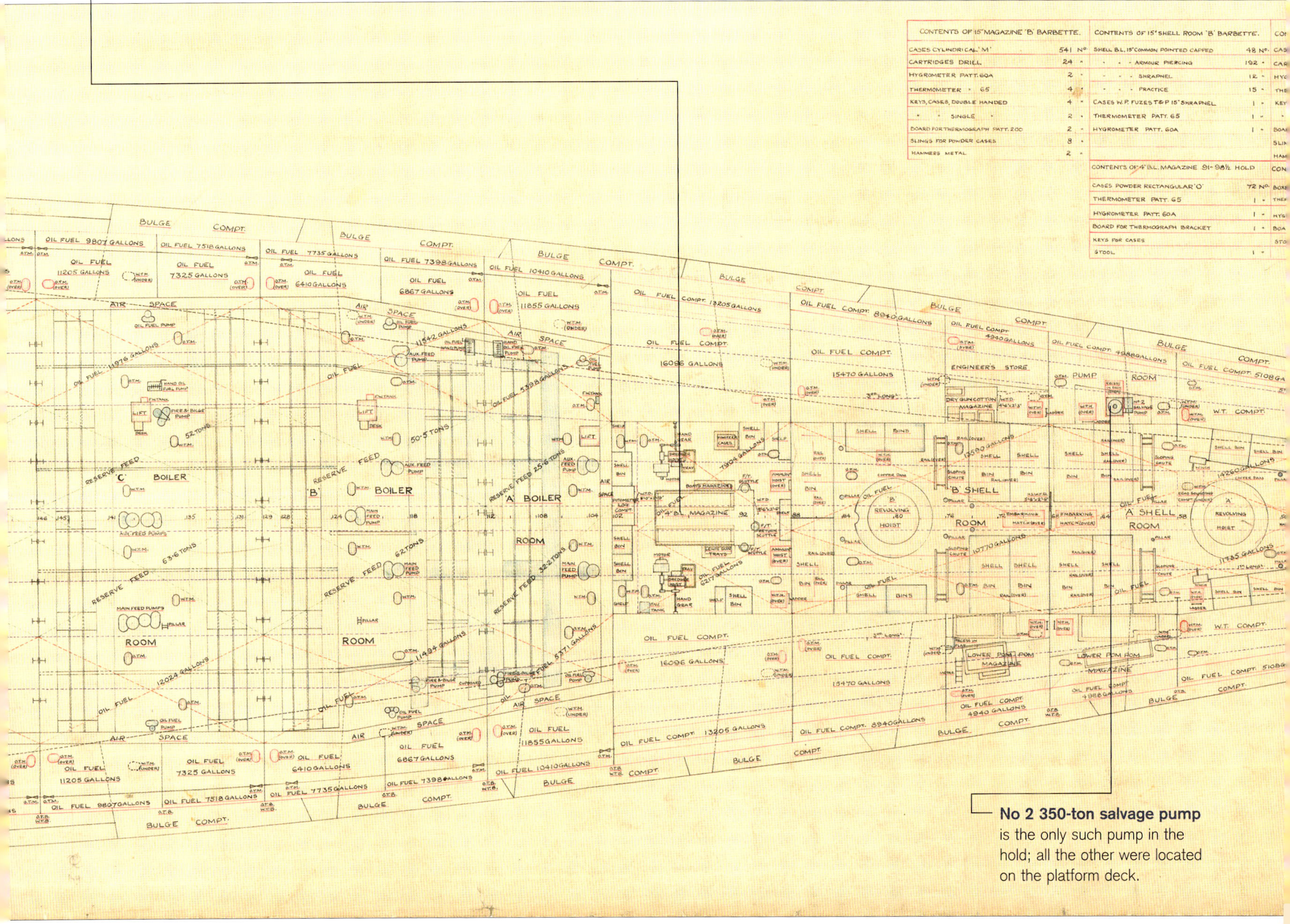

No 2 350-ton salvage pump is the only such pump in the hold; all the other were located on the platform deck.

HOLD

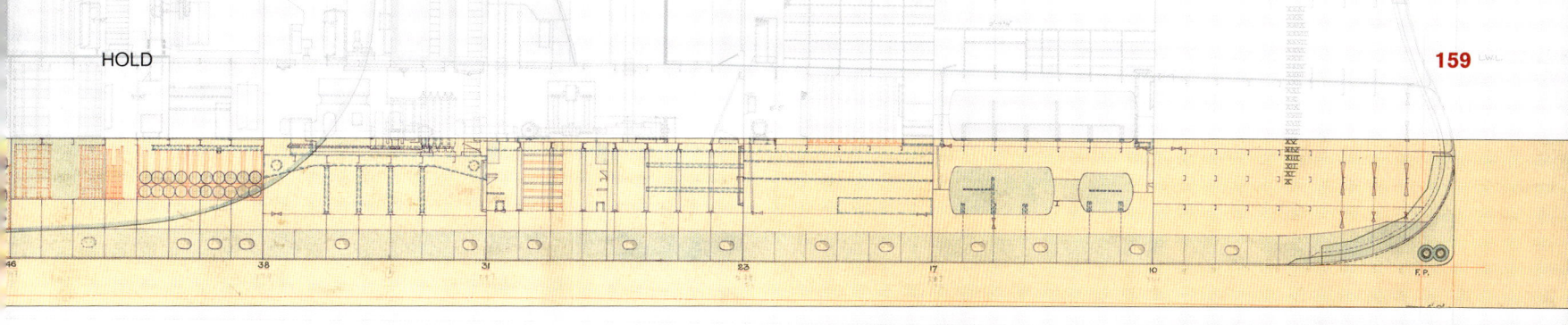

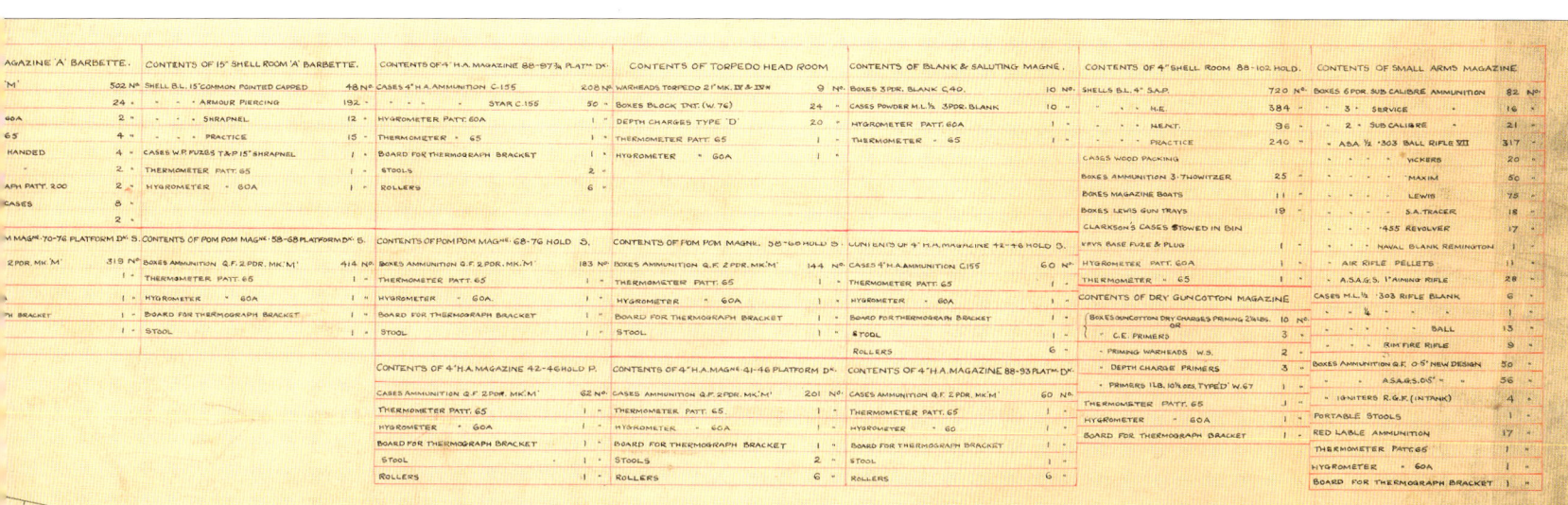

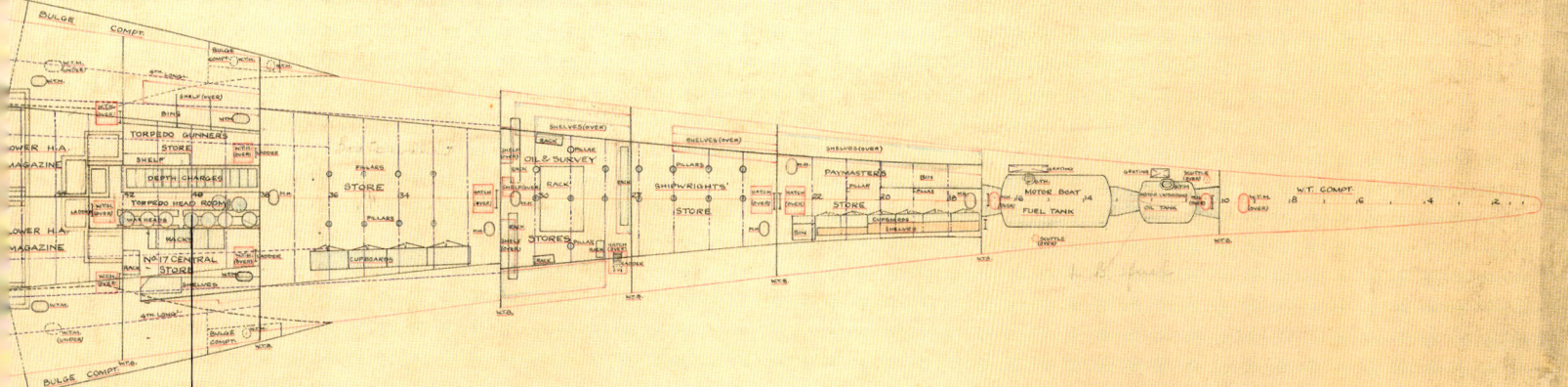

The torpedo head magazine accommodates the nine (eight plus one spare) warheads for the 21in torpedoes. The warheads for the 18in aerial torpedoes were located in the bomb room aft. While these were the standard and safest locations for the warheads, they obviously needed fitting to the torpedo bodies when surface action was expected at which time the warheads were protected by the armour mantles around the outer ends of the tubes – the 21in being in the tubes and the 18in above the four forward tubes. The depth charges, to starboard of the warheads, were to arm the ship's 45ft FMBs when on harbour picket duty.

SOURCES

NATIONAL MARITIME MUSEUM (BRASS FOUNDRY, WOOLWICH ARSENAL)

Repulse and Renown Ships Covers 341, 341A, 341B, 341C
General Covers 314, 314A and 314B
Renown and Repulse Specification Book
Pengelly, H S, Workbook, Box DNC11
Attwood, E L, Workbook, Box DNC3
Mason, H R, Workbook, Box DCN37

THE NATIONAL ARCHIVES (KEW)

HMS Repulse ship's logs: various entries 1916–1941. ADM53 series
DNC Records of War Construction – Renown and Repulse, 1919. ADM1/8547/340
Manual and Addenda to 15in Mk I mounting, 1932. ADM186/315
Manual for Power Worked Mountings, 1921. ADM186/255
Handbook for 4in BL Mk IX and IX★ Gun on Triple Mounting Mk I, 1916. ADM186/214
Manual of Gunnery for H M Fleet, Vol III, 1933. ADM275/29
Naval Rangefinders and Mountings 1921, Vol 1. ADM186/253
Director Firing Handbook, 1917. ADM186/227
Handbook for High Angle Control System Marks 1 and 1★, 1930. ADM86/295
Annual Report of the Torpedo School: various entries during 1916–36. ADM189/36-56
Reports of Post Jutland Committees. ADM137/2027, 2028 and 2029
Protection of Magazines. ADM116/2348
Disposition of Aircraft on Naval Duties, 1918–19. AIR1/670/17/124
Grand Fleet Gunnery and Torpedo Orders. ADM137/293, 2010 and 2015
Steam Ships of England. ADM186/837
British Navy Part 1, Battleships and Battle Cruisers 1922. ADM186/59 and 60
Programme of Large Repairs, 1934. ADM1/9774/107
HM Ships and Armaments April 1938. ADM186/179
Particulars of HM Ships 1940-41. ADM239/68–71
Confidential Admiralty Fleet Orders (CAFOs) various entries 1921–1941. ADM182 series

OFFICIAL ADMIRALTY PUBLICATIONS (HMSO)

Naval Electrical Pocket Book, 1933. BR157/1933
Stokers' Manual, 1927
Machinery Handbook, 1941. BR77
Admiralty Manual of Seamanship, Vol 1, 1922, 1926, 1932 and 1937
Admiralty Manual of Seamanship, Vol 2, 1923 and 1932

BIBLIOGRAPHY

Attwood, E L, *Warships* (Longmans, Green, 1911)
Burt, R A, *British Battleships of World War One* (Seaforth Publishing, 2012)
———, *British Battleships 1919–1945* (Seaforth Publishing, 2012)
Campbell, N J M, *Warship Special 1: Battlecruisers* (Conway Maritime Press, 1978)
Cronin, R, *Royal Navy Shipboard Aircraft Developments 1912–1931* (Air Britain, 1990)
D'Eyncourt, Sir E H W T, *A Shipbuilder's Yarn* (Hutchinson, 1948)
McDermaid, N J, *Shipyard Practice* (Longmans, Green, 1911)
Newton, R N, *Practical Construction of Warships* (Longmans, Green, 1957)
Northcott, M, *Ensign 8: Renown and Repulse* (Battle of Britain Prints, International Ltd, 1978)
Raven, A, and Roberts, J, *British Battleships of World War Two* (Arms and Armour Press, 1976)
Roberts, J, *British Battlecruisers 1905–1920* (Seaforth Publishing, 2016)
Sturtivant, R, and Cronin, R, *Fleet Air Arm Aircraft, Units and Ships 1920 to 1939* (Air Britain, 1998)

ORIGINAL PLANS USED IN THIS BOOK

BATTLE CRUISER DESIGN, MARCH 1915

Sheer drawing (¼in = 1 foot)	J9432
Sectional drawing (½in = 1 foot)	M1003

REPULSE (General Arrangements 'As Fitted' 1916)

Profile	J9371
Shelter & Flying Decks, Bridges, Etc	J9373
Upper & Forecastle Decks	J9372
Main & Lower Decks	M1001
Hold & Platform Deck	M1002
Sections	J9374

REPULSE (General Arrangements 'As Fitted' 1936)

Profile	J9433
Shelter & Flying Decks, Bridges, Etc	J9434
Forecastle & Upper Decks	J9435
Main & Lower Decks	J9436
Hold & Platform Deck	J9437
Sections	J9438
Rig	J9439
Wireless Telegraphy Rig	J9440

REPULSE (Aircraft Arrangements 'As Fitted' 1936)

Stowage Arrangements of Aircraft, Cranes & Aircraft Spare Parts	M0940
Embarking and Discharging Arrangements	M0941
Course of Torpedoes & Bombs	M0942

DETAIL DRAWINGS

Triple Mounting Mark I for 4 inch BL Guns, Sectional Elevation and Rear End View	J9423
Triple Mounting Mark I for 4 inch BL Guns, Side Elevation and Plan	J9424

National Maritime Museum ship plans

Exact scale colour prints of ship plans can be purchased online from **http://prints.rmg.co.uk** or please contact **pictures@rmg.co.uk** for scanning services.